Cᵈ
(JF)

The Changing Face of Multinationals in Southeast Asia

The rise of computer-based technology and the growth of the Internet, instantaneous global communication channels, corporate mergers, changing education levels, and the dawn of new-age terror networks are some of the factors impacting the way multinational corporations have reappraised their structures and strategies for the twenty-first century. Gripped by the region-wide economic meltdown of the late 1990s, Southeast Asia stands at the cusp of this new, unprecedented era of global change.

Written from a rarely glimpsed insider's perspective, this book reveals *how* and *why* the world's foremost companies have sought to revive and develop their fortunes in this emerging and strategically critical region. Using the region's downturn as the "engine of reform," our cohort of corporate practitioners epitomize the sea change in corporate attitudes toward Southeast Asian business units. From the boom years of the 1980s to the early 1990s, many of these units were lauded for their speed and flexibility, and were handed unprecedented levels of autonomy. In the immediate wake of the ensuing crash, however, corporate head offices sought to impose "international" best practice, in order to bring these "errant" units back in line with global corporate norms.

This book recounts their story. Using practitioner insights, the authors outline the initial corporate-oriented programs of change, and trace in detail, using often explosive first-hand accounts, the subsequent waves of indigenous managerial resistance. The authors go on to explore the resultant "compromise" business methods, in the light of which the book proposes a "cross-vergent" framework for strategic thinking, composed from the best of both Western and Eastern managerial cultures. Drawing on the authors' combined experience of corporate methods in the region, the book represents an agenda-setting analysis of the cultural foundations of international management strategy. In an era of increasing speed, risk and uncertainty, *The Changing Face of Multinationals in Southeast Asia* draws a blueprint for sustainable competitive advantage, based upon inherent synergies that can be gained from an integrated East–West corporate approach.

Tim G. Andrews is Senior Lecturer in International Marketing, Bristol Business School, University of the West of England. **Nartnalin Chompusri** is Marketing Officer at the Bristol Business School, University of the West of England. **Bryan J. Baldwin OBE** is Chairman of Trafalgar International, Global Investments Ltd, Evergreen Comware and Director of PCI International.

Working in Asia

General Editors:
Tim G. Andrews
Bristol Business School, University of the West of England
and **Keith Jackson**
School of Oriental and African Studies, University of London

This series focuses on contemporary management issues in the Asia-Pacific region. It draws on the latest research to highlight critical factors impacting on the conduct of business in this diverse and dynamic business environment.

Our primary intention is to provide management students and practitioners with fresh dimensions to their reading of standard texts. With each book in the *Working in Asia* series, we offer a combined insider's and outsider's perspective on how managers and their organizations in the Asia-Pacific region are adapting to contemporary currents of both macro- and micro-level change.

The core of data for the texts in this series has been generated by recent interviews and discussions with established senior executives as well as newly fledged entrepreneurs; with practising as well as aspiring middle managers; and with women as well as men. Our mission has been to give voice to how change is being perceived and experienced by a broad and relevant range of people who live and work in the region. We report on how they and their organizations are managing change as the globalization of their markets, together with their business technologies and traditions, unfolds.

Drawing together the combined insights of Asian and Western scholars, and practitioners of management, we present a uniquely revealing portrait of the future of working and doing business in Asia.

Titles in the series include:

The Changing Face of Multinationals in Southeast Asia
Tim G. Andrews, Nartnalin Chompusri and Bryan J. Baldwin OBE

The Changing Face of Chinese Management
Jie Tang and Anthony Ward

The Changing Face of Multinationals in Southeast Asia

Tim G. Andrews, Nartnalin Chompusri
and Bryan J. Baldwin OBE

Routledge
Taylor & Francis Group

LONDON AND NEW YORK

First published 2003 by Routledge
11 New Fetter Lane, London EC4P 4EE

Simultaneously published in the USA and Canada
by Routledge
29 West 35th Street, New York NY 10001

Routledge is an imprint of the Taylor & Francis Group

© 2003 Tim G. Andrews, Nartnalin Chompusri and Bryan J. Baldwin OBE

Typeset in Times by Keystroke, Jacaranda Lodge, Wolverhampton
Printed and bound in Great Britain by MPG Books Ltd, Bodmin

British Library Cataloguing in Publication Data
A catalogue record for this book is available from the British Library

Library of Congress Cataloging in Publication Data
Andrews, Tim G., 1968–
  The changing face of multinationals in Southeast Asia /
Tim G. Andrews, Nartnalin Chompusri and Bryan J. Baldwin.
    p. cm. – (Working in Asia)
Includes bibliographical references and index.
    1. International business enterprises–Asia, Southeastern.
2. Corporations, Foreign–Asia, Southeastern. 3. Investments, Foreign–
Asia, Southeastern. 4. Financial crises–Asia, Southeastern. I. Chompusri,
Nartnalin, 1970– II. Baldwin, Bryan J., 1937– III. Title. IV. Series.
    HD2901 .A514 2002
    338.8'88599–dc21

                                                            2002075175

ISBN 0–415–26095–7 (hbk)
ISBN 0–415–26096–5 (pbk)

I would like to dedicate this book to my wonderful children:
Antony, Helen and Ariane

Bryan J. Baldwin OBE

Contents

 # Acknowledgments

The authors would like to express their gratitude to the multitude of corporate respondents for their gracious assistance in the research of this book.

Special thanks: Johnny Johnson, Richard Mead, and our commissioning editor, Catriona King.

# Introduction

- Aims and rationale
- Focus "roots"
- Perspective
- Scope
- Method
- Style and content
- Structure

> Once you think you know Southeast Asia, you've just
> made your first mistake.
>
> (Castrol International Executive)

> The only certainty is uncertainty.
>
> (Eastern proverb)

Loosely translated from the Thai, the latter quotation provides as good a
starting point as any for a book on multinational corporations in
Southeast Asia. This is not to suggest that there are no clearly discernible
and emerging trends. But it certainly summarizes events of the past
decade, during which the bubbling optimism of the mid-1990s quite
without precedent gave way to the long, gloom-laden months of 1998,
when most of the region was caught in the iron grip of economic and
financial collapse. As the precursor of the region-wide downturn and
subsequent contraction, Thailand provides the starkest example of this
change. Just a few short years ago Thailand was viewed by the world's
foremost financial institutions as an emerging tiger, with one of the
highest economic growth rates ever witnessed. In early 1995 *The
Economist* projected Thailand to be the world's eighth largest economy
in 2020, and a year later the country's economic planners took the
almost unbelievable step of actually writing 8 percent growth into the
next five-year plan (Keeratipipatpong, 1998; Phongpaichit and Baker,
1998). To most observers it seemed the Asian miracle would go on
indefinitely.

The export slump of that same year gave a stark warning of what was to come, for within a few months the Thai currency was battered and finally unhinged to sink to well under half its previous value. By year-end 1997 the vast majority of existing multinational corporations (MNCs) in the region were coming to terms with an undreamed of – and yet very real – specter of a shrinking market, rising cost structures and excessive staffing levels. In retrospect, the regional crisis was only a number of key forces in a wider, increasingly global context with which business corporations have had to contend. The flotation of the Thai baht itself has now emerged as merely one effect of the resounding impact of instantaneous and hitherto largely unregulated flows of huge amounts of footloose capital around the globe, itself a consequence of the rapid development of electronic technology. Of understandable concern to the governments of developing economies is the continuing spectacle of investors being able to move billions of dollars among nations in search of better opportunities at the touch of a button. Assisted in turn by the rise in instantaneous flows of market information, this freewheeling money supply has the ability to pump-prime and then undermine a nation's macroeconomic performance, as illustrated by the recent destabilization of economies such as Thailand and Indonesia.

In this respect the postcrisis recovery process in Southeast Asia comes at a time of dramatic global business change at the confluence of a new and previously unheard-of set of meta-level forces. Added to the technologically derived efficiencies in global communications and information flows – instanced by the explosive growth of computing power and mobile telephony – MNCs are also faced with the prospect of overcapacity in their home territories against a backdrop of declining interest rates and recessions. This has prompted many large corporations to diversify their investment portfolios away from their saturated home markets and toward the establishment of operations in the developing economies of the Asia-Pacific region. Concurrent developments are increasing the pace and ferocity of global business competition, instanced by the continuing industrialization and deregulation of emerging markets. In seeking to adapt to this new world order, corporations have sought to merge into conglomerates of unprecedented size as a means of holding down costs and extending global reach. Attempts to implement business process standardization and transparency measures are viewed as the logical extension of this activity, as managers seek to maintain central control of huge and often unwieldy enterprises.

In practical terms, the extent and rapidity of these changes have placed corporate business executives in uncharted and often confusing new territory. The past decade has witnessed a strategic reevaluation by multinationals from a cross section of industries of their strategic goals on global, regional and domestic levels. This is well illustrated by the Western corporate reaction to the recently shifting business climate in Southeast Asia. The emergence of an unstable, uncertain global market arena has led many such companies to seek to rethink the way in which their operations are both forecast and measured, seeking to deal effectively with previously unheard-of macro-market scenarios. The refusal of Western-headquartered multinationals to accept this newly destabilized regional business environment as the norm underlies what are seen to be their attempts to force a uniform standard upon their global structures and *modi operandi*. These attempts will form part of the backdrop to the tempestuous scenes of corporate life "at the coalface" described later in this book.

In summary, the Asian economic crisis was in many ways a catalyst for corporate readjustment to the plethora of changes already occurring. Southeast Asia had become a focal point for the spate of global corporate restructuring programs. On the ground we are witnessing the canon of global competition pitted against the traditional "Asian way" of doing business. This has found expression in the conflicting set of forces for global coordination on the one hand and those of local flexibility on the other, of business practice standardization pitted against localized adaptation. Locked into this shifting balance of forces is the debate as to how far business theories and concepts drawn primarily from the industrialized, market-oriented (often Western) economies can be extrapolated for use in the economies of the East. Assumptions made among corporate executives have often tended to oversimplify developments and overemphasize technology's impacts. But at the downstream level we are faced with the same problem; that is, just how a Western-headquartered MNC would implement its global strategies in countries traditionally set against the idea of change.

Aims and rationale

In broad terms the objective of this book is to provide a rich and detailed account of how and why multinational corporations are changing their strategies and structures in postcrisis Southeast Asia. We have therefore concerned ourselves primarily with the identification and exploration of these key trends with which a cross section of MNCs are having to contend, rather than merely seeking to provide yet another survey catalog of the region's corporate cohort. Our focus is upon the ground-floor *implementation* of these changes in practice, seeking to delineate and understand the local reactions to the respective corporate measures and how, in turn, these companies have sought to resolve ongoing disputes over time. With our emphasis upon the experiences of insiders in the field – including our own – we shall provide some of the first and most in-depth empirical data ever compiled within the Southeast Asian context.

The macro dimensions of the regional economic downturn have already been documented and analyzed more than adequately by numerous authors (e.g. Godement, 1999). Yet there has been little attempt to explore the situation "in the trenches." The perspective and role of the indigenous labor supply in the acceptance of these corporate-imposed changes in the postcrisis years have been particularly overlooked. This book is thus an attempt to redress the balance. In extracting a surgical slice of the multinational corporate fraternity in the region we have sought to build on the work of these economically oriented scholars by adding "flesh" to the bone structure of previous survey-oriented analyses.

Taking advantage of our detailed personal knowledge and largely unhindered access to the internal workings of a cross section of Western- and Japanese-headquartered multinationals, we investigate more profoundly than is usually possible the indigenous reaction to these destabilizing macro-management developments. Although the book is based at the micro level of analysis – and addressing the emerging nucleus of the Southeast Asian trading bloc almost exclusively – we anticipate that in complementing the macro emphasis of the existing cross-national management literature, the observations traced herein may provide valuable insights for both students and business practitioners engaged in similar commercial environments, particularly those of the developing world.

Focus "roots"

The original impetus for this book came from the experiences of all three authors within the multinational corporate fraternity in Southeast Asia, particularly across Thailand and the Greater Mekong Subregion through the onset of economic meltdown. Although each of our respective corporate units had become almost habituated to double-digit sales and profitability growth, viewed with the benefit of hindsight these levels of success had made these organizations increasingly insular, as their indigenous methods and working cultures were for years left largely unquestioned by their respective parent corporations. In this respect the crisis initiated by the crash of the baht in mid-1997, while exposing and aggravating their inherent shortcomings, was in a sense perceived by corporate headquarters as a timely trigger for reform.

As the business conditions in Asia deteriorated – and with little prospect of a full recovery – Western corporations were prompted to reframe their approach and perspectives to individual markets in accordance with international norms. Previously held corporate tenets were hastily reassessed as new management guidelines sought to deal with this newly destabilized business environment. Under increasing pressure from shareholders and analysts back home, corporate executives based in the region took measures to tighten corporate central control at their local subsidiaries, viewed under the more critical light of business stagnation as "highly idiosyncratic" and "obstructive" local fiefdoms. Against the trend for adapted, localized management practice, key Western multinationals attempted to "synchronize" their Asian business units in line with global business practices and values. Their aim in strengthening the central "steerage" of group activities worldwide was to avoid any future upheavals of central strategic priorities. To this end, indigenous senior management was directed to "discard past practices" in order to survive, a phenomenon we witnessed not just within our own immediate work environment but also in those of business associates, Western acquaintances and suppliers. Indigenous business practices once lauded as "ideal" for their flexibility during the "boom" years were being dismissed as "suspect," "wayward" and even "unprofessional" now that the regional bubble had finally burst.

In the months and years that followed, a steady stream of organizational restructuring programs began to emanate from the headquarters of prominent Western- and Japanese-headquartered multinationals. Initial cost containment measures included the scaling back of investment plans and current expenditure, necessitating redundancies among their local personnel (something that was to prove highly contentious). Medium- and longer-term measures involved restructuring the sales and marketing departments, along with the instillation of both "transparency" and "accountability" measures in order to improve competitiveness and ameliorate relations between corporate headquarters and their local Southeast Asian subsidiaries.

In practical terms, the prior corporate preoccupation with tailoring structure and practices in line with cultural norms was roundly ditched in favor of an ethnocentric management retrenchment policy. However, far away from the group executive drawing board, the practical implementation of these directives for convergence was to prove much more difficult. Corporate initiatives were often successfully diluted and even blocked in the activation of the elusive but resilient force termed the "Asian way" of management practice. A major characteristic of this crisis-torn Southeast Asian corporate environment in the years since the crisis has thus been this interface between traditional, relations-based Asian managerial methodology on the one hand against the demands of Western-sponsored strategy revision and transparency programs on the other.

Perspective

One major thesis of this book is that the postcrisis standoff between Eastern and Western models of business practice encompasses a far deeper clash of cultures, founded in turn upon fundamental societal values. Although the newly issued corporate directives had focused solely upon the imposition of global business norms, in practice they were confronted with having to engineer a revolution in management culture in the attainment of their stated group objectives. But whereas the more perceptive international business scholars (e.g. Bigoness and Blakely, 1996; Neal, 1998; Rao and Hashimoto, 1996) appear to have realized the importance of rendering managerial practice congruent with local cultural values in order to influence critical organizational outcomes, it appears from our combined on-the-ground observations that their corporate counterparts have woefully failed to follow suit. Yet the numerous examples of international joint ventures that have run aground on cultural differences signal the dangers of extrapolating foreign corporate directives across contexts, especially during traumatic periods of societal and economic hardship.

Cultural differences engender serious profitability-threatening difficulties, from management underperformance, to low morale, to active resistance to parent company directives. Traditional business customs are rightly depicted in the relevant literature as evolving at a glacial pace through generations and centuries and beyond, as opposed to the fleeting swings in business cycles and management policies (Schneider and Barsoux, 1997). Yet practical discussions of the impact of basic cultural elements (language, social structure) on business practices have consistently been underestimated by ethnocentric global corporations. Time and time again we have watched as otherwise competent expatriate managers were exported from their Western home bases into the Asian cauldron of 1997–8 with simplistic and practically useless preconceptions about the nature of culture and cultural difference. Almost inevitably, in the majority of cases their already tentative and suspicion-fueled relationships with fearful local colleagues rapidly deteriorated and eventually broke down.

Part of the problem, it seems, is the way that "culture" has been interpreted, particularly in the fragmented, polarized body of literature on doing business in Southeast Asia. On the one hand there is a prevalence of short, "how to . . ." texts that center on the superficial conventions of social discourse. These appear to be aimed at the short-term corporate expatriate and tend to line the "business/management"-headed shelves of local bookstore chains. On the other hand we are confronted with theoretical, leaden treatises based primarily on survey, quantitative, statistical data aimed primarily at the select business school libraries of universities. Not surprisingly, the loose definitions of culture employed in the two sets bear little resemblance to one another, not least in their loci of emphases. Graphic warnings on the dire consequences of pointing one's feet at a local manager or of patting a subordinate on the head are difficult to locate within the confines of Hofstede's positivistic cross-cultural set of value dimensions. Among current business practitioners in corporate Asia the trend seems to be one of seeking to downplay the role of "culture," claiming that very often the issue is simply exaggerated, either within the local business press or within the cozy confines of "touchy-feely" human resources departments. Founded on the view of "culture" taken from the "how to . . ." guides, this view is one with which we largely concur. After all, just how often, in the day-to-day running of a business, is a Western executive likely to find himself in the position of losing all respect from his local management having accidentally pointed his foot forward in order to activate a floor fan?

In terms of the ground-floor managerial practices that are founded on these differences, however, the consequences of their underestimation is all too real. What we need to remember is that this "crossing of cultures" does not entail the reconciliation of alien absolutes; it is merely about differences of degree, of essential similarities arranged in different priorities. Our own perspective focuses on the cultural congruence – or otherwise – of the postcrisis change in working practices and priorities imposed from overseas. Focusing our book upon insiders' perspectives and experiences also necessitates an exploration of the day-to-day consequences of cultural distance. In the months and years which have followed the initial implementation of corporate change programs, we have begun to trace and explore the emergence of new "synthesized" or "cross-vergent" business practices which have involved a compromise of priority and objective between the initiating Western head office and the local Southeast Asian management (Andrews and Chompusri, 2001; Ralston et al., 1997). Our overall aim in this examination is to explore the underlying issues with which multinationals in the region have had to contend – and not with a constantly changing set of macro variables. What we believe has emerged is thus a rather more profound study of "doing business in Southeast Asia" than could ever be gleaned from the "instant" guides.

Scope

There is currently a dearth of texts relating to multinational corporations in Southeast Asia. However, there exists a notable series of macro-based texts relating to China (e.g. Luo, 2000), as well as a number of texts on "how to do business . . ." in some of the region's prime economies, notably Singapore and Malaysia, Thailand, the Philippines, and – more recently – Vietnam. In dealing with such a potentially vast and diverse mass of data which constitute the postcrisis activities in multinational corporations operating in Southeast Asia, it behoves us to state from the outset the self-imposed boundaries to our framework.

The four manufacturing engines of Southeast Asia are Malaysia, Indonesia, Thailand and the Philippines. A major thrust of this book will thus be to examine the changing face of multinationals in these key strategic areas. However, we have rejected the simplistic desire to focus on these countries either exclusively or necessarily above those of the less developed areas (with the exception of Singapore, about which much has already been written). We have instead chosen to focus on a more balanced and interesting cross section of the more and less industrialized areas of the region in order to give the reader a better "feel" for the differing issues with which major companies are continuing to grapple.

To this end, we have divided the region into "tiers" of emphasis. Our primary tier comprises the Greater Mekong nucleus of Thailand, Vietnam and Laos with related examples from Cambodia and Myanmar (Burma). This is then backed by a second tier of the three other manufacturing bases of the region, namely Malaysia, Indonesia and the Philippines, with added examples from Singapore.

In selecting Thailand as a prime focal hub for this book we are merely mirroring the trend expressed by many of our MNCs in their increasing utilization of the country – both as an operational hub and as an export platform for their Southeast Asian development. This practice has filtered down to the sometimes controversial strategy of assigning Thai managers to set up and control operations in Vietnam, Laos, Myanmar and Cambodia. Because they share similar Chinese-oriented business values (of which more below), it is generally assumed among foreign corporations that Thai managers' management styles and practices are relatively similar to those of managers in other Asian countries. The ability to understand the factors affecting Thai managers in their adoption of certain practices is therefore held to be tantamount to providing regional executives with insights as to business practice norms and values throughout the region.

In cultural terms this is of course a highly dangerous assumption to make, for Thailand is in many respects an anomaly in Southeast Asia. Historically, Thailand boasts the distinction of being the only country in Southeast Asia never to have been colonized, throughout the country's eight-hundred-year history. Further, Thailand was the precursor for the Asian economic meltdown of 1997–8, as the sharp decline in consumer and industrial market demand across Southeast Asia was felt most abruptly within its national borders. There is also a marked perception among regional corporate executives that Thailand has proven the most resilient and "difficult" of Asia's markets in which to implement Western-oriented management practices as a means of boosting economic recovery. Although the countries of Southeast Asia share a region-wide business culture dominated by the ethnic Chinese, in homogeneous terms the Chinese in Thailand have been assimilated into the domestic way of doing things to a far greater extent than those in neighboring countries, even adopting softer Thai mannerisms and Thai-sounding surnames. As one regional human resources controller put it, "even among the top managers in Thailand it's impossible to see who is Thai and who is Chinese, they look so much alike, much more so than in other areas I've dealt with." Taken as the "extreme case" in Southeast Asia, Thailand thus forms an appropriate core base for the demonstration of how overseas corporations have had to adjust their original programs of organizational and business practice realignment, for the problems encountered and the resolutions achieved were in many cases simply magnified from the situations encountered in the surrounding countries.

In industrial terms we have chosen to concentrate on prominent, well-known multinationals, and hence our focus is unavoidably skewed toward Western-based organizations, with notable contributions from Japan. The Western-based Southeast Asian subsidiary is of profound interest owing to the dynamic, often troublesome blend of West-meets-East at the organizational coalface, something that can have a profound impact on all aspects of the business. In this respect we then of necessity include the cases of several indigenous business enterprises in their role as joint venture partners, several of which have become respected multinationals in their own right.

We have also chosen to focus almost exclusively on the consumer side of industrial activity. Retail-oriented corporations provide a sample that has been more particularly affected by the Asian market downturn, given the sharp contraction in consumer demand. They are traditionally not as prone to corruption as the less documented business-to-business sector, and moreover the names of consumer multinationals tend to be far more established in the minds of the populace, and their widespread recognition is reinforced by the increasing focus on brand awareness and development. Finally, we have confined ourselves to *planned* – as opposed to spontaneous or organic – change interventions within our featured multinationals, concerning ourselves specifically with *macro-*level company changes – that is, those that affect the whole organization – as opposed to any "piecemeal dabbling."

Method

In our attempt to provide an in-depth, on-the-ground exploration of corporate consolidation in Southeast Asia we are seeking to capture and express in print some of the breadth and diversity of cause and effect that we have witnessed. With our focus of necessity based at the micro level of analysis, we have subordinated theory to practice and rigor to relevance. Using this method, we feel we can add insight and richness to our current understanding of how corporations can best implement their programs of organizational and strategic change.

As we have already noted, cultural awareness and understanding play a crucial role in this process, necessitating our adoption of a broadly "qualitative" research design in order to uncover the key players' views on the key issues, rather than simply identifying and then listing the "things" themselves. It should also be noted that throughout the course of this research project our environment of analysis was in a state of flux and uncertainty, which further rendered the traditional academic emphasis on the positivist, "closed lab" approach both unsatisfactory and inappropriate. The data interwoven into this book were garnered from field interviews and observation sessions conducted from 1997 through 2002 and reinforced from secondary material derived from internal corporate sources and external literature and reports. Our respondents were drawn from a representative sample of the managerial hierarchy at both corporate and business unit/subsidiary level, providing a diverse yet surprisingly cohesive set of perspectives and experiences.

Information gathered from respondents and (ex-) colleagues was collected on the presumption of anonymity, both for themselves as individuals and – on occasion – for their companies. In these latter cases the choice we had to make was between either accepting the "official" diluted data and the use of the company names, or the real-life accounts with the accompaniment of a pseudonym. It goes without saying that in order to preserve the undiluted quality and depth of the material we were acquiring, we opted for the latter. As often stated, research areas that are traditionally closed off from exterior access are often the most original, utilizable and rewarding. This is especially the case with regard to such sensitive and traumatic events as programs of organizational restructuring and downsizing – upon which companies are understandably reluctant to provide much information. In this respect we felt that in the circumstances our decision was a small but very worthy compromise.

Style and content

By focusing upon the real-life perceptions, opinions and experiences of managers in the field, we have sought to render the text as accessible as possible, both to the business student and to the practitioner, and, more broadly, to the interested general reader. In practice, many of the issues discussed are intrinsically complex, but we have sought to utilize plain text wherever possible, avoiding unnecessary jargon and technical terminology. We have also sought to intersperse the main text with anecdotal evidence drawn directly from the field, typically of a case company or from an individual manager's personal records. All three of us have contributed material to these boxed excerpts, either collectively or from our own individual research and/or experience.

The reader will also come across a particular set of boxed excerpts headed "Executive Insights." These have been composed almost entirely by Bryan and are predominantly drawn from his singular experiences at the helm of Castrol (Thailand) through much of the 1980s and 90s. Further anecdotes have then been added during the composition of this book, typically through Bryan's network of contacts across the region. Intended to provide a bit of "light relief" from the main body of text, these first-hand accounts are often strikingly candid and detailed, allowing the reader a rare glimpse of the key issues chief executives are typically faced with in the Southeast Asian business environment

Structure

Part I – comprising Chapters 1 and 2 – serves to further lay the foundations for the rest of this book, detailing the geographic, cultural and historic backdrop to the region, as well as providing an overview of the incumbent MNC cohort. Part II then provides a detailed analysis of the changing organizational structures and working methods adopted by MNCs in the postcrisis business environment. To this end the emphasis is on intracorporate change; that is, corporate-imposed attempts to downsize and consolidate regional operations, as well as to seek to "harmonize" traditional human resource functions and the use of information technology in line with global corporate norms. Continuing efforts to restructure and redesign local business units/subsidiaries will be explored against the backdrop of several key macromanagement forces, as elucidated in the Introduction (notably, regional economic slowdown, overcapacity and the growth in electronic technology). We shall focus initially on the first wave of organizational restructuring programs to emanate from global corporate headquarters, then analyze the local resistance to these directives, and end with an exploration of the emerging compromise or "cross-vergent" business practices that have come to the fore in more recent years. Each stage of the process will be viewed from the critical perspective of cultural (in)congruence, outlining the pertinent ramifications "from the trenches" in each case.

Part III – Chapters 8 through 11 – moves away from this internal focus to a broader, more eclectic examination of how these corporations are seeking to change their relationships with the world outside, expressed here as the local business environment. More precisely, we shall focus on the evolving MNC *marketing* strategies in Southeast Asia, triggered by increasing global pressures to rationalize domestic product/service offerings on a region-wide basis. An introductory exploration into how the "marketing function" is both perceived and executed in Southeast Asia precedes a discussion of how global corporations have sought to bring back "to heel" the idiosyncratic marketing mix methodologies of their local business units. We focus in particular on the four classic elements of the marketing mix, with a separate chapter devoted to the controversial topic of the need and relevance of the marketing function. The book is then brought to a close with a concluding section that seeks to provide both an overview of the discussion so far and a number of suggestions for the future.

Part I
The Southeast Asia regional bloc: salient features

This opening part of our text provides the contextual backdrop to the core focus of our research. More precisely, we utilize the following two chapters to describe and explore the salient features of the Southeast Asia regional bloc, discussing how and to what degree these inherent characteristics affect the entry and development strategies of the world's foremost multinational corporations.

In structural terms Chapter 1 seeks to overview the Southeast Asian market environment, beginning with a brief description of the region's economic and political heritage. The ensuing – and hugely significant – financial collapse of recent years is then delineated, specifically as regards its origins, duration and long-term effects upon regional commercial activity. We move on to explore some of the deeper, culturally suffused parameters of business development across Southeast Asia, followed by an outline of how the region is now opening up toward a more globalized, deregulated trading environment.

Chapter 2 narrows the focus, progressing toward a more detailed depiction of where, how and why the incumbent multinationals are developing their global business strategies within the region. We begin by tracing the recent influx of foreign direct investment in Southeast Asia, facilitated by the economic downturn. Subsequent sections then delineate the changing domestic industrial landscapes, specifically as concerning their relative attractiveness as current – and potential – targets for multinational business development. The chapter ends with a brief survey of the varied modes of entry employed by incoming MNCs, detailing the traditional dilemma of whether to opt for a local partnership arrangement or proceed by setting up a wholly owned corporate subsidiary.

1 ASEAN business context

- Overview
- Crisis
- Cultural foundations
- Opening up

Overview

The current East–West interface at the front line of corporate Southeast Asia has its precedents in the cultural and historic background to our focal region. Because of its distinctive location, lying as it does between India and China, two areas with huge populations and quite distinctive cultural characteristics, Southeast Asia is positioned to serve as a crossroads over and through which trade passes, along with the movement of peoples, ideas and innovations. In many respects this still happens today and forms an integral part of the region's identity (see Ulack and Leinbach, 2000). Banded together to form the beginnings of an anticommunist trading zone, the Association of Southeast Asian Nations (ASEAN) bloc now consists of the original six market economies of Brunei, Indonesia, Malaysia, the Philippines, Singapore and Thailand – with a total population of 330 million – latterly joined by Vietnam's 80 million, and the three other reforming socialist economies of Myanmar, Cambodia and Laos.

This regional grouping is depicted, along with China and India, as one of the world's leading emerging markets by the US Department of Commerce. By some accounts ASEAN is currently Asia's most attractive region for the overall development of consumer industry. On paper, at least, ASEAN is larger, in economic terms, richer, and moving faster toward trade liberalization than either India or China. It also harbors vast and largely untapped potential for expansion, largely at its northern frontier, where Vietnam, Laos, Myanmar and Cambodia remain predominantly agrarian and have only just been opened up for trade. Even in the manufacturing powerhouses of the region such as Malaysia and Thailand, there is tremendous scope for further development by moving toward more sophisticated, specialized and higher value-added manufactured exports (Ulack and Leinbach, 2000).

The evident heterogeneity of the ASEAN region, characterized by differences in industrial development, political organization and ethnicity, makes the task of defining what constitutes a "Southeast Asian" mode of working all the more difficult. Unlike those in the more developed countries of the West and in Japan, business systems in Southeast Asia tend to be relatively dynamic and constantly evolving, owing to both their "immaturity" and their rapid growth. Indeed, the transitory nature of ASEAN can be evidenced by its evolution both from a command economy to a market-based one and from a collection of rural, agricultural societies to ones that are increasingly urban and industrial.

In general terms, although the region contains some of the world's fastest-growing economies and most rapidly changing societies, it also includes some of its poorest nations. The political dichotomy that has characterized the region in the past decade finds expression in the contrast between the technological and trade-driven development in Singapore through to much of the disorder, disputes and isolation shown at the region's northern frontier. Indeed, except for Singapore, the countries of ASEAN are still depicted as "developing," although sometimes Malaysia and occasionally Thailand are described as "newly industrialized." In industrial terms these differences are instanced in the respective nations' manufactured exports, which tend to be dominated by textiles, clothing and leather goods in the least industrialized countries but with an increasing prevalence of consumer electronic and electrical goods elsewhere.

Crisis

Described as Asia's major economic emergency of the past fifty years, the economic crisis which began in Thailand in fiscal 1998 was a massive tectonic shock for the ASEAN bloc. Although few now say they had thought the region would escape the inevitability of a business cycle downturn, all now admit to having been taken off guard by the severity of the turnaround, which devastated the region and diminished its values, bringing to a halt two decades of gradual poverty reduction and improvement in living standards.

Economic activity across the region shrank by some 40 percent over two years as companies struggled to cope with tightening marketing margins and increased competition. As a case in point, the automotive industry suffered markedly from the rising costs of importing kits and parts in the wake of the currency devaluation. Like so many others, this particular industry experienced an especially severe downturn in Thailand, where sales fell by as much as 75 percent in the first year of crisis, a situation that was to result in mass layoffs across the automotive and spare parts industries through 1997 and 1998. As the IMF frantically sought to arrange and implement its second largest ever bailout, local journalists began spinning images of sick geese, trembling tigers and exhausted dragons to depict the worsening predicament. Phongpaichit and Baker (1998) astutely compared the end of Thailand's boom as being like a "car crashing in slow motion."

Cultural foundations

The geographic focus of this book comprises a highly complex, diverse and ever-changing web of economies. Yet in spite of these differences, the countries depicted are systematically similar in many ways, sufficiently so to make our analysis both feasible and useful. Concurrent with our overall "take" on the issue of evolving MNC practice in the region, the ASEAN group of countries are grouped together for analysis here mainly in terms of their shared *cultural* characteristics, broadly defined as those beliefs, practices and values that are widely shared in the local subsidiaries and joint ventures and which stem from these countries' religions, proximity, history, climate and education. Although there are recognizable cultural differences between the countries, they also exhibit a clustering of cultural tendencies which meld them and render them distinct from both the Western and the Japanese environments. The common root which threads through their respective management cultures lies in the Chinese overseas connection and their particular brand of economic and business capitalism.

Although comprising barely 10 percent of the region's population, the Southeast Asian Chinese are thought to control over two-thirds of its retail trade. Their unparalleled domination of Southeast Asian commercial activity is further expressed in Chinese levels of ownership within the region's private sector. Even in Indonesia and Malaysia – where the Chinese have been traditionally vulnerable to exclusion and persecution – they are said to hold the vast majority of these countries' corporate wealth. In recent years the public profile of ethnic Chinese capitalists in Southeast Asia has become raised, partly as a result of the economic rise of China, which has attracted large investments from Chinese business domiciled in Southeast Asia (see also Hugo, 2000).

Traditionally viewed as good local partners for incoming Western multinationals, ethnic Chinese managers in ASEAN are widely perceived as being more astute, sophisticated and motivated than the majority of their indigenous counterparts. As such, they have tended to reach commanding positions in the urban business centers of their respective commercial communities. More importantly for us, the integrating effect of the Chinese presence in Southeast Asia means that the overriding managerial assumptions and practices in the region stem from the interaction of capitalism on the one hand and the patriarchal Chinese family system on the other, the foundations of which persist in the postcrisis "shake-up" despite the superficial erosion of certain Asian traditions (Hafner, 2000). In the region-wide sharing of these core values and norms the Western MNC could – in theory – expect to be faced with broadly the same type of grounded business mindset whether operating in the Philippines, Laos or Indonesia. Indeed, the dominant presence of the overseas Chinese is often cited as a positive force for harmonization in a region otherwise fragmented into heterogeneous "clans" instanced by the Bumipatra Malay and the Javanese Indonesia businesses, to which we shall therefore be making only passing reference in this text.

The transnational networks particular to the ethnic Chinese in ASEAN provide a form of indigenous capitalist organization distinct not only from the West but also from other Asian business systems, instanced by both the Japanese *keiretsu* and the South Korean *chaebol*. These modes of managerial organization and practice are indicative of deeper culture norms and values, and in order for multinationals to implement their programs of change successfully, it behoves them to try to understand them, to examine what makes them tick. Much of Chinese business culture stems from the communally held premodern belief system termed "Confucianism," after the Chinese philosopher Confucius (K'ung Fu-tzu). In the extant literature, as well as from our respondents in the field, the consensus view is that the cornerstones of Southeast Asian society are expressed in "relationships" and the "seniority system," which stems from belief in, and respect for, the destined order of things. Hence the Chinese business organization has quite rightly been termed "personalized" or "personified," with the underpinning philosophy of Confucius setting out a framework for all types of interpersonal relationships.

Given the lack of a well-functioning legal order and ethnic bias, this emphasis on personalizing or particularizing exchange relations along kinship or ethnic lines, termed the *guanxi* network, provides an indispensable alternative. The ethics embedded within its confines function as a quasi-equivalent to contract law. *Guanxi* refers to consanguineal ties, as well as friendship and business ties, based on mutually beneficial exchanges. Business links are forged through these informal networks or gray-market mechanisms rather than through official channels, and they provide special treatment for those within the kinship groups.

What Western executives find particularly difficult to comprehend, let alone utilize, in their local business dealings is the ethnic Chinese elevation of relationship over and above that of task. Unlike in the West, relationship building is the essence of strategy in Southeast Asia, not a by-product of it – whether with customers, suppliers, joint venture partners or even government officials. Western executives tend to feel it is a bonus if a personal rapport develops from a business venture; it is certainly not something to be expected or even required. However, the Western stress on keeping things "strictly business" at the workplace is likely to confuse, even offend, corporate managers across Southeast Asia. The indigenous Chinese view tends to be that without the trust that arises from personal relations, it becomes increasingly difficult, indeed impossible, to trust the business associate to uphold the contract or perform their jobs. *Guanxi* in this sense is held as essential for business survival. Local executives understandably prefer to hire family members and relations because they believe that their trustworthiness and integrity have been already vouched for. Informal social controls are then relied on to keep employees in line. One of the problems with this mode of working – as perceived by Western executives – is that it tends to foster and encourage varying degrees of internal corruption, the word itself supposedly colloquial Chinese for "grease."

Face – and by implication status – are the major expressions of the second of our identified "cornerstones" of the local business arena, namely the "seniority system." Stemming once again from the philosopher Confucius, social harmony is thought to be best attained through everyone recognizing his or her place in the world. In this sense the social context defines the individual, as distinct from the Western view, in which the individual defines his or her context. A primary contrast between Eastern and Western cultures is this relative focus on the good of the group in the East versus the good of the individual in the West, cited as

Executive Insights: "Happy Christmas . . ."

"During A. D. E. Jones's tenure as CEO [chief executive officer] of Castrol (Malaysia) Ltd in the late 1980s and early 90s he arrived home one Christmas Eve to find some very nice antique-style chairs delivered as an apparent Christmas present. Furthermore, it turned out that they were from a supplier.

"On the first working day after Christmas, Jones called the supplier, thanking him for the gifts – but adding in no uncertain terms that Castrol would be unable to accept them, and that he was sending them back. He signed off the telephone conversation with the terse closing statement 'Oh, and by the way – you've lost the business.'"

the foundation for the centralized, paternalistic and loyal nature of Asian-based organizations. By reason of this group orientation, high levels of importance are attached to conformity and social status in Eastern cultures, and direct conflict is often avoided and highly frowned upon. In maintaining this social harmony Confucius apparently legitimized the strong hierarchical order that continues to dominate the ethnic Chinese business culture. In the broader, societal context respect for tradition, ancestors and age were among the main values of old China and still hold enormous sway. Social status can be gained from their possession and, in certain cases, acquisition of a number of ascriptive factors including age, gender, regional origin and, to some extent, ethnicity. Individuals tend to be deferential to those whom they see as socially superior, and those in a superior position, in turn, have social obligations to their inferiors.

Not surprisingly, this whole set of Confucian tenets translates easily and naturally into the corporate sphere. The family setup is especially important, and is often cited as being the key competitive asset for business success. Power is centralized in the father or parents, who have the authority to command members of the extended family (often nested within a single department) to pool their labor and to allocate these resources for collective security and benefit (see also Lim, 2000). The centralization of decision-making power in the patriarch or the family holding company is held to facilitate quick decision making and implementation, as well as flexibility and risk taking. The "typical" Chinese senior executive thus tends to be relatively power centred and secretive, considering "openness" a weakness in the serious struggle of business competition. Loyalty, obedience and respect are expected in strictly ordered hierarchical relationships and there is close supervision and a high degree of control over subordinates. Young managers are predictably rare.

With relatively high power levels invested in the local managerial role, quick decision making within an executive's sphere of control is to be expected. However, among management committees of peers, the recognition of similar standing within the organization can quickly lead to a prevailing culture of consensus and extensive consultation. Southeast Asian managers rarely say "no" in these situations because refusal causes loss of face. And whereas loss of face is arguably distasteful in any culture – business or otherwise – it is patently far more serious in a set of societies characterized by expressions such as "better to lose money (or even life) than to lose face." In practical terms, negative decisions are of course made and, moreover, relayed to those concerned. However, the process tends to be more opaque and discreet, causing Westerners often to misunderstand and misinterpret these indirect modes of communication, criticizing their lack of speed and efficiency.

Executive Insights: "Belt Up"

An interesting example of loss of face occurred when my boss authorized me to purchase a new car. I took my driver, Khun Sawat, with me to the Volvo showroom on Sukhumvit Road in Bangkok and chose a silver 240 saloon. Driving a safe car is important in Bangkok, and Khun Sawat said he liked the Volvo. This was before seatbelts were compulsory, or even popular, and I explained the system to Khun Sawat. I told him that I would feel happier if he were to wear the seatbelt, but that if he objected or felt uncomfortable, the Volvo mechanics would disconnect the flashing light which operated when it was not being used. He said he'd be happy to wear it.

"A couple of weeks later, people told me that when Khun Sawat took them around he would connect the seat belt first and then sit on top of it. The problem was that when Khun Sawat went to the British Club or anywhere else there were a lot of drivers, and he would lose face wearing a safety device taken to mean I obviously considered him an unsafe driver. I therefore decided to produce a small sticker to be placed on the dashboard of all company vehicles bearing the message 'It is Castrol group policy that seat belts be worn in the front seats of all company vehicles so equipped' both in English and in Thai. Khun Sawat could now point to a company policy from his strange foreign boss that required him to wear the belt at all times. Face saved! We also then paid 2,000 Thai baht to all employees who used their own cars on company business to put seat belts in the front seats of their own vehicles."

A further critique of the seniority system voiced by corporate expatriates concerns the practical impact of high power distance on the productivity levels of rank-and-file employees. The traditional emphasis on hierarchy appears to discourage people from taking responsibility or from risking mistakes – unless they happen to be positioned right at the top of social strata. This is neatly summed up by one respondent who bemoaned the continuing predilection among senior corporate executives for trying to run their corporate divisions as if they were "corner shops," insisting on their sole right to approve even the smallest of decisions. We should also note the prevalent perceptions that the local managers and their departments are reluctant – even unable – to form self-directed teams. This is claimed by theorists such as Niratpattanasai (1997) to stem from the fact that in an agricultural society in which farmers worked in their own fields there was very little call for "teamwork" (in the contemporary sense of the word).

In summarizing some of the behavioral differences witnessed above, we conclude this section with the consolidated findings of a "Work Values/Character Assessment Survey" which was used by the Western headquarters of a major US oil conglomerate in order to establish the divergence in business practices and values between head office and its ASEAN subsidiaries. Distributed in 1996 for corporate cross-cultural training purposes, this internal survey was annotated and scored by both indigenous and US-based management representatives. It appears to demonstrate that whereas Western head office personnel are over-whelmingly "results driven," "serious," "assertive," "punctual," "self-disciplined," "diligent" and "meticulous," their ASEAN counterparts display a set of business characteristics depicted as "process oriented," "relationship driven," "informal" and "respectful." Key difficulties expressed by corporate staff involved with Southeast Asia center on the perceived "lack of forward planning" by the local management, along with their concern for business "form and procedure" over "outcomes," and a "mysterious" emphasis on nonverbal cues to impart opinion and feeling.

Opening up

The economic crisis served to accelerate the deregulation mooted in the 1997 World Trade Organization (WTO) agreement, and has opened up protected markets and monopolies far more rapidly than at first envisaged. The very authorities that had previously ignored the largest foreign

Executive Insights: "Project Lubrication"

"Some Western expatriates working in Southeast Asian markets often complain – and with some justification – that large-scale industrial and infrastructure projects have to be 'lubricated' by between 10 and 15 percent of a project's total cost, paid in brown paper envelopes passed under the table. Not surprisingly, hard facts to substantiate these claims are very difficult to come by, and most decent Western managers would not know how to even approach the issue of paying 'commissions.'

"However, I know of an ethical yet tough Canadian expatriate who refuses to get involved in this kind of practice. During the past eighteen months he has worked ceaselessly and with perseverance to complete a feasibility study and business plan to build a privately owned refinery complex on the eastern seaboard of Thailand (to come on stream in 2004). In fact, it is because of this CEO's international reputation for straight talking, straight dealing and successful projects around the world that international financiers have already decided to back it. It can be done in markets like Thailand, and the Superior Oil Refining Group, led by Nels Nordstrom, will prove it."

corporations were now inviting them to participate in local markets, eager, along with potential local partners, to benefit from their larger cache of money and experience (see also Granitsas and Bickers, 1999).

Reflecting this about-turn in perspective, the balance of power between incoming multinationals and host-market governments has also begun to shift. Contemporary MNCs now have an unprecedented choice of emerging markets in which to invest. The main beneficiaries of the surge in external capital inflows in ASEAN are Indonesia, the Philippines, Malaysia and Thailand, yet the pace of deregulation is uneven. However, even the widely perceived "laggards" of Vietnam, Cambodia and Laos are now passing laws facilitating and promoting overseas investment. The result has been that foreign investment in Indochina has accelerated markedly in recent years and has served to restore quasi-market domestic economies. Investment has surged in private-sector involvement in tourism, commerce, small-scale industry, construction, banking and telecommunications. It is claimed that Vietnam has passed more laws in the past ten years than in the previous two hundred (Borton, 2000) – a factor causing attendant problems among increasingly confused and uncertain multinationals within the market.

Given the wide disparities in income and industrialization between the core and periphery economies of ASEAN, the increasing openness of protected markets is unlikely to lead directly to economic integration of the region. In the meantime the less developed economies of Laos and Cambodia have pinned their development strategies on integration into the "Greater Mekong Subregion," which will link the economies of Laos, Cambodia, Myanmar, Vietnam, Thailand and southwest China. Nonetheless, the planned regional tariff reductions from the beginning of 2000 as part of the ASEAN Free Trade Agreement (AFTA) can be seen as a crucial first step along this path, stimulating expanded trade, cheaper imports and cheaper prices as a consequence. It will also inevitably spark a flood of cheap garments from Indonesia and the Philippines into Malaysia and Thailand, also prompting cheap clothing to be reexported back from China into ASEAN.

At the time of writing, however, these intraregional trade flows have not been picking up as quickly as was hoped. The free trade agreement itself has also been dogged by exceptions, multiple deadlines and other confusing elements that have made selling the concept to outsiders difficult. As a regional organization, ASEAN appeared divided and slow in responding to the crisis, and the overall appeal of the region appears to have faded. International investors seem to be moving away, railing against the lack of objective and clear rules in an Asian economic environment that to them appears to be rigged. The cozy ties which remain between government and a coddled business class are berated as a drag on innovation, competition and, ultimately, economic growth. External criticism has been most keenly felt with regard to the well-publicized liberalization of the region's automotive industry. At present, tariffs of up to 300 percent on imported cars allow Malaysia's fledgling industry to hold out against the world's car giants. Yet that protection is soon to fall away, as part of the plan to liberalize trade within the region, mandating the reduction of import tariffs on cars and car parts, and paving the way for the expected surge in multinational suppliers. The plan is theoretically held to be the key to revolutionizing the entire industry, but increasing doubts have been expressed as to its realization – especially since only Thailand and Indonesia had scrapped their local-content requirements by the 2000 WTO deadline. All that can be foreseen is a series of interim deals between individual carmakers and governments, at least until 2005, when Malaysia will be forced to drop its protective shield against the likes of General Motors and Ford (both of which are already producing in Thailand). The immediate results for both carmakers will be the new-found freedom to import their parts from the lowest-cost, highest-quality, most innovative producers anywhere in the world (see also Goad, 2000a; Holland, 2000; Legewie, 2000).

The ASEAN bloc is also witnessing the concurrent liberalization of another strategic segment, that of the telecommunications industry. Triggered by the economic crisis and the relentless march of technology, Western firms – including British, French, US and German telecommunications companies – are scrambling for new licenses, pledging hundreds of millions of dollars to build the necessary regional infrastructure in the process. Global corporate customers increasingly want seamless cross-border service, and dealing with a single regional service provider for telecommunications in ASEAN would be a step in the right direction. But Asia's patchwork quilt of economies in very different stages of development – plus its self-protecting governmental policies – makes this difficult in practice, rendering the region in danger of becoming a perennial laggard behind the rest of the world in competitive consolidations (Granitsas and Bickers, 1999; Wilhelm and Slater, 2000). Regional Internet-protocol technology in Southeast Asia is also developing at different rates in different countries, although apart from in Singapore and – to a much lesser extent – the Philippines and Thailand it is virtually nonexistent, despite the vast potential for future expansion.

The financial crisis in Asia has compelled local governments to attract foreign capital in order to strengthen the financial positions of their economies and increase their financial leverage. To this end, the previous restrictions on regional cross-border mergers and acquisitions have been lifted. MNCs are now induced to invest more heavily in the region, given the low asset values of local firms, often at prices extremely unfavorable to the local sellers (e.g. Zhan and Ozawa, 2000). Yet in spite of the benefits that foreign direct investment inflows can offer an emerging economy, during the crisis fallout, foreign multinationals were demonized across Southeast Asia as unwelcome vultures feeding off the misfortunes of indigenous markets. The subsequent withdrawal into nationalism pervaded the immediate postcrisis environment, as serious concerns as to the wisdom of selling national assets "on the cheap" increased. Failing to contribute to local productive capacity, acquisition of local capital by global oligopolies is understandably perceived as merely a transfer of asset ownership from domestic to foreign investors. The resentment felt by the indigenous populace is exacerbated should the companies "up for sale" represent key domestic industries, exemplified by the Bangchak petroleum company in Thailand. The situation is further inflamed when – as has become the norm – foreign entrants then wish to "consolidate their operations" and lay off staff as part of a program of restructuring, or even of closing down local facilities.

2 Rise of the multinational

- History and current operations
- Moving in

History and current operations

With its combined consumer potential of 500 million inhabitants, Southeast Asia has been vigorously targeted by some of the world's foremost consumer multinationals for years. The long history of colonization in the region, by Western powers in particular, has served to smooth the path for later economic expansion. Western MNCs are the oldest-established "modern" enterprises in Southeast Asia, beginning with colonial-era multinational trading companies and export plantations. Unlike in Japan or the so-called "tiger" economies of Korea, Hong Kong and Taiwan, where indigenous firms played the leading role, these foreign corporations have been instrumental in promoting the development of Southeast Asia. Even before the investment liberalization of the late 1980s and 90s, the Western MNC had come to occupy a major, if not dominant, role in the modern sectors of Southeast Asian economies. During the early decades, Western investment in the region was most attracted by the region's abundant natural physical resources and cheap labor, and the possibilities they provided for competitive exports to world markets. But since the 1970s the presence of Western MNCs has steadily increased as these economies have grown and developed new sectors, and barriers to foreign trade and investment have been progressively reduced. This is typified by the series of studies indicating that at least half of domestic economic growth in Thailand since the 1980s has been the result of foreign direct investment (FDI), with foreign multinationals responsible for over one-third of the country's subsequent export flows (e.g. Leinbach and Bowen, 2000).

This surge in FDI across the region has propelled Southeast Asia's economies far beyond the point to which their indigenous technologies would have taken them. Governments across the region's developing economies hope to duplicate the success of Singapore in harnessing MNCs to achieve rapid, sustained economic development. Barely a generation ago, multinationals in Singapore were mainly low-wage, labor-intensive employers. Since then they have expanded the size, scope and sophistication of their operations, with today's jobs comprising a wide range of skills-intensive and knowledge-intensive positions (Leinbach and Bowen, 2000).

We found that, viewed from the perspective of the corporations themselves, different kinds of companies are drawn into the region for different, often sector-specific, reasons. Some have arrived to establish manufacturing plants to serve the local market. Others have come to take advantage of the region's natural regional resource base, instanced by the oil refineries in Singapore set up by foreign MNCs to tap output from Indonesia and Brunei. The most important activity cited is in utilizing Southeast Asia as a production base for the worldwide export of product, often through the sourcing of local components (Leinbach and Bowen, 2000).

Multinationals headquartered in the West and Japan are generally far superior to their local counterparts in technological and organizational competencies, from which much of their industrial power is drawn. Chinese-dominated Asian conglomerates have in the past competed largely through pricing and low wages, neglecting the huge effort necessary to move forward in terms of management practice and technology. The global trend toward technological and environmental synchronization – promoted by international trading and standards accreditation bodies – is also shifting the local balance of power to the foremost corporate predators. The smaller domestic – and even regional – competing firms lack the kind of specialist teams necessary to handle these increasingly stringent sets of regulatory procedures.

In the context of the recent economic crisis the prevalence of foreign corporations remains undiminished (and has by some accounts been enhanced). The net result of regional ownership caps being lifted has been an unprecedented wave of acquisition throughout Southeast Asia. With their immense financial weight, some of the world's top corporations, headed by the US giants Procter & Gamble, Gillette, Coca-Cola and Eastman Kodak, have spearheaded the stampede to buy out or take increased stock in partly owned subsidiaries or competitors at "fire sale" prices. Yet far from being mere cases of asset stripping, the vast majority of the larger acquisitions appear to be long-term strategic investments in the region. This is typified by these corporations' reaction to the long years of economic recession and market contraction, as they struggled to cope with tightening marketing margins and spiralling operating costs. The inevitable streamlining and restructuring processes that followed – often directly overseen from corporate head office – is again indicative of their commitment to the market.

In the more developed economies of the region a concurrent slant on MNC investment has been the growth of the increasingly large and affluent middle class. Albeit temporarily dampened during the immediate aftermath of the crisis, this continuing trend has led to a higher demand per capita for more complex, higher-priced consumer durables such as automobiles and electronic houseware. In this context an increasing number of MNCs are being drawn to the region by its consumers. As wage levels in the region continue to rise, some MNCs currently using ASEAN as a low-cost exporting platform may well reinvest elsewhere in time, but others will be drawn in their place by the region's growing spending power. Along with the arrival of firms such as Ford, Nestlé and General Motors, this development will act as a catalyst to the transition from a labor- to a more knowledge-intensive manufacturing base in coming years.

In the current ASEAN industrial environment, multinationals are prevalent across a wide spectrum of industries. A glance at the roadside billboards on the short taxi ride from Bangkok International Airport to the city center gives a typical cross section of the industries represented, from the automotive muscle of companies such as Ford, Honda, Volkswagen and Chevrolet via related manufacturers such as Michelin and Bridgestone through to electrical and communications firms Singer and Siemens, electronics producers NEC, Nokia, Panasonic and Philips, and on to the Swiss consumer giant Nestlé.

In general terms the automobile, electronic and petrochemical sectors have led industrial recovery in the manufacturing centers of ASEAN, accounting for up to 30 percent of the region's total export value. Market leadership in sales volume terms for automobiles is still held by long-time residents Toyota and Honda, the latter with over half of all sales in the ASEAN bloc. Recent reports suggest that their dominance is set to continue – even increase – as global carmakers commit themselves to developing ASEAN's role in their global supply networks (Bangkok Post, 2002). There is also a growing presence of Western car giants in the region making deeper and deeper inroads into what is expected to become the world's largest car market one day. This is typified by the emergence of the "Detroit Three" of Ford, General Motors and Daimler-Chrysler with production facilities based in Thailand, as well as BMW and the imminent arrival of France's PSA group and Renault, and Alfa-Romeo from Italy, all with long-term manufacturing intentions for the region.

Petrochemical and oil-refining companies comprise another major area of activity, and in particular from European-based multinationals. The world's major oil companies, such as Shell, Exxon-Mobil and BP, are drawn to Southeast Asia to be close to the rich fields of Indonesia and Brunei. Petrochemical companies such as UK giant ICI are looking to come closer to their markets so as to avoid the prohibitively high transportation costs of raw materials. Electronics firms from Europe with substantial export-oriented manufacturing facilities in Southeast Asia include conglomerates such as Philips and Siemens, both of which produce semiconductors in the region. Indeed, Siemens – a world leader in electrical engineering and electronics, with a worldwide workforce of nearly a half million employees – offers its entire range of products, systems and services in a number of key domestic markets. France's Alcatel, NEC from Japan and Nortel from the USA also compete in the electronic communications industry, supplying telecommunications equipment such as cable optic fibers and Internet systems.

Comparative multinational dominance is also characteristic of the cosmetics, pharmaceuticals and construction sectors. L'Oréal, Estée Lauder, Amway, Avon, Clairol, Procter & Gamble and Unilever lead the field in cosmetics, the latter two companies also dominating the regional consumer goods industry (along with Colgate-Palmolive). Because its people are rumored to be among the biggest "pill-poppers" in the world per capita, the region has also been something of a magnet for pharmaceuticals multinationals, with all the key players in attendance (including Glaxo-Wellcome, Hoffmann-La Roche and Bristol Myers Squibb). The multinational stranglehold of the construction and construction chemicals industries is spearheaded by the likes of Kumajai and Bayer. These industries are also typical in the geographic duality expressed among the major players, with MNCs controlling the lion's share of business, leaving perhaps a dozen smaller foreign and domestic companies to divide the remaining market chunk. There is a further split within the consumer-based sectors, with foreign and transnational firms together with a few successful domestic companies operating in the larger cities, with small and medium-sized enterprises scattered across the rest of the country.

Among the more fragmented sectors – textiles, food production and shoes – US firms in the region concerned with electronics, textiles, shoes and so forth have not always been the largest investors, as is instanced by the local food industry, where the big European corporations are dominant. But the presence of American firms is widely regarded as being of prime importance to the region as their global marketing strength (e.g. Nike or Reebok for athletic footwear) means that locally manufactured goods have secure access to worldwide markets. Within the nonmanufacturing sphere one notable example is the case of the life insurance industry, which continues to grow at phenomenal levels across the region, fueled by the widespread opening up of the region's markets, which has created a high level of domestic savings among wary and uncertain consumers. The recent crisis has added to this trend, making life insurance packages an enticing investment for families amid the financial instability and corrupt inefficient banking sectors. In this environment the existing multinationals are witnessing policy sales far ahead of expectations, with market leader AIA (of the American International Group) the main beneficiary in Southeast Asia, ahead of Western rivals Prudential, CGU, Royal Sun Alliance, AXA and others (see also Cohen, 2000b).

Moving in

Market screening

In a climate of relentless global competition, multinationals are increasingly concerned with assessing the locational advantages of their regional bases and pockets of development. The region tends to be screened initially on a number of key variables, usually initiated by macroeconomic factors, investment climates and level of political stability. The overall competitiveness of individual countries is then determined in part by the efficiency of its existing telecommunications infrastructure and the openness of its labor markets in allowing easy access to skilled foreign labor. Although decisions tend to be linked to sector, experience and size of operation, we shall attempt nonetheless to venture a number of tentative generalizations.

Much of the recent industrialization in the region has been fueled by footloose capital. Unlike the kind of production facility which requires a large nearby supply of natural resources such as tin or coal, most of the manufacturing operations set up by MNCs in ASEAN require only one major local resource: labor. MNCs therefore have greater latitude in deciding where to locate such plants. In recent years the developed and industrializing parts of Asia have experienced the brunt of rising wage costs. In this context, manufacturing firms from such countries as Singapore and Malaysia have begun to relocate some of their mainly labor-intensive functions to the peripheral, lower-cost countries such as Indonesia and the Philippines when their host countries become too expensive or when new and even less expensive sites such as Vietnam and Cambodia open up. Conversely, the more highly skilled positions, management, control of capital investments and technology and profits remain in the corporate head offices in the "core" countries (Leinbach and Bowen, 2000).

Singapore

Beginning with the more established markets of the region, Singapore is still obviously quite attractive as an ASEAN hub of operations, being a highly urbanized global feeder port and a center for state-of-the-art human and physical infrastructure. Many incoming corporations still opt for centers such as Singapore along with Hong Kong for their comparatively "regional" flavor when set alongside their developing neighbors. This is particularly the case in specialized high-technology industries such as those for top-grade chemicals. However, with the rise in information technology and the "multitasking" of increasing numbers of employees, this concept of having regional "centers" at the top of the development chain is progressively disappearing as outmoded. Specifically, Singapore tends to be comparatively expensive, highly regulated and with an obviously limited domestic market. As one regional expatriate observed,

> "Using Hong Kong or Singapore as your regional base just for copycat reasons, because everyone else is there, makes no sense. The improvements in telecommunications over the last decade have definitely made and will continue to make these places increasingly redundant save for the odd few specialized sectors. There are other countries now which have better air travel, lower renting costs and lower salaries – it's always best to look hard before you leap."

Malaysia

Across the border, Malaysia has suffered in the postcrisis corporate environment, being reduced to relatively low levels of foreign multinational investment initiatives. The country has tended to be difficult for incoming firms, owing to its ethnic heterogeneity and the concurrent impact upon employment regulation. Executives bemoan in particular the enforced quota of Bumipatra Malay locals who are required to serve on joint venture boards. In the words of one Dutch senior manager from the petrochemical sector,

> "These kind of rules are simply not compatible with an economy that is claiming itself to be liberal and open to foreign investment. With a joint venture you need to be as sure as you can [be] that the people who direct the company are loyal first and foremost to the company. But . . . these artificial regulations which stop us from choosing our own staff because they are good and no other reason mean you [are] never sure about loyalty."

The prevalence of distinct racial groups is also cited as a marketing research problem, evidenced by the need for the manifold translation of questionnaires to accommodate these differences. Malaysia also tends to lack the kind of investment-friendly tax laws that are offered by, say, the Thai board of investment, with its eight-year tax breaks and attractive industrial zones. Finally, Malaysia still has its currency – the ringgit – pegged to the US dollar, which is sending alarm signals to a plethora of potential foreign investors in case the ringgit should ever be allowed to float, particularly when one considers what then happened to the Thai baht in 1997.

Indonesia

Before the crisis, Malaysia – along with Indonesia and the Philippines – was a relatively attractive destination for foreign MNCs, but all countries are to varying degrees being perceived as having been adversely affected. The country most seriously affected of this group is Indonesia. Precrisis Indonesia was courted by potential investors for its large domestic market and abundant, low-cost labor. It was felt that the Suharto government provided good macroeconomic management, and the country was viewed as being socially stable and rich in natural resources. Concerns expressed at the time centered on the fact that English was still not widely spoken, and that skills, education and productivity levels needed much improvement. The observed close linkages between the politicians and the domestic business environment, although considered to pose potential obstacles, were not the primary concern. At the time, companies were often more concerned with the country's dependency upon imports for key business sectors; it had few supporting industries.

In recent times these priorities have been upended as multinationals have continued to count their losses from past associations with the now defunct Suharto family. Unlike its recovering neighbors, Indonesia continues to be rocked by political unrest and social instability. With a net divestment of foreign direct investment and a reduction of private capital flows, the country's precarious financial future still hangs in the balance; it is perceived by many foreign corporations as a "bad bet" for current projects. The paucity of corporate restructuring projects tackled in the postcrisis period, during which the host government has actively tried to save local firms from bankruptcy, has also been roundly criticized by foreign investors as akin to "dithering procrastination" as regards the tasks in hand. In its favor, Indonesia is still one of cheapest markets in the region – even the world – and is getting cheaper, prompting renewed interest in companies seeking to relocate their labor-intensive operations. Indonesia does not have the overinvestment problem of so many of its neighbors and can still claim to be in only the first phase of industrial infrastructure development. Despite its ongoing political and economic instability it is also claimed that in terms of its openness to foreign investors, Indonesia is progressing in ways that could not have been predicted a few years ago (Zhan and Ozawa, 2000).

The Philippines

Evolving slowly into a pluralistic state, the Philippines, unlike its Southeast Asian neighbors (with the exception of Thailand), had not one but two Western colonizers in Spain and, latterly, the USA. The impact of these two colonial influences means that the country today is described as the least Oriental country in the Orient, suffused with "three centuries in a Catholic convent and fifty years in Hollywood" (Ulack, 2000). However, sharing a fair proportion of core Asian values and beliefs, the Filipinos, latterly depicted as merely "Americans with suntans," would be more accurately described as "Asians with blue jeans." Economically portrayed for many years as the "sick man" of Asia, the country has not thus far made the social and economic progress that the other original

ASEAN members have. However, in part as a result of this lack of developmental integration, the Philippines has not been as negatively affected by the regional crisis. Otherwise, the country tends to suffer from its geographical location, being perceived by incoming corporations as being "out of the way" compared to the more central sites enjoyed by Thailand and Malaysia.

In the past few years the Philippines has begun to improve its situation and there are increasing signs of its desire to integrate more fully into both the regional and the global economies. Foreign companies are increasingly attracted by the country's tax breaks, skilled but inexpensive workers, and political stability. MNCs such as Philip Morris, the cigarette manufacturer, Ford Motors and Philips Electronics have chosen to set up and then expand their production facilities outside Manila, in some cases shifting production from elsewhere in Asia. In terms of its comparative human resource input, the Philippines enjoys an educated, highly literate workforce and offers a surplus of flexible, English-speaking skilled workers at relatively low wage rates. Indeed, the use of English as the country's lingua franca, and the country's growing reputation in the information technology sector, are viewed as big competitive advantages which the country tends – if anything – to undersell.

Among the many multinational experiences in the Philippines, the case of UK financial conglomerate Jardine provides further illustration of its "on-the-ground" attractions:

> "We've had three joint ventures in the Philippines, and to be honest they were all fairly supportive of what we wanted to do. OK, they may have been argumentative – but they always backed us up whenever things came to a head. But in Malaysia it was like we had three different partners and it was really just one disaster after another . . . in Thailand we had the CP/Central group as partners, and although it was OK, the feeling was that they took us just for what they wanted. In the Philippines my experiences are that there is much more loyalty . . . although there is corruption, at least it's a kind of clear form of corruption – I mean the amounts required are clear from the beginning of negotiations and it tends to stay that way."

Thailand

In many ways Thailand is one of most attractive countries in ASEAN because of its comparatively large domestic market, low labor costs, large base of suppliers, acceptable infrastructure and the pro-business attitude of successive domestic governments. Earlier and better than many of its regional neighbors, Thailand adopted a policy of facilitating the foreign acquisition of indigenous firms, repeatedly lifting upward its cap on foreign ownership levels. The country has gained a reputation over the years as being relatively more open to investment by foreign multinationals, many with their eye on Thailand as a strategic base for exporting to emerging Asian economies and beyond. The vast majority of expatriates we interviewed also thought that Thailand had done the most toward reforming its indigenous corporate sector and economic policies in the wake of the regional crisis.

Unlike Malaysia or Indonesia, Thailand has successfully identified and promoted its key industries in order to remain competitive in the global market. Already termed "the Detroit of the East," with the removal of all local content requirements Thailand's automotive industry is now set to become the region's assembly hub and export platform. As one of the fastest-growing vehicle markets in Asia – and the world's largest market for trucks outside the USA – the likes of Honda, Toyota, Ford, GM, Renault, Mazda, Alfa-Romeo, PSA and Daimler-Chrysler have either begun or recently announced their respective plans to make Thailand the center of their Asian auto strategy, producing units for Japan, ASEAN, Australia and even Europe.

Thailand is also recognized as being a potential export hub for other key sectors, instanced by the electrical and chemical construction industries. The latter is typified by the 1997 entry of the UK company Fosroc, which has recently set out plans for Thailand to become the marketing and production arm for its expansion into Indochina. The Matsushita Electrical Company also sees Thailand as its future export hub, and intends to turn the country into its manufacturing and export center for home appliances worldwide. Recent economic and political trends in the regional mainland have facilitated the country's role in the emerging markets of its immediate neighbors. This has stimulated recent multilateral consultations about ways to expand subregional economic cooperation among the five nations of Thailand, Vietnam, Cambodia, Laos and Myanmar, plus Yunnan in southern China (which together comprise the Greater Mekong Subregion).

Stable and united under its constitutional monarchy, Thailand's famed homogeneity is matched by its reputation for having a more liberal approach to lifestyle freedoms than any of its immediate neighbors. This has certainly made it a favorite among a large contingent of visiting Western and Japanese expatriates, for whom a multitude of lounges, bars and restaurants are tailor-made. According to one US insurance executive,

> "Big corporations send their guys out on two-week trips across the region in order to view the field, help make the final decision as to where they're gonna set up their operations. And these red-blooded males are essentially looking at where they're gonna have to spend the next few years of their lives . . . so does the 'candy-store' nightlife in Thailand sway them in its favor? Yeah, I would say so, at least to an extent . . . whether or not they care to admit it of course is another matter."

The traditional drawbacks to Thailand have also been partially rectified in recent years. The country no longer has a shortage of suitably skilled people for modern industry, and the traditional language barriers with regard to indigenous English language ability have been considerably reduced. Important factors such as transport, schools and hospitals have been heavily upgraded and modernized over the course of the past decade. Air travel is also that much cheaper and convenient than elsewhere in the region. Problems that remain include the poor inspection record of its production facilities, little recognition of international standards, and comparative linguistic isolation. Recent doubts have also been cast over the country's continuing commitment to its investor-friendly business climate, with a recent government seeming to want to shield local industries from global competitive forces, exemplified by the imposition of a number of regulations upon foreign retail establishments (e.g. Makro, Tesco and Carrefour). Broader concerns among foreign corporations are variously stated as resting with the frequent and corrupt electoral process, high levels of corruption in the government itself, and the intricacy of the bureaucracy. The consensus of expatriate perceptions focuses on the apparent lack of transparency and the apparent smokescreen of vested interests with which incoming multinationals have to contend. Deceit, half-truths and uncertainties in business dealings – both with indigenous employees themselves and with the local authorities – are held to be prevalent in a nation claimed by many to be by far the most corrupt in the region.

The practical dilemmas thrown up by these factors – both in Thailand and elsewhere in the region – are neatly summarized by a senior oil industry executive for the region:

Executive Insights: Jail Bait

"In 1981 I was handed down a six-month jail sentence, suspended for two years. This was because the Castrol Thailand Finance Department had sent in a routine monthly stock report to the Thai Ministry of Commerce two working hours late, a document which I had never seen and never signed. Due to lingering tensions in Southeast Asia following the Vietnam War, motor oil stocks were regarded as a strategic issue. Many other people were also arrested, and Ray Weiland of Esso had his story spread all over the English-language newspapers. Our joint venture partner, Loxley Bangkok, possibly could have intervened but didn't know until it was too late, so I went through the obligatory finger-printing procedure at the Chinatown police station.

"Eventually I was summoned to attend the un-airconditioned courtroom, wearing my suit and tie (British to the last!) and flanked by my secretary and lawyer. While we were waiting for the judges to give their verdict, the courtroom filled with all manner of people accused of rape, murder, drug offenses and so forth – mostly in handcuffs and leg-irons. In addition to the suspended two-year sentence, the company and I were each fined 20,000 Thai baht. And while this episode did not prevent me from later obtaining a resident's visa and – later still – Thai citizenship, it is worth noting that laws relating to the liability of CEOs for minor bureaucratic mistakes are still on the Thai statute book."

"Incoming expatriates are always averse to the need for 'greasing the wheels' here, particularly with US companies like Exxon-Mobil, where they even have meetings telling staff bound for the region not to get involved with these dealings or else . . . [so] their guys here have a definite problem in coming to grips with the local business processes, although with no power to prevent it, what you see is still the same speed-up of permit approvals and so on as per normal, it's just that it's done through 'intermediaries.' Basically, if you're having problems with where you're positioning yourselves on a Western morality scale in Thailand, then you should be elsewhere . . . . The simple fact is that if you do not grease the system then you will end up being uncompetitive."

Vietnam, Laos, Myanmar and Cambodia

Our remaining focal nations – the transitional countries of Indochina – were not considered to encompass factors attractive for foreign direct investment on the part of multinationals, even prior to the crash of 1997. Vietnam, Laos, Myanmar and Cambodia all lack the necessary infrastructure facilities, their respective telephone and other telecommunications systems being well below the standards expected by foreign investors. All four countries suffered negative impacts from the crisis nonetheless, primarily through the sharp decline in investment inflows that had previously been sourced from other East Asian countries.

Although still handicapped by rigid one-party systems, Vietnam and Laos have at least gained a reputation for relative political stability and economic reform over the past two decades, despite being partially crippled by the dire lack of infrastructure. But Cambodia and Myanmar remain blighted by chronic instability characterized by years of suppression of dissent in Cambodia, and a cruel and unresponsive regime in Myanmar, a somber backdrop to any potential advantages. Indeed, for all their modest economic achievements in recent years, neither country ever tends to progress through the first stages of any company's regional market screening process as a consequence (see also Bartels and Freeman, 2000).

In per capita terms, Vietnam, with its 80 million inhabitants, has become the second largest market in Southeast Asia, with an economy five times the size of Cambodia and Laos combined. The country's population almost doubled in the decade up to 1996, and three-quarters of the nation's people are less than 25 years old, making it an attractive potential consumer hub. In keeping with the government's commitment to the *doi moi* policy of economic openness, Vietnam has changed quite radically from a planned economy to a market economy, albeit one with vaguely socialist leanings. With a recently signed trade agreement with the USA – and negotiating entry into the World Trade Organization – Vietnam has become a prime target of incoming foreign multinationals, instanced by the entry of Procter & Gamble with the promising potential of a large consumer market and investment-friendly laws. Once on-the-ground operations have commenced, however, such companies often find themselves confronted with more complex and difficult market realities than they had come to expect, notably the formidable bureaucracy and dire internal infrastructure. Concerns have also been expressed with the subtle but very real linguistic and cultural differences between north and south Vietnam, necessitating the translation and adaptation of marketing research questionnaires. US executives also tend to be wary of lingering antipathy on the part of the country's governmental hierarchy toward the USA itself, its corporations and its corporate representatives (see also Quang, 1998). However, we have found the consensus opinion on Vietnam's bureaucracy to be, in the words of one European executive, "at least when they say 'no' in Vietnam you know that this means 'no.'" This was favorably compared to Thailand, where the web of deception and uncertainty were perceived as considerably more serious.

Tiny Laos, with barely 5 million inhabitants, is also worthy of note for its now widely recognized regional geostrategic location. Regarded by the likes of Unilever, Shell and Castrol as the stepping stone into the southern provinces of China, Laos has become a focus for foreign multinational activity far out of proportion to its size. Both Shell and, latterly, Unilever have sought to take advantage of Laos's location as the hub of the Greater Mekong Subregion, the only country to have borders with all five other nations. Perceiving Laos now not so much "landlocked" as "land-linked," both companies have striven to attain dominant shares in a market that they feel is bound to become the transit center for trade to pass effectively from Thailand into both Yunnan province – with its 40 million inhabitants – and the rest of the Mekong Delta.

Mode of entry

Corporate selection of a perceived "optimal" mode of entry into Southeast Asia represents a primary decision affecting the future development and, ultimately, success of the company's investment in the region. Often the first question asked by senior executives is whether to opt for a joint venture (JV) arrangement or a fully owned corporate subsidiary. The choice is partly dictated by legal requirements or protective measures in the new market, which may, for example, necessitate an agreement with a local business partner. Our main focus here will be on the strategic components of the decision, however, and we shall explore the pros and cons of each mode in turn.

The wholly owned subsidiary

Like the more high-profile JVs, a wholly owned enterprise demonstrates a firm commitment to the local market. Global corporations – from the soft drink giants Coca-Cola and Pepsi to the shampoos of Unilever to the motor oils of Castrol – are increasingly drawn to set up local production facilities in order to be closer to the front lines in what is becoming one of the world's most lucrative consumer markets. The vast majority of multinationals featured in this book aim for the maximum possible shareholding in order to optimize their on-the-ground control, often refusing point-blank a minority position whatever the circumstances. In practical terms the wholly owned venture is also preferred as a means of avoiding potential conflicts of interest and business methods with troublesome local partners over how to run plants, deal with quality control and, if necessary, lay off workers. Traditionally localized functions such as distribution and sales are increasingly being outsourced, further reducing the dependency on local expertise. Foreign corporations are aware of the fact that joint venture agreements need continual nurturing and maintenance, often punctuated by culture-bound internal management differences, described as quite simply "the most unpleasant aspect of any overseas operation."

From the host nation perspective this spread of foreign factory transplants – with its biological metaphor of "foreign practices" accepted by "host bodies" – has traditionally been distasteful to the majority of local governments. In the precrisis years the "greenfield" investment was, generally speaking, the only acceptable means of direct foreign entry. The current trend for mergers and acquisitions would have been unthinkable in previous years, despite their long-held propensity to generate employment opportunities, enhance technology transfers and expand domestic exports. From the multinationals' perspective the increasing factor of overcapacity and high costs in their home markets has served to make ASEAN an attractive region for the establishment of production facilities. The financial turmoil in Asia also provided a golden opportunity for MNCs to enter local markets, fueled by reductions in asset prices, regional liberalization and the sharp depreciation of currencies. This provides a stark contrast to the economic "boom" years, where multinationals in practice were often confronted with excessively inflated resource prices. This is instanced by the case of Q8 in northern Thailand, which intended to set up a production facility in the country province in Chiang Rai. As one senior executive reported,

> "We were looking for a plot of land on which to build a refinery, land
> that wasn't even particularly close to the city – what city there was.
> And then we were quoted this price which kind of looked OK on paper
> until we'd got it back to the office and had it translated. We couldn't
> believe what we were being quoted – it turned out as being on a par
> with a plot of land in central London . . . absolutely incredible."

Yet with the recent destabilization of global markets, MNCs have pressed ahead with the consolidation of their cross-border production networks in order to better cope with future worldwide changes in demand and supply patterns.

The urgencies created by the regional financial crisis have also changed these host countries' view of cross-border acquisitions. The Thai authorities have even gone so far as to provide companies majority-owned or wholly owned by foreign companies with the same investment incentives as their indigenous competitors. On the ground, however, it is interesting to note that this apparent willingness of Southeast Asian governments to relax equity ownership restrictions is also viewed as being due to their realization that the ownership transfers in theory do not, in practice, translate directly into transfers of control. Indeed, the majority of our local respondents appeared to be only slightly concerned about whether local ventures fell into domestic or foreign hands, perhaps for this reason.

Foreign MNCs have had to assume that their continuing acquisition of local venture stakes puts them at risk of negative local publicity from influential quarters, and have been careful to avoid being seen as "predators." For example, taking a longer-term perspective on the situation, the UK construction chemicals group Fosroc entered the Thai market in 1997, correctly anticipating its attraction for local businesses seeking foreign capital to help them survive in the tough operating environment of the time. For Fosroc the advantage, then, was the easier attainment of local customer goodwill. Yet from a broader perspective foreign – and particularly Western – multinationals are warned of a concurrent longer-term reassertion of less Westernized, more "Asian" cultural practices in the commercial arena once the tide finally turns and the region fully recovers. "Short-sighted" Western firms that have enjoyed a "cheap and easy" entrance into the local market will then find to what extent this feeling – likened to a "knife through butter" – will prove to have been a fleeting, temporary experience.

A further factor in favor of local production/assembly comes from the traditionally high import tariffs across the region, well illustrated by the region's automotive industry, which by the early 1990s was the fastest-growing auto market in the world. At the time, most cars sold in the region were assembled locally from imported kits in which most of the components were manufactured overseas. This is exemplified by the Volvo company, which until recently had imported completed units into the region before switching to assembly in Thailand via imported kits in order to cut down prohibitive tariffs and taxes. Increasingly, however, the volume of sales in the region's more lucrative markets has reached the kind of levels that justify the development of full-scale vehicle production, a trend instanced by the arrival of BMW, Ford, GM, and so forth. Volvo has also hinted at a future move in this direction, with tentative plans to expand its range to incorporate left-hand drive trucks for Indochina (see also Leinbach and Bowen, 2000).

Cola Wars in the Lao People's Democratic Republic

Coca-Cola was one of the first global companies to set up manufacturing operations in the newly opened economies of Southeast Asia. Seeking to establish a presence in the strategic entrepôt of the Lao PDR in order to serve the northern areas of the Mekong Delta, Coca-Cola initially decided upon a sole distributor arrangement, in contrast to the full-scale manufacturing facility set up by Pepsi. In export terms the choice of sourcing product from Thailand or Vietnam was in practice determined by the Lao authorities' policy of increasing trade with Vietnam and China at the expense of Thailand – typically through the imposition of 50 percent import duty reductions on products from Vietnam. Coincidentally, the first privately owned Lao company to benefit from these reductions was the KP Trading Group, Coca-Cola's initial choice of sole distributor for its soft drinks range. The assumption among KP executives was that these same 50 percent reductions would also then be granted for the company's products, enabling them to compete directly with Pepsi. However, at the time of going to press, these concessions had for the third time been categorically refused by the Lao administration, most recently on the grounds that the Vietnamese government was not reciprocating the arrangement. This refusal by the Lao authorities effectively renders imported Coke wholly uncompetitive against the locally bottled Pepsi. Even more damaging for Coca-Cola is that without these duty concessions the price of its product from Vietnam is now higher than the price at which Coke is sold to the bigger wholesalers in Thailand, encouraging a gray trade of Thai-based product and further complicating the company's relations with the Lao authorities.

The view from Coca-Cola and KP representatives is that these reasons are little short of a smokescreen for the longer-term protection of Pepsi in Laos as per its "special" arrangement with the Lao authorities, and in particular to shield Pepsi from any encroachments by its global arch-rival. The one glimmer of hope that exists for Coca-Cola is that even the apparently "bosom buddy" rapport between the local government and Pepsi appears in some sense to be cooling in the postcrisis years. Stemming in theory from Pepsi's refusal to set up a second factory in the southern trading city of Savannakhet, recriminations were also heard to fly following the shortage of Pepsi product for the capital Vientiane over the 2000 Christmas period, when Pepsi's various orange and lemonades dried up. More importantly, at the time of going to press we have learned that the Lao government has now repurchased the entire Lao brewery company.

The joint venture

The main thrust behind opting for the JV entry mode in ASEAN is in order to complement the "know-how" of the incoming foreign multinational with the "know who" of the local partners. In spite of their undoubted global power – in terms of capital, technology, branding and management technique – once "on the ground" in Asia, all business ventures depend on the collaboration and cooperation of local experts with their knowledge of the market. The prevalence of international joint ventures in the region reflects this need for local relationships to be cultivated, particularly when seeking to secure adequate distribution channels for incoming product. Foreign companies, typified by Siemens, which has stressed this point, are then also able to benefit from a learning curve which will assist them in the acquisition of host country-specific knowledge, for example the marketing skills and tactics appropriate to the local culture.

From a cost perspective, the outlays in forming a rapport with an established local player tend to be incremental when set alongside the huge lump-sum expenses experienced by MNCs seeking to start up from scratch. Existing staff will already have contacts, communication will be easier and the administration will already be in place. Experienced multinationals will also seek to maximize the positive local image to be acquired when entering into a partnership with a local company, promoting the "Asian" aspect of their local operations and enhancing their appearance as the "good local citizen." Local partner selection will then involve a screening of the prospective candidates' sought-after qualities, typically depicted as industry knowledge, visible external success, local power and/or local connections with the relevant facilitating authorities. Chinese-managed local enterprises often excel in these matters, with the social networks and personalistic patron–client relationships with local governments already firmly in place. These nurtured ties are often the key asset required in any JV-type arrangement by foreign companies in need of local resources (e.g. labor and land) and market knowledge, all of which are facilitated by such governmental connections

In any case, the JV is a business vehicle well suited to the Chinese stress on *guanxi* networks and business collaboration. Unlike in the West, where all business alliances have to be seen as temporary, Chinese-partnered JVs can – as with Castrol Thailand – last for generations. Other examples in more recent years have been the joining hands of the

Executive Insights: A Partner for Life?

"Being in the right place at the right time plus a fair amount of good luck are useful contributors to success in Southeast Asian markets, but by far the most important factor is attention paid to selecting the right local partners. If you have already experienced a few years of strategic alliance with a local company – perhaps in the form of an agency or distribution agreement – then you already have a head start, but if not, then your research must be careful and thorough. Fortunately, in the information age reliable research is easier to obtain. Certainly there is a little more transparency of data in Southeast Asia since the crash of 1997, but considerable care is still required, and information should be checked from more than one source. It could be dangerous to choose a partner without making many visits to the field – not only for discussions with prospective partners but also simply for checking around. This applies equally the other way round, because multinationals may have the wrong strategic rationale for entering a new market, or, due to a lack of local knowledge, may have got the timing completely wrong.

"Openness and honesty are excellent starting points, but beware that whilst openness may form an important part of an MNC's corporate culture (because of auditing standards and corporate governance rules in its home market), this may not be the case in Asian companies, often notorious for their multiple bookkeeping. Additionally, family-controlled companies in Southeast Asia often float part of their organization on local stock exchanges, thereby sometimes manipulating results to the detriment of minority shareholders. So, if you have some indirect experience of the market through a strategic alliance – use it. Do your research well, and double-check it, for finding the right partner can be the start of a very successful and profitable venture."

Chareon Pokphand group with the technical expertise of foreign entrants, including telecommunications giant Nynex and PepsiCo. In the postcrisis environment, tying up with a big foreign corporation has been especially attractive as many local firms have needed the new capital these entrants can provide in the restructuring of their debt-ridden and often insolvent operations. This is typified by the Siam Cement group, Thailand's largest indigenous conglomerate, which recently sold its majority holding in four auto companies to the Toyota Motor Corporation.

The maintenance and development of an international joint venture (IJV) between indigenous and foreign companies has built in complications, again founded on cultural incompatibility. Often, in the initial formation of the JV, chief negotiators from both sides are worldly chairmen or chairwomen or CEOs with years of international experience. But further down the organization there may well be an often underestimated grassroots reluctance to accept that new ways or new products are

Shell in Vietnam

Shell often opts for JV arrangements for its "upstream" operations where spreading the risk of often tens of millions of dollars of investment, plus the nurturing of favorable governmental relations, is considered essential. Downstream, however, the use of licenses and/or partnership arrangements is often the only way of securing initial market entry. Such was the case in Vietnam at the beginning of the 1990s, where governmental regulations had necessitated the formation of no fewer than five separate companies. Of these, to ensure a presence in gas, bitumen, lubricants and chemicals, three remain as JVs to the present day, although difficult initial relations have improved, owing to the progress made with *doi moi*, as well as the flexibility and increased dependence on foreign capital engendered by the economic crisis. The remaining chemical and lubricant divisions – the former once a licensing agreement, the latter a joint venture – have since become wholly owned business units. The company is also traditionally wary of using local partnership arrangements in its downstream, consumer-related businesses. The lack of control inherent in a JV, coupled with the rigid and complex bureaucracy associated with governments in the region, has acted as a practical hindrance to the company's being able to oversee its ground-floor operations the "Shell way."

In the case of its lubricants business, the initial JV was with the state-owned PetroVietnam Petroleum Development Corporation in conjunction with an influential local landowner, tasked with setting up the local blending plant. Initial disputes stemmed from the local business partner's apparent insistence on hands-on involvement in the overall strategic direction and operation of the venture, the adoption of a role Shell representatives felt that it was eminently unsuited to undertake. Corporate objections were strongly raised when it was discovered that the local partner was even launching its own products, some of which were in direct competition with those of Shell. This bad feeling then reached a head when the company's blending plant was appropriated by the local partner, the eventual reacquisition of which is said to have necessitated the involvement of both the Dutch and the UK ambassadors to Vietnam.

The latter development had also soured relations through its reminder to Shell of the post-Vietnam War years when the military equipment essentially fueled by Shell was then redeployed after the fall of Saigon to appropriate every one of Shell's domestic petroleum outlets. During the ensuing years of recrimination and dispute the first serious foreign competitors had begun to arrive, instanced by the likes of BP and Castrol. The latter's habit of selecting suitable JV partners – in this case the Saigon Petroleum organization – was also seen as a huge advantage and it was left to Shell to pick up the pieces of its once dominant market share via the receipt of its lubricant license, finally granted at the end of 1995, some four to five years after its two main British rivals.

appropriate or even "better," whatever the circumstances, especially when to both sides the local product and management systems have been held out to them as being the "best." The ongoing resolution of these issues between incoming and indigenous employees and the nurturing of healthy, cooperative working practices is more a human resources (HR) problem than one of strategic formulation, however, and will therefore be discussed in more depth in subsequent chapters.

Executive Insights: A Well-Made Marriage

"Castrol's entry strategy into Thailand was pretty much straightforward. Loxley had been the local agent for Castrol lubricants in Thailand for many years and had its own Lubricants Department. Khunying Chatchani Chatikavanaji (née Lamsan) and Victor Good, Castrol's International Director, therefore simply cemented an existing relationship. Both sides put in £60,000, with Castrol providing the managing director and the know-how, and Loxley providing the staff from their Lubricants Department and their customer records. Although Loxley had the majority shareholding they allowed the new joint venture to concentrate on the business and only very rarely intervened.

"From small beginnings in 1972 Castrol Thailand had by 1996 become the fourth most profitable Castrol company in the world after the US, German and Indian subsidiaries. The Castrol Thailand staff of around 470 were then making profits of £11.7 million and the company had no long- or short-term borrowings. Even following the 1997 economic crash, the 2000 profit levels were still at £12 million, but at the more disadvantageous exchange rate of 60 baht to the pound, instead of 40 as in 1996. An excellent performance considering the post-crash economic environment – the initial vision of Khunying Chatchani and Victor Good flowered into a successful and profitable joint venture largely due to openness and trust on both sides."

The mix

The final main trend we have identified concerns the numerous global corporations that continue to acquire ever-increasing stakes in their ASEAN JV operations yet refrain from buying them out completely. This is typified by the approach of Japanese MNCs such as Toyota and Mitsubishi, which have held back from buying their entire stakes in their respective JVs with Siam Cement for fear of losing Siam Cement's connections and the access to contracts, licenses and other intangible benefits the loss might engender (Keenan, 1999). It would appear that the more developed the ASEAN economies become, the less value the local intermediary function has for the foreign partner. This is evidenced in Daimler-Chrysler's recent effort to reduce the role of its long-term Singapore distributor, while still searching for local partners in less-developed Asian countries. Corporate executives view local partners as being extremely useful within the initial two to three years of a local project, helping to negotiate a way around the varied bureaucratic and political minefields that these countries often comprise. But as the business progresses, the MNC develops its "feel" for the local environment, reducing the influence of the local partner. Yet it is doubtful whether the overall "routing" of a local partner from an agreement makes any sense, even in a country such as Singapore, where local Chinese networks remain strongly in place and may reassert themselves as the region recovers. The only way executives say they would now contemplate such eventualities would be if, as well as their "fair" offering price, these local partners were able to give valid assurances as to their remaining as a "local friend" in years to come.

These current "partnership" deals fall somewhere in between the classic IJV and the wholly owned foreign subsidiary, with local partners increasingly having to accept the minority role. This is even becoming the case in the highly protected Malaysian car industry, where the national automaker Proton is actively courting a tie-up with one of the big "Detroit Three" manufacturers, claiming that the selling of assets to a strategic partner would maximize state proceeds as well as helping it to consolidate its precarious position in a regional market increasingly dominated by foreign giants. This trend has gone one stage further in Thailand, where locally owned firms are being heralded as a "dying breed" as the multinationals take an increasingly hands-on approach to existing local ventures. Nissan Motors, for example, has increased its investment in its Thai operations, making it the major shareholder in Siam Nissan with the expectation that the Renault group – with its 35 percent share in Nissan – will eventually take advantage of these facilities in order to assemble its vehicles in Thailand. The Italian car group Fiat has also announced its intention to take over the distribution of its vehicles from Thai Prestige Auto Sales in the establishment of a local manufacturing facility.

Other examples from a cross section of industries abound, even if we consider Thailand alone. The Castrol corporation – latterly acquired by BP – has increased its stake in its Thai unit from 49 percent to a majority holding of 60 percent. Elsewhere, the Estée Lauder cosmetics company – first introduced to the market almost a decade ago as "Elca" – was initially established and distributed with the assistance of the Central retail group. But in the wake of rapid sales expansion the company has now largely taken control of its own organization and distribution channels. Large capital injections by foreign partners in the electronics industry have significantly diluted the Thai partners' holdings, and in particular with the Thai affiliates of large Japanese and Korean firms such as Thai Samsung and NEC (Thailand) (see Zhan and Ozawa, 2000). The Thai insurance industry provides another example of how in practice ownership stakes can be increased by foreign firms. With an official ceiling of only 25 percent, before the crisis, companies had traditionally relied on other, more "informal" means to acquire a minimum of 49 percent of a local company, such as the utilization of Thai nominees to disguise share ownership. This trend continues in the current environment of raised ownership levels – again a reflection of the desire to gain a quasi-subsidiary operation, although the arrangement is still officially a partnership. UK banking group Standard Chartered took the move of "merging" with the Thai Nakorhthon Bank following the crisis, although nobody we spoke to within the industry views the current arrangement as anything other than a "takeover." The 49 percent ownership ceiling before the crash has since given way and it is estimated that the UK group controls over three-quarters of the current venture. As a footnote here, the same bank is reported to have attempted the same kind of coup in Indonesia with the Bali Bank, only to have the operation scuppered via the local partner's family contacts, coupled with the rising xenophobia within the country as a whole.

In the emerging economy of Vietnam, foreign multinationals engaged in expanding their stakes in local JVs have also come up against indigenous hostilities. Procter & Gamble, having established its brand name within the domestic market, was accused of deliberately setting out to make its JV a loss-making unit so as to force the local partner to reduce and even give up its stake in the operation. In a marriage troubled by contrasting priorities from the very start, the current situation is that the local partner now holds barely 7 percent of the holding, and this as a face-saving gesture, again perhaps due to fears of reprisals from the Western corporations (see also Quang, 1998). In a similar situation the Coca-Cola company in Vietnam has also progressively bought back the capital contributed by the local partner in recent years, and this has been cited as a main reason for the failure of any one of Coca-Cola's JVs in Vietnam to make any money. The reasoning holds that this is due to the corporation's strategy of investing "big" for the years ahead, adopting the typical Western "blaze of publicity" approach and seemingly willing – even desirous of – incurring losses over the first few years in order to establish the brand. The Vietnamese side simply does not have the strength to match either the initial outlays or the losses this kind of strategy incurs, and progressively withdraws from the operation.

Exportation/Distributorship: Unilever and Castrol in the Lao People's Democratic Republic

The complexities involved in utilizing sole distributors to build market presence are typified by the experiences of Anglo-Dutch consumer goods colossus Unilever and UK lubricants specialist Castrol. Both corporations had decided to pursue a policy of brand establishment and market development in the Lao PDR from the mid-1990s, partly in response to the opening of the Thai–Lao Friendship Bridge across the Mekong River, which forms the border. Both also chose to use their existing Thai subsidiary base, deciding upon the use of a distributorship arrangement in view of the size and lack of development of the target country. At the time there were thought to be no more than five import licenses in existence, so it comes as no surprise to learn that both companies sought to develop their extension plans via the same sole distributor. This locally based organization, Connell Bros KP Laos Company, was in itself an IJV formed from a well-known Lao family group ("KP" after the paternal head of the Philapandeth family) and the US trading house Connell Brothers, and had been active in the region for well over a century. With the establishment of this JV in 1995, the Western input afforded by the Americans prompted both Castrol and Unilever to themselves appoint the new organization as their respective sole distributors for the capital city of Vientiane using its initial resource base of three trucks and twelve staff.

Castrol, as already noted, is renowned for its selection of suitable agents, and nowhere more so than in Thailand with its partner of well over a generation, the Loxley conglomerate. Set up initially as an agency, the partnership was cemented with the establishment of a JV in 1972 and has flourished up to the present day. Even after the effects of the Asian economic meltdown, Castrol, as a premium brand, still enjoys a remarkable domestic share of some 15 percent overall and market leadership positions in several segments. Its more than a dozen branches across the country have enabled Castrol's annual turnover in Thailand to grow exponentially since 1980; it now exceeds US$65,000,000. As an illustration of the importance of Thailand, Castrol's first overseas "Technology Centre" was opened just outside Bangkok at the end of 1993, a test facility which is used to test and develop motorcycle lubricant formulations for the whole of the Asia-Pacific region. Not surprisingly, with the appointment of the Connell Bros KP Group (CBKP) in Laos, it was hoped that some of the magic gleaned from the Thai experience would shine off onto Laos. Despite Laos's tiny potential consumer market of some 5 million inhabitants, Bryan – as divisional CEO of the time – stressed to the Castrol group his view that the company could ill afford *not* to be in Laos owing to its wider geostrategic potential in the Mekong region. However, to this day the company has resisted agent calls for a depot to be built near the Thai border town of Nong Khai, and Castrol remains content to ship product up from its Bangkok blending plant.

Unilever's forays into Laos began in 1993 with a market visit and a follow-up meeting with the KP family president. Initial agreements centered on the KP group being appointed sole agent for the distribution of Lux toilet soap in and around the capital, Vientiane, via the larger market wholesalers. With the US partner to the JV on board from 1995, these targets were then revised and increased to encompass the multiple Unilever product brands distributed across the whole country. Initial product imports for

CBKP were sourced from the company's Malaysian factory until additions to the rapidly expanding product range meant that at one stage there was one type of shampoo from Malaysia, two more from Vietnam, deodorants from the UK and teabags from Singapore. This eclectic sourcing method proved to be increasingly difficult to operate, given the rapid growth in sales, and moves were therefore made to consolidate all Lao orders from one central source. Despite the absence of any duty reduction on the part of the local authorities, Thailand was chosen for its geographic proximity, perceived to enhance operational control of export procedures. In recent years adjustments have been made to reduce costs, instanced by the unsuccessful trial importation of Pepsodent toothpaste from India, with negative consequences for the movement of domestic stock. Yet the switch toward manufacture of the company's Viso detergent in China has continued; it is carried down almost 1,000 kilometers by truck to the Lao border and then onward in domestic vans for the remainder of the journey into Vientiane, off-loading product in the main cities *en route*. Needless to say, these shipments receive the full 50 percent reduction in duties.

Part II
Organizational change

The following five chapters focus on the deepening corporate imposition of internal transformation upon multinationals' ASEAN business units. With the benefit of hindsight these changes can be viewed as an essentially multistage sequence. Hence, although different companies obviously followed their own pace and timescale, we are able nevertheless to examine a cohesive pattern of organizational change through a cross-sectional tranche of the Southeast Asian corporate landscape.

As far back as the 1950s, Western theorists such as Kurt Lewin (1951) viewed the process of organizational transformation as comprising three main stages, loosely termed "unfreezing," "moving" and "refreezing." The first step in the achievement of lasting change is to unblock the current or traditional working system, a process usually requiring some kind of confrontation and expressed here in the postcrisis spate of downsizing and layoffs. After the company has waded through this painful process of cost control, the second stage focuses more on the actual implementation process of the overriding corporate objectives – loosely depicted as "moving." The final stage – "refreezing" – seeks to make the changes stick and is expressed in the process of behavioral and strategic reevaluation.

This second section begins with an overview of the initial "fire fighting" involved in the wake of the regional market downturn. At this juncture both foreign and local companies made unprecedented moves toward large-scale redundancy programs, laying off staff, downsizing the administration and closing up-country branches. These emergency actions were then followed by the progressive imposition of more in-depth organizational restructuring programs in preparation for a more deregulated, globalized economy and the long-awaited upturn in the business cycle.

Beyond these measures to rebuild the remaining streamlined units, foreign MNCs have been forging ahead with information technology development and data tracking control. In order to revitalize their remaining human resources and renew their core competencies, these corporations have also sought to build and share new capabilities, "supercharging" HR practices across borders in order to facilitate the adoption of corporate "best practice" worldwide.

3 Organizational downsizing

- Cost control: initial measures
- The onset of layoffs: rationale for change
- First-wave implementation
- Longer-term measures

Taken in its usual context, the phrase "organizational downsizing" is viewed as being just another euphemism for "layoffs." Business corporations are understandably cagey when discussing both the design and the implementation of their own programs for dealing with such eventualities, especially when administered across borders. Although periodic layoffs can be seen as merely symptomatic of the downside of global business cycles, the severity of the programs imposed in the aftermath of the Asian crisis necessitates caution with regard to individual and corporate identities. With respect to the highly sensitive nature of the material collated for this chapter, we have agreed, where requested, to disguise company identities, keeping to the broader denomination of industry type and country of origin.

Driven in part by the dramatic changes in the market environment, a number of foreign corporations have in recent years embarked on programs of rationalization and restructuring in order to maintain profitability levels. But for many foreign corporations the crisis also provided a timely excuse to push through centrally preordained revisions to the working structure, often planned for many years but never hitherto executed on the grounds of the region's phenomenal success. In this context many corporate chiefs were fairly candid on the downturn's role as an "engine of reform," although of course the methods employed and the problems faced within the ranks of their local employees were just as severe.

Whatever the motivation, the rapidly deteriorating regional business environment forced a cross section of MNCs to contend with a shrinking market, rising cost structures and excessive staffing levels. Many found themselves forced to request unprecedented cash infusions from corporate

headquarters in order to "tide themselves over" until the market recovered
– a shock for the local workforce, convinced their Western affiliations
automatically made them awash with capital. The major lack of flexibility
which ensued meant that in practice local MNC units were unable to
progress with their budgeted market plans and the vast majority of
expansion projects were either put on hold or cancelled.

Cost control: initial measures

Region-wide decline in unit revenues prompted a more conservative
approach to financial management, with urgent programs of cost control
instituted in order to rationalize and streamline day-to-day operations.
Initial attempts by companies to cut costs included the spin-off of
noncontributing affiliates, a freeze on staff head count, a cut in
advertising and promotion fees, and collaborations with competitors in
some areas to reduce fixed marketing costs. Senior local managers we
spoke to at the time stated that they had undertaken forward-looking plans
to "refocus their business priorities." Yet when asked to explain the nature
of those plans, the answers proffered were mostly general and
nonspecific, suggesting that they were grabbing at any activity that might
foster cost savings and mark time until the crisis abated.

Among the initial cost-cutting measures we witnessed were attempts
made by a host of companies to reduce power costs by shutting down all
lights and air-conditioning units – for the duration of the lunch hour, for
example, during which the office was to be vacated. But as one corporate
representative observed, "The whole thing's crazy. We are a trading
company. We *rely* on people calling in to place their orders with the sales
guys. So shutting up shop like this is not just illogical – it's astonishing,
whatever the circumstances." Other examples of such piecemeal measures
include moves to monitor all up-country telephone calls and faxes, revise
existing regulations for the level of air-conditioning, and encouraging
staff to shed unnecessary undergarments in order to make themselves
comfortable in the warmer air. The distribution of free hot beverages by
company maids was also stopped, and a ban initiated on the use of new
paper, with all internal documents being circulated either electronically or
on recycled foolscap.

There was a marked increase in the cancellation of corporate Christmas
and New Year events toward the end of the first two years of economic
downturn, beginning in Thailand in 1997 and 1998. A number of local

units took the unusual step of setting up a quasi "hardship fund" with the proceeds from these cancellations, distributing the estimated costs of their respective events to the lower-end employees earning less than a set monthly wage. Yet far from assuaging the anxieties of rank-and-file employees, these moves served as a hint of deeper, more far-reaching changes to follow, accentuated by the widespread cancellation of the annual year-end bonuses.

Ensuing cuts in local entertainment budget caused the first signs of friction among local sales teams, now forced to reduce their customer expense accounts. Much of the bitterness expressed at this juncture stemmed from the fact that a seeming majority of foreign corporations seemed unwilling to cancel – or even reduce – the "special" expense accounts afforded to their expatriate teams, including business-class air travel, the local provision of accommodation and education, and the membership fees of certain premium clubs (e.g. the British Club in Bangkok).

Indecent Exposure

Apart from the minor costs to be saved by the "recycling" of internal documents, there were a number of embarrassing incidents that emerged as a result of staff being ordered to utilize both sides of any company papersheet. Such occurrences were noted within a surprisingly high proportion of foreign corporate units in the months after the economic collapse, prompted by the unwitting use of confidential memorandums and account forms by administrative staff and secretaries. These typically comprised the accidental furnishing of customers with such documents, usually due to a junior member of staff feeding the "wrong" side of a recycled papersheet through the departmental fax machine. But other cases involved more personal "disclosures," exemplified by the personal expense accounts of a senior corporate manager being made public knowledge to a number of key customers and – perhaps worse – throughout the internal company networks. The executive in point was a Japanese national working for the consumer lubricants division of an American oil company in the region, responsible for the formation of long-term connections with Japanese automotive representatives (Toyota, Honda, and so forth). Although competent in his use of English he was nevertheless prone to errors of nuance, typified by his use of the word "RELIEF" to describe a substantial sum of money paid upon one particular monthly expense account. The amused speculation caused among his US colleagues as to the meaning of this term was matched only by his embarrassment as the form was rendered public knowledge, again through forming the unexpected "other side" of a recycled promotions leaflet.

Credit management

Reductions in inventory levels were a major part of most local retrenchment strategies, especially among production units habituated to running at capacity levels. Unfortunately, this unwillingness to hold "dead stock" soon also filtered down to their customers as wholesalers and retailing outlets began to feel the squeeze. To cope with the deterioration in market conditions a number of local firms announced their plans to turn to "just-in-time" inventory systems, especially those units parented by large Japanese conglomerates where such a system was internally well established. Others claimed to be shifting their focus to the export market in their avoidance of hard-pushed domestic customers, a move rapidly extinguished as the crisis spread throughout the region and beyond.

All companies were obliged to focus their attentions on the credit balances of their major customers. The failure of customers and clients in the local Thai market to pay for purchased goods and services was met by local units from a cross section of industries with a number of reductions on credit payment limits, typically from ninety to sixty days. Usually imposed from either regional or global head office, this shift in emphasis caused serious resentment on the part of a large number of local managers who berated this short-termist approach, warning of the potential serious damage inflicted upon their hard-won company–customer relationships. Yet in spite of the unusually vocal objections from the local management teams, these measures were supposedly to be implemented typically across all business segments and without exceptions.

Within the consumer segment, wholesalers were placed under close watch to minimize risk, reinforced within many industries by a corporate insistence on returning to "Cash on Delivery" terms, accompanied by trade discounts, usually minor ones, as a compensatory gesture. Western-parented companies across the region in particular decided to instigate these terms on all new accounts in certain segments deemed to be "critical." Other popular measures included offering special deals on ancillary products and reducing the number and scope of planned and existing consumer promotion campaigns.

It is interesting to note the corollary "Asian" approach of the indigenous competition, where existing credit payback arrangements were often left in place. For these companies the change lay in the shifting of their loci of interest to customer segments with relatively sound payment records until the crisis period "blew over." A number of local managers saddled with the dictates of foreign corporate interests lamented the "impersonal" way in which their long-standing customers had been treated during these initial, panic-ridden postcrisis measures. As one expressed it,

> "It's like they don't understand at all the way we do business with the customer here. A lot of these people have been with us for many years and through all the good and then the bad before . . . sometimes we help them, sometimes they help us because we know each other long time and then we trust each other. So when we say to them we have to do like this and then we see the other competitor who don't do the same what can the customer think? He feel like we don't care, and if he feel like that he go somewhere else; he never tell us why, but he never order from us again."

Staring at the void: redeployment and "ER"

In a quest to avoid staff layoffs at any cost, the typical Southeast Asian manager (a man, let us say) wrestles with the essential dilemma confounding corporate leaders at the time. Essentially, he knows deep inside that his respective company will have to off-load excess staff, but is torn with the knowledge that in cultures such as theirs such moves are deeply shameful for the individuals concerned, and only to be considered as a final resort. The tendency has therefore been to take smaller steps, relying on a process of attrition to reduce staff numbers. Measures such as "redeployment" – essentially, the shifting of redundant staff members into inactive posts they disliked, in the hope that they would resign – became habitual at this juncture, as did the more general method of nudging people into taking "early retirement." Indeed, with the increasing institutionalizing of programs of early retirement during three years of crisis, the words "early retirement" or "ER" became increasingly common among local – as well as corporate – employees in the region.

Indigenous managerial commitment to "natural turnover" methods was felt to help save face for all concerned, an extremely important consideration in aligning corporate strategy with the regional business culture. Furthermore, such measures also save money, obviating the need for employers to pay out the required three-month salary package. Other measures employed included the drastic review of overtime procedures and reductions in the use of temporary staff. Self-imposed executive salary cuts were also instituted as a potential means of being able to "weather the storm" and retain their employees. Cuts were also recorded by local media columnists focusing on companies such as the Bangkok Bank in Thailand at the start of the crisis in 1997, which were held to be engaged in finding ways to avoid "mass layoffs" and adopt a more "Asian approach" toward restructuring tailored to the "country's corporate culture" (Bunyamanee and Yuthamanop, 1998; Kositchotethana, 1998a, b). Less noted was the mirroring of such activities among foreign multinationals in the region; a fair proportion of them sought for ways to reduce variable costs as a preferable alternative to reducing staff numbers – instituted "whatever they may think about us," as one Western manager exclaimed. Looking back, it seems fair to suppose that whatever their internal fears for the future, in the immediate months following the crisis, corporate representatives across the region were hoping that such actions would be enough to achieve the operating savings required.

The onset of layoffs: rationale for change

As the crisis wore on, it became clear that the initial measures, described above, were simply not going to be enough. The vast majority of foreign multinationals thus began making tentative steps toward the imposition of a significant shakeout of personnel. To begin with, a number of open invitations were drawn for staff to register their interest in taking voluntary redundancy. By year-end 1997 Thailand and Malaysia had already witnessed their first formal waves of corporate downsizing, and existing staff across the region were beginning to see replications as inevitable, evidenced by the ongoing reports of such occurrences in the press. Morale during this period was inevitably low among our respondents, although a significant proportion clung nonetheless to the idea that the whole "layoff thing" was in essence a Western problem and would eventually fail to be implemented in the same way in Asia.

As the economic situation continued to deteriorate, Western-parented units were coming under increasing pressure from their respective headquarters to realign their employee needs. Incoming corporate "auditors," while voicing their muted satisfaction at the ways internal costs had been slashed, were concerned with the lack of complaints they were receiving from senior local executives, a phenomenon they claimed to be "profoundly worrying." The need to downsize local workforces was given credence by the visual evidence of "excessive" personnel, typified by the number of drivers, maids, receptionists, guards, cleaners, and so forth at the average domestic head office. Far from being an audited expression of organizational need, this spiraling head count was held to derive more simply from the operation of Chinese-dominated workplaces upon broad family lines, with relatives and friends being permitted to appoint staff to their own expanding fiefdoms, regardless of their competence or skill levels. Almost universally depicted by foreign corporations as making for "sluggish," "bureaucratic," "bloated" and "inefficient" working procedures, such practices were criticized for their excessive layers of management and this overemphasis on creating personal departmental empires.

In the immediate shadow of change, these reductions began to be defined more in terms of "rationalization" and "rightsizing" among senior corporate management, which was perceived as further evidence of underhand dealing by affected local employees. The programs of staff cuts drawn up at this stage were being sold to local chiefs as a purposeful reduction in the size of the organization's workforce – held as distinct from organizational decline in its overriding aim of improving long-term competitiveness. To this end, a number of key corporate groups began the trend of "efficiency benchmarking" through the region, comparing local performance ratios in the portrayal of exemplary performers for what each group wanted to achieve regionally, country by country.

Against this backdrop it comes as no surprise that many – if not all – foreign multinationals operating in this crisis-fueled environment viewed the crash not just as the direct cause of cost-reduction programs but also as a catalyst of the imposition of changes sought in the furtherance of global business practice synchronization. Companies instanced by the likes of Shell, Castrol, Unilever, HSBC, GlaxoSmithKline, Colgate-Palmolive and Chubb were quick to make the best of a shrinking market, investing in assets or upgrading existing – often outmoded – domestic facilities in line with global best practice at the same time as seeking to off-load excess personnel.

First steps

One reason MNCs were able to plan ahead in such a manner is the regional lack of a coherent, motivated labor movement that might have sought redundancy term agreements. The promotion and maintenance of a relatively unorganized, cheap and uneducated workforce was held by many observers to have constituted a traditional element in the maintenance of foreign multinationals' comparative advantage. Although

Southeast Asian economies are universally held to house a collectivist culture, there generally seems to be a lack of class consciousness among workers in the countries of the region (with the possible exception of the Philippines), and the notion of unions and collective bargaining was never a dominant feature of the industrial landscape.

The reasons behind the delays in announcing local programs of layoffs were thus deemed to lie elsewhere. For one thing, foreign multinationals have been very wary of being held liable to lawsuits or other such discriminatory measures by the respective ASEAN Labor and Social Welfare Ministries. Conscious of the inconsistency of law implementation across the region, companies were quick to take stock of the rapidity with which the Thai authorities had passed "protectionist" labor legislation within just a few months of the economic crash – designed to protect indigenous employees from the perceived slash-and-burn tradition of Western companies. In this context it also became commonplace for industry-wide foreign representatives to band together in the initiation of tentative contacts with government, anxious as they were to avoid any potential repercussions for their own downsizing programs. Yet the varied levels of reassurance afforded by domestic authorities could do little to overcome the more deep-rooted resentment of such measures on the part of the local workforce, in turn a corollary of the indigenous business culture itself. From the foreign corporate perspective these internal attempts at "diversionary dithering" were quite simply put down to the Asian habituation to a cozy, noncompetitive business environment, characterized by family conglomerates accustomed to being shielded from market forces. In this context the local preference for early retirement and "lateral placements" was simply a reflection of this, of "clinging to the old ways."

From the local perspective, however, such business methods had proven themselves as having led to the decade-long rise in regional prosperity. At a level far beyond that of "collective bargaining" and "class consciousness," the real reason for the lack of local unionization was the fact that the more fundamental Chinese maintenance of business relations at the cultural and familial levels traditionally obviates the need for any formal "worker solidarity." Senior local executives were anxious to stress that business dealings in Southeast Asia have always been founded on a carefully nurtured "web" of relationships, both within and external to the local organization. The maintenance of this "operating circle" is regulated within the context of a strong hierarchical system, itself reinforced by the indigenous, cultural adherence to the "middle way" to help solve problems and potential conflicts. Reflecting the influence of the varied forms of Confucianism and Taoism, this means of regulating work relations has helped to keep the indigenous people of the region on the path between extremes in life in the restraint of their feelings and emotions.

The essential corollary to this process is the local emphasis upon communal harmony and unity, translated into the workplace as the most important managerial objective. In simple terms, conflict avoidance is held to be paramount, and the office is no exception, rendering the local reactions to distasteful foreign programs of corporate change extremely difficult to gauge. Verbal and nonverbal communication in general among the indigenous populace across the region is rightly stressed as being "disarmingly indirect," of a subtlety and complexity most confusing to outsiders. In negotiations some of the most crucial messages may even be given silently – the hapless Western manager assuming s/he has achieved some kind of consensus, whereas in reality the nonverbal expressions and nuances of speech point very much to the contrary. In this context, foreign managers are advised not to "jump the gun" in such discussions and to play the game of patience. The continuity between past through the present into the future is a major issue in ethnic Chinese business culture, and things tend to change slowly, change being based on the principles of unity and tradition.

A further difference in the local and corporate attitudes to downsizing is summed up in the notion of "family." Patriarchal departmental heads in Southeast Asia consider their subordinates an extended clan built up on the ethnic Chinese notion of reciprocated favors and long-term face-giving between superior, subordinate and colleague. Aptly characterized as "management by entourage," the activities within these organizations are generally coordinated by the family patriarch and a close circle of trusted associates. Against this backdrop, employment, if not for life, normally entails a long-term commitment of the firm to the master–servant relationship, with notions of loyalty and commitment seen as the all-important qualities both for staff and for senior management.

The announcement of company layoffs therefore involved much traumatic decision making for Asian executives, largely misrepresented in the regional business press behind the postcrisis obsession with notions of "cronyism" and "corruption." Yet the nature of indigenous business relationships – as depicted above – means that any such actions are inevitably accompanied by a significant loss of face. The moral dilemmas faced by senior local teams have been compounded by the stated confidence and faith of many workers in their superiors to "do the right thing" and keep to "wage freezes" and self-imposed salary cuts "for the good of the business," staving off their loss of livelihoods until the good times come back.

As expressed by a local human resources manager,

> "Until just recently they insist us to recruit good staff and staff for everything nearly as quickly as we can . . . [and this] involves a lot of work for my team, especially because after they insist we must keep hold of staff and not lose them to the competitor. Now they telling us to give the advice of how the laid-off staff can find the new job somewhere else . . . completely the opposite, in just a few weeks."

Asian workers tend to work for a boss and not a company, and the local word for the "love" of a good boss was one which we were constantly hearing right across the regional corporate spectrum. The difficulty involved in the laying off of these staff is further heightened by traditional assumptions concerning the preservation of the superior–subordinate rapport. In times of hardship, as well as of prosperity, both parties tend to hold to the benefits of their ongoing relationship, recognizing that because businesses need to meet unexpected changes in circumstances, such a basis for interaction must be flexible. They therefore take actions that will help develop the relationship and eschew actions that might disrupt it (even if in the short run it might be advantageous to do so).

To this end, a consensus of indigenous executives opined that the Western concept of restructuring and downsizing ran counter to this need to preserve harmony and unity. A fair proportion of those we spoke to were under the impression that it would be better to work for a Japanese MNC in such an environment, where the "Asian nature" of the board would at least make it adopt a more culturally congruent approach to layoff implementation. The feeling was summed up by the operations director of a Thai-based French telecommunications firm:

> "The way of business here means that this kind of change have to take much time . . . we can't just take the *farang* [Western] model and chop, chop, chop. We have to reduce our costs, we know. But we are looking for the minimum costs per unit of service . . . [and] . . . for us this does not mean just the headcount."

Indigenous attitudes toward employee layoffs were often underlined by tailored legislation to impose high separation costs upon downsizing employers. Foreign executives tended to feel that this environment was largely responsible for the continuing jobs-for-life business culture, loath to give way to the "new world" of individual career development. But many Western executives were also prepared to concede that the extent of the downsizing was in many ways the price to be paid for their failing to invest in globally oriented staff development training.

Whatever the case, the looming threat of economic hardship and uncertainty for masses of ordinary staff employees sank morale to an all-time low. The local offices of many foreign MNCs were witness to a series of anonymous and vitriolic letters that began to circulate courtesy of such self-appointed groups as the "Committee for the Protection of Local Employees" at Castrol. These letters furnished proof – if proof were needed – not only of the deep anger and shock toward the changes being proposed, but also of the subtle but pervasive polarization of the workforce along cultural divides. In this climate fears were also being expressed among a wide cross section of expatriates for their physical safety, particularly in countries such as Indonesia, where incidents of hijacking, kidnapping and assassinations were seen as being all too common in such circumstances. Psychologically, at least, many of their counterparts in Thailand, Malaysia and the increasing spread of countries affected were also beginning to feel the strain. The resentment expressed by domestic workforces stemmed in part from the belief that these "expensive foreign expatriates" were somehow set on destroying their cherished local methods of working, which until very recently had been the target solely for their praise and admiration.

First-wave implementation

Procedures

The majority of foreign multinationals were eventually to downsize their local operations, rendering the Asian experience of mass layoffs a commonplace and continuing postcrisis feature. The Royal Dutch/Shell oil company was the first of the major foreign oil firms to embark on large-scale redundancies in the region, taking the unprecedented step of shedding nearly 30 percent of its 1,000-strong Thai workforce. Within the services sector the UK-based Standard Chartered Bank was soon to follow suit, with 700 layoffs from its staff of 2,100. Both companies claimed that their actions embodied the major reorganization of their local operating units in response to the crises affecting their respective industries. Their reasoning was that such short-term "loss of blood" would improve their productivity levels and their longer-term resilience in dealing with a "wholly revised" market environment.

Across the industrial spectrum the major targets of these initial downsizing "waves" were unwieldy administrative staff, typified by the high proportion of departmental secretaries. But in contrast to the muted reception concerning the reduction in maids, tea-ladies, messengers, stationery assistants, factory workers, part-timers, and so forth, the off-loading of secretaries caused particular hostility from the managers affected. Notwithstanding their often close – even familial – personal relationships, a manager's secretary was a mark of his/her status within the organization, and the subsequent loss was tantamount to a demotion, with a significant loss of face. The Western corporate tendency to provide departing workers with financial packages in excess of the minimum legal requirements was in this respect clearly a misinterpretation of the core problem, that concerning the feelings of the managers and employees who *remained*.

A substantial number of corporations did not even progress this far, seemingly intent on antagonizing their local workforce as a show of strength. This is exemplified by the number of "hatchet jobs," where termination notices were distributed by unsuspecting administration staff to the desk of targeted personnel late on Friday afternoon, leaving those laid off with nowhere to direct their questions and just an hour or two's time to clear the office. The presence of extra security guards stationed at the various departmental doorways and around the offices of their – usually absent – departmental heads did nothing to soften the blow.

Perhaps the most infamous case of such an approach stems back to the methods employed by one US oil company around the beginning of the crisis. According to witnesses, the procedure – not known in advance by anyone except for the Western CEO and his regional superiors – took place one Friday morning cloaked under the unusual occurrence of a fire alarm. Having only gone through the internal drill for such an event the previous week, staff naturally assumed the alarm was genuine and hurried down the stairwells and onto the car park driveway down to the office block forecourt. Once it was clear that no one was left in the building, an announcement was made to the workforce detailing a local program of nearly two hundred redundancies. Those who were to remain had their names read slowly off a list and were instructed to reenter the building via a line of security guards in front of the main ground-floor entrance. Those left outside at the close of the list were refused entry, even for the purposes of clearing their desks, a task already executed by the guard forces scouring the building. They were instructed to clear the forecourts and to return home; their affairs and final documentation sets were either to be sent to their home addresses or taken care of by their remaining colleagues inside. It perhaps comes as no surprise that the foreign managing director responsible for the procedure was away "on business" at the time, returning on the Monday morning with the task all but complete.

A representative sample of implementation methods employed through a cross section of local industries highlights the case above as being an exception. Common methods were to pin an announcement to a notice board informing staff as to the existence of a "program of separation," of which they would be able to "take advantage" were their name confirmed as being on the list by their head of department. The Castrol variation of this method was to allow a week's grace between the display of the list and the day of leaving, billed as a time for "farewells to friends and colleagues." The problem with this method was obviously the surge of emotions elicited among staff during what was depicted in hindsight as one of the "longest weeks in the history of our company." There were also problems with the manner in which the announcement letters were being translated into the local languages, especially in countries such as Thailand, where the attachment to "saving face" is paramount. The emphasis on "inquiring" as to whether you were eligible to join the "separation" program was in practical terms a risky exercise, with a mistaken assumption inevitably seen as an expression either of a desire to leave the company or of being justifiably insecure in one's present performance. Either way, the whole procedure was depicted as a "lose–lose" scenario for those who were due to remain, and for this reason a substantial number of redundant employees were unaware of the fact until their final hour or so within the office, accounting for a final Friday afternoon deemed nothing short of traumatic by personnel who witnessed it.

Other methods included the announcement of a "casualty" list in departmental meetings drawn together for the purpose of the exercise, the outgoing staff being summoned by what became quickly feared as the "call of death," again from their head of department. There the gathered staff would be given reasons for the company's actions and usually invited then to see their superiors at a prescheduled time that same day to collect their leaving packages and vacate the premises. The other favored tactic on the part of foreign multinationals was to inform staff of their dismissals via email, again broadly governed by universal foreign corporate guidelines which seemed overall to encourage the collective notification of staff, whether orally or via block computer message. This "plural" emphasis, regarded as "impersonal," was criticized in some local quarters as being culturally inappropriate, with the preferred method being a discreet private meeting or letter (in order to help maintain what little face was left to those affected).

In the rare instances where a foreign corporation had delegated the downsizing process to its indigenous management team, we noted a striking difference in the pace and style of delivery, more akin to how the traditional Asian company would go about handling such events. In many ways the corporate ploy of "dumping" the execution of its layoff directives on the local management team caused even greater local hardships than if the job had been done from afar. Local HR teams had simply never been faced with the challenge of retrenching hundreds of competent employees. Their relative lack of experience of such matters was held as being a major factor in the subsequent months of "dithering" over the issue. With little or no authority to question the corporate-imposed dismissals, the local team would approach the issue with extreme caution, as instanced by the repeated use of voluntary redundancy pleas.

Whereas the majority of Western corporations downsized their units in progressive stages, the local preference tended to be for "one big swathe" followed by a post-layoff period of mourning and reharmonization. The eventual "single-package" layoffs, although perhaps less financially generous that those from foreign MNCs, were often bound by executive promises to then avoid any further layoffs, which were portrayed as being simply too dangerous for company morale.

Among the much-touted "best ways" to lay off staff was the reiteration of the need to plan programs carefully well in advance. The need for early maintenance of open lines of communication was stressed, it being clearly explained to staff why the layoffs were deemed necessary and what the company hoped to gain by them. Employees identified for dismissal should then be notified as early as possible of their fate in order to demonstrate fair and honest treatment, held in contrast to the worrying number of cases where employees had read or heard of their respective company's plans in the local media. Caltex was praised by a number of executives within the oil industry for the way it meticulously emailed local staff all the way from US headquarters, updating them every two days as to what was being discussed and, of course, making them feel that their predicament was being taken seriously. This implied emphasis on being open via continuous communication channels was also noted within the services sector, as UK banking giant Standard Chartered took over the Thai Nakornthon Bank but then sought to allay the suspicions of its new workforce by gathering and addressing the entire staff on the very first morning of their joint operation. As well as seeking to establish mutual trust, the move was also made for the incoming executives to obtain accurate feedback from their employees on their potential reactions to the imminent program of downsizing they were about to unroll. But it is interesting to note that among several observers and employees involved, this was actually perceived as a mistake, and that in contrast to the Western textbook promotion of "open communication," in Southeast Asia this method served merely to "frighten" staff and increase indigenous reaction against their foreign employers.

From protest to resistance

The levels of resistance elicited among indigenous workteams stemmed not so much from the programs of downsizing themselves as from the manner by which they were implemented. This appears to reflect the view that Southeast Asian management practice places greater emphasis on form and procedure than on outcomes. Western-oriented layoff programs were widely criticized as representative of a short-sighted knee-jerk reaction to changes in the wider environment. Having grown up with the traditional top-down management system, Asian managers viewed the Western-led staff reduction programs as almost alien phenomena when imposed in their close-knit, traditional business systems. Respondents pointed in particular to Western deficiencies when handling the matter of "face," where the very acceptance of externally imposed change is construed as a "loss of dignity" by senior local executives. Ethnic Chinese managers tend to be acutely sensitive to the regard in which they are held by others and obsessed with questions of prestige and esteem. Causing someone to lose face in this manner can have severe consequences; at the very least, cooperation will cease and retaliation may ensue.

The failure by foreign – especially Western – corporations to foresee the level and intensity of resistance to their plans appears also to stem from their perception of the "Asian man" as a creature bound by his/her *karma*, accepting without question his/her fate in this life as the mirror of his/her conduct in the last. According to a cross section of our respondents, this way of perceiving life is still felt to be ingrained in the minds of the local workforce, forever holding them back from unleashing their anger or hurt concerning the perceived injustices of modern working life. Hence the collective shock engendered by the vehement protests on the part of the local workforce, laced with anonymous faxes outlining their grievances and threatening retribution.

As a case in point, a group of senior expatriates from a French telecommunications unit described their anxieties upon discovering copies of a newspaper cutting pinned against their office doors one Monday morning, outlining the recent case of an attempted "drive-by" motorcycle shooting of a Western manager who upset local sensibilities with his attitude toward their dismissals. "It was a warning for me, and of course I am concerned for my family," one said, "but things have to go on here; I have a responsibility to continue with my job and with my life."

Local grievances were typified in the responses we acquired from the remaining indigenous managers left at Castrol Thailand in the wake of the "separation program" of April 1998. The resentment expressed hinged upon the fact that of the staff dismissed, not one had been from the ranks of the "expensive" expatriates, the only Westerner to leave being himself employed via a local package. Notwithstanding the fact that all such positions were viewed at headquarters as being technically indispensable, the assumption among the Thai managers interviewed was that the Westerners had all been informed of the impending restructuring plans, each of them safe in the knowledge that they would be secure under the direction of "one of their own" (i.e. the CEO of the time). The broad feeling was that these foreigners were simply passing through the Thai unit in order to boost their international careers at the expense of a local business which they were now seeking to dismantle.

Indigenous executives across the spectrum commented upon the issue from a broader, almost sociological perspective. Asian society was held to have become corrupted by the West, in part because of the unscrupulous dealings of the regional governments, which seemed happy to allow the economic and cultural colonization of their countries in return for prodigious sums of hard currency. Critiques were voiced concerning the encroaching Western approach to business, in which the longer-term stability and harmony of society was being sacrificed in the heady march for short-term business profits. As one Malaysian executive stressed,

"Restructuring is just the most recent of the fashion in business that come from America. But you only have to look at how we can measure this restructuring to know how much it have harm upon the community . . . just look at the number of people who have no job now or who have nothing for to feed their wife and children – this is the measurement of restructuring."

The heartbreak and anger expressed by the remaining bosses of off-loaded staff – particularly from the older generation – become even clearer when one factors in the cultural foundations described earlier in the chapter. Local business employees are traditionally loyal to a boss rather than to a corporation, but on the ingrained assumption that the boss is protective of them. In Southeast Asia the senior manager is like the head of a family, and by implication holds considerable responsibility for the personal lives of his/her constituents, at a level far beyond that of his or her Western counterparts. Effective Asian managers treat their colleagues as akin to respected relatives, and even the pronouns they use tend to reflect this relationship across the region. In the normal state of working they expect hard work from their staff but in turn will tend to cover staff members' mistakes and reward them lavishly. Doing good deeds for one's subordinates builds up a boss's store of goodwill, normally regarded as an invaluable resource, both in the obligations and loyalty he or she can expect in reciprocation, and in the contribution it makes to the overall harmony of the company – and therefore society – as a whole. Within this context, although local units often utilize highly systematic and rationalized management systems, their management practices are still rooted in the more unstructured style of the family enterprise, with patronage loyalties rather than bureaucratic norms tending to determine workplace relationships. Unlike in the West, where hiring and promotion decisions are supposed to be based on skills and rules, in the Sino-dominated business cultures of ASEAN, people are integrated into strong, cohesive in-groups which protect them in exchange for unquestioning loyalty.

These intraorganizational links – traditionally viewed as the "bedrock" of a business – have been severely shaken by the unprecedented imposition of "foreign" methodologies for dealing with economic recession. Local managers' despair at witnessing the trampling over of age-old cultural traditions is reflected in a number of domestic Health Ministry reports across the region of record suicide levels among corporate managers (particularly in 1998). The trauma was further reinforced by the societal tendency to lack official security systems for those most affected, ironically the result of just this communal harmony, which had previously shielded people from the need to depend on state support. The consensus view among foreign, local and social theorists appears to be that such social safety nets and assistance should be made more available to the indigenous workforce. It is held that in the modern globally driven business arena it is patently in the interests of multinational corporations as well as host governments to ensure an effective program of social measures aimed at softening the impact of these programs of change.

In general we found that resistance levels expressed among local managers were fairly muted in business units housing a high percentage of expatriate managers. Taking advantage of unusually high quotas for such personnel, corporations from a range of industries and country-bases seemed to "get away with" direct protest and lingering resentment on the part of their remaining managers, even where the bout of layoffs had been notably severe. Respondents largely confirmed our observations on the matter, stating that both the number of expatriates and their unusually long tenures at the local units had provided a foundation for the institution of more "globalized" working procedures.

More serious instances of indigenous resistance came in the light of the perceived dismissal by Western executives of local pleas to "slow down" in their efforts, chillingly instanced in the now infamous "elimination" of an Australian senior auditor for Deloitte Touche, shot by a gunman in revenge for his company's efforts to restructure a number of debt-ridden sugar mills in Thailand. This case almost single-handedly shattered Western corporate insouciance concerning the problem, typified in the reaction of arch-rival Grant Thornton, which immediately pulled back on its own similar contracts at Thai-based organizations. At around the same period another serious bout of violence erupted among the normally passive and nonaggressive workforce at the local Sanyo plant, who burned it to the ground one night following the company's decision to cut back on its annual bonus scheme.

Longer-term measures

Procedures

Initial layoff "waves" within the vast majority of our featured corporations were followed by a region-wide policy of reassessing existing staff by means of performance appraisal, traditionally shunned among Asian employees (as discussed more fully in Chapter 5). Utilizing the corporate-approved input/output process matrix, senior expatriates were charged with streamlining the existing organizational structure and required to reduce the layers of management to four or five levels from, typically, almost a dozen. These flatter job structures were held to facilitate both efficiency and flexibility, the latter to be achieved through the "casualization" of the organization's operating workforce, with emphasis laid upon the use of subcontractors, temporary employees, part-timers, and so forth. Foreign multinationals, by this stage wising up to the threat of local resistance, quite astutely judged these latest measures to be trouble-free, because of the ever-expanding reserve of unemployed workers fresh from school.

Once they were familiar with the skills/needs analysis the MNCs were looking for, regional units were then instructed to "optimalize" their manpower needs on the strength of individual employee capacities. This so-called "rightsizing" of the remaining workforces was handled in a number of different ways among multinationals in the region, but usually via the identification of potential "casualties" on an annual case-by-case basis, executed either through hired consultants or from internal headquarters. The local heads of department were typically to be presented with an "objectively determined" list of staff deemed to be excess to unit requirements. As a case in point, the US personal care giant Gillette conducted a skills/needs analysis of its ASEAN units, only to find itself with an apparent surplus of almost 1,000 employees! Needless to say, further reductions ensued, and the company rapidly laid off another 160 workers across the region. In another, perhaps more drastic method, some companies laid off their entire workforces with the aim of making them reapply – and then compete – for a new set of positions now deemed necessary, again via the use of input/output skills analyses. Often a company would lay off huge swathes of employees but then still find itself lacking in certain previously unaccounted-for areas, necessitating the reemployment of selected individuals to fill these new-found shortages.

Among the first to be shed in these minor layoff programs were, not surprisingly, some of the remaining secretaries from the initial culls in the first years of domestic recession. There were also attempts made to dismiss the more unproductive, usually aging, administrative staff lacking either English or information technology skills with which to progress into the "globalized" future. However, the major targets of this spate were to be from the higher echelons, and in particular the costly middle-management positions now deemed to be obstructing the progression toward flatter, more nimble organizational structures. These tended to be "off-loaded" individually or in small groups over the ensuing months – and sometimes years – until the markets slowly picked up through the turn of the millennium.

In terms of implementation methodology, "losing" such senior staff was inevitably going to be hard, and in some sense even more difficult than the more wide-ranging cuts of the first waves. "Face" was obviously a prime concern; deference to age was another. Older workers in the region tend not to listen to younger managers, which effectively slows down the whole process, rendering the long-term objective of replacing unskilled, older employees with younger, better-educated ones a year-long battle.

Lower down the ranks, the ongoing dismissals of "expendable" staff continued to cause upheaval, not just for the people affected but, crucially, among their protecting "group" or department. In terms of procedure, the usual method was either an email or a telephone call from the HR department inviting the staff member for a meeting, whereupon s/he would be informed of his or her fate and told to leave. More controversial methods were exemplified by the approach of a local administration department within the Malaysian office of a European food company. A section of staff were gathered together and informed of an imminent layoff program, meaning that at least four of the dozen employees in attendance would need to leave. Addressing each of the participants in turn, the manager then assessed their future potential to the organization, essentially stating who was of any use, and who was not. The two office telephone operators present were told that only one of them would be needed in future, and that it was up to the two of them to decide who would go; they had to inform HR of their decision by 5 P.M. that same evening.

Methodological "cross-vergence"

The dominant view of corporate downsizing as a universally applicable paradigm is being challenged in postcrisis ASEAN, principally on the grounds of cultural alignment. As a result of the long and often bitter struggles to reshape ASEAN corporate ventures "optimally," Western executives are beginning to accept the strength and resilience of the indigenous working mindset, recognizing that surviving employees were capable of obstructing business outcomes through their instinctive manipulation of internal working networks. Previous methods which had willfully neglected the Confucian importance of preserving face and "right" relationship were now being reassessed in light of their apparent part in the fragmentation of staff along cultural – and hence national – lines. Corporate representatives were quick to admit that the financial advantages of downsizing – while irresistible from afar – were being negated on the ground by a demoralized and resentful workforce.

Certainly there are weaknesses in the local Confucianist mentality. The ingrained sense of duty between superior and subordinate has led to a number of instances where executives would leave the company only to be "followed" by their immediate working team – whatever the potential hardship. The traditional Western corporate dismissal of such values compounds the problem even further, potentially leading the company to lose both manager and staff, and with them a whole chunk of organizational contacts and memory via this underestimated disruption of informal networks and unofficial routines. The process whereby Asian employees develop through time, molded by the examples and intellectual capital provided by their senior management mentors, is of paramount importance in the regional business context. Time after time this has then been wholly undermined by the misplaced multinational emphasis on short-term "results-oriented management" which downplays the importance of the human element in management, thereby cutting the corporation's "pipeline to the future."

Hence the importance of implementation reappraisal, the practical result of which has been the rise in formulation of compromise or "cross-vergent" methods for dealing with future "soft" management issues. Such methods appear to be especially appropriate in dealing with the longer-term feelings of insecurity and distrust on the part of remaining employees fearful they will be the next to go. In practical terms the perception among both corporate and branch employees was that these "second waves" of layoffs have been conducted in a relatively "humane" manner, with more attention being paid to the sensitivities of indigenous management.

Corporate illustrations

Examples abound of this continuing trend toward compromise. Many MNCs began opting for expatriates with proven experience and sensitivity to the Asian environment, typified by the arrival of a Chinese-born executive to head a major US petrochemical group in Vietnam. The ensuing compromise measures he actively encouraged within the organization were perceived by the local workforce as a form of "payback" for the loss of face they had been made to feel under the previous incumbent. Local staff were also keen to stress that for themselves these "concessions" meant a real beginning of a Western-initiated cycle of "right relationship," typified by the long-term approach to the giving and receiving of favors in kind held as crucial for the smooth operation of the company.

A similar choice was being made at the Thai branch office of a UK lubricants multinational, where the newly instituted CEO was portrayed as being far more "flexible" and "willing to listen" than either his predecessor or his industrial counterparts. As well as his return to the traditional predilection for "management by walking around," this new chief was also far more willing to discuss policy issues with the indigenous directors, and to progress a more consensual approach to key company decisions. Further, his active policy of "sharing the misery" when it came to further layoffs was demonstrated by his self-imposed office staff reduction, halving his secretarial assistance from two persons to one, a move immediately welcomed as being a gesture to assist in the current corporate de-layering policy.

Paternal Fixings

Charinrat is a junior sales assistant at the Thai branch of a German electrical goods manufacturer, although her future in the months after the crash of 1997 seemed to lie elsewhere. Selected for two corporate bouts of layoffs, she appeared to the neutral observer to be consistently underperforming and plainly lacking in the stated skills requirement list distributed among departmental heads. Yet to this day she remains at her post, having been protected and bargained for by a particularly vocal sales director, adamant that she should stay whatever the circumstances. But why?

The key to her survival lies in the past to this case, Charinrat being the daughter of an ex-senior sales manager tragically killed in a road accident. Appealing to local paternalistic responsibilities at a depth beyond Western business norms, the sales chief involved insisted that the company reciprocate the loyalty of service given by her father. Dismissive at first of issues deemed extraneous to corporate concerns, as the months became years, regional head office progressively softened their stance concerning such cases, finally affirming their acceptance of her remaining, so long as she was transferred to a related, new vacant post deemed to be within her capabilities.

Similar incidents were recounted at a wide range of ASEAN branch offices. One notable case concerns an elderly marketing administration manager, earmarked for dismissal at a European pharmaceuticals group because of her relative lack of either language or computer skills. In this case, although the lady was still eventually off-loaded, this was done on the strength of protracted headquarter–subsidiary negotiations, resulting in her being presented with a special, personalized severance package for reward of service. Though seemingly insignificant, this compromise with local managerial values was again much appreciated in that it appeared to enable local staff to start forgetting the previous "negative feeling." Corporate respondents confirmed the compromise attained in this instance, affirming that from their own perspective "two steps forward, one step back" was preferred to "no progress at all."

As time progressed, concessions were also made as to the choice of casualties in further small waves of "rightsizing," many of which were being imposed in the wake of globally oriented mergers and acquisitions, instanced by the takeover by BP of the Castrol lubricants group in 1999. In the previous year another oil giant, Exxon, had decided to merge with its old rival Mobil, the former group being anxious to streamline its operations, including that of its profitable Thai business, where the company has maintained a presence for the best part of a century. At this juncture there were also scores of employees who had survived the previous programs owing to their perceived "closeness" with key expatriate managers, only to find themselves now being off-loaded in this second wave of reductions. This is typified by the controversial dismissal of a female advertising manager at a Western automotive company, once held as epitomizing the corporate tendency to "shield their own" unfairly while local staff were being shed. Further examples are found in the increasing trend toward the replacement of exiting expatriates with locally picked replacements, again in consultation with the senior local managers involved. The decision to allow the local team to make their own choices was a move that was warmly welcomed as being not only just but sensible, and was – again – taken as a gesture of genuine working compromise. As one senior marketing executive expressed it, "Within the day-to-day battle with our competitors the generals should always be allowed to choose their own troops." A high proportion of managers recruited as part of the "skills/needs" analysis programs were also noted to have departed of their own accord within a relatively short space of time, presumably aware of this simmering resentment on the part of the remaining local team. Needless to say, these vacated posts also tended to be filled by locally favored personnel, including a fair number of those recently departed. These former victims of the layoffs thus tended to reappear within the changed organizational structure but on less favorable terms – instanced by the case of the graphic designer off-loaded from a US chemical company's publicity department who was later reemployed on a freelance basis.

4 Corporate consolidation

- Status quo: the precrisis years
- Postcrisis consolidation
- Implementation: culture's consequences
- Implementation "cross-vergence"

Corporate needs to respond to the dual strategic demands of integration on the one hand and responsiveness on the other become increasingly complex in culturally distant markets. Nowhere is this more so than in the mix of commercial environments that constitute the ASEAN trading bloc. In the precrisis boom years of the 1980s and early 90s it was the latter – "responsiveness" – element that had held sway. Group reports and brochures of the period expounded at length on the companies' goals of becoming "multilocal" or "multidomestic" and the optimum policy of bringing in the best of their international expertise while making sure that it was "absolutely right for the local people."

At the time, many of these subsidiaries were effectively being shielded from direct market forces, either via the connections of their local partners or – more indirectly – from macroeconomic policies designed to protect domestic industries. Coupled with a strategic emphasis on customized business orientation, these forces combined to make the region the world's foremost growth area. Yet with the cataclysmic crash of 1997 such perceptions were ditched and shattered almost overnight. The onslaught of "meltdown" and market contraction forced a spate of wide-ranging strategic reappraisals, pushing hard the need to pursue maximum firm-level efficiency through the downsizing of staff levels and the consolidation of regional operations.

The first step upon this road – as delineated in Chapter 3 – was to trim away the fat that had accumulated during the boom days. This included the reduction of excessive staff and operations, and the more general need to "undiversify" and focus on core activities. Even in countries which had appeared to sail through the crisis, such as Singapore and the Philippines, there was this pressing need to cut costs, restructure, and sharpen business focus in preparation for the more competitive industrial landscape of the future. To this end, the notion of "downsizing" can be viewed as one single step in the rejuvenation of indigenous business operations, restoring profitability levels to a minimum threshold before turning to the longer-term need to enhance competitiveness.

In this context it was clear that a cosmetic fix was not to be the answer – that something more fundamental was now needed. Fortunately, the falling interest rates and stabilizing currencies at the turn of the millennium provided these business units with the breathing space they needed to consolidate and restructure their operating systems in line with their parent corporate norms. This entailed the simplification of management processes and the reallocation of resources among divisions in order to improve their productivity. MNCs also sought to upgrade their local technological capabilities, enhancing product design across the region in order to regain competitiveness. Moving toward the oft-cited corporate dream of creating one single, seamless organizational culture, a core ingredient of corporate postcrisis agendas was to bring the operating practices of Southeast Asian business divisions into line with those operating already in North America and Europe.

Under increasing pressure from shareholders and analysts, corporate leaders began to demand a tightening of control at their ASEAN subsidiaries. To this end, merely adjusting or fine-tuning the existing organizational structure became patently insufficient. Multinationals in Asia cover a range of businesses and product/market divisions, and are seeking to bridge – or at least accommodate – both. The changes being progressed have entailed a shift in focus from the traditional concentration along geographic lines toward a "type-of-business" emphasis, facilitating the overarching convergence of worldwide business practice. The shift is aptly expressed in corporate moves toward the reorganization of Southeast Asia into global business "streams." On a conceptual level the shift in emphasis turned away from the geographic to a product-oriented focus – again in an attempt to converge business practices across the region.

In pursuing this objective, multinationals in the region have had to address both the "hard" and "soft" elements, so-called, of the targeted organizations. As defined by – among others – Peters and Waterman (1982), the term "corporate hardware" focuses on the products, technology, formal reporting relationships, roles and clusters of activity within an organization. By contrast, the organizational "software" centers around the corporation's "culture," with an emphasis on values, attitudes, beliefs and behaviors. The latter involves seeking to integrate the business norms and values held among Southeast Asian managers with those shared by the "global corporate fraternity" – in other words, nothing less than a regional management revolution.

Status quo: the precrisis years

To begin with, we must first describe the so-called Asian way of doing business, exploring why it was so lauded in the precrisis period only to become denigrated and dismissed in the wake of economic downturn. In answering this question we must address two main factors. The first centers on the recent explosion in computer-led communications. The second concerns the very success of the region itself. The former is typified by the example of Unilever's regional expansion during the 1980s and early 90s. Before the advent of electronic communication links, the substantial cultural and geographical distances involved in ASEAN development signaled huge challenges for the organizational control system.

Complete and accurate information about branch unit performance and methods was particularly difficult and expensive to obtain. In this situation corporate head office had no choice but to allow country managers to make key decisions on their own, giving them the autonomy to respond to local conditions as they saw fit. In organizational terms this "hands-off" corporate arrangement helped form the complex matrix reporting systems typical of companies such as Unilever, allowing the firm to leverage its massive resources to tackle local markets while avoiding getting unnecessarily bogged down in bureaucracy.

Southeast Asian organizations tend to be more loosely structured than their Western counterparts, being founded on cultural emphases on hierarchy and relations-based networks. With little tolerance for Western notions of "the professional manager," these units have traditionally eschewed the dependence on financial analysis and risk management as being "alien" and contextually unnecessary. In processual terms power normally resides in the senior executive to a degree unheard of in the West, with every decision – no matter how small – requiring his or her stamp of approval. One of the downsides of such traditional methods is that they tend to permit more "creative accounting" and lingering corporate suspicions of opaque, underhand business practice. During the precrisis decades the perception was, increasingly, that such cultural foundations were ill equipped to deal with the manifold structural developments required to keep them nimble and responsive. With the progressive lack of "personal contact" possible between the unit chief and his or her subordinate, executives found that their authority became progressively circumscribed. One way around this was for local managers to try to organize themselves into close-knit, "insider" groupings or fiefdoms, usually by rank or, more commonly, by department. But a major drawback of these hardening lines of divisions was that they were becoming increasingly inflexible and unproductive, characterized by overlengthy meetings, decision-making procedures and excessive monitoring.

A second major reason for the increasing operational detachment of these ASEAN branch units was the unquestioned success they enjoyed through much of the 1980s and early 90s. While seemingly assured of near double-digit GDP growth, the "hassles" of doing business in Southeast Asia were easily defrayed. Local firms tended to be left alone by head office in the wake of such impressive profit figures and their country managers granted considerable leeway. In this context the overall organizational culture and working practices of many Southeast Asian subsidiary divisions became steadily more "indigenous" as day-to-day power was progressively invested in the local management committees. Western multinationals would even pride themselves upon their respectively high proportions of indigenous managers, keeping their expatriate executives to often well below corporate quota levels.

Postcrisis consolidation

What triggered the ongoing program of regional consolidation was undoubtedly the Asian market downturn of 1997–8. Yet calls for the full integration of these units came in the light of market developments that occurred well beforehand, spearheaded not just by the growth of electronic global communications and instantaneous movements of freewheeling capital but more subtly by the progressive shift in consumer purchasing powers and habits. The rise in precrisis incomes had already begun to push regional demand toward higher-grade products and services, as illustrated by the growth in brand-name sales on the high streets of ASEAN countries. Regional regulations had begun to put wider

"Jonathon Fry joined the Burmah Castrol Board in 1978 from Unigate as Planning Director and later was appointed Managing Director of the Burmah Castrol Chemicals business following the hostile takeover of Foseco. By the time he made his first visit to Thailand in 1987 he was Chief Executive of the group's lubricants business. He arrived via Malaysia and I met him at Bangkok's Don Muang airport with Miss Castrol, who placed the traditional lotus flower garland round his neck to "protect" him during his stay. The press was there and we received good coverage of his visit in the local and English-language newspapers.

"When we got in the car for the trip to the Oriental Hotel, I gave him a half-inch-thick bound folder. This included a letter of welcome, his full program, our latest monthly results (which were good) and a one-page profile, including photograph, of each of the Thai directors on our joint venture board. Next came a one-page profile of the senior twenty-five Thai employees he would meet, and this too included photographs, their job responsibilities, ability in English, level of education, family background, and so on. The last part of the booklet was a checklist of who he would meet at each function during his short stay. There was nothing in it about me.

"Having read the booklet, Jonathon said, 'Thank you, Bryan, that's very good! Tell me, what were you doing before you came to Thailand?' I replied that I had been the Lubricants Controller in Burmah Castrol Europe, based in Hamburg and later in Swindon. 'Was that your first job in Castrol?' he asked. Somewhat angrily I said, 'No, Mr Fry, I've been in Castrol for thirty years. Don't they brief you before you come out?'"

pressures on the production and sales of certain commodities over others, instanced by the environmental moves toward higher-priced, low-smoke synthetic oils in the domestic automotive industry. Concurrent moves made in the field of organizational management were perceived as heralding the time when global conglomerates – through their shareholders – would finally get to grips with the inefficiencies and overmanning of their ASEAN operating companies. The progressive recasting of headquarter–subsidiary relations was applauded as representing constructive signs heralding greater professionalism and transparency in the future.

Integrating hardware

Consolidation of corporate hardware across Southeast Asia denotes the changes made to the "bone structure" of organizational relations. With the deteriorating economic situation serving to widen the gap between the "haves" and the "have-nots" in many affected countries, Western multinationals voiced their conviction that the idea of having self-sustaining business units in each of these countries was no longer tenable. Corporations sought to adopt a global view to find the most effective way to work, instead of having geographical trading entities under separate management. Western-based corporations began to reverse their traditional focus on business strategy adaptation, now claiming to have "overcommitted" their resources to individual domestic markets. The "business streaming" policies enacted by a substantial number of consumer-focused enterprises reflect this shift, redividing their East Asian units into a unified regional network as opposed to the existing country-centered, geographic focus. Western-style management structures were imposed to reflect this return to the matrix organization, intended to put an end to the emphasis on internal politicking and shifting it back onto the core global product base, returning better value to local customers. Evolving regional markets were also deemed to be in need of business streaming in order to cope adequately with their increasing product segmentation, advanced in turn via the rise in telecommunications and cross-border product knowledge and promotion campaigns.

The return to the matrix structures of old embodied in the switch to business streaming is aptly illustrated by the "class of market" approach taken by the Shell oil company. Its new-found emphasis on functionalization necessitated a separate manager for each business, with corresponding geographic responsibility on a regional – rather than domestic – scale. Under the company's new chairman this restructuring of responsibilities was a key weapon in the corporation's assault upon its ASEAN units. In a similar vein the Bayer chemicals group began to refocus its Southeast Asian structure, integrating domestically based subsidiaries in the provision of regionally focused operations. Key corporate services such as procurement, information systems, finance and accounting, control, personnel, and corporate communications were merged in line with the company's global policy to streamline operations.

Such moves have been replicated by MNCs across the postcrisis industrial landscape, instanced by the "resynchronization" packages progressed by companies such as the US oil major Caltex and the French telecommunications giant Alcatel. These have almost always involved the restructuring of operations into new and distinct profit centers to enhance transparency and strengthen locally utilized accounting systems.

Continuing corporate mergers have only served to accelerate this process in the pursuit of increased synergies and economies of scale, driving down costs and creating new products and markets in the attainment of enhanced global shareholder returns. This is well illustrated by the BP takeover of Castrol, after which the aggressor kept its own supply chain, product formulations, computer systems and reporting structures intact, simply tacking extant Castrol operations on to its flank. Similar moves stemmed from the acquisition of Volvo's Mitsubishi stake by Daimler-Chrysler, already the world's largest manufacturer of commercial vehicles, enacted in order to strengthen its regional market share.

Executive Insights: Merger Mania

"During the past five years or so, the world has gone merger mad. If it carries on like this for another decade we shall all be working for one global company named God Incorporated! Almost every industry is being affected: vehicle manufactures, steel, pharmaceuticals, insurance, banking, petroleum, advertising, etcetera. Is it because the current gurus at INSEAD and Harvard preach that big is beautiful? I personally believe that few of these current mergers will succeed, perhaps because the companies involved become too unwieldy for effective and sensible control. But what are the practical effects?

"The Daimler–Chrysler merger has already become an unmitigated disaster, not because the basic strategy was unsound, but because of cultural differences. And if the Germans and Americans can't work together effectively to ensure customer satisfaction and improved shareholder returns, what chance have the big guys got of adapting to the much more culturally diverse markets of Southeast Asia? These days the customer, the organization's only source of revenue, no longer knows who owns which company or who owns the brand he or she buys. And customers *do* have expectations from the corporate cultures of the brands they have come to trust.

"British Petroleum, since acquiring the one hundred-year-old Castrol brand in 1999, have spent a fortune trying to find out what makes Castrol tick. They could have taken the trouble to find out before they paid five billion dollars for it, and some people could have told them for nothing and in just a few sentences. It is – or rather *was* – 'employ the best people you can, train them as well as you can in the culture as well as the mechanics of the job, look after them, and make sure that the customers are happy with the value for money they get, and they'll come back again and again. If you look after the business properly the share price will look after itself.'

"Is the current merger mania fueled by greed? Are the people at the top, whose salaries and benefits are not to be sneezed at, motivated by the fortunes available by maximizing the value of their share options? Many directors of Castrol are reported to have retired with many millions of pounds. And BP still do not know what makes the Castrol brand tick, and the chances are that the hundred-year-old brand will suffer the same fate as Duckhams at BP's hands.

"What happens to the subsidiaries and joint ventures around the world? Do the chairmen or CEOs of these mega-groups based in their ivory towers in London or New York know much about the people their decisions affect? Aren't they too far away from their staff who know these strange, far-flung markets, and, more importantly, aren't they too far away from their customers? If so, profits will be hard to sustain. It is my strong belief that the corporate giants of this world will have great difficulty maintaining close contact with their customers, and that there is a wonderful opportunity for smaller and medium-sized enterprises to truly care for and motivate their staff to become customer-oriented in the traditional sense."

A detailed rationale for business streaming is perhaps best illustrated by the example of various multinationals within the petrochemicals and oil industries, usually considered to mirror the wider economic climate. The lately acquired British lubricants specialist Castrol is a case in point. Its organizational structure had hitherto had a geographic emphasis, with the ASEAN bloc a key subsector in its Asia-Pacific operations. Within each individual market the company was further split into a Retail division on the one hand, and a CIM (Commercial, Industrial and Marine) division on the other, each with its respective director of operations. Business streaming centered on the fact that the processes involved in each of these divisions were becoming so different that it made sense to try to enhance this critical facet – rather than simply seeking to ignore it. The company divisions therefore further split into the current "streams" defined as Commercial (trucks, commercial fleets and off-road vehicles), Industrial (power generation, mining, metalworking, etc.) and Marine, each with its own managerial hierarchy. The Retail segment was then divided into Consumer (cars and motorcycles) on the one hand and Premium First Fill on the other, this latter section capturing exclusive contracts with globally based luxury franchised dealerships such as Porsche and Jaguar. The Castrol corporate group worldwide comprises four worldwide profit centers, one for each core stream, responsible for their own strategy and results on an international scale. In power-base terms, whereas the balance used to be between the CIM and Consumer units in each local division, this has been simplified to encompass the local, regional and central/global powers. The new structure is designed to weaken the local sales teams' hold upon their domestic territories via the more balanced allocation of resources. The overarching objective is for the company to maximize the profit potential of each of these businesses by refocusing its international resources on the different requirements of each sector in the most cost-effective manner.

At the local level the reporting structures have changed so that each "stream" forms part of a deeper, region-wide focus, with a longer chain of command throughout the Asia-Pacific region. The stream controller in each domestic market is now faced with up to four bosses right up to the regional stream director based in Hong Kong. In practical terms, the previous divisional directors' scope of responsibility was narrowed into that of a single stream (as opposed to the old CIM separation) and their relative status correspondingly devalued. This is also reflected in the reduced role given to the new "country managers" – formerly CEOs – who also now report directly to the regional heads of respective business streams. Formerly charged with the securing of best prices for domestic base oils, in their current roles these chiefs are mainly figureheads with an essentially administrative role; they ensure, for example, that financial operations and product formulations comply with local laws.

The implementation of product groupings being placed back ahead of geographic territory was reflected further down the ranks, with the realignment of domestic sales/marketing divisions at a number of Western corporations in line with home office norms. Castrol again provides a case illustration, with the reorganizing of its consumer division in several key ASEAN markets including Malaysia and Thailand. Traditionally, these countries had been split into two- and four-wheel sales and marketing functions, with concurrent geographic separations of respective sales territories. In the case of Thailand, which had been split into central, northern, northeastern and southern regions, there were two senior sales managers for each of these divisions, one for motorcycles and the other for cars and pickup trucks. However, with the implementation of business streaming, corporate-induced changes engendered a realignment of this "two-" and "four-wheel" product/territory split into the corporate norms of Automotive, Motorcycles and Agri-trucks. In practical terms this new structure effectively shifted resources away from the "Central–Bangkok" focus to a more balanced allocation of resources nationwide. Each new senior sales manager was now to be held responsible for one division to span the entire country, which meant that their number was effectively reduced from eight to three, each with a product counterpart to be drawn from their three newly appointed consumer marketing managers.

Viewed on paper, such structural changes come across as being easy to formulate. But in reality such mechanical restructuring translates slowly into everyday practice. Though it is tempting to view the task of managing the restructuring process as one of sketching alternative chart structures by moving boxes and redrawing lines, all too often management theorists – and even practitioners – lose sight of the real organization behind these structural representations, casually underestimating the underlying interactions and relationships, which may have taken years to develop. As noted by Bartlett and Ghoshal as far back as 1989, there is a continuing need to beware of the assumption that changes in formal roles and reporting relationships will force concurrent changes in the organizational linkages and decision processes, in turn reshaping the way individual managers think and act. The underlying key is to address the "people factor," the human element in organizational change, in order to facilitate the kind of behavioral changes required at the "front line" of business practice, and it is to this that we now turn.

Integrating software

Consolidating corporate Southeast Asia involves much more than simply cutting costs and rationalizing supply chains. Firms have sought to modernize their business processes to make them more competitive, particularly with regard to Web-based technologies. Communication lines have been broadened to provide the relevant intracorporate information to staff throughout the region. Corporate priorities for their regional units have shifted to focus more directly upon cash profitability, efficiency, management training and corporate governance. Specific measures designed to reform the latter issue have included enhanced enterprise monitoring and improved disclosure and accounting practices. But the behavioral changes required to fully implement this shift in focus imply a more fundamental development of the requisite business culture, in order fully to integrate these organizations into the corporate networks of their parents. This will involve, of necessity, the dispensing of many hierarchical layers of management and the implementation of wider spans of control via functional teamwork. Management roles will need to become less hierarchically rigid and more flexible, drawing together small teams of staff across departmental boundaries.

Ostensibly to provide staff with "wider on-the-job experience," respondents generally cited such a reshuffling of managers, supervisors and even secretaries as representing the first step in the breakage of intradepartmental loyalties, in turn to help foster a more "team-spirited mentality." Their impressions were reinforced on the ground by the initiation of "interface" agreements between departments designed to encourage – and at the same time regulate – communication. Attempts within the region to "tighten up" the working practices of indigenous employees are typified by the specimen guideline documents issued during this period, which emphasize the need for units to "speak with one voice" throughout the world and especially in East Asia at this difficult juncture. Stress was placed upon the inculcation of quality global products and agile, high-speed procedures. Western MNCs wished to be seen by consumers as young, dynamic and forward-thinking, anticipating the needs of the marketplace. The desired "modification of attitudes" among local employees was designed to make the business culture more "open-minded" (and in particular to anticipate any future market shifts), characterized by a "spirit of initiative" and "simplicity in working relationships." In future relations with trade purchasers and potential new customers the term "integrity" was to be key, a veiled reference toward some of the murkier dealings between local sales representatives and their dealers. The internal push for "good governance" and "transparent" working methods was typified by the uncharacteristic and unexpected branch dismissals of sometimes highly proficient employees (especially sales managers) perceived from headquarters as epitomizing the corruption they were looking to eradicate.

Implementation: culture's consequences

As previously noted, much of this region-wide consolidation was not specific to Southeast Asia, but stemmed from a wider global push for corporate integration, fueled by improvements in electronic communications. Nonetheless, the levels of success achieved in the local context were critically determined not just by technology levels and head office influence, but also by indigenous business norms and values – themselves indicative of the underlying societal cultures. The relative cultural distance between Eastern and Western modes of practice has meant that in the majority of Southeast Asian markets change has taken over three years to set into practice. The general response to externally imposed transformation has been by all accounts typically "Asian" – a slow, cautious approach designed to avoid wrenching social change wherever possible.

In broad terms the type of change result sought by the Western multinationals was typified by that attained by Mercedes-Benz. Seemingly as a result of the parent firm's professional management programs and technology upgrades, Mercedes-Benz has become the only European marque to make the top-five car brand rankings in the ASEAN block. Yet even with this type of apparent success, the danger in Southeast Asia is the strength and resilience of local business methods, which are liable to steer local employees back toward their old, ineffective patterns of working. Concern has been increasingly expressed by foreign MNCs anxious about these opaque resistance levels, held to be the "invisible force" leading to stagnation. Longer-term success – the *institutionalization* of change – was found by these companies to depend critically on *how* their respective programs had been implemented. MNCs have increasingly begun to appreciate that their methods must be congruent with the local culture if they are to last. Attaining local commitment and organizational stability requires the fusion of local managerial values with corporate strategic priorities, often overlooked and easily underestimated. The given system of "control" rooted in the Southeast Asian social fabric, and the hierarchical nature of its business culture, have tended to put the brakes on Western notions of empowerment and work teams – notwithstanding lengthy corporate efforts to the contrary.

"Software" implementation

The lack of organizational transparency alluded to above is reflected in the structural cityscapes of many Southeast Asian megacities. Substantial numbers of glittering, brand-new office blocks conceal the almost Dickensian feel to the operations performed inside, another testament to the difficulties of forcing local employees to manage their activities in a loosely "Western" style. Corporate-oriented shifts toward "professional working practices" – the crux of most software integration packages – were greeted with smiles of indifference and skepticism by local respondents. The vast majority of those we spoke to expressed their view of the changes made as being purely cosmetic, saying that they would simply "wane" and "melt" when judged against the hard criteria of time. As one local manager put it,

> "Conformity has always been the center of our society. Business and everything is always based around the group, around the family, and

> this cannot change . . . so whatever new rules and regulations people
> talk about because of the economic situation here, they are just
> talking; nobody believe the changes will come in reality . . . because
> there are too many things to keep everything the same as before."

The case of Thailand is again of especial interest in this context. At the
surface level the Kingdom would appear to be the ideal candidate for
the successful reception of Western marketing practices and values. In
Thailand, home to an established constitutional monarchy and a
democratic, pro-business political system, the slogan "open society –
dynamic economy" was for years promoted as the Thai governmental
motto in the precrisis boom. Beneath the surface, however, Thailand has
kept its cultural roots largely intact, being the sole Southeast Asian nation
never to have been colonized by a Western power throughout its eight-
hundred-year history. The ensuing depth and homogeneity of the
domestic societal culture has caused a myriad of problems for incoming
foreign multinationals, and in particular during the postcrisis years.
Whenever local employees have perceived corporate-induced changes as
a threat to the core beliefs of their organization, they have resisted its
implementation, even in the context of an unexpectedly severe economic
downturn. Initial and limited changes observed to local behavior patterns
appeared to revert back to type when imposed values proved inconsistent
with cultural norms (Andrews and Chompusri, 2001).

Even where corporate attention was paid to this issue, it was found that in
practice a significant loss of managerial control was still occurring at
each descending level of external supervision. Against this backdrop,
even for perceived "successes" it was found over time that very little had
changed in practice. Multinational corporate claims to have eroded
"corruption" (as they perceived it) and cronyism within the unit by the
summary dismissal of "misbehaving" sales managers were laughed away
as the ploys of local directors to appease headquarters and prevent
further, maybe deeper, investigation. In any case, and as was stated to us
by indigenous managers across the region, "corruption" was a purely
Western construct, with no translation in local languages, where the
concept was taken merely as a form of *guanxi*-oriented networking. The
perceived extent of the challenges which lie ahead is illustrated by no less
than the former Thai governmental senator and chairman of the country's
Financial Restructuring Authority, Amarit Sila-on. Although the
following excerpts – delivered to the British–American Chamber of
Commerce – may be regarded as simply "playing to the attendant
gallery," there is little doubt that much of what was said resonated

strongly with the experiences of those present corporate chiefs. Sila-on outlines what he considers to be the "key values" within the indigenous societal framework society which, he claims, not only hinder current corporate restructuring efforts but also "threaten to erase the little, if any, gains made so far":

> "The social values I am referring to are cronyism, collusion, corruption and complacency, which I call the four modern Horsemen of the Apocalypse. These values – which have been collectively known as management Thai style or the 'Asian Way' – are so deeply entrenched in Thai society that they exert tremendous influence on all political, economic and social activities. These social forces converge in ways to protect the status quo and to block changes. Cronyism allowed well-connected players to circumvent competition. Collusion is another technique to convert competition into cozy cooperation, while Corruption was often relied upon to remove competition altogether. Complacency, finally, was the result of no competition."
> (Sila-on, 1999; see also Backman, 1999)

In the "trenches" of organizational upheaval, meanwhile, the main problem was the local ambivalence toward not so much the changes themselves as the means adopted to promote them. This ambivalence seemed to center upon the corporate choice of country managers for the task, usually deemed on the ground as involving wholly unsuitable individuals. Much of it stemmed from the perception of Westerners' arrogance in their seeming refusal to adjust their global change formulas for the good of the local conditions. This refusal was typified – albeit in microcosm – by tales of the local insistence on the credibility of the traditional, indigenous ways of working practice. This was set against the retort of corporate representatives that the organization was part of an *international* group and therefore had to adhere to *international* business practice guidelines.

Many local employees expressed distress at the foreign tendency to "look down" upon them and their indigenous working methods, specifically as somehow "underdeveloped" and in need of outside direction. An example of this was the practice at certain organizations of taking down from the walls existing local posters outlining domestic management philosophies in favor of global corporate alternatives. Such acts of confrontation adopted by incoming expatriates of the period clashed with the indigenous stress on harmony and consensus in reaching all major decisions. The aggression and loss of face engendered by such moves was also roundly condemned for its lack of cultural sensitivity. A number of branch subsidiaries were unhappy with the "global" corporate style of business practice, resented for its cold, impersonal stress on computer-aided communication in place of the traditional face-to-face discussion. The short written directives seemingly favored by the majority of incoming expatriate managers were in marked contrast to the regional emphasis on leader visibility and "MBWA" ("management by walking around"). Indigenous employees from a cross section of branch subsidiaries depicted these "new" Western styles of working as variously "secretive," "autocratic," "dictatorial" and – in translation – "noncommunicative."

Further, Western corporate consolidation strategy appeared to turn on the idea of approaching the issues sequentially rather than simultaneously, focusing primarily on financial restructuring as a means for mobilizing the energy for change. The phrase "Let me straighten out the business first, then we can worry about the people" (or words to that effect) was attributed by a number of respondents to their respective expatriate chiefs and held as being typical of an ethnocentric corporate approach. Yet the consensus among indigenous employees was that this second stage – the "emphasis on people" – never actually materialized – beyond of course the dismissal of all those individual team members identified deemed to be "blockers" of the process.

The major thrust of Western multinational change was perceived as being upon the readjustment of working systems rather than on the people and this "softer" side of management practice. Exemplified by the "input/output" matrix referred to in the last chapter, corporate programs claimed to focus on the underlying drivers of cost and staffing (i.e. the "what" before the "who"), suggesting that a failure to adhere to this maxim would lead to lower levels of unit productivity. Yet in their rush to restructure programs, Western companies have tended to overlook – and certainly underestimate – the importance of cultural congruency, in spite of the warnings. The impression of foreign MNCs as concentrating upon global-oriented business systems to the neglect of their people was described and condemned by countless indigenous employees. A broad consensus of managers across the region stressed the need for foreign expatriates to understand the importance of this "human side" to business practice, of the relations-based, informal local approach to performance enhancement. Failure to do so through the use of flatter organizational structures in turn engenders lower, Western-style levels of loyalty among staff. Hence, instead of the high retention levels seemingly nurtured by Sino-Asian approaches to management, the current spate of Western restructuring programs has only served to heighten employee turnover and depress individual job satisfaction.

As regional business commentators have been quick to note, Western corporations typically seek to take a process, unfreeze it, change it and then refreeze it again (much in line with the thoughts of Lewin almost a century earlier). But what might be more appropriate in Southeast Asia would be for them to take a process, unfreeze it and then *keep it unfrozen*, allowing for the fluid, informal-type continuity so characteristic of business in the region (Nivatpumin et al., 1997). In blunter terms, the steamroller approach to corporate restructuring is inevitably going to be a mistaken strategy in a region where gentle persistence and an almost obsessive desire to save face are the everyday norms of office life. In the words of a Filippino automotive executive, "If you come to Southeast Asia and behave just like Jack Welch, then the only thing you'll increase will be the extent of collateral damage. We don't need that kind of method here."

Looking beyond the internal confines of ASEAN branch subsidiaries, the imposition of US-style operating methods and regulations was held to have damaged the local sales teams' relationships with their customers, particularly in the way credit rules had been imposed with lessened scope for the informal, bilateral flexibility held to have sustained individual relationships in the past. The application of "alien" regulations in the ASEAN business context was felt to be feasible only so long as Western MNCs were equipped with superior technology and business-process know-how. Any future slipping of these perceived technical leads would, it was claimed, cause them serious competitive difficulties should they continue seeking to realign the region in this manner.

In summary, imposing egalitarian Western systems and values on socially hierarchical Southeast Asia has engendered a myriad of challenges to consolidating multinationals, most prominently in the areas of communication, information sharing and staff loyalty. Indigenous employee resistance to parent company directives has most often been expressed in severe communication breakdowns, catalyzed by the overwhelming impression among senior Asian executives that they were no longer being listened to. Critically, such rifts may have cost multinationals dear in terms of poor performance, disharmony, inefficient strategy, missed opportunities and suppressed profitability if the underlying tensions have not been dealt with decisively. The vast majority of indigenous managers we spoke to – as well as a similar

Con-Air

An intriguing wave of ill-feeling was triggered among the local respondents of a Thai-based German chemicals conglomerate – intriguing in the sense that it stemmed not from business process change so much as alterations to the office-wide air-conditioning levels. Corporate air-conditioning policies had apparently neglected the traditional local practice of lowering the air temperature in individual offices as one progressed up the managerial scale, so that by the time one reached director level the use of a jacket to cope with the chill was almost a necessity. Not surprisingly, this local correlation between one's rank and office temperature was initially dismissed by regional headquarters as the type of cultural pandering they no longer had the time to entertain. But taking it as an affront to their traditional business values, the Thai executive committee consistently stood their ground upon the issue, with departmental secretaries ordered to adjust local air unit settings each morning before the start of work in defiance of the group default setting. However superficial such actions may appear to the outsider, at this particular organization there was no escaping the tacit loss of face encompassed in the warming of the air about one's workstation. As one perplexed head office envoy put it, "It seems you're simply not a big boy here unless you're attired in a thermal vest and charcoal-gray serge suit. If you ever see the guy in the long fur coat, then watch out!"

proportion of locally based expatriates – were of the view that without motivated local cooperation furnished by an understanding of indigenous value-sets, any externally imposed program of integration would be rendered impotent and powerless.

Business streaming

A number of powerful general arguments were made by respondents as to the unsuitability of carving Southeast Asia into regional business streams. Unlike the practically borderless European and North American continents, the national divisions and interconnections within the ASEAN bloc were felt to be both deeper and far more complex, providing contextual constraints to the wisdom of global business streams. Business streaming in the former areas is relatively easy and can help save costs by facilitating greater customer focus. The process is far more difficult in Southeast Asia, where markets are geographically distant and culturally diverse. Thailand, for one, is widely held as being subject to forces described as "culturally distinct," having never been colonized by a Western power. In stark contrast, the Philippines has been colonized by not one but two nations, drawing cultural nuances from both during nigh on four hundred years of occupation.

The invoking of a region-wide chain of ascending managerial levels for every trifling domestic matter was also held to be unworkable – particularly when the traditionally self-contained ASEAN subsidiaries were habituated to using their own, informal means for resolving personal staff–customer crises. The fear was that in future these kinds of decisions would be subject to time-consuming and inflexible consultation with a regional headquarters perceived as being unsympathetic and culturally uninformed. The concurrent fragmentation of these family-style local business units held cultural ramifications for a region habituated to personalized superior–subordinate relationships beyond the formal reach of global corporate guidelines. Whereas before, the unit chief executive could at least *approximate* to the traditional Asian paternalistic, indulgent, big-hearted boss, the onset of streaming meant that stream heads would often be cross-border executives local managers had never even *met*. The risk with this change was obviously that it would serve to demotivate the local staff, as stated by respondents even in Singapore (where it was claimed to be roundly "hated"). The perceived MNC placing of systems over people left local managers resigned to dealing with faceless unit resources instead of familiar flesh and color, and hence – in their words – never really knowing "who the good guys are." The other main problem, and one often overlooked by incumbent Western multinationals, concerned the case of unit joint ventures. Unlike the wholly owned subsidiary, the JV organization, by definition, comprised not merely the MNC branch operation but also the local partner, which would tend to be a passive major shareholder in a 51:49 operation. And it was this indigenous partner that objected particularly strongly to the notion of business streams, claiming that they desired and required the corporate head of the local organization to be someone with real power with whom they could talk, and not some nominal figurehead bound to a quasi-anonymous boss in Hong Kong.

More general concerns were raised as to the practicalities of planning strategies on a region-wide basis. Local respondents tended to perceive even their own domestic environments as being basically "unknowable" and requiring a great deal of instinctive, flexible decision making to make their strategies work. In practical terms, the costs and inconvenience of regional face-to-face meetings were derided as unrealistic. The alternative – that of interunit videoconferencing – was also dismissed as "wholly unsuitable" for the local market emphasis on personal, face-to-face debate. Streaming effectively requires "virtual teams" of people across country borders, a geometric change from the traditional Asian "huddled group" discussion sessions. One major consequence was felt to be the very opposite of what the Western MNCs were trying to foster, namely the development of cross-functional teams. With team business done increasingly over computers, it was found much harder in practice to produce streaming units which really "gelled," in part of course because of the lack of English language skills on the part of many Southeast Asian managers. The only way around the dilemma was viewed by corporate representatives as being via an investment in "cross-fertilization" programs, sending – even rewarding – branch stream management with weeks abroad in order to help mold their ways of thinking more into line with the MNCs' global preferences. The general lack of enthusiasm among indigenous management toward these schemes was something of a surprise to corporate headquarters. But on reflection, a cross section of our respondents put this down to the fact that the overwhelming majority of managers in the region were from a privileged, well-educated elite who were heavily cosseted from birth in their respective countries. Usually with prior experience of such "business trips" abroad, such executives, habituated to being served by maids, drivers, family and friends, were hardly likely to relish the prospect of weeks spent in places where, as one local manager put it, there was "never anybody to carry your bags . . . it's all do-it-yourself . . . there is very little respect."

A further concern stemmed from the perceived idiosyncratic structure of the domestic customer business. Within the regional lubricants business, for example, most of the distribution outlets are family run with several kinds of outlet being under the overall control of one extended familial organization. The global structural separation between the *Consumer*-based motorcycle workshop on the one hand and the *Industrial*-based sugar mill on the other simply does not hold here. In Southeast Asia both outlets will generally be under one family, and that one family will generally have built up long-term relations with a single senior sales manager and/or one sales representative. In this contact-oriented environment it was held among respondents from all sectors that the imposition of the company–client structure inherent in business streaming could only be damaging to existing relationships and detrimental to long-term business success: as a local Castrol executive stated,

"Having three salesmen visiting one family is not the good way to
develop the business here – or even to hold their business. They will
think you are playing the game with them. In Southeast Asia it is
necessary to keep the relationship stable – this is the most important
thing the Western style never understand."

The subtle but essential notion of "face" provided the final major
problem with regard to streaming implementation – again well illustrated
by the case of Castrol. A substantial number of key sales executives
brought to our attention the consequences of perceived corporate
inattention to this issue among the indigenous divisional heads.
Apparently, with the introduction of regional streams, the former local
heads of combined "CIM," along with the split of their divisions into
three separated concerns, were up against a significant potential loss of
face and even demotion with their newly reduced span of operational
control. Owing to the cultural importance of saving face, rather than
communicating these essential changes to the majority of their domestic
subordinates, many former directors simply allowed their staff to
continue assuming that they were still in control of all three segments
(subject to a mere title change but with no corresponding practical effect
upon their grip upon power). Ironically, this myth was rendered easier to
propagate by misguided corporate attempts to "smooth the transition" by
allowing these former heads to retain their status as "directors." A year
into the imposition of change, the sobering reality to a number of visiting
corporate representatives was that a worrying number of ground-floor
employees were displaying almost total ignorance as to the concept of
business streaming and why it was of long-term benefit for the
organization.

Implementation stagnation was of course the only possible outcome
should the grassroots of each branch unit be aware only of the "negative"
sides of streaming practice. In order to ensure that these long-planned
programs of change did not simply fall apart at the seams, one method
increasingly used by these units as time went on was to effectively
remove those managers perceived as "blockers" to change. The other
way, of course, would be as per the strategy adopted by Caltex. The US
giant had sought to obviate these resistance attempts via a program of
prevention at each of its ASEAN branch operations. Having always
sought to fill its corporate quota of expatriate global managers, Caltex
had already long since successfully implemented such "Westernized"
programs of control as the ISO 9000 quality procedures. With such
reforms up and running well before the onset of postcrisis regional

consolidation, the subsequent decisions to stream and streamline its organizations met with notably less resistance than was experienced at the majority of MNC local subsidiaries.

With the benefit of hindsight, the consensus view on the Asian implementation of corporate business streaming seems to be that although it is a good idea for respective multinationals *internally*, huge problems were perhaps overlooked with its cross-border extrapolation. The overarching corporate objective of purifying business functions on a worldwide basis was hindered and in places diluted in the ASEAN bloc of countries, because of the large cultural distance. In the words of one Shell executive, "In this context the whole thing should have been done a lot slower, bit by bit, rather than trying to stamp it out in one fell swoop."

Implementation "cross-vergence"

Initial attempts to "converge" business practice consolidation methods were followed by year-long gaps, characterized by "divergent" waves of counterimplementation measures. Undertaken by the indigenous management teams, these actions expressed resentment at what they perceived to be unwarranted Western "meddling" in their domestic affairs. The eventual working methods that were to emerge at the coalface are distinctive in their apparent "compromise" or blend between traditionally Eastern and Western ways of business. Denoted here as "cross-vergent" business practices, these were developed and nurtured specifically as a long-term response to disputed initial home office programs of strategic integration. The progressive realization from MNC head offices was that in order to make the changes stick, there had to be, somewhere down the line, the active adoption of their merits by a local consensus of employees in order for them to be successful.

With regard to business streaming, the concession made to the former division heads in the case of Castrol was the allowance that they retain their nominal "directorship" job titles, despite the practical reduction of their responsibilities. The former trappings of directorship status were also adhered to in a number of companies, including the retention of personal chauffeurs and a place on the local executive committee – a concession, it was claimed, to the indigenous importance of saving face. As expressed by one corporate representative,

> "We need to work with the local staff and within their own ways of thinking here otherwise nothing'll ever get done, it's all turned pear-shaped as soon as our backs are turned . . . we need to ensure our policy changes are not simply left to stagnate at the coalface; it's essential now, too much time has been wasted already."

More generally across the regional corporate landscape, the major improvements noted by indigenous management involved the perceived loosening of control over the initial change directives. Several companies sought to initiate compromise via the rotation of senior expatriate executives at the very top of the local organization. The ensuing change of leadership and the concurrent personality changes engendered were held to save face for all concerned, including the corporation itself. Often, the organic shift in management style brought on by the change in thinking was in itself enough to smooth over major sticking points between the local managers and their parent counterparts. In selected multinationals their newly "compromising" chiefs were beginning to pave the way for an effective long-term corporate-societal blend of working norms – including, of course, the concept of business streams and their acceptability among the grassroots local employees. A number of multinational branch units had even taken the considered – and rather bold – move of employing new country managers from among the indigenous ranks. Whatever their cultural origins, its seemed that the incoming "school" of chiefs were generally adopting an approach to business perceived locally as being both more informal and – crucially – flexible. Unsurprisingly in this context, the subsequent chief at a German-based chemicals group appeared uninterested in readjusting the traditional local mores with regard to office temperature regulation, leaving the air-conditioning maintenance entirely in the hands of the individual department heads. More generally, the discernible trend for head office "kid glove" methodology with regard to corporate ASEAN branch offices appeared to be an effective means of dealing with the now destabilized business environment, providing new, tailor-made services to valued and long-time customers, particularly welcomed among the remaining indigenous sales teams.

The eventual compromises attained encompassed a practical redefinition of the role of "country manager" within the newly consolidated hierarchical structures. With the tacit agreement of regional headquarters, an informal – though very real – transfer of day-to-day power back to the local unit heads has become increasingly evident in recent years. In terms of business streaming in particular, domestic chiefs – although officially accountable to the regional stream directors – were allowed to effectively retain control of all internal aspects of their local operations. An unofficial "dotted line" to corporate headquarters was effectively in evidence for the ASEAN domestic heads, permitting the local incorporation of long-standing client–representative relationships and areas of responsibility, while simultaneously keeping the formal arrangements intact. In this respect the new country managers continued to discharge their day-to-day responsibilities as their predecessor chief executives of the precrisis years would have. The manner by which nominal business streams were made flexible to the needs of the existing customer network made for progressively higher levels of change acceptance among indigenous employees – conscious of the apparent concessions made to local market conditions.

Other changes facilitating this "cross-vergence" of business methods stemmed from globally oriented shifts in working practices at the company–customer interface. In the immediate aftermath of the economic crisis, multinational insistence that regional business norms would now begin to converge with those practiced in the West was scoffed at by local respondents. However, in the course of time the traditional power base enjoyed by the local sales force began to wane as the customer business structures themselves "self-adapted" to the changed environment. Corporate and eventually local respondents perceived a change in attitude among some of the larger franchised establishments, particularly – though not in every case – when they were now under the control of a larger multinational conglomerate. Japanese-parented automotive dealerships were apparently now quite keen to distance themselves from the contact-oriented relationship and move toward one based on professional referrals. The traditional Southeast Asian type of business network founded on ethnicity, universality, religion and family was held to be no longer the force it once was – exemplifying the culturally based move toward the Western corporate element of the typical ASEAN branch operation.

In structural terms the key appears to be to develop an efficient global organizational template capable of being adapted to fit local business norms. In this context, although the core of the machine remains uniformly integrated, the external cogs are roundly flexible. Companies cited as having achieved a type of balance in this regard range from the foods giant Nestlé through the US oil venture Caltex and on to the Asian-based bank HSBC. The first of these is held to have successfully combined the enforcement of uniform principles, policies, rules of conduct, and strategies with the local diversification into various needed areas of expertise. As regards management style, the core principles appear to be flexibility and simplicity, aiming to respect the customs and beliefs of different nationalities while simultaneously applying the company's core values to all employees, regardless of origin. To our surprise, the Caltex group was also praised by a cross section of respondents for the flexibility of its regional organizational structure. Unlike the majority of multinational oil companies, Caltex has largely now dispensed with the traditional practice of seeking to dovetail local managerial structures with those of the wider corporation. Reportedly encouraging creativity and effectiveness over any "artificial" constraints to external working procedures, the type of flexibility enjoyed by local managers allows their chosen strategies to be based on the skills of the people actually present rather than on any centrally imposed best-case scenario.

In conclusion, the successful corporate consolidation of its ASEAN-based units depends upon the ability of the parent to accommodate culturally congruent styles of business practice. Such "congruence" can never be a one-way street, however, and hence our focus upon compromise or cross-vergent business practices in which the building up of mutual trust and confidence is paramount. Flexibility and consultation in decision making through continuous information-sharing mechanisms is the key via which the ultimate synthesis of Eastern and Western styles of management can be reached.

5 Human resources management

- Recruitment
- Where the twain meet: expatriates v. local recruits
- Managerial rotation
- The rise of the "younger" executive
- Reward structure
- Appraisals
- Training
- Language

Part of the organizational "software" depicted in the previous chapter concerns the management of human resources management (HRM), often depicted as being the least "Westernized" of any of the elements of Southeast Asian business practice. HRM in the host markets of Southeast Asia is undergoing colossal change in the new economic environment. The majority of MNCs are increasingly holding their staff accountable for how value within the organization is actually created. For years it seemed that operations within the region had been managed "willy-nilly" (as one executive put it) – with even the branch units of the world's foremost multinationals being run as, essentially, "glorified green-grocers," the personal fiefdoms of their managers.

Of course, in the precrisis era of just a few short years ago there seemed little need for the global norms of strict accountability. Branch operations were growing at lightning speed and were hiring new staff nearly as fast. As Slater (1999a) notes, there were jobs in abundance, and bonuses and pay increases were often sky-high – "life was good." The looming crisis that was to lead to stringent cost-cutting, bonus cancellations and layoffs – the focus of Chapter 3 – was an unthinkable nightmare, but one that was about to ignite a fire of radical change in personnel acquisition and control.

One major result of the ensuing Western-oriented change has been to increase the role and power of the corporate central office *vis-à-vis* host-market work regulations and rules. The host-market relationship between management and employees has become more international in character, making the human resource administration more complex, based on a structure brought in from overseas. Increasingly tied up by norms and values that are essentially "alien" in origin, these changes have impacted quickly and deeply upon relations which were previously "Vietnamese," "Malaysian" or even "Asian" in character. The Western corporate focus upon issues of productivity, improving the performance of remaining staff members in order to get the most out of them, has led to the rapid emergence of a whole new set of expectations for a profession that, in Asia, has "traditionally functioned merely to process forms, benefits and new hires."

These changes have been compounded by the corporate swing away from focusing on geographical regions toward globally oriented product lines (as depicted in the previous chapter). The rise of functionalization has emphasized the need for host-country employees to be able to relate to their counterparts, whether they are the Swiss in Hong Kong or the Germans in Singapore. Corporate consolidation – and in particular business streaming – has pointed to the increasing importance of intercultural management practice, making it more and more difficult for local units to cling to their traditional methods of conducting business. The "cradle-to-grave" egalitarianism mindset, characteristic of the precrisis years, has given way to the "novel" concept of being expected to earn wages and bonuses on the strength of objectively determined performance criteria. Indigenous employees are being coached, encouraged and in some cases forced to focus on teamwork, efficiency, responsibility, capability, honesty and open communications – with future promotion criteria being based on merit instead of the traditional criterion of seniority.

Needless to say, the complexity of the ASEAN working environment profoundly colors the picture for existing foreign multinationals. Many employers have had to adapt their human resource rules and practices in order to comply with the varied employment legislation across the region. The rate of acceptance for sophisticated HR methods has been subject to the widely diverging business environments. Some countries – and in particular Singapore and the Philippines – already have a substantial number of Western-style industrial relations in place. The latter's relative amenability is to a large extent the result of its colonial past, the main patterns of recruitment, training, job design, pay systems and labor relations having been established by Western manufacturing entities while the Philippines was still in the hands of the USA.

Whatever the country, societal culture has substantial influence upon local HRM practices, particularly in such areas as compensation and rewards, performance appraisal and staff recruitment. Although the main thrust of the postcrisis changes may have eroded many traditions related to the employment relationship, others seem firmly rooted in the complex texture of individual host-market society. To many commentators (e.g. Lawler et al., 1997), human resource programs – as an "input control" – are a vital area for cultural integration. They must, therefore, be attuned to their cultural contexts if success is to be achieved, particularly via the careful recruitment and development of key decision makers. While empirical research on the appropriate match between specific human resource practices and cultural elements is difficult to find, the available literature suggests that although HRM practice should always be culturally aligned, such differentiation of programs also involves substantial costs in terms of their development, implementation, coordination, monitoring and periodic adjustment (ibid.; Bartlett and Ghoshal, 1989; Lawler, 1996; Muralidharan and Hamilton, 1999).

Longer-term corporate adjustment of indigenous work practice depends for its success on the local tendency to stress "consensus decision making," requiring sustained, intensive communication between all parties. Recent efforts by Western and Japanese MNCs to impose HRM systems in an ethnocentric fashion in their ASEAN operations have generated significant cultural clashes in the workplace. Non-Asian "corporate fixers," sent over from central headquarters, have been widely berated for their patent lack of language ability and cultural experience, typified by their evident confusion at some of the more subtle workplace processes such as *kreng jai* and *bunkhun* in Thailand and *tiwala* in the Philippines. Floundering on incomplete knowledge and the weak information provided by local management, many MNCs have been able only to recommend vague strategies and structures, which are often then interpreted by the senior controlling team in a way that suits their own purposes (see Buranakanonda, 1998) – hence the increasing necessity to initiate policy changes by first seeking to render them appropriate with existing norms and, critically, managerial values. As foreign multinationals have become major host-market employers, these issues have necessitated quick resolution in order not to exacerbate already delicate postcrisis labor market tensions. Confrontations have been notable within cross-border JV arrangements in particular, as host-country and foreign corporate partners battle it out as to the extent of implemented domestic versus global HR norms.

This chapter focuses on the two major strands of indigenous HR management practice: employee recruitment and employee retention. The section immediately following delineates the existing issues surrounding the changing nature of branch-level employee composition, including the continuing debate upon the pros and cons of hiring expatriate as against local managers, as well as the related controversies as to the relative age and managerial rotation of key staff. The second half of the chapter is focused on the development and training of extant and incoming personnel, including separate sections devoted to reward structures and staff appraisals of a cross section of MNC branch operations. Inextricably intertwined in practice, the two main strands of this chapter are separated here purely for the sake of structural convenience.

Recruitment

In the recruiting of key personnel, the usual Western corporate reliance on agency head-hunting and market intelligence has traditionally been problematic in the markets of Southeast Asia. According to the majority of our respondents, the best way around this problem is to focus on first *understanding* and then *addressing* the existing local methodology rationale. The process whereby indigenous norms are then "molded into shape" over time can be facilitated in a number of ways. To begin with, newly installed MNC branch units can aim to recruit relatively young members of the local managerial community – typified by those imbued with a Western university education. The recruitment of locally based expatriates – as opposed to those from either home office or other regions – has also been suggested, the reasoning being that a manager with experience of the host country's culture will be of practical benefit during the first years of a unit's operation, particularly in helping to navigate the often confusing mire of local operating regulations and business culture norms. This is held to be the case even if the individual involved has a completely different product background, based on the premise that it is far easier to transmit knowledge of an industry or product than of an entirely new societal culture.

The acquisition of such potentially valuable Western managers is typically facilitated through the informal – though highly influential –

networks of contacts built up around the various domestic chambers of commerce, businesspeople's groups, Rotary Clubs – and even through the long-running "Hash House Harriers" (the latter self-depicted as groups of "drinkers with a running problem"). Needless to say, these unstructured, motley clans of people differ markedly from the legal trade associations found in the West. But the golden rule seems to be that in terms of expatriate recruitment it is always best to go via your friends.

The difficulties associated with recruiting experienced and suitable functional expatriates from corporate headquarters has been compounded in recent years by the increasing preference shown toward alternative destinations within the Asia-Pacific basin, notably further north to China, Hong Kong, Taiwan, Japan and South Korea. A recent Political and Economic Risk Consultancy (PERC) survey into the movement of expatriates in the Asia-Pacific region found that within the ASEAN bloc only Singapore and the Philippines scored highly on the factor ratings addressed, notably health care, housing, schooling, recreation and security (Bangkok Post, 2001). Thailand, although high on nightlife and recreational activities, scored surprisingly low on health care and educational standards. Vietnam came under considerable criticism for its weak infrastructure, as did Indonesia, which was also berated for its deficient medical facilities and poor security.

Those recruiting local managers have often paid attention to the purported extent of their contacts – either via work experience or from the more traditional *guanxi* connections discussed in Chapter 1. While setting up its branch operations in the region, the Shell oil conglomerate would always seek to employ those with experience working for the respective host-national oil company. In these early stages of recruitment an incoming MNC would also do well to consider the effects of employee loyalty, particularly when the unit consists of a joint venture arrangement. The oft-cited claim that in the ASEAN corporate environment loyalty is considered more important than either qualifications or experience is of import here. Existing local loyalty toward the existing partner in the JV can often create conflict with the foreign multinational, stressing the need for loyalty to the *venture itself*, rather than to one of the partners.

The corollary problem with this issue of loyalty is that local employees are often portrayed as in essence bound to their direct superiors, over and above any commitment to their respective organizations. Asians, it is said, tend to work for their bosses rather than their companies. This is partly because traditional employee recruitment throughout the ASEAN region has tended to be based around the use of personal or family connections, referred to in Thai as *mee sen* (literally, to "have strings"). Such elongated "strings" typically take the form of an extended university alumnus group, or along religious sectarian lines or even down to region of birth. The existence of these groups of employees congregating together within the corporate community often makes for teams within teams which are very difficult to break into. This can result in the resignation of a senior manager, leading to the departure of whole departments, symptomatic of a society in which strong allegiance is shown to one's own "group" within the hierarchical structure. In the current business climate such a loss of trained staff can be particularly difficult, even disastrous, in a region where there is a current shortage of skilled people to fill the growing number of specialized positions (Holmes and Tangtongtavy, 1995; Toews and McGregor, 1998).

The resilience of these local groups becomes apparent when one examines past attempts to override the local recruitment process – for example, by going over the heads of the local HR managers. This is illustrated in a number of relevant cases, for example the recruitment of a Western woman manager to a senior marketing post within a European consumer group's Malaysian subsidiary. Instigated over a period of years by the incumbent Western chief executive, the appointment was organized in consultation with the regional corporate team yet with only minimal reference to the relevant Malay managers. Local resentment over the newcomer was expressed in very clear terms, although in a manner that would be deemed discriminatory in the West. The exclusively male marketing management team claimed that a woman – Western or otherwise – was patently unsuitable for such a role in the domestic environment, especially with regard to a number of the company's key account customers. The fact that the foreign CEO had seemingly overruled these objections – with the tacit support of regional headquarters – was taken as evidence of a wider Western failure to understand the local business context.

More recent examples of such attempts to circumvent indigenous recruitment procedures have centered on seeking to change the structure of company policy itself. This is exemplified by the adaptation of such a policy at the ASEAN units of a major US oil company. Corporate head office had made the decision to "phase out" the traditional lump sum payout given upon retirement, now seen as a hangover from the old "jobs for life" culture. The new policy – again already in place in the vast majority of Western oil companies – pays this same sum incrementally, year on year, from the time the recruit first joins the company. It is hoped that this new method will attract a "new kind of employee," one who is ambitious, who wants to spend the money on bettering themself (e.g. learning a language also of use to the company) while still young, and who would be able to place both company and individual goals in tandem.

Where the twain meet: expatriates v. local recruits

In the words of one senior Shell executive, the "best" kind of joint ventures house a relatively high proportion of two types of employee: the young MBA returnee and the Western corporate expatriate. To this end Shell reportedly had over twenty expatriates on its books in Vietnam alone – well over the usual MNC quota levels of between 5 and 10 percent. The rationale for this approach seems to stem from the company's focus upon the start-up phase of the operation. Aside from any corporate desire to raise expatriate numbers *per se*, the main objective is more to install the systems in place in order to make the ensuing organizational practices as close to global norms as possible. In investing in a high percentage of expatriates during the initial stages of the operation, the Western partner, so the theory goes, has a far greater chance of seeing its systems up and running by the indigenous employees.

This type of approach among foreign multinationals is particularly marked in Japanese-parented local units, which tend to depend upon having Japanese managers in key middle- and upper-level positions. Indeed, over the years the use of expatriates by their Western MNC counterparts seems almost sparing in comparison. Part of the reason for this divergence in method is the assumed – though often contested – cultural similarities between Japanese and Southeast Asian managers expounded by Japanese parent executives. For although undoubtedly they share some measure of societal heritage, in business culture terms the vast majority of our Southeast Asian respondents stress the fact that unlike, say, the Thais or the Vietnamese, the Japanese hold their work to be their central interest in life. Hence, although perhaps more comfortable with Japanese staffing procedures, local respondents were manifestly unhappy and even resentful of the perceived "bamboo ceiling" for local employees of Japanese-based operations.

A shared feature of foreign multinationals is the desire – indeed, the need – to have *some* measure of corporate expertise in key managerial positions. The small number of corporations seeking to develop their respective product markets in Cambodia, for example, have expressed dissatisfaction with the indigenous middle-management incumbents. A cross section of corporate executives felt that such staff were simply incapable of grasping the Western business concepts and methodologies they were required to take on board. The local branch units of several banking and telecommunications companies found they were having to devote around six months of valuable time in order to equip these employees with the basic skills for everyday practice. Laying the blame for this inadequate state of affairs squarely on the local education system, respondents bemoaned the local employment regulations, which prevented them from employing more of their "own" executives.

Viewed from the indigenous perspective, these same MNCs have been roundly criticized for this desire to bring in costly expatriate staff as a kind of "cure-all" for their local HRM problems. Particular concerns were voiced with regard to the tendency for MNCs to try placing their own executives in the very top positions in cross-border joint ventures. More precisely, we found a surprising prevalence of nonresident chairpersons from the corporation's head or regional office being promoted to the boards of these local ventures. Local criticism of these moves was based on the practical failure of such parent executives to contribute to the well-being of the operation. In the words of a senior Thai executive,

> "Surely it is wiser to appoint someone who knows and understands the market. Whether the person is a local manager or whether it is a foreigner, that person should at least have his home in the same country as the business. This is not too much to ask, is it? . . . Not to do this seems crazy when a good, well-known local executive is what you will need in order to deal with the government, deal with employees, deal with customers."

Most Western MNCs tend to focus primarily on securing their own executives in the very top management positions, be it at chief executive, chairperson or general manager level. Yet although this may perhaps make sense at the starting phase of a working agreement, the consensus view is currently that the firm should then transfer the reins to a suitable, mutually agreed local general manager as soon as logically possible. At a more general level, the debate as to the pros and cons of employing expatriate personnel over locally based alternatives hinges on three main issues, namely *cost*, *commitment* and *understanding*, each of which will be delineated below.

Cost

Cost is perhaps the major sticking point among host-country personnel. The wide compensation gap between expatriates and locals has been a constant source of indigenous employee resentment. In purely monetary terms, it is often possible to substitute four indigenous managers for the price of one expatriate – hence the difficulties in finding suitable justification for their continued presence, especially in the postcrisis era of thrift and cost control. Notable concern was expressed to us with regard to the cost of personal chauffeurs for senior foreign managers. As one executive bemoaned,

> "We can accept that the CEO or the directors should have their own driver but what about these other foreign managers? Surely there should be some limit to this benefit? I mean, if after two years of working here they still cannot drive themselves around, then maybe they are just not suitable to living here."

Since the economic upheaval of 1997, MNC branch operations have increasingly turned to the use of "localized" assignments in an effort to contain the costs typically incurred with traditional expatriate packages. Compensation packages offered to locally based Westerners, although competitive, have tended to be more in line with host-country levels, with far less allowance being made for housing, schooling, and so on. This shift toward local expertise has even extended to the recruitment of management consultants, traditionally the almost exclusive territory of the highly paid Western adviser. In practical terms the region has witnessed a thinning out of existing expatriate levels, instanced by the current situation at Jardine, where the proportion of foreign executives is currently running at well below 5 percent of total head count. Several well-known Western multinationals have also decided to pass the leadership torch in a number of their ASEAN units to a native manager, moves that only a decade ago would have been nearly inconceivable.

Commitment

The lack of commitment to a particular country role on the part of an incoming expatriate stems not so much from his/her want of ambition, but rather from the difficulties imposed upon the person by the differing demands of the new cultural environment. The expatriate family man, in particular, is under a particular set of circumstances, having moved his wife and children from Europe or the USA into an Asian metropolis such as Bangkok or Metro Manila. To begin with, he will have much less time to spend with the family. Children based in big regional cities often leave for school at five in the morning or even before. And although they are home from mid-afternoon onward, the busy father will be hard pushed ever to return much before seven in the evening. The local emphasis on functions, social gatherings and customer entertainment soirees makes the occurrence of late, often drink-fueled evenings almost a routine. The "candy store syndrome" so often referred to in expatriate business circles concerns perhaps a more extreme version of this heady lifestyle, populated by establishments proffering ready supplies of beautiful women tailor-designed for the errant Western executive. The initial protestations of new Western executives that they would "never pay" for such pleasures is only too often reversed within the first six months of domestic tenure.

The high level of divorces, family instability and alcoholism is an unfortunate, though all too regular, testament to the destructive nature of these environmental influences. The often underestimated – but very serious – cases of incumbent Western managers who have progressively lost their grip upon reality has been cited as being perhaps as big a problem as the breakdown of the corporate computer hard drive. As expounded by a number of long-serving ASEAN-based managers, the corporate center needs to be prepared for such increasingly common occurrences with the development of sensible and practically oriented contingency plans, especially in a region where continuity of method and priority are regarded as so important.

Understanding

The continuing influx of Western expatriates into host-market organizations has been held to be counterproductive, owing to the patent "lack of cultural understanding" evinced by so many of their number. In a business context, where the local relations network and patronage claims preclude them from having any real influence, it has often seemed senseless among local teams to go on paying them exorbitant wages for what has been perceived as very little output. This feeling is typified in the following observation made by a senior Indonesian sales manager:

> "The most important thing for us in the Asian-style business is the relationship between ourselves and the customer because these are the

people who pay our wage, and the people that we have to respect. But
for the foreigner, the white man, it seems like only the results that
they care anything about, it's not the people . . . but for us here it's a
very different way for us. The process of working together here is so
essential but it's like they cannot understand this, even the white man
who work here for so [long], they always say that they understand us
but the reality is that they cannot . . . they don't even try to learn our
language."

Given expensive expatriates' – at best – "generalized" understanding of
individual Southeast Asian markets, local managers consider them to be
little more than a costly luxury. Ironically, this is increasingly held to
be the case as the domestic market begins to develop and mature –
segmentation deemed to require in-depth and culturally grounded
knowledge of the market. Multinationals therefore perform a balancing
act in the current changing business environment, trading-in the short for
the long term in their hiring of Western executives, who typically require
a minimum of three years to understand the local market to any level of
effectiveness. This lengthy "gap in understanding" is borne out by the
experience of a number of Western consultants from both the pre- and the
postcrisis periods, who emphasized the deliberate local attempts to keep
them "in the dark" for as long as possible.

Initially – and to our surprise – the vast majority of those we interviewed
claim to have been treated fairly, even welcomed, by the local
management team. But with the benefit of hindsight these same managers
now admit this was down to the fact that in practice their roles were little
more than "window dressing" and the positions they were filling merely
cosmetic in import. A majority claim to have been politely bypassed
when any important decision was to be made, only learning of detailed
changes to be made "at the last minute – if at all." Their big titles and
status were held to be little more than moves made to appease the
analysts, head office representatives and international suppliers.
Westerners in Southeast Asia, it was claimed, will never in practice be
allowed to exercise control or to penetrate too deeply into the informal
organizational networks, which are deemed "too secretive, too intricate"
for anybody other than an indigenous native to comprehend. In fact, the
only apparent means by which these "consultants" were actually taken
advantage of was through the breadth and potential of their locally based
Western contacts within the wider expatriate business community.

One role which remains predominantly the domain of the home office
executive is that of the chief executive officer, or "country manager," as

those performing that role are now more commonly described. During the precrisis period these branch office heads enjoyed considerable decision making autonomy, with profit and loss responsibility and the oversight of multiple functions. And although their role is now substantially lessened with the switch to function focus over that of geography, these figureheads still play a critical role in the overall harmonization of domestic human resource management. In order to fulfill this role to the utmost, country business chiefs should be able to function ideally in at least two environmental cultures, namely those of the business unit on the one hand and the corporation on the other, the latter usually heavily affected by the nationality of the corporation. The existing literature also reiterates the point repeatedly made by our informants as to the desirability of employing "corporate diplomats," depicted by Hofstede two decades ago as being infused with the corporate culture, multilingual, and experienced in living and functioning

Executive Insights: Americans in a Thai Bank – A New Initiative

"Apart from the HSBC, which has been in Thailand for more than 150 years – and has recently been granted license to open yet more branches – the majority of foreign banks have had difficulty in maintaining a secure foothold in the local market. Since the 1997 crash some banks have been able to acquire ailing Thai banks and finance houses to give them better access to Thai and foreign business enterprises. In the past, Thai banks have had difficulty competing with the efficiency of foreign outfits. In fact, to open an account with a Thai bank used to be, and probably still is, a bureaucratic nightmare.

"The Thai Farmer's Bank, however – under the leadership of its president, Banthoon Lamsan – has taken the unprecedented step, for a family business, of appointing two experienced and well-respected American bankers to strategic positions. The first, William Fontana, was appointed as the new Executive Vice President of the Bank's Human Resources Group in January 2001. He told me that in other places he has worked – including ten years' international experience – he was always given a lot of responsibilities but without the authority to back up his decisions. However, at the Thai Famer's Bank under President Banthoon he has now been given both responsibility and the requisite authority to back up his actions.

"The second – David Hendrix – is a retail banking marketing expert formerly with the Citibank Corporation for many years. Together, these two appointments strike me as representing an excellent strategy for a somewhat traditional Thai family bank to compete more effectively postcrisis and going into the new century. I hope Banthoon continues to support them and to listen to their recommendations."

in various foreign cultures. As acting liaison officers in the various head offices and/or up-and-coming local ventures, these diplomats are essential in making multinational corporate structures work in practice (e.g. Hofstede, 1980; Quelch, 1992). These roles have been taken one step further in the changing postcrisis era, with the increasing appointment of regional HR controllers with a "foot in both camps" – typically, Asian individuals with substantial experience in Western business environments.

Managerial rotation

The modern multinational corporation subtly but meticulously seeks to ensure that its assumptions and values are transplanted into host-market environments. These values are then doggedly reiterated and maintained through the rotation of senior expatriate managers. But the notion of "managerial rotation" is viewed with considerable suspicion by the apparent majority of indigenous employees, and has become a hotly contested debate in the ASEAN economies. We shall start this section with a depiction of the views of both camps, beginning with the perceived disadvantages expressed by a variety of local market managers.

"Job rotation is no good in Asia, it is amply clear from all the evidence." These are the words of a local representative from one of the region's chambers of commerce. The catalog of severe criticisms leveled at the practice stems from the widespread perception that two or three years spent in a post does not provide adequate time for an incoming expatriate to establish and benefit from personal relationships. This frequent movement of expatriate staff is further perceived to emphasize the *institutional* nature of Western corporate business relationships, over and above their *personal* aspects – features again thought to be culturally inappropriate in the Southeast Asian environment. The shifting of executives from post to post, country to country, with little thought for the likely impact on business relationships is roundly criticized as "short-termist" and harmful to the long-term success of domestic branch operations. The stop–start nature of the domestic company–customer relationships runs against the local stress on societal stasis and unbroken continuity, leaving little room for the kind of one-to-one flexibility traditionally nurtured. As already outlined, all business dealings in the Chinese-dominated ASEAN corporate arena are based upon the development of strong relationships between partners. This can be a complex process involving many more luncheon and dinner banquets and office and factory visits than is usual among Western companies. Western managers may feel that little work is getting done, but in practical terms relationships that are being built will be very valuable in the future.

The second main critique of managerial rotation – as expressed to us – concerns the lack of real control and influence afforded to expatriate incumbents, a far more serious issue to the majority of our Western corporate informants. With only a limited tenure in their respective positions, expatriates can easily be led "as blind men" by experienced indigenous teams of managers with their own internal agendas (indeed, this has often been labeled the corporate "mushroom" policy of keeping one's local expatriates in the dark and "feeding them on bullshit"). Conflicting sets of priorities between expatriates and locals often mean that the former will be told more or less what the latter think they want to hear. And then when things go wrong, it is the foreign executive – usually with ultimate responsibility for unit performance – who will get the blame.

Expatriates generally arrive at their respective branch units with some new system or working method they are adamant they will set in motion, habitually where others before them have failed. Yet the locals are all too aware of the practical realities of such claims. Expatriates, after all, are typically on fixed-term contracts – they come and then they go. But the indigenous team know from experience that when the current expatriate leaves it is *they* who will then be charged with operationalizing the system as they see fit. Local managers thus tend to appease the foreign representative, safe in the knowledge that come a year or two, the present incumbent will be replaced. As a direct result of this, the average local manager sees little need for the acquisition of cross-cultural skills. Indeed, s/he is shielded from the need by this utilization of corporate managerial rotation, even in the modern multinational office.[1]

---

1 The fact that this state of affairs is often portrayed as akin to the "tail wagging the dog" puts one in mind of similar charges leveled at the UK political establishment. Whereas the elected politicians generally serve a maximum of five years, the civil servants behind the scenes often, indeed usually, stay on throughout the course of their long and secure careers. Exemplified by the Permanent Secretaries at the head of each governmental ministry and immortalized in the TV series *Yes, Minister*, the realistic probability that the country's political establishment represents a self-perpetuating machine can be put down to this power-draining rotation of democratically elected public servants as against their bureaucratic counterparts.

In their defense of managerial rotation, multinationals in the region hold fast to the notion that it effectively embodies both the structural and the personal aspects of local human resource objectives. The internal rotation of indigenous management is held to be a positive factor in the recent push to eradicate widespread corruption practices – and particularly at the company–customer interface. The periodic rotation of both expatriate and local executives also reduces the risk of becoming dependent on any one individual in any one role. The practice of regular management rotation acts as a kind of limitation exercise on the potential for local resignations *en masse* in support of a departmental head, so the company is never left scratching its head wondering "well, who's going to do this job now that so-and-so has gone? He was the only one who understood it" and so forth. The development of key appointees in a cross section of positions makes for a more forward-looking, confident and well-managed corporation. The resultant pool of multiskilled teams of executives should also therefore lead to a constant *stream* of continuity in each key position – as opposed to the more stifling, stagnating practice of keeping one person in one post. Breaking down in practice the traditional patriarchal structure in domestic markets, the rotation of pivotal executives has facilitated the switch to the functionalization of global organizational structures, placing a business or product focus ahead of the former reliance on cozy, corruption-prone local networks.

Structural benefits aside, the rotation of managers can also help to reduce the problems with "errant" expatriate managers (as delineated above). The oft-noted tendency for incoming Western managers to "lose the plot" in some of the more lively regional cities – and the quasi-alcoholism and domestic strife this can engender – can be overcome by a policy of rotating and recycling corporate staff. Viewed as a kind of "contingency plan," rotation policies can assist an organization in its quest to keep its expensive cadre of global troubleshooters firmly "on the rails." Leaving expatriates in a domestic market for indefinite periods can also ultimately reduce their global "usage," particularly in the case of country chiefs. Although taking the time to learn the local customs and working styles can help tremendously in the understanding of a domestic business environment, there is a perceived "fine line" between becoming culturally aware and "going native." With country chiefs the main problem seems to relate to their longevity having bred a locally flavored resistance to adopting newer, global working systems – particularly in the precrisis environment, when the success of the ASEAN branch units meant that no one asked too many questions. But for the functional manager lower down the ranks, the main point is not to "go overboard" in adopting local customs and modes of thinking. Just as such managers had reached the point of feeling they had understood their new country, their parent headquarters would often repatriate them on the assumption they had "gone native." But the loss of such promising future executives and the time it takes to replace them can be overcome through the institution of a system of managerial rotation.

In order to try to balance the perspectives and priorities of branch operations and corporate headquarters, rotation programs have in many cases been substantially revised, generally as a result of the postcrisis corporate acknowledgment of the value of "relations-based" networking. Many multinationals have agreed to soften the effects of their respective policies by making an assessment on a case-by-case basis, often at the end of each three-year position cycle. However, many respondents felt that the ceiling for tenure should be raised across the board to at least five years, ending with a performance review to determine its continuity or change (based on the relevant circumstances). From the general response of our local informants it was this willingness to concede on the part of the multinationals that has made all the difference, signaling the crucial change from "Western rigidity" toward "Asian flexibility."

The rise of the "younger" executive

One final dilemma surrounding the changing patterns of host-market recruitment methodology concerns the postcrisis attempts by incumbent MNCs to "phase in" new crops of younger managers, perceived as being more amenable to Western ways of business practice. Regarded as a highly risky method for exerting control over host-market HRM, such generational transitions are nevertheless seen as essential in order to cope with a current business environment characterized by rapid technological change. Recruiting predominantly younger individuals to high-status positions is felt to adhere to the need for ASEAN units to become internationally competitive, operating according to increasingly stringent international standards.

Many MNCs expressed their conviction that on a day-to-day basis, younger local managers were far easier to direct and apt to show far less emotional attachment to their superiors (over and above that of the corporation itself). Asian youths are seemingly getting a "lift" from the pressures of globalization, and in particular the Westernization of indigenous management techniques. As technological changes begin to engulf local organizations, this new generation of managers is increasingly taking control. Their better grasp of new computer-aided technology and how it can best be used for the company means that older bosses are having to loosen their control spans and accommodate the new electronic mode of business or become increasingly sidelined. Young returnees from MBA courses in the USA or Europe are seen as being better at dealing with non-Chinese customers and suppliers, managing their departments more openly and rendering their units more acceptable to international investors. The overall ability of the younger generation to have its way across the spectrum of ASEAN host-market subsidiaries is being seen as crucial to the survival of locally manned organizations across the region (see also Gilley, 2000).

But although the traditional local patriarchs may be behind the times in technological terms, their wholesale replacement with a new wave of perceived upstarts is by no means as simple as it seems. Often viewed as being more driven than their younger counterparts, the older generation of managers have strenuously sought to maintain their grip on power, utilizing their often formidable power base of key account customers. Compounded by indigenous factors such as seniority, respect and "face," the actual cases of incoming Western-educated managers successfully imposing Western ways of working upon the older organizational members are statistically negligible. The overall attitude expressed to us by our senior indigenous pool of informants was one of horrified disbelief at the "antics" of these new recruits, whom they hold to be too young and too green either to appreciate or to understand fully the vagaries of the local business/marketing environments.

In a local environment where age respect is an in-bred, continuing concern, the loss of face involved for older staff receiving orders from their juniors has also been a contentious issue. In this way much of the Western business education being pumped into this new generation is being effectively circumvented. As one senior JV chairman expressed it,

> "Even the ones who come back to work with the MBA from the USA, still they must obey the older guys here in the same way they have to obey their fathers. In reality here it is impossible for the old man to ask the young man for advice or for the young man to tell the old man what to do. Impossible."

The greater proportion of respondents stated their belief that in time there would nevertheless be a shift in line with the global necessity for

Executive Insights: "Eurasians"

"It would be natural to assume that executives who are the offspring of mixed marriages and who speak languages fluently would be helpful to your organization in bridging the gap in cultures which occur in any MNC. To some extent you would be right, but it cannot be taken for granted. Many such 'Eurasians' are faced with the problem that they find it difficult to fit in with, and be totally accepted by, either group. They might be looked upon as a kind of 'spy' for either camp.

"The same can be said of locals who have been educated abroad for a long time, particularly through their childhood. They will not have the contacts or friends from their school or college days who are now in influential positions in politics, the military, police, businesses or the customs department. They may be looked upon with suspicion because they speak faultless English, so they too may have difficulty fitting in. However, bearing in mind the problems they may have personally, they normally make very good employees and executives because they understand the way foreigners think and have a Western work ethic, but also retain the basic charm of the East Asian. They also tend to be honest in their dealings and believe in speaking their minds – both invaluable assets to any firm."

younger, technologically savvy local managers. The Southeast Asian business culture would, it was claimed, progressively align itself with Western corporate norms in this regard, but this could only come about by education. However, it was felt that this trend would take at least "another generation" to filter through, as the long-time tradition of sons obeying their fathers was not about to change in the space of one decade.

Reward structure

Having delineated the main issues surrounding regional MNC recruitment strategy, we shall now shift our attention to the factors promoting employee *retention* – beginning with an examination of the typical multinational reward system within the ASEAN bloc. The traditional means by which local units were able to secure the retention of their "good" employees was via the development of their loyalty and commitment through job security, social approval and material benefits. Recent attempts to shift the structure of local rewards in the postcrisis context have focused more on adjusting the extant incentive systems, particularly for top management, in order to refocus the indigenous organizational cultures toward encouraging value creation.

As noted in the considerable body of research upon the subject, an organization's reward system specifies guidelines for what employees have to do in order to receive pay rises, bonuses, promotions and praise. To this end it acts as an unequivocal statement of values, beliefs and assumptions (Bartlett and Ghoshal, 1989; Schein, 1987). In the past, the extent of incentives offered to staff – beyond adhering to the constraints of collective societal norms – was fairly limited, particularly in locally based conglomerates. Rigidly hierarchical management systems, the reluctance to dilute company ownership and a traditional disregard for the rights of minority shareholders have meant that local employees were served nothing like the kind of tangible benefits expected in the West. However, in an increasingly tight labor market, MNC branch reward structures are being clearly aligned with parent norms, the usual pay and benefits being supplemented by opportunities to buy shares in the company (Holland, 2000). As a case in point, the Anglo-Dutch consumer giant Unilever rewards loyalty in the company via generous benefit schemes and retirement packages. Because of this scheme the branch units across the region are considered as being home to an especially loyal workforce. From the envelope fillers, drivers and messenger boys at the lowest rungs of the organization right through to the top, there will be the global Unilever emphasis on employee empowerment – with clear links to the overall corporate reward structure.

Described at the beginning of this chapter, general reward structures – promotion, bonuses, appraisal and training methods – common to the ASEAN bloc have traditionally been the least Westernized of all the indigenous work practices (though obviously subject to regional variation). Generally speaking, corporate respondents cited Singapore, Malaysia and the Philippines as being the "closest" countries in terms of local reward structures. These were followed by any one of the emerging Indo-Chinese markets along with Indonesia. As one Western oil executive remarked,

> "We felt most in control in Malaysia, although even in Vietnam we seemed to manage all right in getting the local staff to work in the way we wanted them to. But Thailand was just an entirely different ballgame; it's like we totally had to adjust our expectations of what and, more importantly, how we wanted the team down there to perform day to day."

In an incisive article, Charoenwongsak (1998) sought to explain the consistent difficulties in motivating indigenous staff within the Thai market, highlighting the traditional "patronage" system under which

Executive Insights: Flower Power

"One particular month when sales had been much lower than budget, Castrol's Thai marketing director wanted to boost the moral of the sales team when they returned to HQ at the end of the month. He therefore arranged for the girls in his department to stand all day in the reception area to give a rose to each representative as he entered the building. Sometimes the 'soft' issues can make all the difference!"

rewards were traditionally given for the most useful social connections – as opposed to any objectively defined measure of performance. Secondary promotions were then awarded to those who had been able to gain the most favor from their bosses – again over those with the "best" ability. As a result, "achievers" have traditionally been oppressed in Thailand and corporate environments have been polluted by jealousy and even violence. Adopting the broader perspective, Phongpaichit and Baker (1998) regard this patronage system as the deep-rooted legacy of a long history of absolute monarchy and military dictatorship. Autocratic habits were built into the mindsets of the bureaucrats and politicians, into the working systems of major institutions and then down into the branch units of Japanese and Western multinational corporations

Executive Insights: Changing the Bonus System

"From the time the Castrol (Thailand) Ltd joint venture had been formed, all staff had received a standard annual bonus of one and a half months' salary. In the early eighties times were tough but I argued to maintain current levels on the grounds that everyone was having to work even harder during these difficult times. Fortunes then improved in the latter part of the decade and the bonus had by then crept up to three months' salary across the board. Staff head count had also risen and I felt that the system had become somewhat inequitable as some people made a real contribution and some didn't – as for every business organization.

"Seeking to change the system, I gave a year's notice of my intentions. In future, bonuses were only to be paid if the company had performed well and had met its targets. The amount of bonus for each employee would then be determined by that individual's performance and personal contribution. The average remained at roughly three months' [salary] but based on evaluations by departmental managers some people received the minimum of one to one and a half months' whereas a few high achievers sometimes received five months'. Basically, because a whole year's notice was given of the change, and because the system was seen as being fair, we had no problems at all."

What appears to motivate these senior local managers, particularly the wealthier ones within the management ranks, is not so much money as what Holmes and Tangtongtavy (1995) define as "personal prestige." Examples of this would be, for example, the image of the company worked for, the space of the office, the quality of car, even the coolness of air, referred to in Chapter 4. Another major motivational factor is the number of direct and indirect staff reports, which in part accounts for why recruitment patterns in the precrisis years were perceived by headquarters as spinning rapidly out of control. Lower down the managerial ranks lies the huge import of having one's own mobile phone, and of its continuous utilization even during meetings. According to a number of Western-educated local managers, the tacit refusal to switch off mobile phones during meetings goes back to the importance of "face" and social status. The feeling is that receiving calls in such an environment provides added face, as those present will regard the recipient as being terribly important to be subject to urgent calls in such a manner.

The same logic applies to the issue of company namecards, where the wording of a worker's position within the organization is a highly significant and sensitive issue. As noted by Toews and McGregor (1998), a "fancy" business card that shows the position of "Head of Cash Receipts Department" is strongly preferred to one pronouncing a person to be just an "Assistant Accountant." And a business card made up for the person in charge of accessing the stockroom – typically, "Stationery Assistant" – appears in turn to be better than having no business card at all! Such titles are undeniably useful in the Southeast Asian business environment, however, where they are more likely to facilitate employee access to important external contacts with power and influence. Within this context the implementation of flatter, Western-styled hierarchical structure imbued with "self-directed teams" has caused inevitable problems in the area of namecard allocations. The apparently minor point of having one's card title changed from, for example, "Manager" to "Team Leader" or "Coach" is seen as a serious loss of face on the part of the indigenous recipient. For this reason, many Asian executives have strongly resisted this approach as being tantamount to a serious "breach in confidence" by their foreign parent, and have striven to retain their former titles.

As stressed by one senior Vietnamese executive,

> "Head office is always saying we have too many managers here but so long as they keep what they pay us the same as the other places then

what does the name matter for them? But you see it matter for us, it matter for everyone who concerned with doing the business here and with the competition."

The corporate response to these objectives has been to point out the practical difficulties of having "every other member of staff walking around with a vice president's namecard." Following a successful meeting with a customer, the employee may well find him- or herself being asked there and then to make the decision on a "big deal." The ensuing delay due to the person not having the power in practice to match that suggested by his or her namecard could do untold harm to the longer-term reputation of the branch unit – and, indeed, to the corporation as a whole. One way around this dilemma, currently being tested out at a small number of MNC subsidiaries in the region, is to simply make *two* sets of namecards for every employee of middle manager status and above. That way one card can be sanctioned, where appropriate, for use with the bigger customers and also for the employee's own saving of face around the metropolitan karaoke bars. The other, more down-to-earth card will be the one to be utilized in contacts and meetings involving head office and other branch office meetings, training courses, and so forth.

Executive Insights: "You Can't Have a Policy for Everything"

"We had a sales representative who was killed in a car crash on his way to a regional sales meeting. He had been separated from his wife for a long time and had left two young school-age children he had by his then partner. The Sales and Marketing department were very concerned about these children and told me that all the guys were contributing money to ensure the children's future education. I thought this was a superb gesture and told them whatever they raised would be doubled by the company. They raised 200,000 Thai baht, so a total fund of 600,000 was put in a bank account to be administered by a small committee comprising the finance director, the marketing director, the regional sales manager and a sales representative – the latter being a close personal friend of the deceased and his family.

"Our Thai personnel director was basically against all this because there wasn't anything covering this arrangement in our company working regulations, and there was no precedent. I pointed out to him that even the best-organized governments in the world with their annual accurate budgeting methods are often quick to cough up millions of dollars in aid unexpectedly whenever a natural disaster should occur in another part of the world. You can't try to legislate for every eventuality. I'm pleased to say that some twelve or thirteen years after the tragic car crash, the committee of colleagues is still effective in ensuring the children are properly educated."

Until the early stages of the regional economic crisis the tendency for most incoming foreign corporations was to play around with the local reward practices at their leisure, and certainly with scant regard for indigenous tradition. Assumptions of employees' passivity and moderation in comparison to their Western counterparts seemed to be backed up by the Buddhist and Taoist beliefs found in much of the region, which recommend taking the middle path in life's issues, and with a fun-loving grain of salt, as it were. But the burning and destruction of the Sanyo plant in Thailand by local workers dissatisfied with the changes being mooted with regard to their annual bonuses provided a stark warning on the perils of taking cross-border states of mind for granted.

Appraisals

Staff appraisals are the dominant means by which Western companies decide who is to benefit from rewards of the kind outlined above. Appraisals are set up and maintained in order to measure performance in the Western world, but they have traditionally been overlooked and/or rejected in Southeast Asia. The neglect prior to the crisis of 1997 is partially understandable, with the unprecedented growth levels leading to automatic pay and across-the-board bonus awards. But in the current changing environment – and under increasing competitive pressure – Western corporations have sought to reintroduce the internal stress on making employees accountable for their performance. The perceived need is for cross-functional teams of employees to work as a cohesive, meritocratic unit, over and above the old habits of cronyism and relations-based networks. Although people within the region are working roughly the same number of hours as before, the difference in the current climate is that their performance is being measured more carefully. Emerging evidence appears to show that the perception of Asia's unique precrisis industriousness was little more than a myth, demonstrating some of the highly wasteful practices that lurked unchecked for years alongside the phenomenon of explosive growth. In their dwindling tolerance for people who produce very little at the workplace, foreign multinationals have begun to reward their local staff exclusively on the basis of concrete performance, rather than on seniority or possession of a certain set of skills (see also Slater, 1999b).

A number of practical measures have been introduced with the aim of increasing performance transparency and corporate governance. These include the widespread adoption of job assessments, function gradings and performance-based promotions. Performance review is particularly valued, corporations hoping that it will effectively replace the traditional means of protecting underperformance within local in-groups, helping corporate executives obtain a clearer idea of which individuals are doing well and which are wasting their time. For employees with the ability to adapt, it is claimed, the rewards can be extremely fulfilling. According to a cross section of MNC representatives, working without the safety net of an automatic bonus can be frightening at first but also exhilarating – but only so long as the link between performance and reward is a genuine one (Chandranoi, 1998; Nivatpumin, 1998).

As mentioned above, the traditional Asian penchant for using seniority over performance as the criterion for reward and promotion goes back to traditions of the military, a custom that has percolated down across the years. Whereas Western-headquartered multinationals have striven to emphasize employee competence as a criterion for promotion, ASEAN-market units place more emphasis on the number of years the employee has been in the company, believing that length of service relates directly to a person's competence in protecting the interests of the company. This is typified by the prevalence of so-called managers performing functions which to incoming expatriates seem to be little more than secretarial functions. "Marketing administration executives" in a whole host of Western branch subsidiaries often are aging administrative support staff who have climbed through the ranks over the years on the strength of their having remained with the organization for so long. Performing roles deemed as being on a par with that of a "glorified typist," such incumbents have been roundly criticized for their rigidity of style and lack of either language or computer skills. But demoting these people back down the ranks – let alone off-loading them – is never as simple as it seems (as outlined at length in Chapter 3).

In this environment managerial status is "measured" on factors such as number of people and computers within one's span of control, rather than via any tangible link to performance and profitability. Assignments and responsibilities are allocated predominantly on the basis of perceived reliability and trustworthiness. An example of this kind of mentality was recounted to us from the Thai unit of a European telecommunications company. Seeking to reduce the unit quota of drivers for senior management, a prime candidate for dismissal self-selected himself to the Western CEO, having crashed his vehicle for the third time within the confines of the company parking lot. Corporate surprise at the local HR director's decision to keep him on at the expense of other, seemingly more competent colleagues was met by the explanation that the individual concerned had been loyal to the company over many years. Starting out his tenure filling envelopes, he had progressed to being first a cleaner and then a guard before the eventual shift in role to driving company cars. Praised as a "nice guy" and rewarded for his cooperative spirit, the individual remains with the company to this day – despite Western corporate demands for chauffeurs to be selected on their ability to drive automobiles.

The paternalistic character of Asian business practice also tends to stress promotion "from the inside." Against this backdrop, notions of status, order and harmony are all, inevitably, intertwined. Promotion is based upon seniority and character – there is no fast track for brilliant performers. This final point is well illustrated by the myriad of Chinese maxims to reiterate the point that a person who stands out from the group will be criticized and ultimately prevented from reaching his or her goal: "The tree growing high above the others will be blown down by the wind," and "the gun fires at the first bird in the flock." Being a top performer would bring pride and confidence to a Western employee, whereas in Southeast Asia it may engender embarrassment and shame. Imitation, on the other hand, is a more secure route to success as imitation gives face to those who matter.

Unsurprisingly, none of our local respondents could see any urgent reason to tear up this dutiful system of appraisal and reward – claiming that it had served them well in the precrisis years and would do so again when things "got back to normal." The Confucian ethic at the root of this system, with its emphasis on loyalty to family and friends, was held up as having served to maintain stability within these enterprises through generations – whatever the external economic conditions. In a culture where such notions of character appraisal are held to serve the good of the company (and the wider community as a whole), the entire business of hiring, retaining and firing staff on the basis of "performance" is considered to be at odds with the prevailing societal values.

Many corporations have thus found "performance review" a particularly difficult idea to put into practice in Southeast Asia, essentially because of the "confrontational" quality of the exercise. The Thai concept of *kreng jai*, whereby an individual seeks to avoid potentially traumatic or discomforting situations even where his or her own interests may be compromised, was alluded to as one of many culturally founded factors in the debate. Problems of this nature were found to persist even where the parent corporation had largely succeeded in getting the system instituted and "up and running." This is instanced by the difficulties experienced by locally based expatriates in obtaining accurate, honest feedback from the staff involved. A symptom of the indigenous stress on hierarchy, loyalty and face, is the fact that lower managers were traditionally loathe to suggest ideas openly in meetings, thereby promoting the value in conflict avoidance above the potential for innovation and improvement. In the Sino-Asian tradition the giving of criticism, even constructive criticism, will never be done directly – except, in extreme circumstances, by a very senior person to a very junior person. The Western notion of performing 360-degree or "reverse" appraisals whereby superior–subordinate evaluations are supplemented by the subordinate's appraisal of his or her boss is almost laughably unsuited to the local business context. Even the most optimistic of the reforming Western corporations have been left with no choice in practice but to summarily pluck the "reverse" aspect out of the equation.

In a similar vein, much of what the regional HR controllers were able to glean from the completed reviews was to prove unrealistic and beyond corporate use. Global performance appraisal forms habitually employed a Likert scale for grading purposes, ranking individuals on a quality marked from 1 through to 5. Yet within the Southeast Asian context the returning forms were almost always marked either "1" or "2" – denominating relative excellence – for each and every quality assessed, again stemming from the fear of causing offence or loss of face. Regional market intelligence agencies such as AMI began developing a "discount weightings scale" for their corporate clients in order to allow for this tendency and render the results worthy of global comparison. One method for doing this was simply to expand the Likert continuum from five gradings to eleven and then scale back the points as required. As one executive bemoaned,

> "The problem for us in taking the results here as they are mean that in the global HR rankings all our Southeast Asian branches are portrayed as being filled with staff of either 'excellent' or 'outstanding' capabilities – so where do we go from here? We appear to have, in effect, a severe shortage of 'normal,' everyday personnel. And that's great – except that we shall then be expected for this quality to be translated into performance, i.e. bottom line. And that's when the trouble starts."

Executive Insights: Industrial Accidents

"Khun Ong-Arch was a Castrol sales representative, and I went to his wedding. A month later he was involved in a horrendous car crash which left him paralyzed from the waist down. His parents would not allow his wife of one month to visit him in hospital on the grounds that 'she had brought him bad luck.' I was also criticized because if it hadn't been for the company's seat belt policy (long before they were compulsory) he would have died.

"I went to the Paulo Memorial Hospital in Bangkok and talked with the attending physician. I explained that if this had happened to me the company would almost certainly have flown me to the UK for a second opinion, and asked if this might help in Ong-Arch's case. The doctor, who was UK trained, explained to me the details of the case in great detail. The spinal cord had been broken and Ong-Arch would always be paralyzed from the waist down.

"After about a year he was allowed to go home, so we bought him a wheelchair [and] a special adjustable bed, and gave his replacement company car to the family so they could drive him to and from hospital appointments. In such cases of "industrial accident" in Thailand the victim is paid a certain amount a month for a period of six years from the Workers' Compensation Fund. As this was less than his Castrol salary we made up the difference out of petty cash.

"A couple of years later our marketing director told me that Ong-Arch had become potentially suicidal. Apparently he needed to feel useful again, and so we took him on as an order clerk operating a computer terminal, a job which fitted in well with his previous experience as a sales representative. He needed a rest every afternoon and so a fold-bed was placed in the tearoom as well as an empty 5-liter oil pack provided for urination to save him visiting the toilet. We also employed his wife as a telephone operator so that she could bring him to and from work.

"The staff always looked after him very well, and at the annual New Year party he could always be found in the middle of the dance floor hanging on to his Zimmer frame, swaying to the music with a crowd of office girls dancing around him. We agreed to count his time away as unbroken service, and I shall never forget one New Year party when I had given out all of the long-service awards except one. When Khun Ong-Arch's name was announced I walked from the stage in front of the 500 members of staff to present a gold chain to Ong-Arch at the table where he was sitting. Needless to say, a very emotional experience.

"I never checked how much money the company had spent on Ong-Arch. We always said that we looked after our people at Castrol, and he was a real example for everyone to see. Ong-Arch was 'retrenched' by BP in 2001, but 'rode away' with over three million baht. It is amost five years now since I retired, but he always sends me a Christmas card."

Training

> "We threw the rule book out the window when we started here. There
> were no recruitment guidelines in our office, no fancy systems for
> grading candidates because what we wanted was so simple. Number
> one, we wanted people who were not so old that they were set in their
> ways or that they didn't know how to work a computer. Number two,
> they had to speak English. So we put out an ad in the newspaper and
> then shortlisted all our candidates who were under the age of 30.
> From the ones that were left – and who we met – we made our choice
> on two criteria: spoken English and attitude, and that was it.
> Everything else we trained into them."

The Western corporate faith in the power of management development –
illustrated by the above US oil executive based in Vietnam – adheres to
the Asian perception of foreign MNCs as being "big on training." Even
during the precrisis period, when things were so good for local corporate
units, companies such as the cosmetics giant Estée Lauder were stressing
the need for training at every level of their local organizations, from the
senior managers right down to the part-time make-up artist. Training was
held as being "imperative" should a company wish to get the best from
its people. To this end employees were regularly flown abroad and
relevant functional experts were flown in, not just at Estée Lauder but
across the whole spectrum of multinational interests in the region.

Having completed the streamlining and regional consolidation of
corporate operations, many MNC branch subsidiaries have introduced a
further wave of training initiatives in order to enhance their customer
focus. Caltex's training program for its new retail representatives focuses
strongly on the global corporate notion of "business partnering": seeking
to inculcate staff members with the sense of interdependency between the
company and its retailers. The objective of these programs is to render
sales staff more responsive to customer needs in order to surpass the
competition and become the region's long-term brand of choice.

By way of contrast the comparative *lack* of training within the indigenous
management teams stems back to local notions of performance and
appraisal. With the emphasis firmly on the character and integrity of the
individual employees there is an undoubted expectation, even
assumption, of trustworthiness and loyalty among local employers –
factors which are held to obviate the need for such formal training
programs. However, with the current vacuum in middle management
positions caused – in part – by the continuing exodus of local employees

for greener, mid-size local company positions, such programs of rapid management practice assimilation are becoming crucial.

Branch subsidiaries of well-known Western MNCs are increasingly sending their managers on externally hosted courses in order to learn Western management techniques. The consensus view among visiting expatriates appears to be that whereas the "harder" management skills are improving markedly in the region, there is a major problem with communication skills and attitude. Exemplifying what is held to be the underlying fault of a deficient domestic education system, local employees are perceived as showing an inability to view or accept change as an opportunity. As one respondent expressed it,

> "Their instincts here are always to see any change as a threat, when anything's about to happen you'll see them all retreating into huddles in order to try and resist, every time. . . . I mean, in the period up until the end of 1997 it didn't matter so much, but with the situation as it is now, then it's not something we can simply go on tolerating; they've simply got to accept the need for changing their work methods and this can only come about through the right training."

From our discussion so far, the reader might be forgiven for assuming that all Western MNCs are "training obsessed," in direct opposition to indigenous work teams, who seemingly couldn't care less. However, as with all generalizations, there were a small number of local management representatives who were markedly dissatisfied with the amount and level of training that they were getting from their respective MNC branch units. As an – admittedly rare – example of a senior woman manager working for a French telecommunications company in Bangkok was to state,

> "I think that one of the main reasons the local people choose the Western company is not just for salary but also for the thing like the training and development – because we always think it so much better than with Thai company, that there is much more chance for us to improve what we can do . . . But it seem like this company not care too much about that, not for the Thai managers."

The response of a British lubricants marketer to such veiled accusations was quite revealing:

> "The trouble with training within these units is that the local employees have come to think of it as being a right within a foreign multinational, that we somehow have a kind of unwritten duty to provide all kinds of development courses for the majority of our staff

. . . [but] this isn't the right way to go about it. To my mind, the way to make the training courses here more effective is to begin with an analysis of the needs of the organization, and in-depth, and realistic . . . right now what we have is a lot of companies in the region undergoing training for the sake of training, and it makes no sense. . . . Certainly the current practice of having some kind of centrally imposed budget quota for training which has to be taken up at all costs is downright counterproductive."

Among the vast majority of both corporate and local respondents the main role of training in the current ASEAN environment was considered to be the provision of foreign language courses, especially as more and more corporate communication was being done in English, notably via the increasing use of electronic technology, the Internet and email. The sums actually being spent on teaching English to the staff in need of it are, of course, another matter. But as a general principle, the necessity of improving regional standards – particularly in countries such as Indonesia, Thailand and the Mekong nations – is considered the main priority in making sure capable local staff are not unnecessarily prohibited from progressing to regional management status.

Training methodology: design and implementation

The need to "train up" corporate teams within the ASEAN bloc encompasses not merely language but a range of "soft" skills such as empowerment, conflict management, team building, leadership and dealing with change. But how is this to be implemented in practice, even assuming that the requisite training needs have been both identified and approved? At what point along the adaptation–standardization continuum should such courses be delivered? How far should they be tailored to the domestic branch unit and thereby rendered culturally sensitive – away from the central corporate norm?

Of the choices to be made, one of the first is whether the training should be administered internally or via an outsourced, external organization. Of the two, internally delivered courses tend to focus on imbuing employees with a feel for the overall culture of the corporation – its objectives, characteristics and values. External courses, by contrast, are more suited to inculcating local employees with Western management techniques and ideologies. Coming as they do under a mixture of corporate and societal culture influences, ASEAN branch organizations would ideally be provided with a finely tuned balance incorporating both elements. Further decisions would then involve how either – or, indeed, both – of these elements should best be taught in terms of both design and implementation.

These choices are aptly illustrated by a look at one of the more popular external training courses in the region, the "Bullet-Proof Manager" course designed by the US-based training provider Crestcom. Sold as a franchise holding to interested business executives in a range of domestic markets, the course seeks to provide Western-oriented managerial development of the "soft" skills, as well as sessions focused on effective meetings and proactive planning. In terms of design and implementation, the method advocated is the use of videos, shipped across in English and then translated into the vernacular for the increasing proportion of indigenous attendees. Videos are then supplemented with the use of interactive role-plays in order for local managers to gain hands-on experience as to how the concepts taught might work in practice. Back at the office, the hoped-for changes in local managerial working methods would then cascade down the organization, over time providing a company-wide change in business thinking.

In order to get the best from such courses, there is the subtle – but very real – need to have sensitive program facilitators with a good knowledge of the local culture and its communication idiosyncrasies. The face/status factor across the region can be addressed in a number of ways, exemplified by the practice of relative "status anonymity" during training program meetings among managers from different participating organizations. By placing "unknowns" next to each other, the status problem can be overcome; participants can enact their role-plays with no fear of losing face. Western training franchises seemed especially keen to try to "mix and match" varying industries and managerial levels as much as possible in order to broaden the range of experience acquired.

Corporate utilization of such interactive training providers was perceived by the great majority of our expatriate informants to be much more profitable than the traditional in-house training given by local HR representatives, especially during the precrisis period. The general tendency appears to be typified by the handing out of the glossy corporate brochure to new employees with little, if any, annotation or comment – after which the newcomer would simply file, forget or even dispose of it, confident in the assumption that it would never be referred to again. An extreme case of this is illustrated at the Vietnamese office of a major consumer goods multinational, where the corporate training manual got as far as the CEO's office and no further. Having discussed its relative merits with the domestic executive committee, the Western chief decided that the document would only serve to "confuse" the indigenous managers, and in particular upon their initial entry into the local ranks. The manual was thus effectively rejected, left to gather dust within the murky depths of the basement stockroom.

During the regional "boom" years of the 1980s and early 90s the prevailing attitude was that Western executives based in the region should focus their attentions exclusively on strategic and planning matters, handing the operational aspects of the local businesses firmly back to their indigenous management counterparts. The highly localized feel of most in-house training was reflected in the practical emphasis of employee bonding through the engagement of fun and games. Local induction programs of the era tended to be short, smiling "talks" on the respective departmental functions, interspersed with games such as "pass the balloon" and the art of balancing balls on the ends of drinking straws. Surprisingly vivid health warnings were also often disseminated,

Executive Insights: Looking After the Boss

"Shortly after my arrival in Thailand in 1978 I went on a trip to Chiang Mai in the north to visit important Castrol customers there. I traveled with the regional sales manager and we met with the local representative once we'd got there. One evening after dinner with some customers we went to a nightclub. Walking down the stairs to the club the bandstand was facing us and a girl was singing. She was stunning and wore a very short skirt. Almost involuntarily I said something like 'Wow! Look at that!' Anyway, we stayed there half an hour or so and then went to a couple of other places before they took me back to the hotel. It had been a long day and by midnight I was asleep.

"I was woken up at 3 A.M. by someone knocking at the door, and somewhat bleary-eyed I went to see who it was. Surprise! It was the singer from the first club we'd been to. Well, I consider myself a pretty regular guy, but I would at least like the chance to get to know someone if I were going to make love to them. I said, 'Come in, you can sleep here if you want to, but I've been asleep for three hours and I'm not going to do anything!' In the morning I left her in the room and went down to breakfast prior to another day visiting customers. I explained to the regional sales manager what had happened and told him never to do such a thing again. I explained that if I'd wanted a companion I would much prefer to have found my own.

"Finally, in case you're wondering, when I returned to my room at the end of the day none of my belongings were missing."

fueled by the specter of HIV/AIDS within domestic cities. Footage of scantily clad young women cavorting around steel poles in local go-go bars were juxtaposed with sobering images of the kind of graphic skin disorders associated with sexually transmitted immune deficiency. Often these week-long courses would culminate in a weekend "up-country," either by the sea or in some country garden resort where "jungle walks" and "treasure hunts" were the order of the day.

In this environment the Western corporate emphasis on notions of "teamwork" and core customer-led values was scoffed at by a substantial proportion of indigenous managers. The conceptual substitutions of the latter are often impressive in their ingenuity, however. This is clearly illustrated by the interpretation of Castrol core brand values proffered at Castrol's Thai subsidiary. Portrayed quite accurately as a substance for the reduction of friction between moving parts, the notion of lubrication was then "adapted" to reflect the local importance of flexibility, of "keeping things running smoothly" in the local company–customer relationship. Corporate representatives at several of our respondent corporations were also surprised to learn the types of maxims being proffered by domestic HR chiefs at "executive" management courses, including the – perhaps errant – denotion of the employee as "the most important person" to the firm, over and above the concerns of their respective customers.

Perhaps as a response to increasing competitive pressure, recent years have witnessed attempts by indigenous management to restructure some of their own – heavily criticized – programs of staff development. In some cases openly acknowledging the key areas for potential improvement, memos were circulated by department heads calling for a new focus on "professionalism in all dealings." Locally initiated meetings of HR practice discussed methods by which the traditionally "relaxed," "easy" office atmospheres could be made more productive in order to weather the current market difficulties. Part of this change in outlook was to focus on the hitherto ingrained assumption that MNC branch units were furnished with unlimited resources, gratefully paying their employees for the privilege of witnessing them show up at the office every day. The new emphasis was to move away from this attitude to concentrate more on notions of austerity, efficiency and hard work. Newly designed training courses were to reflect these changes, centering participant activity upon cross-functional teamwork linked by frank and open channels of communication. The intention was to try to phase out the traditional focus laid on hierarchy, status and the family-type insularity – held to pervade current unit divisions and stifle any quest for innovation. Long-term changes in working styles would seek to make the best of assertive Western-style decision making, while at the same time retaining the local penchant for incrementalism and consensus. Local management executives stated their confidence that, given time, the domestic markets of Southeast Asia would become dynamic learning arenas capable of adapting, responding to and even anticipating the fast-changing business environment.

Within the current business climate, however, the kind of lengthy timescales – typically four to five years – requested by the local units in order to fully implement these autonomous changes were never to be granted. Against a global corporate backdrop of mergers and acquisitions there has been a marked clampdown on the levels of adaptation to be tolerated in single markets. Recent home office directives have tended to seek to harmonize domestic working methods, illustrated by the strict and detailed retranslation of global training manuals into local market languages (despite indigenous complaints as to the unfathomable intricacy of much of what was being distributed). This perceived reimposition of global management development programs in the ASEAN bloc began with the region-wide announcement of "refresher" courses to imbue local staff with a "correct" interpretation of core corporate values and competencies.

Not surprisingly, this has led to a concurrent period of corporate denigration of traditional "Asian" training methods. Regarded as something of a joke, these so-called "treasure hunts," "forest-free rides" and "jungle walks" were roundly criticized by corporate representatives (notwithstanding the locally derived benefits from such pursuits). Dismissing the longer-term relevance of these programs, corporate respondents remain unfazed by local concerns over their methods, claiming that in any case such qualms would have all been "forgotten a year from now." Demanding more local emphasis upon management development – as opposed to mere "fun and games" – corporate visitors to the region were scathing of the way training resources were being handled, and in particular with regard to the expedition of local managers abroad. In the words of a US pharmaceutical executive,

> "We have little or no idea of how these little 'jollies' were being allocated; it makes you wonder . . . many of these guys were being sent to the US or to Oz on some accounting or financial management course as a reward for whatever they were supposed to have done

back home . . . and so they go on these things for no practical reason
at all, and then come back and continue the same as before, as if
they'd never been away. . . . To be honest, it just felt like they were
on a double whammy – nice trip overseas and a certificate to put in
their office on return. But as to the tangible benefits, as to what they'd
learned? Well, you tell me."

The steamroller approach taken by frustrated corporations was further
expressed in their widespread removal of previously displayed local
poster boards and newssheets – anything, it seemed, to have emanated
from the indigenous teams in the precrisis years. At the extreme were the
"guides to business success" and "philosophy of management"-type
posters once fairly typical of the ASEAN branch subsidiary. Usually
composed in a type of pidgin English reminiscent of the locally educated
translator, the kinds of maxims on show at this period include "To
succeed you must be flexible like Thai, diligent like Chinese, organized
like American and disciplined like German," "To have success in the
business you must to have the goal as the mission" and "To be happy all
things are possible."

In order to optimize the current switch to corporate-centered training
there are a number of ways in which the requisite programs can be
adapted to align themselves with domestic managerial values without
compromising core objectives. Positive actions in this regard seem to
have centered around the effective "loosening of the leash" by regional
headquarters with respect to local content and style of training
dissemination. The rigid policy guidelines imposed in the immediate
postcrisis aftermath have been notably diluted in a cross section of
MNCs, in recognition of the need for local flexibility at the cutting
edges. The "relaxation" of headquarters attitudes perceived among the
local managers as the economies have slowly improved has led many
of their number to proclaim that "things have settled down now like
before . . . it's better." Interestingly, we have also picked up a
corresponding willingness on the part of indigenous employees to want
to cooperate now more fully with Western management traits, hoping
that such bilateral compromise would prove a useful breeding ground
for the "cross-fertilization" of future training and development
programs.

Executive Insights: Cross-cultural Training

"Before I came to Thailand my company sent me on a cross-cultural management program at the corporate Centre for International Briefing at Farnham Castle in the UK. It lasted a week and covered a number of topics common to Southeast Asia and some 'breakout' sessions for those going to different countries. These separate sessions were covered by returnee expatriates with long experience of living and working in their particular countries.

"Subjects covered in the Thailand section included the overriding importance of the monarchy, the principles of Buddhism, the role of the military, the political system, the incidence of corruption, the benefits of living there and the pitfalls.

"Fascinating, and very useful for people who had never been outside of Europe. A very important tip was never to let a Thai 'lose face.' For example, we were told never to tell anyone off in front of someone else. Now, a sensible and courteous manager would never do this to anyone, never mind a Thai. I know for a fact that foreigners (or *farang* as they are called in Thailand) can 'lose face' as well. I have seen examples of it. Learning some basic cultural rules is of course important, like respect for the institutions, not pointing the soles of your feet at anyone and not touching a Thai person's head (the 'temple of the body'), but common courtesy and good manners will get you a long way. The Thais are usually very forgiving if you make a mistake.

"Later, after a few months in the job, I attended a local cross-cultural management program run by an American anthropologist. This went into a lot more detail about cultural differences, and especially about attitudes in the workplace. It highlighted different loyalties, different expectations and especially a very wide divergence in the understanding of accountability.

"Thais can learn from Westerners about timekeeping, decision making, planning and accountability. But they can teach us volumes about the soft issues in personnel management such as avoiding unnecessary confrontation, consideration of others' feelings and generally caring for people."

Motivation

Crisis-oriented meetings and talks were a notable means by which Western executives sought to try to (re)motivate their remaining employees. Their initial failure to use such means among the majority of MNC branch subsidiaries is indicative of a wider lack of guidance provided to top corporate management within the region. Many CEOs of the period we interviewed admitted that despite their proclamations in company-wide gatherings as to their determination to motivate the local staff, in reality they were only making matters worse. Their employees' resentment found expression in a host of reported misdemeanors, from tardiness and time wasting through to petty theft and even spending errand time at the movies. Moves made to try to ameliorate this situation included the reiteration of the provision of comprehensive cross-cultural training to both expatriate and indigenous management at the very highest levels in order to bridge this ongoing gap at the headquarters–subsidiary divide. Such courses were held as being the ideal platform for the cultural sensitivity needed in order to facilitate the smooth transition of change in the Southeast Asian environment. Effective management within the region was generally held by course providers to encompass the recognition and understanding of local customs and practices, imbuing participants with the essential import of listening, comprehensive consultation, right relationship, face and respect. Southeast Asian managers appear to be united in their dislike of confrontation and their responsiveness to compromise. A Western CEO would do well to learn and take note of these traits early on in his or her tenure – indigenous reaction against a proposal, as we have seen, signals a strong and resilient obstacle (see also Borton, 2000; Quang, 1998).

In terms of management style, Western respondents expounded at length upon their aims to be as friendly and as visible as possible, whatever their technical and/or strategic prowess. In the local environment it is well thought of if a CEO appears in front of the entire workforce at least several times a year, to tell employees what has been going on and to answer any queries – in essence, as was roundly emphasized, "just to show that they care." The essential development of love and trust in the ASEAN business context stems not so much from the provision of bonuses, profit-related pay, and so forth, but from more *intangible* activities that add value to one's tenure in command: attending staff funerals, complying with local requests to wear traditional dress on certain days, performing civic duties at the temple, distributing gifts, and so forth.

Executive Insights: Maintaining Expatriate Harmony

"Multinationals should take considerable trouble in selecting the right kind of executive to take up an expatriate appointment in a country where the culture is very different from their home country. Of course, they have to be good at their job, must be honest with themselves and their company and partners, must be good listeners to shorten the learning curve, should be uncompromising on matters of principle, and above all must be flexible.

"Not only will the culture be different, but so is the language, the script, the way of doing business, the traffic, communications, the weather, the food. Expatriates soon realize that their orders (or rather their requests!) may be misunderstood, and sometimes, if the subordinate thinks the request is unreasonable or inappropriate, even deliberately misunderstood.

"Much time has to be given therefore to building relationships and trust, and to listening as patiently as possible. When people understand and accept your philosophy and objectives they will work hard to make them come true. But all this takes time – much more than it would back home.

"There are social responsibilities too, such as attending staff weddings, visiting employees in hospital, and attending the funerals of your employees' relatives. Then there's entertaining HQ and regional visiting 'firefighters.' You know, 'I'm here from Head Office. I'm here to help you!'

"While all this is going on, the expatriate wife is at home, trying to show her first ever maid how she would like things done. The maid will invariably be uneducated, with no English, unless she has worked for foreigners before. The lady of the house learns that shopping takes longer than at home; she has to schedule the use of her husband's car and driver. She's getting used to air-conditioning inside, the heat and humidity outside, new types of food, and even organizing the kids' lives.

"Hubby comes home later than he would have in his home country, and he's exhausted. This is the ideal scenario for friction. Some women will feel neglected in these circumstances, and there is obviously a limit to the satisfaction to be gained from ladies' groups coffee mornings or sitting at the poolside with a good book.

"The message for multinationals therefore is not only to select the right kind of executive for the job, but also to make sure that spouses are flexible too, and aware of the problems they will face. Marriages fail in any society, of course, but the incidence is somewhat higher with the stresses of expatriate life. However, I know of countless cases where marriages continue to survive because of their love, trust and understanding.

"It has been Castrol corporate practice for many years now to bring the whole family over for a 'look-see.' In one week they can get a good idea about housing, schooling, hospitals, shopping, restaurants, clubs, etc. It's money well spent, for a mistake at this stage can be very expensive in the long run."

Language

The difficulties in cross-cultural communication are compounded by the indigenous lack of English language proficiency in some of the region's key long-term markets. Even managers who emanate from such former British colonies as Malaysia and Singapore still face difficulties in understanding the wealth of different accents, jargon and slang that emanate from Western corporate headquarters. This is largely back down to the region's education system, which has traditionally stressed reading and correct grammar over making oneself understood, thus stifling attempts to try to speak the language by the shy and ill at ease.

Many foreign multinationals – notably Volvo and BP – have sought to bridge this often chronic linguistic difficulty by providing all their staff with free English language lessons. But seeking to narrow the chasm is proving extremely hard, with thousands of MNC factory workers still depending on their floor supervisors' imperfect interpretation of what the top management wants. This practice of dubious interpretation extends to the top of the business hierarchy, where the linguistically challenged foreigner will find him- or herself relying heavily on certain key local personnel, notably their private secretaries and/or personal assistants. The utilization of such employees as the chief's "eyes and ears" can sometimes have dangerous knock-on effects for the health of the business, evident in circumstances where those same staff have their own personal agendas, dictating the perceptions they imbue in their boss.

Language deficiency also permeates the wider company practice of strategic meetings, and in particular "focus groups" used locally to generate problem-solving plans of action. Generally speaking, key meetings tend to be held in English, particularly where the incumbent CEO is present. Solutions are then almost exclusively promoted by the few members fluent enough in English to dare to venture an opinion; the majority sit back in noncommittal acquiescence. The language barriers mean that, in practice, local employees are obliged to listen to the question or proposal being ventured, *then* translate it back into the vernacular, *then* come up with a response, *then* back-translate into English and only then try to formulate the words. Not surprisingly, by the time all this has been accomplished, those colleagues who enjoy greater English proficiency have long since given their answers. Stemming from the indigenous preoccupation with keeping face, local managers will always tend to allow proceedings to continue rather than admit to not having understood a certain issue. Mark the Thai phrase *sia ngern mai wah yah sia nah* (better to lose money than to lose face) as an illustration of this attitude. Against this backdrop the oft-heard local claims that meetings held in English serve only to "choke creativity" begin to make real sense.

Of the few methods being proffered to overcome these difficulties, one way is for people chairing meetings to deliberately allow time for ideas to

worldwide development of electronic technology and its integration into business management has assisted multinationals in the reinforcement and longer-term institutionalization of these programs. In the words of a US oil corporation executive, "These days you can never say a program of parent–subsidiary integration is complete until the *information systems* of the two entities have been merged."

Electronic technology denotes *centralized* technology. It promotes the adoption of homogeneous internal structures and working practices. Centralized information storage and manipulation leads to increasing control on the part of the global corporation, drawing power away from its ASEAN branch subsidiaries and toward head office. A new generation of technological business applications is helping to transform global organizational structures from their current geographically based hierarchies into functional, coherent global entities, filling in the traditional headquarters–subsidiary data gaps. Corporate intranets foster communication within a firm – at least in theory – by directly linking everyone from home office to remote field outlets. Overcoming the traditional barriers of space and time, the Internet, in particular, links company operations and people worldwide, furnishing marketing managers with almost instantaneous information (Lazer and Shaw, 2000; Leinbach and Bowen, 2000).

Most of our Western corporate interviewees were at pains to stress the future of electronic communication within their regional business restructuring programs. Their collective belief is that the "e-corporation" in the years ahead will need to support Web-based business throughout its global subsidiaries, largely via the utilization of more powerful computers, faster telephone lines, easier-to-use software applications and videoconferencing equipment. The worldwide consolidation of corporate structures into "business streams" has worked hand in hand with this process. Indeed, the whole concept of streaming is being enacted practically via the use of computer-based technology. Castrol International – with a host of US counterparts – has adopted the fully integrated business system expressed as the "J. D. Edwards program," designed and run with the use of computerized technology. Operating as the global hub of the corporation, J. D. Edwards works as a product/manufacturing coding system with deep connections into the various divisions or "streams" worldwide. Necessitating the use of similar – if not identical – coding structures throughout the organization, J. D. Edwards is a classic example of how the trend toward centralization is being reinforced by electronic technology. Computer-based business systems also house the potential to link up supply chains as well as facilitating the placing and tracking of both internal and external communication lines, running through to the online design and dissemination of the kind of employee training discussed in Chapter 5.

Electronic mail has enabled a widespread advance in the maintenance of corporate control. E-communication has been promoted by MNCs throughout the region, which deem it ideal for the medium-term replacement of traditionally lengthy, often ambiguous face-to-face meetings and decision making. Email allows overseas-headquartered corporations to have all future decisions stored *in writing* for all relevant parties to see, both within the local unit and across the corporate network. In this context a host of Western and Japanese-based corporations have sought to dispense with all forms of paper-based communication.

Concurrent with this desire to gain control over their increasingly errant ASEAN business units, corporate respondents cited a host of more specific reasons for the promotion and enforcement of computer-based organization technology in MNCs. In theory, email holds the promise of freeing workers from the tyranny of "paper overload" and, as a result, giving them more time to get on with their core concerns. More generally, the efficiency gained in the use of electronic applications has the potential to substantially decrease administrative and transaction costs. Within the extant literature Slater (1999c) discovered that on average managers within the region have to wait almost two hours to see an employee's file – compared to the ten minutes they would then spend reading it! Fortunately, the advent of computer-based technology has facilitated the introduction of "online personnel files," drastically reducing such delays and thereby allowing local executives to manage staff, improve communications and provide training more effectively.

Innovations such as these obviously have a huge impact on globally spread conglomerates, permitting the timely and reliable distribution of information. Intranet sites facilitate the communication of corporate activities, priorities, imagery, global programs and services, internal job posting, and social activities. The visible manifestation of such change is illustrated by taking brief walks through the production plants of some of these developing host-country units, noting the wide open spaces formed from the work of thirty operators being done now with the use of a half-dozen machinists equipped with automated, computer-based equipment. As well as the facilitation of improved online information and communication modes, the goals of such technology are to develop previous productivity gains and, quite literally, to "tune in" local workers to the so-called "new economy" (Slater, 1999c).

So much for the global corporate wish-list. Let us now explore the current corporate realities encountered in seeking to implement electronic technology in Southeast Asia. On the one hand we have the undoubted and continually publicized potential of such technological applications. Depicted as making possible an emerging "revolution" in global business practice, computer technology and commerce has intensified as information technology spreads and personal computer ownership grows across the region. But despite the global hype, the World Wide Web appears less about the world as a whole and much more about specific Western markets. Certainly, for much of its infancy the Internet has been very much an English-speaking, US-dominated phenomenon. Across the corporate world there is a high degree of variation in awareness between, say, Western and Japanese executives and their Southeast Asian counterparts, related in part to the simple economics of per capita income. In this fabled new era of telecommunications development, itself dominated by US companies, the ASEAN economies are seemingly swimming against the tide. By all estimates, local technology penetration in the majority of these countries is, at a minimum, two years behind the West. Yet analysts and economists still insist that Internet technology and commerce is the key to the longer-term, postcrisis revitalization of these continuously sagging markets.

Despite Southeast Asia's overall growth over the past century, most other markets – though not Singapore – follow Thailand's straggling development of information technology potential. Among the majority of our interviewees Singapore is held as being "fair" to "good" for IT usage, Malaysia as "OK" (so long as online training is supplemented by the use of tape cassettes), the Philippines as "fair" (and rapidly improving), Thailand as "fair" to "poor," and Indonesia, Vietnam, Cambodia, Laos and Myanmar as "very poor." Internal variations were often striking, with there being nearly three times as many computers per capita in Malaysia as in Thailand, and almost thirteen times as many in Singapore.

Businesses across the region can no longer afford to ignore the Internet phenomenon – this much is clear. Fortunately, and on the strength of recent statistics, this is a warning that is increasingly being adhered to. The number of Internet users in Thailand alone has, in domestic terms at least, risen exponentially from 600,000 to almost 2 million in two years.

Yet this still represents a cache of users comprising less than 5 percent of the population – as opposed to the 70 percent in the USA or Europe (Waltham and Dasaneyavaja, 1999). Still too small to support serious advantages to domestic business-to-consumer electronic commerce, this growing figure may yet engender significant structural advances within the internal business unit network. Against this backdrop many ASEAN governments once suspicious of the new technology are now encouraging the Internet to grow rapidly within domestic borders, viewing it as an essential tool for prosperity in a knowledge economy where data transfer now holds precedence over traditional industrial processes. With its natural tendency for decentralized coordination, ASEAN countries – through their political leaders – have gradually come to accept and embrace the new technology, assisting in its advancement via the progressive deregulation of related telecommunications industries. In the past decade many sectors related to this technology have grown annually at between 30 and 50 percent. In the future the developing prospect of an integrated e-commerce system is that it will grow by almost double that figure (Kittikanya, 2000).

Local challenges

Setting aside the optimism of local commentators, in reality only a small proportion of the ASEAN population are actually using IT facilities. Generally speaking, the region's growing middle class still cannot afford the price of a home computer. In a number of countries the supporting technological infrastructure access is also comparatively rudimentary, with countries such as Vietnam, Thailand and Indonesia lacking the requisite broadband access that makes usage experience quick and free from disruption. Perhaps surprisingly, the cost of lease lines and access to the Internet is one of the highest in the world, owing to industry monopolies typified by the Communications Authority of Thailand. In themselves these lease lines are essential, as users are otherwise dependent on the often unreliable and clogged up telephone system. With assured access to the Internet on each occasion, lease lines give secure and instantaneous access, yet can only be purchased locally for each domestic ASEAN market. This is held to be one of the greatest weaknesses in local IT operations, and multinationals are being thwarted in their implementation of lease line-supported access (although the prevailing view is that lease lines *will* be acquired, whatever the cost).

The challenge of pushing forward Web-based technology usage has been compounded by the longevity and severity of the Asian economic slowdown. During the postcrisis "clampdown" there was a marked shifting of attention and funding away from the possibilities of e-technology and toward that of mere survival, with a majority of MNCs adopting a cautious "wait and see" approach. This situation was exacerbated by the tendency for local directors to claim a "lack of Y2K readiness" – on top of their budgetary constraints – as the rationale for their continued reluctance to computerize their local offices. Concurrent with the Western skepticism as to the validity of these claims for a "Y2K freeze" were those concerning the necessity of having software packages designed to accommodate both English and local character scripts. The caution observed at MNC headquarters served as a catalyst for the kind of disputes that were to arise in later years and which are delineated below. First we shall explore some of the more practical challenges with which foreign corporations have had to contend.

Practical constraints

A basic hurdle facing MNCs in the ASEAN environment is the continuing lack of indigenous comfort with computer-based technology. Local distrust of the medium has been especially prevalent in the emerging economies, illustrated by their reluctance to install and operate the new technology. At a substantial number of resident companies the introduction of computer systems – typically designed for internal information storage and dissemination – has taken up to a staggering two and a half years to implement, again as a result of resistance initiated by top divisional personnel. The vast majority of our younger Asian interviewees express the view that the older generation's prevailing suspicion of imported technology was one that stemmed from the domestic national education of their particular era. Whereas the younger managers had grown up with the Internet boom, the traditionally centralized schooling system, with its emphasis on rote work and written formulas, would have all but precluded the prior generation from possessing the creative mindset required to "make the leap" to a revolutionary method of working. As one Thai interviewee expressed it,

> "We can buy all kinds of technology tomorrow – but do our top
> managers know how to use it? . . . It's a slow process for the Thai
> people, especially the older people . . . if you rush too much, and

try to change the working too much, you will create more bad things
than good."

In short, just because a local unit makes a "commitment" to harness the
promise of the Internet, this does not mean that this initial enthusiasm
will unfold according to plan. Compared with their Western counterparts,
many hitherto successful Asian subsidiaries appear tentative about
moving online on a day-to-day basis. Certain managers may be intrigued
by these new tools in theory, but instead of scrambling to change their
fundamental business plans, the supporting changes that they actually do
enact are therefore somewhat less than radical. The basic problem is that
although electronic technology can be shown to work, it is quite simply
not being *utilized*, at least not anywhere near its full potential.

Take the use of email as an example, held as quite probably the most
accessible aspect of Web-based office technology. Although loathe to
condemn the obvious practical benefits of the medium, the majority of
our local respondents were of the opinion that the email system was
being both overrated and overused. Confronted with their evident failure
even to read the greater proportion of their messages, local managers
voiced their discomfort with the use of "computer English," instanced by
their uncertainty as to both content and procedure with regard to "Block,"
usually company-wide messages. From the local perspective the ever-
increasing number of messages was felt to be both unnecessary and
seemingly easy to ignore without, as yet, much fear of unwelcome
executive feedback. As Wong (2001) notes, in one respect email has
succeeded so spectacularly that what was once "blissfully asynchronous"
has become "woefully chronic." Within the ASEAN trade bloc, as
elsewhere, even moderately busy users of the system will be faced with
perhaps a hundred new messages a day. Again in the words of Wong, it
now seems that "just as the answering machine gave us a reason to avoid
the phone, email has given us a new incentive to delay work in the
morning: email dread" (ibid.).

The consensus among Western executives is that part of the problem is
the lack of proper "on-the-ground" training. In the words of one CEO,

> "No one much knows how to use this technology properly, and most
> of them don't want to know, especially the big guys, the older guys.
> But even among the young it's like they continually make the
> simplest of mistakes. . . . Take the sending of Christmas cards last
> year – bearing in mind these are predominantly Buddhist or Muslim
> countries, we had our server crash on the back of 4,000 employees

from across the region all sending their favorite online cards, or doggy photos or whatever. . . . And it's the same with other mail. Because of their lack of English language training, or because of something, we have scores of staff who are simply not getting to grips with how to properly filter their inboxes, all pressing 'Reply All' to each and every block message sent – and again causing major problems."

On a related note, even younger managers who appear to have mastered the intricacies of email usage appear to be ignorant in practice as to what constitutes "acceptable" usage practice on the Web, often overlooking home office country laws with regard to obscene or sexist material. Even within the region, a number of cases were reported to us whereby local executives from one country in particular had become incensed with the kind of material disseminated apparently for fun in another. One such Christmas message concerned a rather offbeat depiction of Santa Claus and his "team," the former cavorting half-naked in the snow to a backdrop melody beginning with the phrase "ho ho, fucking ho" and ending with an act of quasi-bestiality involving the protagonist and a member of his yuletide entourage. Respondents have it that one financial manager from the Philippines was especially incensed. She had neglected to install her computer soundcard, which would at least have alerted her to the fact that the message was supposed to be a Christmas joke-song. However, in ignorance of such applied accessories, all she was confronted with was a moving image of Father Christmas dancing with a red-nosed reindeer. Small wonder offense was taken, an account which also reinforces the oft-forgotten difference between the ASEAN bloc and either NAFTA or the EU, namely that the former consists of a set of countries profoundly different in language, religion, customs and moral sensibility.

And hence the oft-made suggestion: that although communication may move at the speed of light, the mechanics of office politics and local mores still inevitably grind on at their own predigital pace. Western- and Japanese-headquartered multinationals are charged with being so captivated in the global transmission of this new technology that they have tended to neglect this invisible yet highly powerful wall of resistance. Fortunately, such traditional barriers to the routine utilization of e-technology are predicted to improve over time. There are also signs that the localized costs, slow speeds and bureaucratic hassles associated with Web-based applications within the region are also now beginning to diminish (see also Headlam, 2001). However, one aspect that will certainly require the longer term to overcome is the "societal culture" factor, a consistently vital influence on the effectiveness of e-technology implementation and one to which we now turn.

Culture factors

Apologists for the region cite a simple lack of knowledge and understanding as being the main reasons for the low penetration of e-technology. But according to our sources the major obstacles remain the ingrained local managerial stress upon flexibility, secrecy and the close control of information. Specifically, there are a number of cultural mores peculiar to the region's business cultures that continue either to hold global innovation at bay or to try to adapt it to indigenous practice. We begin here with a look at the impact of "age respect" upon the computerization of commercial premises. Across the globe the age of e-communication has been promoted and progressed by younger managers, a trend reflected even in the Confucian societies of Southeast Asia. Older executive incumbents have looked upon these – often Western-educated – MBA returnees with feelings akin to horror, demonizing them as upstarts and a threat to traditional business methods. Yet plainly the dismay felt by these old guard representatives stems largely from their fears of being driven out by their lack of now requisite IT skills. Striving to become electronically aware from top to bottom in this emerging set of economies, global MNCs have effectively sounded the death knell for these traditional local executives.

Within the ASEAN bloc, however, this "transformation" has been consistently hindered by the ingrained cultural respect – even deference – toward their elders. Against this backdrop, many of these old guard managers still effectively hold sway within their respective industries, continuing to rely upon traditional, *guanxi*-based communication methods far removed from the world of e-commerce that they remain committed to obstructing (Agence France-Presse, 1999; Long, 1999; Yuthamanop, 1999). Indeed, even the Western methods of managerial information gathering and sharing employed for many years have continued to be shunned. The more developed of the ASEAN markets have long had access to comparatively sophisticated networks of trade associations, newsletters and conferences that inform marketers as to changes in markets, costs, tastes and technology – methods which the older generation of managers have continued to ignore. As a result of this, the introduction of electronic technology has of necessity been a slow and drawn-out process. Although many of the younger managers we spoke to voiced their enthusiasm for the opportunity to become fully computer-literate – and were already using email – there were as yet no plans to institute the kind of corporate directives on internal communication in the way favored by their Western counterparts.

A second cultural facet bearing upon the adoption of Web-based technology concerns the societal differences with regard to "communication" – on both the corporate and the individual levels. By way of example, executives of the US Motorola corporation discovered that despite their countless emails, it was only when they physically sat down with staff and talked the issues through in the traditional manner that "anything got sorted out." As described in Chapter 1, indigenous management promotes and depends upon face-to-face communication. Messages delivered across a computer screen are viewed as abhorrent and inappropriate. This is typified by the horror of one local marketing director at receiving directives from his British CEO while the latter was seven thousand miles away, supposedly on vacation. It is reiterated by the widespread dismay felt among the local Thai management of a major US oil JV, indignant at the expatriate practice of detailing strategy proposals in lengthy, "five-page" emails. Criticized as being insensitive and a culturally incongruent way to motivate indigenous employees, much was made of this need to adopt face-to-face communications, even to the extent of taking staff out to dinner.

Traditional Southeast Asian business methodology is portrayed as an informal, secretive series of networks with a tendency toward centralization and control. The reliance on word of mouth, for both information dissemination and decision making, continues to be cited by respondents as an integral component of competitive success. The computer-generated transparency pushed for by corporate HQ is therefore resisted, being perceived as diminishing the speed and flexibility associated with the word-of-mouth commercial environment. In the words of one interviewee, "email does not promote dialogue." It certainly allows little leeway for the all-important nonverbal forms of Asian communication, a fact that makes local managers feel at a double disadvantage when communicating with foreign bosses via computer. The resourceful tendency of local staff to utilize emoticons to express their feelings is a partial way around this deficiency, but although it is of use between friends and equals in an informal manner, it has been of little benefit in the formal hierarchical structure. Further, although the

Internet may transcend national borders, most Asians would prefer to surf in their native tongue, especially in countries such as Indonesia, Vietnam and Thailand, where English is very much a second language.

The importance of hierarchy, status and "face" within the local managerial environment is a further factor found to have influenced indigenous resistance to electronic technology. Let us begin with the actual installation and use of computers *per se*, never mind that of Web-based communication. Traditionally, and as in the West, managers did not take the time to sit and compose their reports and letters by hand but rather gave dictations or handwritten notes to their secretaries, who would then type them up. In the Western world this practice quickly declined with the advent of word-processing technology and the concurrent spate of corporate downsizing through the 1980s and 90s. The number of personal secretaries declined with the progression of automated technology, there now being, typically, two or three remaining such personnel for an entire Western department. However, this trend has taken much longer to come about in the East, owing in part to this ingrained sense of status and "face" among local executives. Quite simply, it looks good in Asia to have your memos and missives typed and beautified by a personal secretary. Typing one's own documents is taken to be almost tantamount to a demotion, and has vigorously, though often quietly, been resisted and ignored.

In this context the supposed leveling, democratizing benefits of computer-based technology carry very little weight in Southeast Asia. In the West one of the widely heralded facets of Internet use has been its "status-blind" character, affecting the highest executive and the lowliest supply clerk alike in much the same way. The original promise was that email was going to be the great democratizing agent of the corporate world, allowing an instant and – if desired – anonymous exchange of ideas unimpeded by gatekeepers and protocols. All distances – geographic, hierarchical or whatever – were to vanish in the new corporation, thanks to the rise of these new applications. Yet for the Asian manager much of these benefits were unwarranted and the promises unwanted. True to type, the trend within the region has been to effectively circumvent the perceived "incongruent" elements of this new technology. In the teeth of corporate-backed moves for the electronic leveling of pyramid structures, local staff have found ways of reflecting the hierarchy through their messages in terms of both style and content. Internal messages are imbued with subtle status signifiers that serve to divide senders into the same categories observed in traditional face-to-face meetings. So although this obviously does not include body language or interruptions, other ways are being found of acknowledging the inherent social distinctions. To begin with, higher-status employees tend to restrict themselves to short, curt messages, in part to minimize contact with lower-status workers, but also to convey and reassure subordinates as to their comfort with their own authority. These will generally be sent to multiple respondents, save for direct reports, where individual messages will be the key, in part to seek to mirror the one-to-one contact of face-to-face discussion. As in the West, mid-status employees by contrast tend to produce longer, more discursive missives. Hierarchy will also be reflected in the time taken to respond to messages, with senior executives allowed – and even expected – to take much longer than the subordinate in any two-way communication.

Again, much of the above occurs to a certain extent outside of the ASEAN bloc. The differences are essentially differences of degree. Part of the reason the use of email remains so unpopular with older Asian executives is that they are simply unable to signify their status via this medium to the degree that they would like. Older managers are typically some of the least proficient in their mastery of the English language, and therefore shy away from displaying their lack of knowledge upon the intranet for all to see. In a similar vein, employees lower down the hierarchy have voiced their fears about writing email messages in English for fear their superiors may have a clear and unambiguous look at their varying levels of proficiency. Further reluctance to send views, feelings and even just information "through the wires" on a day-to-day basis stems from a societal association of the written word with authority, power and, most importantly, permanence. Indigenous managers are fearful of their words being taken from above as somehow final, definite, "set in concrete," whereas local languages tend, by contrast, to reflect the flexibility and ambiguity of the societal mindset writ large. As a direct consequence, many of our local interviewees admitted quite candidly to deliberately leaving their messages unclear by way of compensation, rather than seeking assistance in clarifying them.

In spite of the difficulties outlined above, many senior managers are actually beginning to make the tentative conceptual leap from viewing the computer age with unbridled suspicion toward seeking to develop and adapt it as a tool that can also work for *them* and on *their* terms. As a tool for business and trade, the Internet is proving an increasingly useful local means by which markets and contacts are progressed and "sniffed out." It has also been suggested – and partly recognized – as a useful method for overcoming shyness at meetings, allowing the chance for employees less competent or confident in English to compose their points and queries in their own time and, if necessary, with assistance. On a perhaps more sinister note, a number of senior local executives have also learned to conform superficially with the corporate demand for a "paperless" office by insisting upon exclusive information purveyance via email, while at the same time effectively ensuring that all vital pieces of data remain within the "inner group" circle upon a strictly word-of-mouth basis. But in another sense this can be seen as an example of indigenous employees finally "wising up" to the practical possibilities of electronic technology management.

Security

Aside from specific cultural constraints, the issue of security poses perhaps the biggest IT headache for foreign MNCs in the ASEAN bloc. The problem of Internet security has particular relevance for Southeast Asia, where computer security is generally looser than in the West and the composite countries simply do not have the relevant laws in place, either to support the development of – for example – online digital signatures or to combat crimes such as hacking. The corollary weakness in confidence apropos Internet usage is bad news in the emerging economies of ASEAN, where e-technology has already got off to a slow start. The adoption of proper security measures is therefore crucial to building confidence in online communication and transactions, and therefore the eventual development of a viable e-commerce infrastructure (Waltham and Dasaneyavaja, 1999).

From the indigenous perspective, a corollary fear concerns the perceived rise in corporate espionage, whether from outside spies or from within an organization's own ranks. In a climate where commercial *information* is increasingly considered to be the most precious corporate asset, older executives are generally wary of going online for fear of unwittingly revealing company affairs, inventory and business strategy. According to respondents, this indigenous reaction is both natural and to be expected. Habituated to the storage of key data within closely knit groups of trusted advisers, the electronic dissemination of precious information – with its concurrent loss of control – is perceived as a serious threat. The reluctance of Southeast Asian business units to have their data processed outside of the region becomes understandable, even though parent headquarters may continue to assure them of the speed and security of central links effected with the use of passwords in encrypted sessions (Crispin, 2000b). But what are MNCs supposed to do? The secure protection of information, although a massive issue, cannot simply be circumvented by resisting the use of e-technology or by staying offline. One way in which office-bound usage has been modified is through the adoption of certain qualifications such as standing back from the holding of large-scale discussions over the company email system. Particularly sensitive data have also been withheld from the system with the informal blessing of unit bosses, again via the use of word-of-mouth dissemination among trusted lieutenants (see also Wong, 2001).

Foreign MNCs have had to grant concessions to local managerial teams regarding the progression of the Western-originated institution of "flexi-hours" and staggered office shifts, supported by the use of company-sponsored equipment from home. Certainly the mere idea of employees sitting at home sending and receiving business data on company-customized laptops is one that has been reacted to with horror by indigenous executives. Even in the Western world, corporate businesses are wrestling with precisely how and to what extent employees should be permitted to enter the company intranet from home without compromising the safety of its system (also Slater, 1999c). To some extent these residual uncertainties are being progressively justified, especially in the wake of increasing employee unease at how their own organizations can deal, if they so wish, with messages previously assumed to be "private." Although they are assured that they can send emails from work in a purely personal capacity, in reality the situation may not be quite as user-friendly. According to both corporate interviewees and recent secondary material, it would appear that when emails are sent across company systems, international law recognizes them as constituting official communication, regardless of the content. In this context, potential unwanted exposure is created each time an employee uses the corporate system to send messages to friends and family. Further, and as with other forms of written evidence, a priori innocuous comments made via email can be perceived as threats, libel or harassment. Idle remarks referring to a co-worker as – for example – a "dinosaur" could in theory become the basis for an age discrimination lawsuit. Other doubts concerning email security abound, typified by cases of wrongly presumed email "loss" on the one hand and "recipient exclusivity" on the other. Although we are periodically reassured that emails do, sometimes, get lost among the worldwide traffic, in reality there is no such eventuality, with search engines of ever-increasing sophistication being able to find and retrieve almost any email from anyone. Emails are also often distributed with neither our knowledge nor consent as a result of forwarding and, or (blind) carbon copying (ibid.).

Again – what are the modern corporation and its employees to do? Plainly, if privacy is held as a main issue, then the same may be leveled against personal telephone calls made from the office, which in a similar vein may quite legitimately be listened into or recorded. The wider issue of surveillance and information tracking among the population at large is also something pertaining not just to corporations but on a grander scale to host-country governments. Within the ASEAN context this has led to there being a type of two-tier system in practice, whereby certain governments – primarily from the emerging Mekong markets – have sought to monitor and censor and simply dissuade local users from venturing onto nondomestic sites, concerned at the dangers incurred by their importing dangerous foreign political ideas.

Response of the multinationals

From the broader perspective, the Western world – via numerous governments and international agencies, trade groups, and associations – have continued to "suggest" to Southeast Asian nations how they might best adjust to the newly "networked world" in order to get the most from information technology. These "suggestions" range from assistance with industrial deregulation (e.g. of the banking and telecommunications sectors), providing better opportunities for computer literacy and Internet usage (e.g. by reducing service fees) and, more generally, promoting e-commerce, providing the necessary funds and giving clear direction, both now and for the future (e.g. Waltham and Dasaneyavaja, 1999). Having weathered the largely unsubstantiated fears concerning the Y2K computer bug, host-country governments are being urged now to view the new technology less as a potential liability and more as a powerful economic and business weapon.

Multinationals themselves have begun to realize that the ultimate test of successful e-technology and, crucially, habitual *usage* among their local units lies with their core assets – that is, their people. Encouraging rather than simply seeking to force Asian managers to adopt the new systems involves essentially changing their hearts and minds, their feelings and attitudes, so that they will support, rather than resist, the new technology.

Interestingly, even Internet experts such as the US-based Dell Computer and Intel corporations have come around to the idea of pushing an all-out internal campaign to make its host-country employees feel more comfortable and confident online. Along with American and Delta Airlines – and even the Ford Motor Corporation – these companies have sought to embrace the Internet one employee at a time. Although the details of each program obviously differ, each of these groups has decided to purchase personal computers for each of its local employees, along with cheap and even free online access to the World Wide Web (Slater, 2000a).

Other measures adopted by MNCs to familiarize their staff with computer-based applications include the provision of terminals placed – for example – in office canteens. Among those staff with their own computer, rendering the company intranet informative, attractive and amusing will then help staff make the transition from looking through their in-trays to logging onto the intranet first thing in the morning. Further down the branch hierarchy, many factory workers are also being given the opportunity to become computer literate via the provision of the requisite facilities on-site. This is particularly relevant in countries such as Vietnam, the Philippines and Thailand where workers tend to live – as well as work – on factory premises.

Regarding the daily usage of the new equipment, a substantial majority of the MNCs have also sought to institute the relevant training programs, sometimes group-wide, sometimes tailored for a host region and occasionally specific to a single country. Many such courses begin by focusing upon managerial-level staff, especially older executives, in an attempt to address and ease their inbred fears concerning both security and the perceived danger of their being shown up by their lack of English. Later courses are then cascaded down the organization as the months and years progress, particularly for finance, HR and administrative personnel.

Adaptations and concessions have been made to the local mindset in order to render the new technology more palatable. The majority of indigenous managers, it will be remembered, have an inherent distrust of electronic documentation. They have grown up and worked with paper all their lives and have learned to trust this medium alone. For this reason fax machines were, by contrast, adopted with only minor delays. Being tangible and noisy, the information they spewed forth came to be depended on by local sales managers, who relied upon the noise accompaniment to ensure they never missed an incoming order or important piece of data. But informed of such idiosyncratic counterarguments, many MNCs have adapted their system of order receipts so that, by way of example, their computer system not only generates an email to suppliers but also automatically notifies the relevant company employee via mobile phone. Similar modification to the day-to-day usage of email communiqués has also been propagated by a number of MNC executives. This is illustrated by the dilution of certain Western practices, for example that of using the intranet system in exclusivity as a means of spreading information. Rather than sending emails to the local guy sitting across the corridor or next door, expatriate managers have been advised to guard against this tendency – and to force themselves to get up and address the recipient verbally, on a face-to-face basis wherever possible. Further to this, in dealing with the deeper problem of English language usage, many Southeast Asian subsidiaries have been equipped to handle intranet communication in their own script, instanced by Malay, Thai or Vietnamese. To an extent this reflects the supposedly wider global trend whereby it has been predicted – rather optimistically – that by 2004 half of all online commerce will be coming from somewhere other than the USA, and that the Internet will eventually become a thicket of contending languages replete with localized content.

Of course, this partial localization of corporate IT packages does not, of itself, guarantee that it will then be accepted. Concessions made may be sniffed at, adaptations ignored for not going far enough. Equally, the foreign multinational may also then decide to forgo such attempts at conciliation, and may instead adopt a strategy of standardized retrenchment. Examples abound. The most extreme recounted to us stems back to the belief that, in any case, older executives with a lack of IT skills are "on their way out" with the rise of the new economy, and that in conjunction with this inevitability, the way around local resistance is simply to remove these "blockers," whether by redundancy packages or via early retirement or function rotation. As in the case of Shell Vietnam, all future replacement staff can then be both computer literate and under 30 years of age.

Fortunately, such diehard impositions of Western values have been rare. The long-term view *vis-à-vis* the local managerial adoption of corporate intranet applications is one suffused with glowing optimism, albeit one aligned with the future rise of the *younger* executive. Western corporate representatives – in particular – have stressed that to their mind the managerial attitudes toward e-technology from both the ASEAN host markets and the West would mix or "cross-verge." Many of our informants have backed this assertion by pointing to the medium-term local decline of traditional nuclear family values – extended or otherwise – and particularly within the confines of the bigger local cities. The rise of electronic communication – and, in particular, of the Internet – is said to have "redefined" the Asian family home via the placement of younger family members in constant contact with Western media and, by implication, cultural norms and values. In this context, emerging generations, although still *physically* at home, exist emotionally outside of it through the mediating effects of this exterior communication.

Concluding thoughts

The vast majority of Western CEOs within the region continue to voice concern over the comparatively small proportion of local managers who actively use electronic technology – and in particular the company email system. Further, the major difficulties among the local work teams are concentrated among the higher echelons of indigenous management. This is in spite of various attempts by a number of Western MNCs to adapt or in some way "soften" their initial e-technology implementation programs.

It would appear that there remains a divergent set of values with regard to new technology. On the one hand we have the younger, up-and-coming employees who seem to assimilate – and even pursue – the latest Web-based applications with gusto. On the other hand there remains an older generation who show continued resistance to technological change – those who retain power at the top. The rapidly gained enthusiasm among junior staff for new computer and Internet-based technology is gradually being transferred to middle management, but it will, surely, be at least another generation before this latest crop of controllers rise high enough to implement these corporate measures properly. Against this backdrop, what seems certain is that the desired local adoption of e-technology will come to pass only with the progress of time itself. Within the boundaries of single-market societies, the phenomenon of electronic adoption can be viewed less as simply a "cultural" issue, and much more as a "generational" one. The question that remains is whether future generations of business leaders, confidently empowered with computer-based technology, will then seek to democratize their organizations in line with electronic methods of information dissemination and possession.

7 Information tracking

- ISO certification in Southeast Asia
- Rationale for accreditation
- General critiques
- Implementation within ASEAN
- Culture-based resistance to implementation
- Tentative resolutions

Multinationals in Southeast Asia continue to implement Web-based technology for a variety of reasons: the enhanced coordination, communication and, critically, control that it offers. In the precrisis environment, MNC headquarters claimed to be suffering from a lack of detailed knowledge as to the activities of their far-flung subsidiary units. But the way in which computer-based technology overcomes these barriers to space and time has enabled corporations to gain clear and precise snapshots of their local concerns. Concurrent with this desire for instant information is the need to implement the technology that would enable this information to be logged and traced *over time*. This chapter progresses our analysis of electronic technology with a complementary exploration of corporate information tracking methods. These are typified by the Total Quality Management (or TQM) movement, which in turn has engendered a wide-ranging series of quality assurance protocols, foremost among which are the International Organization for Standardization (or ISO) 9000 standards.

According to the vast majority of our interviewees, the major asset to be gained from transplanting centrally ordained programs is the greater levels of *transparency* they imbue in their local working methods. Transparent practices, traceable over time, have provided corporate central commands with unprecedented levels of visibility. As part of an overall program of global restructuring, information tracking systems allow the requisite changes to be truly and verifiably maintained. At the "coalface" this is achieved in practice via the use of recording and documentation/database technology. As well as facilitating the tracking of internal business unit communication and information leads, such devices would then also be employed in the garnering of market developments and environmental trends.

The specific focus upon quality systems finds its expression in the renewed emphasis upon overseas business unit acquisition of ISO 9000 accreditation. ISO itself encompasses a global standard of quality certification, in effect a support toward the corporate push for increased worldwide unity of operations. Based in Switzerland, the ISO series is made up of national standards institutes from all countries – big, small, industrialized and developing, right across the globe. As a nonenforceable, voluntary consensus of protocols, ISO 9000 has become a fact of life in the majority of industrial segments – adopted as a national standard by most countries and often required by contractual agreements (Corona, 2001). The USA has for years been a leading influence in the development of ISO 9000 standards, while the European Union has recently adopted these new standards over existing national regulations. ISO has become an umbrella mark and guide for all multinationals seeking to develop their global business processes.

In organizational terms the ISO 9000 series is a set of broad standards primarily concerned with quality management and the control of company processes. Quality management embraces the collective hub of what the corporation does to ensure that its products or services conform to customer requirements and, to this end, is applicable to *all* product and/or service sectors and to *all* organizations. The protocols include requirements on the safety of facilities, treatment of raw materials, quality inspection procedures and even customer satisfaction measures and job descriptions. In practice the ISO system involves each and every phase of a product cycle and the attendant processes, from initial identification right through to final consumer satisfaction. The typical phases in this process would be those set for marketing and market research, product design and development, process planning and development, purchasing, production, provision of services, verification, packaging and storage, sales and distribution, installation and commissioning, technical assistance and servicing, after-sales service, and the disposal or recycling of a product at the end of its useful life.

Since initial publication in 1987, ISO 9000 standards have gone through several changes. Currently they require an organization to address quality planning, customer satisfaction and continuous improvement. In 2000 the

ISO 9001 to 9004 protocols were rationalized into ISO 9000: 2000,
designed to resemble its environmental counterpart, ISO 14000 – thereby
forming a family umbrella of international management standards.

ISO certification in Southeast Asia

Although ISO certification is not, as yet, a legal requirement, many local
companies have decided to expend resources in improving their
operations in order to gain certification. The interest demonstrated across
the region is expressed within the range of public utilities, especially
those with international connections. On arrival at any number of central
airports within the region the first signs a passenger is likely to see are
those displaying the ISO 9002 certified claim for customs services –
along, of course, with those for perfumery and duty-free alcohol. On
exiting the terminal, watch for similar displays concerning official airport
taxi services, again with ISO regalia. The highways to the city are then
adorned with local companies making recent claims to the same award,
along with the billboards advertising Sony, Nestlé, Coca-Cola and BMW.

Local corporations lacking ISO accreditation have been anxiously
hurrying to meet the requirements. This is mostly due to the mounting
pressure from international purchasers and suppliers, which increasingly
demand accreditation for their particular industries. Against this
backdrop, over thirty accreditation agencies from both within and outside
the region are now actively operating for business, promoting their
services on the back of this promised access to importing countries that
ISO endorsement will provide. Many local managers have decried this
trend, suggesting local companies should not be panicked into
compliance with a standard, stressing the essentially voluntary nature of
the exercise. Yet a growing body of commentators in turn oppose such
attitudes. They point to the decline in local competitive advantage
because of just such a reluctance to comply, holding it as a block to
continuity in industrial development and a brake upon the nations
seeking to join the ranks of the newly industrialized countries (e.g.
Marukatat, 1999). A particularly sobering point is made by Tha Hla
(1998) in that as of July 1998 the average ISO accreditation process in
the region was taking over twice as long as for their competitors in the
West. Many employers have exacerbated this problem by slashing their
funds for new quality training programs in the wake of the recent
economic crisis.

The problem stems from as far back as the mid-1990s, when a study of the region's car industry found "inconsistent quality, high costs of production, deviation from delivery schedules and unresponsiveness to sophisticated production technology." On the strength of such reports, a number of local factories began campaigns to achieve international quality standards, backed by government-initiated training and advisory services to upgrade the car parts industry (Crispin, 2000a). But this has been a long and tangled process, fraught with delays and resistance. The implementation of ISO 9000 standards across the region has been a patchy affair for both local firms and subsidiary corporations alike. Generally speaking, the MNC experience has been to push for accreditation in one country at a time, starting with the more developed economy of Singapore and then perhaps Malaysia, where the requisite systems training has been put in place with relative ease. Notable exceptions to the rule include the Castrol corporate fold, for which Vietnam was the surprising first port of success. More typical examples include that of the French telecommunications conglomerate Alcatel, where Malaysia preceded Thailand, in turn preceding Vietnam, with the unit in the last-named country one of the few remaining still to lack accreditation.

In mid-1996 the first ASEAN-based ISO 9000 forum was held in – ironically – Vietnam, attended by well over one hundred representatives from both the international and the domestic business arenas. In a sense this meeting signaled the underlying change in attitudes toward quality that was about to engulf the region. The ISO's then president expounded upon the role of international standards in overcoming the region's technical problems in manufacturing, supply, performance and equipment. Held up to the conference as a common framework of reference for both suppliers and their customers, ISO implementation was promoted for its trade, exchange and technology transfer benefits.

Rationale for accreditation

With so much time and resources now being pumped into quality standards, we need to delve into the underlying rationale for this trend. Why – for example – be so keen to secure ISO accreditation? And why has this trend increased so dramatically? What can a company expect to receive for all its trouble? From the accounts of our respondents, the reasoning proferred is both diverse and context bound. For the sake of clarity we have therefore categorized these responses as corporate center benefits, local employee benefits and perceived advantages for the organization as a whole.

Corporate group benefits

We have loosely subdivided these official corporate benefits into those of *quality* on the one hand and *efficiency* on the other. Beginning with the former, according to a near-consensus of our interviewed managers, quality is now improving in the ASEAN region, with a tangible basis in the emergence of the ISO program implementation. This can be illustrated by any number of multinational subsidiaries, typified by the case of BMW in Thailand. Launched in 2000, the current 3-series aimed at the region as a whole is being assembled for the first time at a production facility in Rayong, on Thailand's eastern seaboard. To the surprise of many analysts, and in line with senior management hopes, the quality level of the models there is rapidly approaching that achieved in Munich.

As the ISO certification is valid only for three years, mandatory six-month checks after the duration of this period then help ensure that the quality standards are maintained. By regularly tracing the various steps and procedures along a manufacturing line, companies can minimize variations and errors, helping to ensure that the final quality of a product matches customer expectations. The basic ISO philosophy rests upon adherence to these basic processual steps. Along the ISO continuum, "that which can be measured can thereby be improved." In order to maximize the impact upon overall quality levels, these facets must encompass management review, internal quality audits, and corrective and preventive action. Performance metrics and statistical controls are also employed in order to ensure accurate benchmarking, itself a time-honored tool both for general competitive analysis and as a catalyst for change. Far from merely cutting out steps in a continually monitored process, ISO can impact upon a company's core competencies, customer expectations and bottom-line performance through reductions in costs and cycle time (see also Corona, 2001).

In reality, of course, quality enhancement is much more than an internal turnaround of corporate operations. Southeast Asian companies are falling over themselves to gain ISO 9000 – and, increasingly, 14000 – accreditation, in large part because of the marketing potential ISO affords

Events such as these have often turned Southeast Asia into a kind of "Ground Zero" for Western multinational quality controllers, forcing them to overhaul their existing regional governance procedures (Slater, 2000b). This has meant keeping closer tabs upon their contractors and suppliers – the type of tracking processes mandated by ISO. In theory such systems should be a potent force for global standardization, yet in reality this is often far from being the case. Within the ASEAN region in particular there is still very little agreement as to how exactly subsidiary factories are to be inspected. As Slater (ibid.) notes, whereas some hire international audit bodies, others will seek local-based firms and even conduct their own internal inspections. The codes of conduct adopted for the purpose are similarly disparate and vague – although at the same time often of priceless importance. Certainly the type of negative publicity surrounding Nike's use of local labor is, in the longer term, potentially destructive with regard to years of brand building and local market development. In this context the use of international standards such as ISO has as yet to make much impact, though commentators have recounted the efforts to create similar systems that focus exclusively on issues of social accountability (e.g. "SA 8000"; ibid.).

General critiques

The common thread linking the benefits referred to above lies in its perspective – looking at the organization from the *center*, viz. head office. So with the following depiction of ISO critiques we shall also remain at this level. One of the most common caveats expressed to us concerning ISO lies with its presumption to guarantee "quality." But can ISO accreditation ever guarantee quality *per se*? Plainly not. A set of ISO systems can only cover the production process itself, along with general levels of internal efficiency. In practical terms a corporation could spend decades churning out low-quality goods based on inefficient, shoddy production procedures while keeping its ISO 9000 certificate firmly nailed to the head office wall.

Such potential inevitably calls into question the benefits – indeed, relevance – of pursuing ISO certification. Another common charge – often laid by implication – is that of elitism. Much of this surrounds the perceived density of the 9000 protocols, which are often tome-like in appearance and unfathomable in content. Of course, ISO must by its nature encompass difficult, complex issues such as supplier certification and systems engineering. Quality assurance, by its very nature, deals with all supporting procedural and related documentation necessary to the process. Yet how much of this is ever really, properly *read*, let alone digested – even among a branch unit's resident quality personnel? How many of an MNC's ASEAN units have ever properly scoured the intricate ISO protocols? How many of its staff understands its dictates, even in theory upon the page? The vast majority of our interviewees appeared to regard this prickly subject with something akin to subtle bemusement. Very few had actually claimed to have ever seen one of the – at times – eighteen-volume manuals being picked up off its shelf. Our overall impressions were that there is a definite and dire lack of understanding by locals of the very complex ISO 9000 protocols.

Further critiques center on the ISO accreditation process as being both intrusive on the one hand and overcostly on the other. It goes without saying that a key element of ISO involves the identification of a business core working thread and the procedures vital to managing – indeed, controlling – the business successfully. Unfortunately, the methods and decisions employed to obtain such data are often regarded as akin to a kind of central strategic dictatorship. The managers – even CEOs – in charge of both headquarters and branch units have been almost united in their resentment toward and unease with such prescriptive courses of action imposed from outside. Although patently beneficial in its overall objectives, ISO is held to feel like an inspection program set to probe into methods of practice deemed beyond its call of duty. Further, such a means of implementation adds scarce resources – notably people, time and extra work – to the business operation overall. For these reasons the oft-cited claim that "ISO reduces costs" *per se* is not as clear as was first assumed.

One final critique concerns the entire ISO inspection procedure, from initial implementation right through to the continuous postaward checks and inspections. Many business managers view this whole monitoring process as being inherently flawed. As one executive put it,

> "It's an open secret that factories put a show on for the ISO auditors. And I'm sure the auditors know this, they see it every day, but what are they going to do about it? At the end of the day they want to be paid like the rest of us; it's not in their interest to fail an existing account on the strength of their hunches as to day-to-day activity."

These suspicions have led many managers to question the current credibility of the whole ISO business in Southeast Asian markets. As one Western executive based in the region remarked,

"Honestly speaking, in the local realities of conducting everyday business how many purchasers actually ask for the certificate? It would seem that it's only electronics and maybe petrochemical companies who are bothered. So you can understand now the dragging of feet for the rest of us wary of wasting our time."

Executive Insights: Quality as a Corporate State of Mind

"Quality is very often a corporate state of mind. How many motorists fill up their tanks at a Jet station in Thailand because the petrol is better or cheaper? Hardly any. Yet I know many people who prefer Jet stations for the simple reason that their wives and daughters do not like the often disgusting toilets at competitive petrol stations. Conoco's Jet stations in Thailand have the cleanest toilets, the most attractive Jiffy convenience stores *and* the cheapest petrol. No wonder they sell more fuel per site than any other oil company in Thailand, and theirs is the only network which is still expanding. They have a quality state of mind and it directly affects the bottom line."

Implementation within ASEAN

The worldwide implementation of the ISO 9000 protocols forms a major plank in corporate moves toward business practice homogeneity. At the local level the practical installation process is, by contrast, inescapably grounded in societal culture. And nowhere is this dialectic more pronounced than in the ethnic-Chinese business arenas of Southeast Asia. On the basis of our combined experience together with that of a selection of our interviewees, we continue our discussion of the perceived benefits of ISO accreditation, focusing on the culture-bound rationale of local managers. We then outline some of the difficulties typically experienced at the practical stage of quality systems implementation within the region.

ISO certification: priorities and rationale

Broadly speaking, the consensus of our local respondents was that ISO accreditation would imbue their company with a certain "edge" over the direct competition, as yet uncertified. But probing slightly deeper, we found a clear divide between those who see "external" benefits as the main advantage of ISO certification and those who focus on the internally based benefits they hope to obtain. Briefly, external influences regarding the decision to become ISO 9000 certified encompass both customer requirements and competitive forces – as exemplified above. The internal benefits, by contrast, center upon the processual improvements and transparency of information held to "drive" a corporation through the ISO 9000 certification process (e.g. Corona, 2001).

Let us begin with our first category, typified by the desirability of ISO accreditation in meeting the increasingly stringent global purchasing requirements. Suppliers to the automotive industry, as a prime example, are now faced with General Motors, Swedish Motors and the majority of Western automotive interests demanding internationally recognized levels of production standards. Within the multinational organization itself, branch units are increasingly having to gain ISO accreditation under the dictates of head office executives, likewise seeking to spread their own global uniform standards across the corporate group.

Indeed, the whole "standardization" mentality affects the implementation not just of ISO but of the whole of the international standards umbrella. Recent attention has been given to the environmental protocols delineated in ISO 14000, especially among Western MNCs long since 9000-certified and seeking to impose ever stricter screens upon their global supply base. In this era of globalization, new technology and product innovation are not necessarily a guaranteed formula for business success. Responsible environmental practice is also regarded as a significant factor, giving added value to products and services. Like ISO 9000, the ISO 14000 standard is held to equip a corporation with the necessary strength to compete successfully in the international trading arena. ISO 14000 accreditation is held as expressing unequivocal proof that a company is both responsible and reliant, acting with integrity and genuine support for sustainable environmental and economic and social development. This holds particular relevance for the electronic, petrochemical and oil industries, all of them under near-continuous scrutiny because of their perceived adverse effects on the environment. The ISO protocols can be seen to demonstrate a company's firm commitment, through actions rather than words, to customers, the local society, shareholders and staff.

Quite apart from their usefulness as an external marketing tool, adoption of such processes is also held to encompass essential benefits for the internal working methods of a business. Take the case of the latter series protocol, ISO 14000. As discussed above, the maintenance of a clean and safe environment in the interests of society brings numerous external benefits for a company – but how about its employees; how about the *internal* benefits? Surely the correct implementation of 14000 procedures will also assist in maintaining a nonhazardous, concerned working environment for corporate employees – not just in Southeast Asia but across the world.

In these terms, quality is often thought of less as being simply a certificate on the wall and much more as a process *in itself*. More than as a simple promotions tool, quality has an inherent purpose, that of measurable, continuous improvement alongside cost reduction. To this end, corporations need to understand the processes *themselves*, and be prepared to verify and validate on a continuous basis the what, when, who, where and why of each process before any stable, meaningful change can take place. Almost by design, ISO 9000 provides the ground rules for documentation and control – establishing a stable baseline of operations. In itself, then, this provides an invaluable rationale for accreditation – quite apart from any externally grounded demand for the certificate. It is therefore essential to emphasize the practical, day-to-day elements of the quality process, to the active tracking and recording of internal working procedures. To this end, companies will not just *say* they are seeking and achieving quality; their processes and end products will *prove* that they are.

In practice, ASEAN managers, along with their headquarters-based counterparts, tend to stress one accreditation benefit to the exclusion of the other. More precisely, the tendency for Western interviewees has been to focus primarily upon the *internal* gains to be made on a longer-term basis. This is well illustrated by the number of examples of MNCs that, while they have already begun to put quality controls in place throughout, have as yet no plans to become formally accredited with ISO. As one executive stressed to us,

> "We have a system in place where we backcheck a minimum of one-third of the work we do here in Malaysia. Now that's three times more than is required by ISO in the USA and twice as much as is done at our head office in Western Europe. So where's the problem?"

More generally, it was put to us that for large, well-known companies with already efficient work systems, the ISO accreditation was hardly of interest. While it was felt that the certification of quality might draw certain types of new customer to a company, in the long run the bulk of these recruits would either stay or not on the strength of the quality received – and not simply upon bits of paper pinned to office walls.

However, the views expressed above were hardly representative of the ASEAN management cohort. At year-end 2000 a majority of Western MNCs all felt that an unacceptably high percentage of their Southeast Asian units still lacked ISO 9000 accreditation. Corporate respondents blamed this ongoing failure on the perceived polarization of attitude toward the accreditation process within the local units. Whereas the corporate-represented emphasis was on the measures for changes *themselves* – in order to obtain greater transparency and control – the Asian local management teams appeared to be merely concerned with "getting the certificate on the wall." Even where local respondents were initially enthusiastic about the internal benefits to be derived from ISO implementation, further probing tended to uncover a deep-down lack of interest in anything "quality linked" beyond having the qualification spread across company letterheads and product packaging. The danger with such an attitude was that it could engender the illusion of internal quality where very little could be seen to exist – exemplified, according to several respondents, by the ISO certification of the notorious Bangkok metropolitan bus service. Hence, although locally tied resources were being poured into the concept of quality systems management, it became increasingly evident that there remained a nascent and deep-seated suspicion of processual change. Particular unease came to be expressed with the "alien" notion of "recording each and every working procedure," a practice that seemed to go hand in hand with the "ISO way" of doing business. Even where some measure of these required changes had been put into place, the fundamental value and assumptions that seemed to underpin them remained substantially unchanged.

Fortunately, this seeming polarization of attitudes still allowed for certain notable "crossovers" in approach. A small number of local managers who were dedicated quality enthusiasts faced skepticism not just from their indigenous counterparts but also from their Western bosses. Safety procedures appeared to be an especial area for ridicule, as illustrated in a substantial number of regional MNCs. For one thing, departmental "safety officers" were almost always appointed among the lesser-regarded of a director's personnel – appointment to this capacity was felt to be a "kiss of death," rather than an added responsibility one could undertake with pride. Safety reports were therefore hardly ever considered seriously, let alone read – even among the incumbent CEOs. As one executive wryly commented,

> "It's hardly ever going to be a high priority for any manager –
> especially in the current market climate. Also – and to be honest here

– how many things can you write about a fire extinguisher every
month? How can you justify the role?"

Similar cynicism greeted the safety officer's administration of office fire
drills – typically involving the evacuation of a multinational's local office
suites located high up in some downtown city skyscraper. One CEO
demanded to be informed as to the precise day and time of the drill on
each occasion – just so he could then either arrange to be away at a
meeting, or simply ignore the alarm. Not surprisingly, the residing
quality team was less than impressed, and certainly gained neither job
satisfaction from nor motivation for their efforts.

Executive Insights: Fire Drills

"We previously occupied the fifth floor of an old building in Chinatown. There were no
fire extinguishers and the staff had never had a fire drill in their working lives. I wanted
both. Extinguishers were ordered and staff trained to use them. Fire marshals were
appointed and as CEO I personally led all staff out of the two possible exits. Everyone
cooperated, although one or two people thought the whole exercise hilarious, something
that made me angry. I pointed out to everyone that one day they would have children of
their own and would prefer them to work for a company which was concerned for their
safety as opposed to one which couldn't care less."

On a more general level, quality management and ISO seek to breed a
sense of accountability down through an organization, prompting
employees to feel responsible for the work they produce, and act
accordingly. Yet the traditional cadre of local managers – and especially
those from the older generation – is not so much interested in "the
environment" or "process documents," considering such efforts a waste
of company money. This view is then writ large across the billboards and
airport plazas across the region, seeking to establish international
credibility while at the same time circumventing the necessary internal
changes. Yet to the genuine aficionado, such a view of ISO certification
as an end in itself is a dangerous mistake. It is held that this view breeds
complacency and neglect. For example, the view may take hold that with
the award pinned to the wall, the company no longer needs to "do the
checks" that got it there in the first place. In reality, certification should
just be the beginning of a longer process. As one local quality assurance
manager put it, "What use is it to the company to stop the process once
we have the certificate? It just means we have paid for all these 90,000
words of volumes and manuals just for some paper. It's crazy."

Practical measures

A further demonstration of the power of local culture concerns the methods by which ISO-type standards have been implemented *in practice*. Held to be the key to long-term employee acceptance, the involvement of grassroots staff in every stage of the process was thought to ensure its clear and open passage. However, many local employees have complained that although they are closest to the day-to-day operation of the business, in reality they had been neither consulted nor trained in the workings of the quality systems process.

Indeed, the process of ISO 9000 acquisition typically began with a home office or regional directive on the matter to the respective subsidiary's chief of staff. Once the chief of staff was informed and trained, his or her knowledge and motivation were then to be cascaded down to the middle layers of management, who in turn would pass these on to their departmental staff. The consensus among respondents was that this is the most fitting and suitable way for the process to occur. Yet in practice this method was habitually flouted, with skeptical executives either loath to filter the correct information downward, or incapable of doing so. "Sideways constraints" served to complicate the issue; these were characterized by the choice of external quality consultants to "assist" the local units in their implementation process. Initially employed on a temporary basis, these quality "figureheads" were often kept on in their respective roles, much to the chagrin of the local managers. Oftentimes the consultant would seek to appoint a representative in each department. But although consultants brought in from outside were resented, when an appointment was made from within, the job would be given, as we have said, usually to the least favored and/or least competent member of staff.

External quality consultants were typically Western in origin, tending to follow the ISO and, indeed, corporate head office guidelines to the letter. Rightly, they were then perceived as a further force toward central standardization and control. Yet most were to express their anger and disappointment at the lack of support from the corporate heads of ASEAN branch units. This lack of support and endorsement encompassed fairly innocuous "oversights" right through to, for example, being left off the company executive committee and kept in the dark as to strategic plans and objectives.

A program of ISO implementation would typically begin with a company-wide presentation of some description, whether in one fell swoop or by turns through the ranks. Usually held to imbue top management with a sense of both the urgency and importance of quality systems, the speech itself would then be followed by some kind of quality booklets and office posters – generally, though not always, translated into the vernacular. Moves were then set in place to disseminate specific training sessions concerning the ISO standards in the ensuing months, sometimes through the block emailing of all staff by top management personnel.

Naturally, such moves were not without their opponents. In line with our societal culture hypothesis, opposition took different forms in different countries. A digested summary of respondent views held that in corporate Malaysia and Singapore, ISO protocols were successfully adopted in that they were at least properly written down and, to varied degrees, understood. The problem – and in particular for Malaysia – was that these standards were then simply never *used* on a day-to-day basis. To this extent Malaysia was often viewed as a kind of mid-point between Singapore and countries such as Indonesia and Thailand. In the last two of these countries, although in some cases executives were adept at copying the regional quality templates, they took very little genuine interest in the comprehension or usage of the protocols. To put it bluntly, they saw little intrinsic value in the process, whatever the reasons given.

Local quality managers complained, perhaps predictably, of gaining only limited support from among their indigenous colleagues. Where a chief external consultant was involved, these support levels and, more importantly, communication difficulties were exacerbated. Within their respective departments these "quality reps" tended to find themselves ostracized among their direct superiors with "more urgent" matters to attend to. With the ISO-prompted stress on transparent documentation there was a notable lack of trust given to the quality teams, which were generally regarded with a mixture of distrust and resentment. ISO implementation programs were felt to cut across informal relationships built upon trust and mutual understanding – neither of which was "recorded in written files" to make them work. This was a feeling shared, on occasion, by many Western subsidiary chiefs.

The ensuing problems concerning departmental job descriptions seem clearer in this context. With the trend toward uniformity and systems reliance, job descriptions have been of tangible assistance to Western MNCs in their practice of rotating senior managers across the globe. Yet within the ASEAN bloc their application was fraught with difficulty. The rapport between an individual Asian manager and, for example, his or her secretary was one that was grounded in personal affinity. Thus it was not unusual to discover a secretary spending time performing the duties of a maid when, for whatever reason, the latter was absent from duty. It is hard to envisage such a change in roles being translated into the comparatively strict guidelines locked into any future description of the job. Similarly, the role of direct subordinates is traditionally founded on flexibility and trust that lie far beyond the task-oriented mentality of a Western manager. Job descriptions were therefore almost unanimously perceived as an unwelcome straitjacket upon a director's rightful control within his or her particular department.

Further implementation problems concerned the role and actions of the individual assessors sent from their respective accreditation bodies to check the process. Certainly the majority of the quality managers we spoke to had been less than happy with the nature and content of their continuous contact schedules. In some of these cases the problem seemed to be linked to that of status. Many ISO assessors routinely demanded to talk exclusively with the CEO of each company. So as well as taking this as a loss of face, many local teams were also to cast doubt upon the thoroughness of the methods employed, the practice of only speaking to the top company member being taken as a sign of incompetence and sloth. Many others wished to know how exactly an accreditation body selected its individual assessors, and whether in practice their appointment stemmed from genuine suitability or merely convenience.

Local managers expressed continuing confusion concerning some of the practices they were being asked to adopt. One of these was the notion of actually seeking to *measure* customer satisfaction. Asian executives were perplexed by the perceived need to try to measure rapports that – by their local definition – were informal, often relations based and unique. Seeking to quantify such a relationship was held to be both pointless and impossible. They also proved to be very costly – typically put together by the two main international market research agencies in the region, AMI and A. C. Nielsen. The documents officially designated as being those linked to the "quality push" could – as we have seen – extend to over eighteen manuals in the most extreme of cases. Even the most diehard Western-style executives felt this to be excessive.

As one manager observed, from the regional perspective

> "The program that gets the most local support from us will be the one which adheres to the line of least resistance. Basically, it'll be the

lowest common denominator that works. So if something's written up which fills more than half a page of foolscap, then it's bad. You need to bring things here to a level that the local staff will warm to. And that means fewer words, more talking, more action. The Asians are the unsung progenitors of the soundbite, believe me!"

Such corporate-initiated ISO examinations and procedures obviously did little for local employee motivation. This was further damaged when the years of preparing for ISO 9000 certification in the form of documentation and systems seemed then to be made almost obsolete by the increasing emergence of ISO 14000. With the global emphasis turned toward environmental issues the credibility of ISO 9000 seemed to have been watered down in the eyes of some local executives – especially as they were well aware of the home office scramble for the 14000 counterpart.

Executive Insights: The Struggle for ISO 9000 – A Case Study

"Castrol headquarters appointed a quality control manager whose remit was to introduce ISO 9000 to corporate subsidiaries and joint ventures worldwide. As a joint venture we – as the unit in Thailand – had always taken quality seriously, from quality ingredients, sound manufacturing procedures, quality products and packaging, regular product testing and customer satisfaction assessments garnered via marketing research. I'm sure we weren't perfect but we all took our jobs seriously and we were continuously very profitable.

"At the initial stages of our seeking ISO accreditation we appointed a Western ISO consultant based in Malaysia, who came to visit us a couple of days every month. Progress was slow and internal resistance was high, mainly because this consultant was looked upon as an outsider who didn't understand the Thai culture, or how the company worked. After a while it became clear we were getting nowhere, so we terminated the agreement and considered the available alternatives. One serious suggestion put to us by a local executive was that a Thai accreditation agency could guarantee the ISO certificate – albeit at a price. However, this was rejected outright, and to cut a long story short we asked our overworked but highly competent expatriate technical director to mastermind the process in Thailand. At about the same time the Castrol headquarters quality chief was himself dismissed, just as he was beginning to achieve some credibility and success – or so it seemed to us.

"As we got deeper into the documentary process of the company-wide communication needs it became increasingly clear that what we needed was a full-time executive consultant to take some of the weight off the shoulders of the technical director. But this new appointment turned out to be a disaster. The new quality control expert knew his job, understood the ISO processes and procedures, but culturally was completely insensitive. If you don't even try to understand the Thais they will eventually become obstructive. This guy caused so many problems in almost every department that he became an embarrassment to the management committee and to me. In the end we had to let him go back to his home country, and by the time I retired we still didn't have the ISO 9000 accreditation despite years of endeavor, considerable effort on the part of our people and, of course, an enormous amount of expense. Shortly afterwards Castrol Thailand did achieve accreditation so perhaps it hadn't all been wasted, but I look back on the episode as a signal failure on my part, not to have organized the whole process in a better way, and for appointing a so-called expert who was completely insensitive to the Thai culture."

Culture-based resistance

Societal culture and its practical implications pervade the whole process of ISO implementation. Nonetheless, this often very potent force has been more marked in some countries – and some organizations – than in others. Typically, both Western- and Japanese-headquartered corporations have enjoyed more success with their quality plans in Singapore than in Thailand. Similarly, within a country like Thailand itself, the results will often differ through industries and companies, and for a number of fairly straightforward reasons. The most basic of these is the number of home office managers per indigenous employee – and for how long this has been the case. Among the noted oligarchy that remains the motor oil industry there were a handful of multinationals in contention – among them Exxon-Mobil, Shell, Caltex, Castrol and Dupont. Within this group there is a substantial variation in the expatriate quotas levels – a difference that was reflected in the corporate experience with local quality systems implementation. In the companies housing a high percentage of Western employees we found that quality systems management had already been promoted on an incremental basis for years.

Much of the societal influence on the perceived success of quality systems programs begins at the proverbial drawing board. The transparency and frankness associated with ISO process implementation are held to be primary values in Western – certainly American – culture. The notion that company information should by default be available and accessible to everyone within the organization who needs it expresses deeply laid assumptions. But do such values hold as dear a place in the collective consciousness of corporate Asia? Are they even acknowledged? The evidence suggests otherwise. Right across the region our own respondents balked at the idea of such democratic transparency and deemed it wholly inappropriate for the local business context. Indigenous business culture has traditionally discounted such ideas, especially in the ethnic Chinese-dominated working environments so predominant in the markets of ASEAN. Even where the idea of frankness and clarity of process was approved in theory, as a practical day-to-day concern it was dismissed at every turn. The majority of our interviewees were even prepared to defend the old, autocratic working methods whereby a departmental head had literally to sign for everything that went on in "his" domain. Again, for all their drawbacks, such methods were, on the whole, deemed to be "correct" in the patriarchal, familial-style environment of Southeast Asia.

Furthermore, the emphasis on informal contacts, the relations-based character of Asian business methods, means that rapport with business customers is paramount. The contrast with the business climate predominant in the West – whereby commercial success mainly stems from referrals – could hardly be more pronounced. In ASEAN countries the perception of quality within a company, while it may promote and enhance positive referrals, does very little, if anything, to circumvent an existing long-term business rapport. Hence, the intrinsic desirability of ISO 9000 accreditation is perceived as being only marginal in the emerging markets of ASEAN. Local managerial reaction to the so-called "international standards" of business method was one of indifference bordering on hostility. As expressed by one executive of mixed Western and Asian origin,

> "The most important characteristic of the local business culture is that it's contact oriented . . . the idea of having a merit-based organization founded on these quality programs is considered here as being an idea from another galaxy. . . . Most dealings here of any import tend always to be hush-hush and liable to revision and change at the drop of a hat . . . it's reactive to external events, not proactive, and always has been. . . . The idea of having to write everything down for some *farang* certificate with the letters ISO stamped on it is irrelevant here."

Local attempts to circumvent – and effectively sabotage – the regional ISO certification process have been much in evidence in the postcrisis period. Sometimes they involve the hiring of locally based accreditation bodies unknown to the wider international business community, but with suspected links of an "informal" nature to the company's senior management. These types of arrangements were typified by the apparent "wallflower" appointment of a part-time Western consultant merely for the sake of appearance. Although formally certified with the ISO 9002 award, these local bodies take only a matter of six to eight months to grant certification (as opposed to the year-long international norm). In this context many Western MNCs have become suspicious as to the apparent game plan of their local subsidiaries and have since tightened their monitoring of these accreditation companies – for example, with the later acquisition of ISO 14000. Accreditation bodies are now almost always international companies unanimously selected on a central corporate basis, with the global quality account an emerging mirror of its more established advertising-agency counterpart.

Further changes have also been made to the ongoing evaluation process – especially where the original accreditation body has been a locally selected company. Held to be a critical component of the overall quality systems process, such recurring checks on the processes employed have tended to be practiced on a six-monthly basis. Yet even where centrally chosen international bodies were utilized, there have been problems with how such checks are actually operationalized in practice. Take the case of the French telecommunications conglomerate Alcatel. This MNC had chosen the world-renowned BVQI (Bureau Veritas Quality International) company from France as its ISO accreditation body. Yet at the business level both the original assessors and the follow-up evaluation critics have all been local employees – whether Malaysian, Singaporean or Thai. The tendency has then been for the assessors to deal primarily with the quality assurance manager from the subsidiary branch involved – who again would tend to be of local origin. Furthermore, such assessors were also effectively customers, even long-term customers, having often been at the accreditation process with a particular company since its initial program implementation. There to check processes and to monitor improvements, these agency representatives were also there to be paid and, inevitably, to maintain business relations with the company. If we read between the lines in such cases, the possibility for societal culture to color these relationships remains as potent as it has proven elusive.

Managers within the ASEAN bloc have traditionally depended on such people-centered business methods over and above the Western preoccupation with systems and processes. In contrast, the foreign MNC has focused on coordinating its working practices on a global scale, practices that can be interchanged and transplanted much more easily if they are clearly definable within the confines of written documents. A systems emphasis is held to encourage uniformity and facilitate the cross-border rotation of managers, a view that is shared by the majority of our local respondents. The flipside of this perceived "systems obsession" on the part of home office is that it is felt to be a harmful factor diverting valuable time and resources away from the far more pressing need to be alert to the needs of the indigenous customer base.

Theoretically, ISO certification provides assurance for an organization's customers that the company's corrective action and complaint resolution processes are doing what they say they are doing. But are the majority of customers in Southeast Asia interested in such claims? Or are they, rather, bound by the traditional norms of reciprocated favors and respect in their relations with suppliers? Possibly the current business environment denotes a varying amalgamation of both, with efforts of extant MNCs being to shift the emphasis toward these global standards. Part of the problem concerns the interpretation of certain terms, themselves an expression of the surrounding culture. According to the quality gurus, what is *measured* is, *ipso facto*, *improved* – yet to the Asian managers a relationship, by its very nature unique, informal and flexible, defies measurement. Quality programs often state the need to determine customer wants and to translate these wants into the language of the corporation. We have often read that understanding the customer's requirements is the "key to all quality." But, again, such claims are viewed with disdain and as often as not dismissed among the local managers in the region – adamant that the global culture of a corporation can never align itself in full with the values of each individual ASEAN market. The standards set by ISO are of necessity a force for standardization and central uniformity – hence by their very nature a contradiction of the front-line practical dealings with domestic customers.

Executive Insights: Relationship versus Accreditation

"My Thai wife owns a middle-of-the-range European car. The maker has a workshop very close to where we live and it certainly has ISO accreditation. She firmly believes that their servicing is well below standard and that their objective is to keep her going there every two or three weeks to have something else done. However, her brother-in-law has been going to a nonfranchised workshop for years now, without any problems and at a reasonable cost. She tells me she'll be taking it to her brother-in-law's workshop in future."

Furthermore, the inherent speed and flexibility deemed crucial to local working practice were felt to be hindered by the Western-led preoccupation with written procedures. This hindrance was exacerbated by the onset of quality systems program implementation. In the words of one local manager, ISO was felt to stifle and kill traditionally small and nimble business structures divided by department. Quality management, as it states, depends on "predictable processes," a "closed loop corrective action process" and a "formal communication methodology" (Corona, 2001) – not one of which appeals in any shape or form to local management. Once again, the problem lies in the varied perceptions of the notion of "flexibility." Corporate critiques of local business methods center on their being depicted as both opaque and unfathomable. Western quality chiefs expressed their unease with the perceived lack of accountability in the traditional Asian methods, one executive remarking that it was practically impossible to find out "just *who* was doing *what*" – especially within the subdepartments, for example that of "Accounts Receivables" team. Yet according to indigenous respondents the Western – so-called "formal" – communication process, expressed in interdepartmental "interface agreements" and held to be integral to the quality process, was derided from the outset as being wholly inappropriate. Similar sentiments were stated with regard to the drafting of an "input/output" matrix along with departmental job description sheets – again held to determine resource needs based on a foundation that emphasizes system over people. Workable relations in the Southeast Asian context depend on informal concepts of give and take, of face, of status, respect – *kreng jai* and *bunkhun* in Thailand, *tiwala* in the Philippines – and a host of other cultural peculiarities. To support these relations the corollary need for flexibility largely rules out the written documentation procedures required of ISO. Simply put, to the average ASEAN manager, ISO, rather than being a "quality stick" with which to be beaten by headquarters, should rather encompass the best way in practice to run a business organization. To this end, although the need to follow a corporate mission statement is generally recognized, so is the practical need for contextual compatibility.

Tentative resolutions

A compromise in headquarters–subsidiary attitudes toward the ISO accreditation implementation process has been partly achieved in recent years. Changes have evolved in a number of organizational spheres involving actions maintained by the corporation, its local branch units and even by the local accreditation bodies themselves. By the second year of economic crisis and with mounting pressures from governmental agencies – from both within and outside of the region – these formerly "relaxed" and informal certification companies with suspected ties to local corporate management were now having to sharpen up their approach. Tightening their own procedures toward the Western/ international standard, these local certification bodies, so long regarded as a soft touch, were no longer willing to play the "relations game" and hand out certificates on the partial basis of personal acquaintance. Against this backdrop the majority of local managers have had to rework their own ISO implementation procedures, bringing them more toward the requisite internal process changes themselves, as opposed to the former preoccupation with, as one respondent put it, the "window dressing."

Some of the implied criticism of these locally based accreditation bodies has also rendered the extant MNCs severely sensitive to the corollary charges of underhand dealings. Certainly it is widely felt that the potential damage done to a company via the practice of effectively "buying" ISO certification would be incalculable. Multinationals have become almost obsessively protective of their brand and wider public images. The – admittedly troublesome – proof of such corporate activity is hence almost unheard of. The habitual resolution of these concerns has been to utilize an international – rather than local – accreditation agency such as SGS or BVQI, and if possible on a global scale. However, and as Alcatel and Castrol – among others – have discovered, such measures are not always enough to ensure guaranteed credibility, at least not in practice. Corporate respondents based across the region have thus stressed the need to be both rigorous and vigilant with the standards and practices employed by both the local agencies themselves and, moreover, the local branches of even world-renowned quality bodies.

Further improvements in acceptability levels, according to a consensus among local staff, stems from a progression of another sort, this time from the heart of the MNCs themselves. As ISO certification has gradually been acquired among increasing numbers of regional subsidiaries there has been a subtle but discernible trend for corporations to then allow their "feet to leave the pedals." A host of multinationals have chosen to relax the stringency levels of their day-to-day quality protocols – not through any slipping of standards but rather as a conscious attempt to render their actions congruent with the societal working norms so far as common sense will allow them. To this end, then, the prior demands for process documentation, job description updates and the like on a quarterly basis were either put on hold or watered down and made an annual concern. In a similar vein, the general amounts of paperwork and resources deployed at the local units of MNCs to both "quality" and ISO were progressively decreased.

The once strict and standard systems and procedures were in effect now being blended with an indigenous culture that stresses flexibility and fluidity. The habitual regulation boundaries have thus been consistently adapted and revised in practice across the spectrum of Western MNC concerns within the region. Traditional working methods, far from being crushed, exist now hand in hand with international business templates in order to optimize the local use and promotion of the quality enhancements set to serve the global market.

Part III
Marketing

In this third part of the book we shift away from the internal, intracorporate focus of Part II and toward the external interface that a multinational business unit in Southeast Asia requires in order to manage its indigenous customer base. The focus of this section is therefore primarily on *marketing*, as the conduit through which the global subsidiary corporation interacts with its domestic environment. Marketing has also traditionally been the strategic function over which local managers have had the greatest control – and poses perhaps the most complex success factor for a contemporary multinational operating in the ASEAN trading bloc.

The chapters in this section will deal with the two salient – though often intertwined – marketing issues affecting multinationals in the region. Both of these are suffused with the age-old debate regarding the relative benefits of global standardization on the one hand versus local adaptation on the other. Our first major line of analysis concerns the differences in business culture between East and West that have been brought to the fore as a result of the Asian economic downturn. As we have seen, the business contraction and heightened instability of the region have led many foreign multinational head offices to seek to bring their "wayward" Asian fiefdoms back into line with corporate marketing norms. These measures – imposed from both Japan and the West – include the reimposition of practices such as tighter documentation control, increased strategy planning, more in-depth marketing research and a reorganization of the current sales and marketing department layouts. Unsurprisingly, many of these measures have been vigorously resisted by the extant local teams on account of their cultural incongruence. Some of them have been modified over time to reflect this – and some of the "hybrid" East–West business practices outlined in previous sections have been mirrored.

Against this backdrop, our second main line of inquiry reexamines the continuing dilemma of how far a corporation can standardize its regional marketing mix without falling foul of individual market-culture differences. In this context we rest exclusively with the local subsidiaries and their domestic-centered dilemmas. For most MNCs, including the big names such as Shell, Procter & Gamble, Coca-Cola, Sony, General Motors, IBM, and so forth, it has always been a shifting battle of global versus local. On the one hand, the rapid industrialization across much of ASEAN during this period has brought unprecedented wealth and power to the region's consumers. A sharp increase in the variety of brands available has transformed Thailand, Malaysia, Singapore, the Philippines, even Vietnam, from a seller's market into one favoring buyers. Partly as a reflection of the nascent individualism seeping into the region's markets, domestic markets are beginning to exist, even thrive, on choice. In general terms Asian consumers are now a younger, middle-class group and their minds are seemingly more open to the global market, holding on far less to any feelings from the past, partly as a reflection of their enthusiastic embrace of new, Internet-based communications media. Needless to say, such changes are consistently publicized by extant MNCs looking to standardize their regional marketing strategies.

But among the domestic management teams there remain powerful dissenting voices. Such critics point out that the so-called rising, choice-oriented Asian middle classes are – and have always been – but a tiny domestic minority. Given the wide disparities in income and industrialization between the core and periphery economies of Southeast Asia, it is therefore unrealistic to expect economic integration of the entire region in either the short or the medium term. More generally, the fundamental complexity of the Southeast Asian markets acts as a continuing and deep-set barrier toward regional uniformity beyond a certain – as yet ill-defined – point on a shifting continuum. While standardization strategies make good sense when applied to a single country – even continent in some cases – the ASEAN bloc houses wide cultural divergencies. The differences within it are held to be larger than those between some of the countries and the USA or Western Europe, itself a somewhat chilling factor affecting retrenchment.

Further, even these domestic markets are depicted as hosting a plethora of internal social and economic divisions. Much of the rapidly gained wealth ascribed to certain of these nations tends to be highly concentrated in one single city, namely Metro Manila in the Philippines, Bangkok in Thailand, Kuala Lumpur in Malaysia, and Vientiane in the Lao PDR. The vast majority of the rural populations have, in stark contrast, gained little or nothing from the years of rapid industrialization. In societies riven with status pointers the agrarian majorities are looked down upon by the urban elites, who show little more than contempt for the peasant culture and lifestyle. Indeed, to the Southeast Asian urbanites the terms "peasant," "villager" and "provincial" are used to imply a lack of education, ambition and sophistication, while from the village or province the city dweller appears to be cosmopolitan and knowledgeable of more modern ways (see also Goss, 2000). Evidently, these important – though often overlooked – societal tensions play a big role in any domestic product positioning strategy.

With the above in mind – and anxious to find a suitable "third way" – the region's corporate cohort has sought to synthesize these opposing forces in the portrayal of a combined – "glocal" – alternative. Yet the twin forces of regional economic collapse and ever-intensifying competition have effectively blown apart any possibility of reconciling the global and local strategic alternatives. In the immediate wake of the crisis the forces for retrenchment, rationalization and standardization were the stronger. More recently – and perhaps fortunately for the local work teams – far-seeing corporations have looked to buck the trend and opt for a more localized market approach.

Reflecting these prime concerns for ASEAN-based multinational corporate operations, our chapter structure for this part of the book runs as follows: Chapter 8 begins our depiction of marketing with an explorative foray into the function itself, and in particular with the changing way in which its role and status are being portrayed and perceived across the region. Included in this account is an explanation of how the incumbent organizational departments have been rethought in the light of recent environmental forces. An attempt will also be made to explain some of the deeper, culturally rooted modes of thinking which imbue indigenous work teams with their respective "takes" on strategic planning, its importance and desirability. Delving into the classic elements of the marketing mix, Chapter 9 examines the shifting global/local forces behind the product positioning debate – encompassing the related issues of brand and price positioning. The ancillary concerns of advertising, promotion and distribution are then pursued through Chapters 10 and 11, which conclude this part of the book.

Throughout these final chapters the underlying focus is on attaining the optimal balance between the twin pillars of global standardization and local customization as the key to sustainable competitive advantage. Viewed as an elusive and shifting point upon a "global–local" continuum, the correct balance of the opposing poles lies, first, in the *identification* of such a point. Many of the factors that determine where this point lies vary from market to market. They will depend on such variables as the maturity of an economy, customer understanding and so forth. Depending on such factors – along with corporate objectives and values – MNCs from Japan and the West tend to lean firmly to one side or the other.

8 The marketing function

- The traditional marketing function
- The rise of Western marketing methodology
- Indigenous resistance
- "Cross-verging" market practice: hybrid working methods
- Localization: general pointers
- Strategic planning

This chapter focuses on the intrinsic properties of the marketing function itself. In particular, we shall take an in-depth look at how the function is perceived and acts both in the home offices of prominent MNCs, and in their domestic Southeast Asian units. As a corollary to this theme we shall also trace the attempts made to impose the "Western" concept of the marketing function and how such imposition was achieved via the reorganization of a number of case-study sales and marketing departments. Focusing on the stage of practical implementation, we shall outline the local challenges to these plans and seek to provide an account of the underlying determinants – the local rationale.

The traditional marketing function

The habitual makeup of a Southeast Asian subsidiary's sales and marketing department comprises a strong Western expatriate influence in the marketing function and a concurrent control of the sales operations by these expatriates' indigenous managerial counterparts. In strictly nominal terms, of course, this may not always be the case. There are many examples of local executives who are billed as "marketing directors," "market development executives," and the like. But in real terms, is the work they actually perform day to day in the realms of "marketing" or, more narrowly, "sales"? – for therein lies a key difference. Traditionally, Asian business culture has tended to give more weighting to the sales function as incorporating the critical company–customer interface. In the Western sense of the word, "marketing" as such has been given barely even a back seat in the strategic hierarchy. Among the vast majority of senior ASEAN-based sales directors the marketing function has been perceived as little more than a backroom administrative function in support of the core sales team.

Acting at the "front line" of customer acquisition and management, the sales function has, by contrast, been held to comprise the key to business success. Basing its work on the local emphasis on long-term and informal networks of business relationships, the sales team will build its expanding core of customers largely via unwritten communication – word of mouth being the obvious example. To this extent the sales teams have traditionally been held to understand customer needs at a far deeper level than their marketing counterparts could ever hope to emulate.

Chinese-oriented management "strategy" is based on a strategy of low margin, high volume to penetrate markets and to guarantee a steady flow of profit. Central to the achievement of these goals is the use of networking within the Chinese community. ASEAN-based marketers therefore need to get to grips with these relationship networks to have any chance of success. Unlike in the West, buyers and sellers in Southeast Asia are seen as active participants in the business transaction. The buyer is not limited to a passive role, and can seek to influence the nature of the marketing inputs that are offered. Indigenous buyer–seller relationships are often long term in nature and tend to be based on mutual trust rather than a formal contract. Because of the intrinsically complex nature of local client–sales relationships – at least, to the untrained eye – marketers and purchasers may be more involved with supporting and maintaining these than with actually buying and selling.

Yet this begs the obvious question: with what, then, have local marketing units traditionally occupied themselves? As we have said, when compared to the sales, finance and production functions, marketing is often looked on as playing a relatively insignificant role in the overall prosperity of the company. In Southeast Asia marketing has traditionally revolved around the duplication of corporate promotion material and the organization of shop signs and posters. There has been little in the way of advertising and promotional campaigns – still less of their postevent evaluation. Similarly, brand-positioning strategy is a most recent and Western-oriented activity, one that has traditionally been overlooked as of little on-the-ground relevance. So far as market research has been concerned, much of what has constituted in-house market share percentage achievements has been based more on gut feeling than on statistical analysis. Much of the type of data habitually utilized in the West is almost nonexistent and should be taken only as the grossest of approximations. This is particularly the case with some of the less accessible nation-states of the Mekong subregion – namely Vietnam, Cambodia, Laos and Myanmar (see also Goss, 2000). In the latter three countries even the World Bank publishes very little information.

The rise of Western marketing methodology

It seems surprising to talk here of the emergence of Western-style methods. Yet there are indisputable signs that in the postcrisis ASEAN business environment, "marketing" – in the Western sense of the word – is being accepted and embraced as of increasing importance. So why is this the case? Partly, certainly, it has been adopted to meet the new and almost alien challenges of Southeast Asia's own changing and modernizing home markets – founded on their rapid industrialization over the past two decades. As the domestic markets of Southeast Asia continue to develop, they have become simultaneously more sophisticated and more stagnant. Growth in the wake of the crisis is on the rebound and consumption has been creeping back up to previous levels. Asia's consumers have become more discerning. They want better value for money and more attention paid to the quality of service. For the Japanese and Western multinationals this obviously poses numerous advantages – not merely for the growing necessity of pushing home office marketing methods but also for its intrinsic push toward regional standardization possibilities. As numerous executives expounded to us, the marketing dynamics in Thailand, Indonesia, Malaysia and the Philippines are essentially the same – and have been broadened in the postcrisis years.

Within this environment there is an apparent desire for MNCs to take fuller advantage of their global competitive assets – specifically in terms of new products and superior production processes, on top of their marketing skills. Taken together, these advantages have enabled them to differentiate their products through innovation and design rather than just price competitiveness. Using the regional downturn as a catalyst for the imposition of some of these skill-sets, foreign MNCs have increased their influence at the ASEAN business unit level. Some of the changes involved at this juncture have involved fundamental changes in strategic direction. Foremost among these stands the example of the Anglo-Dutch consumer goods conglomerate Unilever. Having localized heavily in the

1980s, Unilever has recently retrenched its traditional position and is now in retreat, slashing its portfolio of 1,600 brands down to less than 400. More generally, debates were held with regard to redirecting ASEAN business units away from their traditional, sales-oriented, volume emphasis and toward the profitability criteria of their global head offices.

Other – more usual – examples are less extreme. A number of Western marketing managers working for local business units have cited a reinforcement of home office transparency policies within the marketing planning reports. Traditionally, it was claimed that the expatriate CEOs of regional units had often tended to "shield" their local management teams at corporate budget meetings. This stemmed from a number of factors, usually those of impressive sales growth figures coupled with a regional aversion to providing detailed written market reports. However, in the immediate postcrisis environment centralized audits conducted in the region uncovered alarming discrepancies in some of the data being proffered. Whereas corporate figures for such issues as market share were between, say, 5 and 7 percent, the corollary percentages issued by locally employed market research agencies were up to double this amount. Unsurprisingly, home office representatives from the companies involved voiced their suspicions of "foul play" and "number massage" to give a false – more favorable – impression of their progress. Further criticisms were made of local units that still resisted home office marketing strategy for their lack of compliance and cohesiveness.

Revision of marketing practice

Moves were initiated from both Western and Japanese headquarters designed to simplify and standardize existing reporting procedures. This desire on the part of global MNCs to integrate their documents was intended to achieve a uniformity in understanding, ensuring that corporate head offices receive consistent and reliable data sufficient for regional and/or worldwide comparison. The onset of economic collapse drew a wave of more "hard-line" programs of change, with many multinationals demanding the issue of timely, regulated "strat-plan" documents in line with global business norms. Broader directives concerned the requisite formulation of management information systems in order to be able to supply this information. Western conglomerates, in particular, were anxious to secure updates on how their ASEAN divisions were to split their marketing budgets between the various product ranges and also on the various media. Locally employed market intelligence agencies were also systematically replaced during this period, or backed up with corporate-sponsored alternatives engaged to undertake research fieldwork in line with global norms. Normally either the AMI group or A. C. Nielsen was used.

At a more informal level, Western MNCs looking to have their domestic marketing practices replicated sought to institute more frequent marketing strategy meetings. The former CEO of Castrol (Malaysia) Ltd provided us with one of a number of examples of this:

> "The usual practice in K[uala] L[umpur] under the old regime was to have just one meeting every week. This would be held on a Monday morning and it would last one or maybe two hours. What I wanted was for each department to hold their own internal meetings every morning from 8.45 to 9 o'clock. In order to make sure that this was being done and . . . to maintain momentum . . . I'd make sure I'd attend as many of these as possible, although of course without letting the local heads know in advance which particular meeting I'd be attending."

In order to help instigate more of a Western interest in and approach to what were previously alien marketing concepts, several other "off the record" techniques were described to us. One involved the "strategic" placing of marketing-oriented posters, books and articles around the relevant unit's premises – with understandably mixed results. At one particular company the office of the newly recruited marketing manager came to double as a kind of marketing theory library for his direct reports. Moves were then also made to institute more Western-driven marketing training programs – often at the expense of the "fun-style" training course of the past (as outlined in Chapter 5).

Departmental restructuring

One major new initiative concerns the widespread corporate reorganization of existing ASEAN sales and marketing departments, depicted as having been "offbeat" and "idiosyncratic" in the precrisis decades. Much of the focus involved bringing these errant organizational subsidiaries "back into line" with regional and/or global corporate guidelines. The consensus among our expatriate informants was that it was necessary to equip these units with a strengthened marketing team at the expense – if need be – of sales. At several corporations – including the majority of our Japanese cohort – this wholesale division of the sales and marketing functions was avoided, as were external recruitment programs to bolster existing skill-sets. Nonetheless, each and every organization claimed to have shifted more unit resources to the marketing function in the Western sense of the term.

Prior to the crash of 1997 the typical ASEAN-based sales and marketing setup would have its sales and marketing functions intertwined – but with sales to the fore. Among the departmental director's trusted lieutenants would be a senior sales manager who would also act as the department's strategist. The requisite – and often periodical – corporate advertising and promotional campaigns would be drafted and enacted in-house – as were all necessary planning documents, often as merely a sop to home office demands. Among an overall department of – say – a dozen managers, perhaps two or three at the most would be given the "marketing" designation to describe their role. These particular staff members would then usually be viewed as occupying a "less essential" role than their sales counterparts. Typically they would be concerned with signage coordination, stock control and liaising with external advertising agencies.

In order to break this traditional sales grip on power, the subsequent split of these existing operations was often accompanied by a realignment of reporting procedures and a program of external recruitment. To begin with, a host of "new marketing" positions were placed under the direct auspices of the relevant unit's chief of staff. Depending on the stage and extent of business streaming employed, the combined department itself was then repositioned to a regional level to be coordinated in strategic and organizational terms by corporate regional controllers. Within the domestic unit itself, a number of externally appointed marketing managers were then drafted in – sometimes at the direct behest and approval of the incumbent CEO, often in spite of the stated policy of "head count freezes." Typically, a hand-picked – sometimes head-hunted – director, whether of local, Western or "mixed" descent, would be drafted in to oversee both divisions. This executive would then him- or herself be charged with bringing in several other new managers to shore up operations. And whereas the previous sales chiefs were usually allowed to retain their former titles and perks as a sop to the regional stress on "face" and "status," the effective demotion of their roles was evident for all to see.

As well as this movement of top managers into these expanding marketing divisions there was a concurrent shifting of roles among the

Executive Insights: Overpromotion

"Reorganization is always difficult to 'sell' and implement, because in both East and West there is always an element of loss of status and loss of face for someone. Only when a company is growing quickly and everyone involved is promoted is this not the case. Americans may be a little more ready to accept the need for change, as US companies tend to have less constrained 'hire and fire' policies than their European counterparts. Employees of US companies don't appear quite so fazed about being fired, as they are more likely to be out the same afternoon looking for a new job and – pre-September 11th – would invariably land one.

"But in the East it's a much more delicate matter. What is effectively a demotion has to be disguised as a sideways move if possible, and privileges and perks be maintained or even improved to minimize any loss of face. It's more difficult when someone has been overpromoted within a fast-growing operation. Overpromotion happens everywhere and in almost every company, and putting it right always causes pain and strain and – of course – cost. In fact, while existing employees should always be considered first for promotion in my view, recruitment from outside of someone with additional skill-sets is always preferable to overpromoting someone who may not have the capacity both mentally and physically to take on additional responsibility. As with all HR issues – proceed with care!"

lower ranks. This is illustrated by events at the Malay, Indonesian and Thai offices of a European telecommunications equipment manufacturer. Within the new sales and marketing structure each "marketing manager" was now to have a direct sales counterpart in terms of both territory and product groupings, as part of the new-found aim to get both functions working more closely together. At the Thai office the new end-of-month company "beer busts" for marketing staff to enjoy with their sales representatives back from the field proved to be an informal yet integral part of this process. Finally, the in-house recruitment notices utilized at this – and a score of other – foreign MNCs in order to obtain the "appropriate" staff provide further illustration as to the gradual shift toward the Western-oriented marketing approach. Placed in both the local and the English-language dailies – and sometimes exclusively in the latter – the adverts would almost always specify the possession of an MBA qualification (preferably from a US university) and a high standard of English language proficiency.

As regards the average sales representative, along with the majority of lower-level staff coordinators and supervisors these were subsequently trained in home office-style marketing techniques, either via an approved

Coca-Cola on the Mekong

Coca-Cola's recent push to expand its presence in the Mekong Delta markets has been widely documented in the local business press. Held as the polar opposite to Unilever's decision to retrench its product range, Coca-Cola has entered on a bold, trend-bucking policy of domestic marketing localization, rightly depicted as a bold new chapter in the company's regional history. Coca-Cola's objective within the Mekong is to replicate and widen the 2:1 profit-share leadership it has achieved in the Vietnamese city of Ho Chi Minh. In the attainment of this goal, the company strives to capture what it depicts as "every potential consumer opportunity" via the execution of a "five-star" channel strategy. This strategy seeks to mix and match the classic elements of the marketing mix in a new concoction of measurements and ratios. Stated otherwise, Coca-Cola's main thrust seeks to connect *when* ("activity") and *why* (i.e. "need") consumers drink beverages with *how* they shop for them. In order to do this there must be a two-pronged focus on marketing *within* as well as *outside* the location denoted as the point of consumer purchase. Coca-Cola claims that if it can actively market *inside* the store to all the consumers' beverage needs occurring *outside* the store, then it will effectively drive both incremental purchases and consumption occasions. The corporation aims to pull ahead from simply putting its brands within an arm's reach of desire to "creating desire within arm's reach." Via the route of quality differentiation at the point of purchase, Coca-Cola seeks to win local consumers on the strength of the global brand name in tandem with a viable strategy of distribution congruence. A host of "MITs" (Merchandising Impact Teams) have since been trained and prepared to ably assist in the realization of Coca-Cola's ambitions across the Mekong Delta. We await the interim results of this localized campaign with some interest.

external body or by visiting corporate specialists – or a combination of the two. At the lubricant marketer Castrol's regional branch offices, the globally coordinated induction had often been bypassed in previous years – a reflection, it was held, of the idiosyncratic nature of the respective domestic markets. But this was "restructured" in the postcrisis years in favor of an instituted series of region-wide "refresher courses" that focused on core corporate values, instanced by the stated values of being "marketing led," "technology focused" and of "premium quality" caliber: "The Lubricants Specialist."

Indigenous resistance

As a corollary to these changes, it behoves us at this point to touch upon the indigenous unease and dissatisfaction felt at the stage of implementation. The progressive transference of "the marketing function"

from the former sales directors to the new marketing team was a
particular cause of bitter resentment, recrimination and even resignations.
Even the nominally innocuous switch from a "volume" to a "profitability"
emphasis was regarded with marked consternation, especially among
sales teams habituated with meeting and beating the old-style "unit-
shifter" targets. Against this backdrop the challenge ahead – and in
particular for the Western-parented companies – lay not so much in the
redrawing of structural boundaries, as in successfully *operationalizing* a
long-term adoption of change among the local teams. Its successful
institutionalization and enactment among the locally led sales teams –
with their powerful hold over key account portfolios – was therefore of
primary concern.

The sense of being wronged felt by many indigenous marketing managers
was compounded by their insistence on their own in-depth knowledge of
their respective markets – knowledge they would claim could never be
replicated by the incoming strategic "experts." Many of the corporate
"audit teams" sent in the immediate postcrisis period were strongly
criticized for their lack of understanding as to the wants and needs of
customers in the ASEAN bloc. Such criticisms were held to have been
borne out by the subsequent difficulties encountered when trying to
implement some of these new practices in the field. According to
numerous local sources, this evident lack of understanding is well
illustrated by the failure of expatriate marketing personnel to appreciate
the strength and ability of indigenous competitors. Local firms, it is
claimed, are often the most dangerous competitors owing to their speed,
knowledge and comprehension of their native environments.

Through the *guanxi* network local companies can readily gain access to
the necessary market data, for instance on how to scan, interpret and
verify contextual changes and uncertainty. Their inbred familiarity and
experience with the local environment equips them with information
which would otherwise prove both elusive and extremely costly to a
foreign entrant, especially in a region where the indigenous traditions and
practices are so different from those in the West. On a broader level,
Southeast Asian business culture tends to be more strategically flexible
than its occidental counterpart. Local marketers are therefore imbued with
the ability to configure their processes more ably to the local environment
– and certainly with greater success than via using the Western-favored
"arm's-length" approach (Luo, 1999; Muralidharan and Hamilton, 1999).
Within this context the successful trading operation tends to depend more
upon relationships with customers and suppliers – however much

influenced by Western theories and practice. Such "bamboo networks" continue to afford the local sales representatives team an "ear" as to what the local customers really want and need. Through these *guanxi* ties the input of the traditional sales and marketing managers should be one that Western parent firms seek to take advantage of and utilize – rather than simply attempting to conform to global corporate norms.

Not surprisingly, the imposition of a policy to split the sales and marketing functions – and in particular that of seeking to enhance the latter at the expense of traditional methods – drew a strong and sustained reaction from a cross section of subsidiary employees. A number of former sales directors pointed with a mixture of wounded pride and resentment at their seemingly forgotten decade-long run of rising volume growth achievements. Added to this were their initial feelings of incredulity when confronted with the "new-style" marketing activities under the direction of the so-called experts – tasks which they themselves perceived as being both pointless and fanciful. These were instanced by the apparent time consumed by the new marketing teams on "playing with computers," regarded by the sales teams as being a waste of limited resources.

Further critiques by these disgruntled local managers focused on the profiles of the personnel being drafted in. These new, young recruits with their Western MBAs were criticized for their perceived lack of on-the-ground international business experience. With their supposed expertise in marketing theory and diplomatic competencies, these new managers were being asked to demonstrate both their local business understanding and their so-called mastery of intercultural awareness. The severest criticisms were reserved for the "top dogs," often expatriate chiefs who had been drafted in to head up these newly realigned departments. Often posted on a fixed, relatively short-term contract in the crisis aftermath, these executives were berated for producing perhaps a half-dozen reports at great expense and of ultimately little use in either acquiring new local customers or, more importantly, maintaining relations with existing ones. They were compared unfavorably with the local Malay, Vietnamese or Indonesian managers who, for a fraction of the pay and prestige of their newly installed bosses, remained unheeded at the real "coalface," yet were deemed to be much more knowledgeable of the local business environment.

With their traditional sales-driven approach, indigenous marketing teams reiterated their claim to understanding the traditional customer interface and the desires of the market much more thoroughly. To the fore of their responses was the distinctly Chinese-oriented importance of the relations network between the sales representative and his or her customer, particularly in regions where the ethnic influence of first- and second-generation Chinese was especially strong. Over the course of the years that followed, some of these remaining sales managers have remained steadfastly of the opinion that the original postcrisis changes imposed by the big Western MNCs were culturally incongruent in both their objectives and implementation methods:

> "For my mind I cannot see how the foreigners can tell us how we think. How can they know how the local people decide how they buy something and how much they will pay? . . . and all of this kind of thing. How can anybody know how the local people think if they are not from the local country? We still waiting for them to tell us this."

Much of the local employee resistance to MNC directives occurred on a semisecret basis. A fair amount of it incorporated a stress upon local networking skills to hold on to existing customers in the traditional manner. By way of example, corporate attempts to redefine "product territories" were rendered impotent by the continued sales usage of their traditional customer ties. It was found that these were much stronger and deeper than corporate home office had initially envisaged. At one company we discovered evidence of a covert "counteremphasis" whereby added staff and resources were switched from the more profitable metropolitan hubs back to a renewed focus on the predominantly agrarian, up-country provinces. Confined to the relative safety of the ad hoc

Executive Insights: It's Your Country

"I said to them, 'Okay, we have a problem. What do you think we should do?' Then comes a period of silence, because you're the boss and expected to know all the answers. So, I went on, 'Look – this is your country and you'll be here long after I've left, so what do you think we should do?' Often the suggestions would be quite novel and surprising, so the next question is 'Why do you think we should do it that way?'

"This process helps the expatriate CEO to learn about local thinking processes and about the people and customers' expectations. It also helps the local executive to think things through – if he hasn't already done so. More importantly, whatever decision you reach together, you'll both have contributed and you're more likely to gain clear commitment on the line of action you've decided to take. And you're likely to be right!"

Castrol (Laos) in Training Mode: A Communication Cauldron

Following years of underachievement in this least developed of Mekong markets, Castrol (Laos) Ltd sought to establish its brand once again via a planned market relaunch in the summer of 1996. Prompted by a series of criticisms from its existing distributor in Laos, Castrol plucked a new recruit from the UK and gave him the sole task of developing this poor and scattered market. One of his first tasks was to rekindle relationships strained by years of neglect, and then progressively to nurture and train the relevant Lao representatives. A simple enough task, surely? But this was not to be.

Castrol's agent in Laos was – and still is – the family-owned KP group, chosen mainly for the solid governmental contacts and business expertise of its chairman. In 1994, one year after the initiation of this rapport, this Lao organization became part of an international joint venture formed with the US trading house Connell Bros Co. This new organization – renamed Connell Bros KP Laos – then set about working with the new Castrol executive in the redefinition and achievement of a fresh set of market objectives. As part of this development program a team of Laotians from the KP local offices were sent across the border to Bangkok in order to take part in a week-long "Castrolization" training program. And this is where the fun began.

Communication between the Laos and Thais itself was not such a problem. Indeed, the Lao language is almost identical to the dialect spoken in the northeastern Isan region of Thailand. However, as already noted, the executive overseeing the operation was an Englishman – and anything but fluent in either Thai, Lao or the Isan dialect! Fortunately, a relatively educated member of the Lao team was able to get by in a passable level of English – and instructions and limited small talk were thereby relayed back among the team. Unfortunately, on the fifth and final day of the program this senior member of the delegation failed to materialize at the Castrol office – apparently owing to having "overindulged" at one of the city's infamous watering holes the previous evening. The remaining team members were on a field trip around the Castrol Pitstop outlets – guided by their UK overseer, pondering the seemingly insurmountable linguistic barriers that now divided them. Quite unexpectedly, however, it transpired that another, older member of the Lao team, although unable to speak *English*, was able to communicate in broken *French*. Again, and purely by chance, so was our UK guide – which rendered things slightly less difficult. The reason for this latter linguistic achievement was, of course, the fact that Laos was for many years a former colony of France – French still being widely spoken among the educated older generation.

Toward the end of the tour, channels of communication were again seemingly broken by the loss of the Francophone in a downtown department store (Castrol's newest and fastest-growing distribution outlet). Resigned to an endgame marked by hand signals and silence, the UK executive was astonished to find that from among the Lao team there was yet another language being proffered – possibly as one final way out of the continuing communication predicament. To his dull and tiring sense the political foundations for this addition – later explained by an international colleague over dinner – seemed both logical and predictable. For, as well as the traditional French colonial influence, there was a second wave of cultural and territorial control exerted in the second half of the last century: that is by the Soviet Union. And yet, while the group members were standing in an increasingly perplexed huddle about the Castrol wares in the downtown branch of Central Plaza, the proffering of a multiphrase depiction of intent in the *Russian* tongue came as the proverbial straw to break the camel's back. With a hasty retreat into sign language, the remaining members – including the exhausted UK leader – quickly fell into the simplest common language known to man: enduring fits of laughter!

departmental briefing session, sales representatives were advised to spend more time in the field and less at head office, only to come back for a maximum of three nights at the end of each month for the departmental rally and also to be made aware of the new marketing plans and promotions for the month ahead.

Market research

In the wake of the cataclysmic events of 1997, a cross section of Japanese and Western-based multinationals sought to exert increasing levels of control upon their ASEAN subsidiaries' marketing strategies. A major plank of these initiatives involved both the gathering and the presentation of market data in an attempt to render the process both effective and transparent. This is exemplified by BP's reimposing its global consumer categories of "enthusiastic," "appreciative" or "uninterested" upon its newly acquired Castrol ASEAN units. Yet there were major problems encountered in making "effectiveness" and "transparency" into mutually inclusive factors.

At the simplest level the kind of data-sets so esteemed in the West are both expensive and time-consuming to compile in Southeast Asia – especially in the less developed markets of the Mekong Delta. There have also been serious queries as to the inherent reliability of the research presented, queries concerning, in particular, the *manner* by which data are collected by local agency teams, as well as how information is proffered by respondents.

Foreign MNCs have traditionally opted for the acquisition of large-scale data sets – e.g. via questionnaires – which generate standardized data at a relatively limited cost. The inherent problem with such methods is that the evidence gleaned is often superficial and predetermined. This disadvantage is magnified in ASEAN markets, mainly owing to the ethnocentrism of the questions posed, compounded by the underestimated problems of utilizing translation/back-translation techniques in overcoming linguistic difficulties. Many of the core questions highly relevant to Western audiences can carry very little weight in Southeast Asia – even given a decent stab at translation. For this reason, unexpected findings are difficult to generalize and validate. People's responses in Southeast Asia tend not to fit the pigeonholes imposed from methods employed in the West. Campaigns held in the home country which have elicited clear and sharp segmentation landscapes may seem more blurred and ill-defined when applied to ASEAN markets. Quite simply, the mindset of respondents does not necessarily match that of the inquirers.

At the general level, global corporations have for too long been duped by the logic of "you get what you pay for" in markets expressing high levels of cultural distance. Marketing services regarded as "modern" put their faith in the quantitative research technique underpinned by intimidating sets of statistics. Yet in the field, local marketers have stressed the viability of instinctive, intuitive data-gathering techniques based on the day-to-day feedback from sales representatives, test introductions and years of personal field experience. Apart from this variance as to what actually constitutes *valid* market research, further difficulties have then tended to emerge once new corporate policies are implemented at ground level. Research generated today and relating to the future relies on the past – at least to the typical mindsets of the West. But digging up the relevant data at many ASEAN units has proven to be extremely problematic. Assuming there was any depth of documentation stored in the first place, often this had been hastily composed with little attention paid to accuracy, merely for the sake of paying lip service to yearly corporate budget directives. This is understandable – especially since the information was assembled during the boom years of unprecedented market growth and profitability levels (trends, after all, that were expected to continue).

In the immediate postcrisis period, visiting market audit teams – of both internal and external origin – were often perplexed by the lack of substantive, *written* market data. Again, especially in the mid and lower-end markets from Thailand down to Myanmar, respondents were dismayed by the difficulties involved in finding, for example, up-to-date maps of critical urban hubs, as well as written lists of business suppliers, contacts, customers, and so on. Local managers were characteristically unrepentant – why look for bits of paper when it was all stored in their heads? Further complications arose in seeking to identify and compare the relevant cost components involved, and in seeking to translate home office guidelines into local terms on the back of the plethora of opaque and fragmented (mis)information with which these teams were being presented.

The regularity and depth of the responses to newly drawn market survey questionnaires are a further source of contention. As a result of societal idiosyncrasies, certain industries gained a far higher response rate than others. For example, when people are asked about their personal cars, response rates have traditionally been very high. The car, in East Asia, has always been a critical determinant of one's all-important status within society – adding valuable, visible "face" to the title on one's business card. Obviously, with the rise of "vulture sales" in the face of the regional economic downturn, this trend was jolted somewhat, but the fundamentals remain: cars have much higher status connotations than those for one's brand of shampoo, life assurance or coffee. Yet even where answers are given in equal depth, problems still remain. Like the use of Western "job evaluation" techniques outlined in Chapter 5, the use of the familiar Likert scale of preference gauging on the Asian consumer threw up obstacles to valid cross-national comparison. For example, of five gradings ranging from a 1 for "very good" through to a 5 for "very poor," respondents would, typically, rarely use any figures below a 2 or maybe a 3 – seemingly for fear of causing offense or loss of face. Held to be opaque and inscrutable, the Asian-raised consumer tends to express what he or she perceives to be the "correct" answer. Hence, when seeking to contrast these data with those garnered from the West, a "discount scale" was initiated by the larger international market research agencies.

One way out of this conundrum – increasingly utilized by Western MNCs such as A. C. Nielsen and AMI – is to support and qualify existing data with new information gained from a series of more *qualitative*-based techniques. The classic method has been to use the focus group throughout the region: small, selected teams of representative consumers. However, current thinking has again moved toward tradition – even in this respect. Of our local management informants the majority decried the validity of this method – sensing it to be "fake" and stilted. They placed more weight on random interviews of locals in the street, claiming that these bore far more value as being more "real" – especially when conducted at an in-depth level.

Such case studies – founded on interview and observation – provide data at closer levels, revealing unforeseen issues and rationales. Care must be taken with presented stimuli, for cultures vary in their focus. Often it is stated that Asians tend to center on the visual at the expense of what they hear. This is held to be in direct contrast to the situation found in the West. Yet even here a high degree of sensitivity fails to overcome more basic barriers. Such methods are comparatively expensive and require an extensive knowledge of the society and its language in order to interpret the findings fully – findings that themselves are then hard to generalize beyond the boundaries of the region. This leads us back to stating why the local managers continued to balk at changes, perceiving them as typically crass and naive. As one respondent put it,

> "Why spend all this time and money on these things you call research? The only way to know and understand your market is to know your customers. This is what we say for many years, and this is what we want here. Because up to now we get our data through our distribution channels. We use our people because they have the relations with their customers. And all your graphs and policies cannot compare to this way, never . . . no matter what the situation of the economy may be. The customers they know themselves – and who can know them more than this?"

Marketing meetings

A similar variation in perspective caused a host of other difficulties for foreign MNCs seeking to try to render "marketing" a uniform discipline. Examples of how Western-style meetings were imposed and structured give us one clear illustration. Corporate demands – on paper seeming to be astute and commonsense recommendations – tended in practice to betray ignorance of "on-the-ground" business cultures. To begin with, the very concept of the "marketing meeting" in much of the developing countries of ASEAN bears little if any resemblance to such meetings undertaken in the West. Western expatriates come from environments which encourage frankness in meetings, and quality feedback – and expect to find the same abroad. And yet in much of Eastern Asia meetings are always very formal affairs where the junior staff and management sit and listen to departmental directives issued by the respective divisional heads. In this respect there is little input or contribution of ideas by staff unless they are specifically invited to participate – in which case, comments made are brief and respectfully discreet. Because of the elevated importance of "respect" and "conformity," question-and-answer sessions are hardly ventured because of the fear that this may be taken as a criticism of the "superiors" present. The avoidance of confrontation often means that whatever the outcome of a departmental meeting, employees present may – if they either disagree with a notion or find it impossible to enact – simply choose to instigate differing measures, ones agreed among their own little subgroups within the unit. For this reason, the corporate call for more meetings to be held was greeted at the local level with a mixture of bemusement and skepticism that they would ever see the light of day.

Market objectives

The sales-led mentality of the incumbent ASEAN management structure has traditionally nurtured a concurrent stress on volume sales over profitability. Employee targets measured month by month at the majority of regional subsidiary groups have tended to foster a culture in which the mass-market, bread-and-butter product or service has taken priority over the top-end, premium range. This ordering of priorities, not surprisingly, has often been at odds with MNC home office preferences. Faced with a booming set of market environments through much of the late 1980s and 90s, MNCs generally sought to try to "trade up" the local consumers – as well as simply selling them more. But with the ensuing downturn of the regional economy this long-term aim was sorely tested. With a reduction in their purchasing power, consumers claimed as having traded up now turned back to cheaper alternatives. Nonetheless, the dogged MNCs have – in the main – stuck firm to their long-term strategy goals.

To this end, sales commissions were restructured, and increasingly so in the postcrisis years. The methods used, although sometimes opaque, were often fairly simple. At Castrol Asia-Pacific, traditional commissions based solely on calculations of the number of liters sold were switched to encompass the gross profit levels earned by individual product lines. Notwithstanding such logical adjustments, however, local resentment simmered. The changes were considered inappropriate and unfair in the local business context. In the case of Castrol (Thailand), concern was expressed about the differing levels of purchasing power throughout the domestic regions, notably in the north and northeast of the country. The feeling in the senior sales team was that this Western-oriented policy had been instituted without proper attention being paid to the vagaries of the Thai customer base.

To paraphrase one executive, traditional home office policy has been to allow its ASEAN subsidiary units to work according to their own goals and methods based on *local* customers and their *local* buying behavior in the context of *local* competition. The system of rewarding volume sales on a month-by-month basis, far from being "backward," was stressed by this respondent to be an appropriate motivating factor: "This way it success for us all in the past – so why do we want to change it now?"

Other indigenous business units – from other industries, other countries – spoke in a similar vein. The management team of an Indonesian-based Western trading house voiced their own concerns with objective changes imposed from overseas. Foremost among these was the concept of "maximum profit flow" and the diversion of emphases with which it became associated. The local critique of such objective changes raised the anxiety felt among local managers about the attendant scrapping of traditional targets of market share attainment. Chasing market share with sales teams at the helm was deemed to have been a major plank of the unit's prior success levels. Ditching such aims was therefore both incongruent and steeped in risk. The rationale was largely twofold: first, market share is held to be just and entails a fair split of the country – similar to the opinions put foward at Castrol Thailand. Second, the "profit shift," where rewards are linked to margins made, tends to favor the major cities at the expense of the nation's geographical rump. This is because wealth, resources and purchasing power levels have spiraled upward in the cities in the wake of economic prosperity and growth. Wealthier city inhabitants tend to "trade up" to higher-margin products as a result – leaving managers responsible for their less developed up-country counterparts at a serious disadvantage.

Ironically, although professed with some vigor among our Indonesian informants, this factor is actually more pronounced in several other countries in the region – notably in the Philippines, Laos and Thailand, where the stated "primacy indexes" (i.e. difference between first and second cities) are among the highest in the world. Respectively, Metro Manila, Vientiane and Bangkok dwarf their nearest rivals in terms of both wealth and population size. And even Vietnam shows a parallel concentration of resource, albeit housed in two cities – namely, Hanoi in the north and Ho Chi Minh in the south. The broader concern with pushing profitability targets over those of straight sales is summarized by an employee from the oil group Mobil – itself subject to the creed of maximum profit flow for a number of years:

> "[Head office] always talking about this, to make maximum profit, to make 12 or 15 percent return on assets around the world, but here in the real place we also have to make sure our price is user-friendly in

practice, for the local man. So we also work back from this end as
well, from the customer back to the figure – because the customer
pays my salary, pays your salary."

"Cross-verging" market practice: hybrid working methods

In the months and years since our original rounds of interviews, the
balance of power between MNC headquarters and their once "errant"
Southeast Asian business units has shifted once again – but this time
toward a compromise. In particular, corporate envoys and incumbent
expatriate executives gradually came to acknowledge the importance of
local business mores and practice, and the contextual rationale that
underpins them. The Chinese ethnic ties that cross-weave much of the
regional customer base have led a substantial number of MNCs to rethink
their core "marketing-led" ideologies in favor of a more Asian, "sales-
based" approach. Of especial interest here is the way in which a cross
section of multinationals have effectively "blended" their home and
locally based methods in order to gain an optimal mix of market aims and
methods.

In practical terms these concessions from home office bases led to their
actually encouraging the local sales teams to spend more time in the field,
as per the indigenous tradition. According to the corporate executives
questioned on this relinquishment of their initial postcrisis standardization
policies, such moves were designed to enhance the group's edge in the
local relationship networking "scene," working with – rather than against
– indigenous business methods.

Held to reiterate a corporation's long-term "commitment" to a particular
market, a main plank of Western concessions revolved around the notion
of nurturing Asian-style business networks while *simultaneously*
imposing Western-style market planning techniques back at the office.
Such methods are depicted – simplistically? – as the "win–win" approach
to successful regional business operations. For example, the expatriate
managers of some companies, such as Procter & Gamble in Vietnam,
were lauded for adapting their US management communication styles to
reflect the vagaries of the local environment. In terms of general
marketing strategy, the company was seen to partially implement the
recommendations of locally based corporate analysts. Sticking to their
standardizing policy with regard to overarching strategic policy, Procter &
Gamble proved themselves also able to follow a diluted adaptation

approach with regard to sales and marketing strategy, tailored to local societal norms and tastes

A number of more precise, detailed activities were instituted by MNCs to make the best of existing bonfires of current marketing practice. A cross section of expatriates outlined their plans – some already adopted – to restructure the salary scales across their newly divided sales and marketing departments. Not surprisingly, the sop to the traditional working ways was to increase the commission bands for the sales teams – in practice allowing them to earn up to twice as much as their marketing counterparts. Held to be a long-deserved reflection of their often "crazy" lives based around customer functions and antisocial hours, the measures were also perceived as being a tacit shift toward the traditional local definitions of "sales" on the one hand and "marketing" on the other, with the preeminence swinging back to the former.

One other example of how the two functions were rebalanced concerns their respective working interface arrangements. More precisely, a host of companies came around to the practice of enacting both *direct* and *indirect* lines of communication between the two departments – not merely between themselves but, crucially, with customers on the one hand and the incumbent Western CEO on the other. In the majority of cases a direct line of working between the sales team and its customers was established, a move which was viewed with particular satisfaction by weary sales managers, with their traditional emphasis upon business relationships. By contrast, the customer lines to the new marketing team were of an almost exclusively indirect nature. All contact with the company's customers was henceforth to emerge exclusively via their sales counterparts, effectively shielding the marketing personnel from the customer interface.

To offset this "imbalance," the sales team was to hold but a "dotted-line" or indirect working rapport with incumbent – predominantly Western – chief executives, as opposed to the "direct" line given over to new marketing. This was judged by respondents to be a satisfactory – if not optimal – compromise solution for the companies involved; it permitted them to take advantage of both group and subsidiary "best working practices." Local managers felt that they were supported now in doing what they did best: maintaining relations networks among their indigenous clientele. The new marketing teams, usually similarly satisfied, were keen to stress that the new structure provided them with a new base of power via their direct line to the respective country manager – a factor which would in practice make the sales team wary of "crossing" them.

Finally, the running disagreement over the imposition of profit targets was also partially settled, at least in certain sectors of the corporate landscape. We note with interest the move by a host of resident MNCs to keep the profitability stress intact in the higher-income cities while at the same time "phasing in" the traditional idea of volume sales through the poorer regions in order to reflect the country's high wealth disparities. This was also applauded by respondents as "leveling the field" between sales representatives, making the attainment of objectives equally and fairly achievable throughout the whole country.

An Equipment Services Division in ASEAN: Castrol's Secret Weapon

In the year prior to the crash of 1997, Castrol's successful Thai unit decided to try to introduce an Equipment Services Division, following the example of its operation in Malaysia and modeled on the highly successful UK model. "ESD" consisted of a special team of managers positioned as a major attack weapon in securing long-term contracts with existing and potential automotive dealerships. As in the UK, this newly instituted division was to work from within the sales and marketing department, with responsibility for equipment, technical advice and workshop design facilities.

Among the Thai management team of the era, however, the whole system was rejected as being contextually inappropriate. Why? To begin with, the local market segmentation structure was held to be quite different from either its UK or its Malay counterparts. The lubricants industry in Thailand is loosely split into seven separate distribution channels of which the franchised dealerships account for a relatively low percentage of revenue. This contrasts with the UK, in which the market predominantly comprises large franchised dealers who are more in need of workshop design and equipment advice and by whom the concept of "ESD" can be understood.

Furthermore, the working processes assumed by the ESD unit were held by the vast majority of interviewees to be culturally misaligned. The formality, professional and official nature of the ESD setup – deemed in the West to be its strong point – was branded "useless," "unsuitable" and "damaging" in an environment where customers were gained and held almost purely on the basis of personal relationships. The notion of drawing up a contract for the supply of "free" equipment to outlet owners in exchange for their selling Castrol lubricants exclusively was deemed unenforceable in practice. Thai customers, unlike their Western counterparts, are regarded as having little knowledge of – and even less respect for – the law, a fact borne out by respondents with numerous tales of gun threats in situations where local representatives had sought to try to make them comply with what were perceived as alien rules and regulations.

Faced with these continuing local objections, the ESD unit – and its corporate-chosen head in particular – was effectively ignored throughout the crisis year by local senior management. Quite apart from its planned role in theory, in practice the unit was shunted to having a powerless, almost symbolic role within the organization. The Thai management team were essentially and vociferously opposed to this perceived attempt at breaking down their traditional and revered methods of sales control. In view of this unexpectedly severe backlash, in a change of heart the ESD unit was eventually broken up toward the end of 1997. This move was further welcomed when the component parts were redistributed among the existing power structure. For example, "workshop design" was placed under the control of an old and well-regarded local sales executive. "Equipment loan" itself was then transferred toward the local administrative staff – mainly drawn from marketing. A direct sales counterpart was then charged with simply *recommending* equipment to specific dealers – as opposed to loaning and stocking it directly. Among Castrol local representatives this "back-off" by Western headquarters was taken as a sea change in corporate attitude toward the efficacy of the Thai-style reliance on traditional, informal customer relationships.

Localization: general pointers

A fundamental charge against foreign MNC entrants concerns their failure to take account of local variances within the region. The differences in culture not just between the West and East but also within ASEAN itself has become a major source of contention. Many world-class MNCs are often guilty of the simplest of oversights. As recounted by its former Lao distributor, the consumer goods giant Unilever appeared unaware of local natural forces in the country that affected sales. High upon the list of these was the often chronic inland flooding in the southern region. Capable of displacing up to 10 percent of the country's populace, the floods would often stop dead sales of soap, shampoo and toothpaste. This in turn affected retailers and filtered over to the sole distributor, who was loath to order fresh stock until the rains had ceased for another year. Seemingly unaware of the extent of such domestic "acts of God," the MNC involved still pushed for increased sales.

Another external force often underestimated by MNCs comprises the reach and machinations of local politics and governmental regulations. Take the case of Laos again. Exposed to Western-style advertising from Thai television across the border, the Laotians express as much – if not more – interest and desire for Western products as do their Thai neighbors. Nevertheless, such simple observations hide a nasty sting: the one-party, loosely Marxist state which still controls the nation's resources. Committed to retaining what they perceive as being age-old cultural traditions, the Lao authorities have maintained a highly vocal anti-Western stance. In fact, only very recently has this at last begun to change in earnest. But still the old red tape remains across Laos and much of the rest of Indochina.

The US coffee vendor Starbucks is reportedly marching across China, Malaysia and Singapore with cloned outlets offering nearly identical decor and service (Cohen, 2000c). Yet in an unexpected development, this has not been possible in Vietnam, owing to a hefty 50 percent government tax applied on imported roast coffee beans. Vietnam has also served to perplex the mightiest of Western MNCs seeking to enact a regional – even domestic – marketing mix strategy within its borders, because of the underestimated but very real variations between its north and southern regions. Such differences in taste, resources, even language also plague similar campaigns in Malaysia and Indonesia. The complexities in seeking to centralize marketing strategies across the region are compounded by the kaleidoscope of dialects and languages. This has huge implications for the coordination of product names – and even more so with central-source computer-based coding systems such as the J. D. Edwards program, employed by MNCs across the globe.

Of course, to some degree the nature and operation of the marketing function in Southeast Asian markets depends upon the class of product or service being proffered. Nevertheless, as a rule of thumb, when dealing with the ASEAN bloc a corporation with external origins would do well to be flexible and diverse with its product range in order to meet local customer wants and needs. Many products and marketing campaigns that have worked in the rest of the world have fallen flat in Southeast Asia. To this extent marketing localization is an often inescapable – albeit costly – fact of doing business in the region. Indeed, for both Coca-Cola and Unilever, ASEAN has been a fervent testing ground for localization policies. Similarly, and taking stock of their experiences, today other well-known MNCs, including Procter & Gamble, Colgate-Palmolive and Shell, are also seeking to buck the trend of postcrisis rationalization and follow the adaptation approach, tilting their marketing and sales strategy toward local culture and taste. The sheer diversity of the region, in terms of culture, language and living standards, has forced a whole host of companies to modify their worldwide strategies for the ASEAN marketplace.

The case of Coca-Cola – deemed the "world's most successful brand marketer" – provides perhaps the clearest and most recent example of this as the company seeks to transform itself into a localized "total beverage" company, adopting Asia as the testbed for this new strategy. Indeed, it is estimated that currently around 25 percent of Coca-Cola's products in the region simply cannot be found anywhere else in the world. With sales of its flagship brand stagnating in the wake of the crisis, Coca-Cola's marketers have radically shifted their line of focus, setting aside their all-time favorite beverage in pursuit of the local demand for teas, waters and fruit blends. Perceiving itself as being newly "responsive" to the indigenous consumer, this "think local, act local" strategy constitutes an unprecedented change for what was once, after all, little short of a one-drink firm. As late as the turn of the 1990s the firm wanted to become universal and to "give the world a Coke." So why the change? And what of the pitfalls – could variety cost Coca-Cola its focus long term?

Our respondents think not – whether they are expatriates or locals. All of them claim from business experience that a foreign firm in Southeast Asia must both act and think local. Who, after all, buys the drink in the first place? Local consumers with their personal thirsts, who go and buy Coke from their nearest retailer. And in order to maximize the local nature of its business the company has repositioned its hubs of decision making and responsibility "closer to the front lines" (Far Eastern Economic Review, 2000). In practice, whereas strategy selection was previously controlled from the group's Atlanta headquarters, aspects such as products and advertising policies are now made "on the ground." This has enabled the company to become much more flexible and responsive to consumer needs, regaining the lost months spent awaiting headquarters' approval on everything from price formulation to packaging (ibid.). Whereas before, Coca-Cola was a sitting duck for the more nimble competition, in recent months it has produced a number of best-selling local drinks.

Other notable companies have been reviewing the wisdom of their immediate postcrisis emphasis on uniformity, partly stirred by the ancillary factors of copycat local branding and a traditional lack of innovate new products aimed specifically at the local consumer. Further – and despite the mooted "globalization" – the region's crucial automotive industry is also experiencing problems. The main manufacturers are discovering that car models aimed simultaneously at all major markets continue to fail to reach their – already somber – sales predictions. As a region ASEAN still tends to thrive on tailored models with varied specifications from the "global norm," mostly to do with size and touch. It would seem that a number of global players such as General Motors and Ford are rediscovering the notion that the adapted product suited to Asian tastes can be a valuable weapon in the fight for market share.

In the consumer goods industry similar trains of thought are beginning to make sense to the likes of Gillette, Unilever and Colgate-Palmolive. The decision by the last of these to centralize its research and development function in the wake of the regional downturn has thrown up some unexpected difficulties. Adding sunscreen to its line of shampoos sold in Thailand, to give a product that served both functions, did not, for example, win it many new customers – and certainly served to perplex a fair number of existing ones! In a similar vein the Swiss giant Nestlé found itself in difficulty with a country-wide sales drive for its renowned instant coffee in Vietnam. Foremost among the problems was the nation's startling north–south divide. In the north the proximity to China has engendered a strong tradition of tea drinking. Yet this does not hold in the south – where the French colonial influence has kept an aftertaste for coffee, and tea is given out for free with meals (see also Cohen, 2000c).

Once a very hegemonic corporation, the automotive superfirm General Motors has also adopted the localization tack, at least in terms of its "softening" business values. Once firmly set on a strategy of acquisition, GM is currently displaying a more relaxed attitude to its local dealings, and placing new-found trust and expertise in domestic alliances. Indeed, its overall attitude is now closer to that of its US counterpart, the telecommunications equipment maker Lucent Technologies. The latter's strategy – best described as "multidomestic" – assumed that markets vary and are segmented on domestic lines. In order to tailor its products to meet these needs, Lucent has also based its fortunes on a decentralized, responsive organizational structure.

Strategic planning

A cross section of MNCs view the centralization of their strategic planning methods, facilitated by developments in computer-based communication technology, as a core plank of their long-term ASEAN objectives. Included in this aim are corporate moves to strengthen central control over local business unit data. Group headquarters were determined not to be "duped" by optimistic local figures, as many of them had been in the past during the crisis years. Executives craved what many termed "globally competitive procedures," underpinned by speed, business and customer intelligence.

Traditional methods, corporate critiques

What do Asian managers understand by Western notions of strategic planning? This is a question that continues to perplex expatriate troubleshooters. Divisional sales and marketing teams are seemingly habituated to an unwritten mechanism of mutual protection within their traditional networks of associates. Such a defense structure has tended to shield them from the negative, uncertain aspect of market forces. The stated need to "plan ahead" in the postcrisis environment has thus largely been taken to mean little more than a heightening of awareness to the possibility of future market downturns.

But what of routine planning? Previous methods and documents were held up to us by numerous Western and Japanese executives and roundly criticized for their ad hoc, incoherent nature, typically thought out no more than a single month in advance. Traditional ASEAN "planning" – except, seemingly, in Singapore – was felt to be almost wholly reactive in nature. Many of our informants also pointed to the vague, piecemeal, largely spontaneous decision making routines that often characterized domestic operations.

The common thread here was the extent to which the global MNC headquarters stressed their desire for more precise, proactive marketing planning – with a tighter level of control. Using the collapse of late 1997 as the catalyst, an increasing number of corporate groups were now openly voicing their dissatisfaction with both the timing and the content of ASEAN domestic strategy reports. Against this backdrop there has been a discernible push for more detailed written plans and data sets, similar to those engendered from the home markets. Group tenets such as "key drivers" or "critical success factors" – to name but a few – are now being held up as a mirror to the demands being made of Southeast Asian subsidiary units, to be identified and acted upon through "proper," thorough market research.

What respondents did not want a repeat of were the short, dogmatic phrases traditionally being put forward as both a rationale for and an analysis of monthly divisional activity. Take the case of Castrol (Thailand), illustrated by the following (disguised) excerpts from precrisis marketing budget documents: "There is no special trade promotion for this month, but we play with another 7% price increase rumor for automotive market," or "We continue our 4T/Si-flow coin redemption campaign," or "we start the 2T white pack Ghost/Jump TV commercial

. . . and the SLS free gift at department store campaign" – and so forth. The perceived lack of forward planning evidenced by these papers was mirrored in the concurrent by-competitor analyses sheets: "Mobil has offered cash payment terms of 15 days with 5% discount for their new 2T vista," "Caltex have their 'buying volume collection' campaign starting from Oct–Nov 1996" and "Shell has informed of price increases which will be effective from Oct 15th with special trade promotions for wholesale dealers."

Corporate solutions

The consensus among MNC home office representatives was that they wanted the enforcement of stricter and more detailed planning and strategy guidelines. Not surprisingly, most of the Thai managers and expats we spoke to "on the ground" claimed to have taken this as a further attempt by headquarters to "tighten the leash" on their "unpredictable" ASEAN subsidiaries. At the "conceptual" level this stated need was founded on various theories and maxims, perhaps best summarized by the oft-cited maxim "Proper Planning Prevents Poor Performance.'

At the practical level, group representatives spoke to us of the necessity of having the "systems in place to capture essential market intelligence," and the importance of "company-wide teamwork and cooperation," with other departments such as operations, finance and technical forming an integral part of the overall planning process. The guidelines (sometimes hastily revised) which were issued in the wake of the crisis were designed to be worked via their detailed communication to the relevant sales forces in order to ensure grassroots involvement and a shared commitment to succeed.

As a general practice, most of the domestic unit reports were already incorporated into the MNC's regional plan for the Asia-Pacific hub of operations – sometimes referred to as "East Asia," more uncommonly as "Southeast Asia." The tightening of control on future country submissions was often quite intricate and detailed – with guidelines not only as to structure, but also as to content. What follows comprises several of the more detailed directives given in these revised guideline texts. In line with the express wishes of our informants we have disguised both the origins and the industries of the multinationals referred to. The information is presented in a summary, digested form. We begin with structural directives, instanced by notes provided for the country contents page to be formed of headings/sections devoted to – or with more emphasis upon – "projected performance," "trading environment," "financial commentary" and "marketing action plans." The latter were to include such things as a current and future market map or analysis, outlining in detail a company's position at that time, where it would like to be in three years and, crucially, how it intended to get there. Group executives were keen to point out that the guidelines devised for the region should in principle apply to any unit and to any market. However, we witnessed the inclusion of a number of provisos drawn as a concession to local mores, which in effect allowed for the indigenous management teams to adapt the guidelines – where appropriate – to their own particular needs.

In terms of set timetables for the revised data requirements, the usual trend was for detailed reports to be submitted for corporate approval at monthly, annual and three-year junctures. For some business units this involved a marked increase in written output. Many firms had only ever operated on a maximum of a one-year time frame, and the idea of a strategic marketing plan to be drafted three years ahead came as something of a shock. The annual marketing plan of action was to be compiled and submitted generally by the respective country manager or CEO. This latter document was to provide summaries of targets and tactics, a list of tasks to be performed and the names of people responsible for enacting them. Finally, as well as the traditional monthly report, many of our MNCs were also keen to institute a "marketing database," to be set and updated in spreadsheet format at prescribed intervals.

With the overarching structure once agreed, the stress was on additional – and similarly formatted – subsections and more detailed demands. For instance, take the "SMART" addendum – common to most Western corporations. This acronym seeks to summarize group marketing objective facets: they should be "specific," "measurable," "achievable" but stretching, "results oriented" and "time bound." Further, such SMART marketing objectives were to be drafted not merely for each report but for each marketing segment in which the respective company was competing, outlined in terms of volume, profit, value and market share.

In certain corporations the regional guidelines distributed contained an especially precise, detailed and regulated set of demands for both structure and content. One company's headquarters had gone so far as to effectively draft the entire report – leaving merely a series of blanks for the local directors to complete. Take the case of the "new-style" projection summary instituted as from late 1999, and the following "model" scenarios – complete with blanks: "199X was a more difficult year in volume terms but with better than expected consumer margins, making for a TP result $x\%$ ahead of budget and $y\%$ up on 1997," with subsections made up of phrases such as "at the expense level, higher distribution costs were offset by savings following the recent office consolidation initiative and the overall expense ratio to sales was $X\%$ below budget."

Particular attention was given to the financial side of the unit: "We are budgeting a 1999 volume of X million units ($+y\%$ over 1998) and a trading profit of $\$Z$ million ($+X\%$)"; "Expenses will rise by X million – $y\%$ – with a disproportionate increase in XX offset by a marginal increase in YY."

Local critiques: the backlash

Initial moves to integrate these reporting procedures in postcrisis ASEAN corporate subsidiaries came under severe criticism – particularly for their perceived inflexibility. During interviews held at this period, directives issued to "structurize" sensitive information within a rigid corporate framework were attacked as being detrimental to the flexible, instinctive business methods on which the majority of the region's subsidiaries were considered to have built their success. Many marketing managers remained suspicious of so-called "objective" market research and planning, which they viewed as an inappropriate use of resources in the region, where managers claimed to possess a "natural" feel for the market. In this context, quick, "instinctive" decision making had always been considered the prerequisite for marketing success in an environment which was locally held to be both unknown and unknowable.

Such an assumed level of understanding was also claimed to reside only in those of an ethnic Chinese cultural heritage, an implied and very serious constraint on personnel recruitment. The apparent desire by Western corporate executives to "bind" themselves – and others – in "plans" and "graphs" for greater planning and control was considered to be a mark of naïveté in a business context where nimble flexibility reigns supreme. Indeed, on countless occasions we were told that this "misplaced" commitment to linear planning methods was a wasteful and potentially very dangerous constraint upon local business instincts handed down through generations.

The traditional practice of simply augmenting monthly and yearly volume sales was held to allow sales managers to nurture "proper, flexible" relations with their clients. Within this context, targeted decisions can be made quickly on a case-by-case basis by the individual sales representative responsible. The new stress on rigid credit limits, financial targets and levels of support proffered was claimed to have caused a strain on many valued customer relationships. And for what? Viewed through the eyes of one senior sales executive, discoursing upon the working practices imposed by his US director, the dilemma was simple:

> "You can see what my staff must to do now with their time. This computer for writing the documents for HQ . . . [but] instead of this, why can't they send us something to help our team sell another 20,000 boxes a month? . . . What is the point of them using my people to create this kind of thing? . . . It may be very beautiful but only our target sales by the month will pay our salaries."

Broadly speaking, it appeared that the financially driven, Western stress on results had come up against the indigenous Asian priorities of harmony, relationship and tradition.

Antecedent foundations

Lifting up the surface on this divergence in perspective, our research suggests that in Southeast Asia the underlying stress is on marketers becoming *perceptive* and *flexible* in order to meet and exceed the expectations of the local customer needs. Further, this is categorically set against the Western norms of forward planning and analysis, dismissed as being contextually unworkable. The extant literature upon this topic, meager though it is, sheds some light upon these differences. In a study from the mid-1990s, Schneider and Barsoux (1997) put forward the notion that managers from an Anglo/Western background tend to believe that their environment – and particularly their business contexts – can be analyzed and known. For this prime reason, Western managers are attracted to techniques such as strategic forecasting, scenario planning, and so forth – and tend to emphasize the importance of "industry reports" and "market research." Armed with this information, they then have faith in their ability to predict, and hence control, their environmental context, and the external course of history (ibid.; see also Shoham and Albaum, 1995). By contrast, managers from Eastern cultures perceive a greater uncertainty when faced with similar environments, believing they have less control over what will happen. They are thus more inclined to "go with the flow," to adapt, and to react at speed to change. Such data as are used at all are gathered not via spreadsheets but through informal channels and personal relationships. These are then interpreted through intense, face-to-face discussion and debate, in the belief that multiple perspectives and broader involvement will help in dealing with risk and uncertainty (see also Erramilli, 1996; Schuster and Copeland, 1999).

Such deeply founded differences further translate into interminable headaches at the level of operation. Traditionally, when dealing with the region, MNC headquarters have problems in getting local managers to accept – let alone use – their home office-led models and analysis methods. Asian managers have tended to dismiss and/or ignore these methods as oversimplified and myopic in scope – and in particular for their own domestic markets. Moreover, market research in the region has always been a hit-and-miss affair. The mass of statistics available is both unreliable and inconsistent. But whereas this bothers group home office, the locals have tended to stay unfazed, happy with what has been termed "fuzzy focus." Indigenous managers do not plan; they react, and with speed. The mindset in Asia is to resolve what has happened first, with little regard for the Western "proactive" stress, based on "what if" as opposed to reality. This tends to work when done at speed, of course. And speed is held to be an intrinsic part of the local stress on business relationships, traditionally founded on trust rather than legal contracts. Local business units, when left to their own devices, are held to outperform Western companies in configuring their strategies to the external environment.

The rationale for "business instinct": origins of difference

But why is this the case? Where do the diverging mindsets outlined above originate? At the superficial level, there were several reasons given to us. To begin with, the Chinese-oriented business approach prevalent across the region has its foundations in the family business. Within the family business the need to plan and draft contingency arrangements is much reduced. Managers simply do not change at anything like the same rate as in the modern multinational. Further, with information stored among loyal, trusted kinsmen, the need for such things as approval processes and systems procedures is almost circumvented by the scope for informal, day-to-day business conversation. Within such an environment the tolerance for ambiguity and uncertainty is also that much higher – and planning for the sake of colleagues an obvious waste of resources.

Plumbing slightly deeper, we have been struck by the apparent *cultural* dimensions to the debate. This concerns in particular the perceived importance and viability of the need to plan ahead – the crux, surely, of the traditional "sales versus marketing" conflict which has been played out across much of the ASEAN corporate landscape. Western culture, so it goes, has tended to foster the cult of progress and change. The mere notion that change can actually be controlled, and especially via technological means, is one that is traditionally alien to the indigenous Asian manager. In this sense, "marketing" is a very Western, US-based skill. American culture has been characterized as "cybernetic," appreciating the use of planning and quantitative techniques, looking for feedback, and considering mistakes as moments of learning rather than failures.

This stands against the overriding perceptions held in the East. Certain deeply founded aspects of Southeast Asian business culture run counter to the nature of strategic decision making as conceived in the Western setting. To the Western eye, Asian managers are typically rather fatalistic in outlook, a characteristic related to their sense of the world as an externally, rather than internally, controlled set of unknowable movements. Against this backdrop the Western preoccupation with uncertainty evaluation takes a back seat. The idea that one can lay out strategic moves step by step in some preplanned sequence is contextually preposterous – even more unlikely than elsewhere.

The fundamental divergence in outlook we are arriving at is also embedded in the personal lifestyles of the individuals involved – including, of course, our own. The Southeast Asian "take" on the value of strategic planning is reflected in the average employee's view upon what constitutes "career development" – and quite how he or she can influence its fruition. An extreme example of how the local mindset tends to dismiss the need to plan is embedded in the native Thai male's expenditure patterns – instanced by the "typical" city *tuk-tuk* driver, quite capable of earning 200 baht in any one day only to spend 300 in the same evening.

But again, why these varied outlooks? The apparent consensus among our respondents lay at both the educational and the agricultural levels, the latter being a precedent to the former. Simply expressed, the foundation to the Southeast Asian business culture lies in the region's *rural* culture, tailored by its climate. A quasi-sociological perspective suggests that the abundance of natural resources and relative lack of natural extremes or disasters across the region has meant that there has never been the need to plan ahead to fight with nature. Unlike in the West, planning has never become a deeply ingrained necessity (see also Niratpattanasai, 1997). Work and leisure within the domestic frontiers of the region have evolved around well-defined climatic, religious and farming seasons. Understandably, then, in such a context the concept of "strategic planning" in the modern workplace, taken with a rural mindset, seems pointless. Planting and harvesting times cannot be changed but appear as an infinite cycle of seasons. As a corollary to this, time management – indeed, planning itself – is not then viewed as being a linear, unidirectional process as it is in the West. This explains in part the criticism voiced concerning local timekeeping and deadlines.

Furthermore, the tendency to *react* to external events – to eschew notions of "proactive" planning – is also held to stem from the physical environment. Broadly speaking, the region comprises resources in depth. As per the old maxim, common to the region, "Fish are in the water here and rice is in the fields." This perceived and inherent lack of want reinforces the cyclic certainties that underpin the local business culture. Cycles give rise to reassurance, in turn promoting stasis. The static nature of the domestic cultures is perhaps most aptly illustrated by the structure of the languages. Take the case of Thailand and the following common dialogue: the question *"mii arai mai?"* (i.e. "is anything up/the matter?") invariably precedes the response *"mai mii arai"* (i.e. "there's nothing up/the matter") – a simple yet relentless means by which the daily stasis is constantly reiterated.

The third way: "hybrid" mindsets?

Our analysis has rolled out the main determinants of marketing planning practice across the East–West business culture divide. With such fundamental variance, can there possibly be a meeting of minds concerning this dilemma – a compromise between the two? The answer – "yes, but only to an extent" – was partially engendered by the unprecedented regional collapse of the late 1990s. Consider the phenomenon of corporate strategic plans devised in the mid-years of the decade, replete with three- and five-year projections to see them through the turn of the millennium. In the wake of economic crisis these plans – almost without exception – were rendered worthless, ridiculous even.

Against this backdrop, substantial numbers of respondents – of both Eastern and Western origin – have begun to question the wisdom of imposing global "strat-plan" formulas in the ASEAN environment. Local managers in particular were reemphasizing the stated "environmental congruity" of their traditional, sales-led methodology for sustained business success. Much of their rationale stemmed from their inherent perceptions of reality. More specifically, and paraphrasing the words of one especially coherent regional sales executive for Alcatel, Western methods were simply no longer aligned with the tangible global business trend. Why? Because of their root-source fallacy, that of believing external events can be both *predicted* and *controlled*. Predictions, after all, are inextricably founded in the past – past trends, past events – and then drawn up in the present for utilizing in the future. But in a world characterized by spiraling risk and uncertainty, such linear methods may no longer be viable – indeed, may serve only to distort, rather than assist in a company's strategic plans. So what of traditional methods, then? And why would they be more appropriate? According to respondents, their main strength lies in their inherent flexibility, characterized by rapid word-of-mouth dialogue – as opposed to the perceived Western insistence on ponderous written systems and procedures. To this end, Asian managers have always reacted to the present – rapidly, via nimble networks ensuring a near-legendary speed of maneuver. Further, it is claimed that this may well represent the key ingredient for future competitive strength in a world business arena plagued by instability, a world where attempts to be proactive can justifiably be regarded as akin to "shooting oneself in the head."

Not, of course, that the majority of our Western expatriates were of the same mind – far from it. But over the years that followed the initial business collapse of 1997–8 a host of corporate representatives from a regional cross section of industries gradually came to accept the inherent cultural difficulties of "planning" in a historically plentiful region where the contextual preoccupation with trend prediction was almost nonexistent. In practical terms this has led – at least until now – not so much to a revision of market planning fundamentals as toward a discernible relinquishment of initial "hard-line" working proposals. Hence although MNCs' local subsidiaries are still charged with regularly satisfying regional headquarters that corporate strategic planning guidelines are being adhered to, there has been a progressive reduction in the written material demanded of them, far less that in some of the immediate postcrisis "coordination" initiatives. A compromise blend of planning report structure and content practice has emerged whereby the rush of reports and figures initially demanded has receded back to a steadier and more adaptable output of locally conceived summaries and reports.

Respondents – again, of both origins – also noted the concurrent relaxation by Western executives toward the guidelines on planning meetings – possibly due to their witnessing such events! Hence, over time and in practice – although not necessarily with any change in written procedure – a broad grouping of MNCs have been allowing a certain relaxation of home office planning directives. This has effectively allowed the local teams to circumvent many of the original controls on structure, content and overall levels of detail. We also witnessed the tacit acceptance of certain idiosyncratic domestic inclusions within a cross section of local unit report documents, mostly regarding the emphasis on individual customer requirements and feelings.

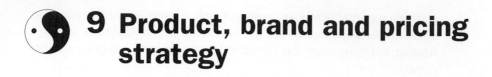

9 Product, brand and pricing strategy

- Traditional practice
- Multinational brand repositioning strategies
- The underflow: forces for adaptation
- "Cross-verging" brand perspectives

Most MNCs in ASEAN countries consider themselves to be marketers of premium-bracketed products and services. There are exceptions, of course – although rarely admitted. The simple truth is that even where such a company's products are considered to be fairly "average" in their home market, in Southeast Asia they are nearly always competing at the "top end." An example is Marks & Spencer, the UK retail group. In such a context, brand awareness, strength and development are key areas of concern for ASEAN-based foreign multinationals, and especially those from a "developed" country base.

Rarely does an MNC enter a market just to "fill an existing gap." Contrary to popular belief, such gaps never really exist. Even services and products created via quality innovation will be nurtured and developed only via proper branding. The modern MNC thus looks upon brand values as an intrinsic market "given," a core driver impacting any take on planning strategy (ranked alongside market objectives, available working capital and core corporate value-sets). In this context MNCs are prepared to spent huge amounts of the budgets on long-term branding objectives. Even cost leadership is viewed as a corollary to branding strength – affording business units more flexibility with regard to resource allocation, encouraged as an occasion to reinvest in brand development.

When MNCs enter the ASEAN bloc, a major pillar of their strength lies in their ability to utilize often globally recognized brand names in order to capture market share. In contrast to their local competitors, MNCs generally do not rely on distribution, customer relations or even pricing competition, which are all subsumed to the strength of branding. This is the case across a multitude of industries: food and beverages, tobacco products, pharmaceuticals, and health and beauty. Nescafé and Pepsi have built initial market share on brand strength almost exclusively (Nestlé now boasts of five production plants in Malaysia alone). The Swedish Motor Company (now part of Ford) trades on the back of its global "safety" image – embodied in the Volvo brand as the summation of an integrated quality approach. Much the same is true of other highly regarded brand identities: IBM and Intel, Motorola and Nokia, Coca-Cola and General Electric, Microsoft and McDonald's.

Once established in a local market, MNCs set about encouraging local consumers to "trade up" to premium product brands. This is obviously easier with some products than with others. As markets become more prosperous, the demand for better cars will increase – as with motor oil. But what of bottled water? For in spite of the product's appeal as a high-volume, essential and easily understood product, it is generally low margin, tough to transport and indistinguishable from the competition once out of its package. That is why companies such as Danone from France and Nestlé place so much emphasis on their branding techniques.

In a similar vein, the US oil giant Caltex, in its quest to become the "brand of choice" for consumers in the region, has progressed a brand "repositioning" strategy – pushing the four factors of perceived quality, professionalism, service and efficiency. In seeking to realign its brand image and values with those of its perceived future customers, Caltex in the region portrays its customers as both young and of a "high-tech" standing. Anxious to attract such people so as to ensure ever-increasing market shares, the company has sought to redesign its brand logo – the "red star" – as a recognized symbol of performance, strength and excellence, an expression of the company's self-perceived identity. Bolstering its affiliation with the growing Asian "yuppie" segment, the company has introduced the color green into its famous star – as a more laid-back, less formal sop to the younger generation, backed by an environmentally friendly approach.

More generally, multinationals have given prominence to the idea that global brand is ideally suited to the ASEAN customer mentality. Much of this reasoning stems from two sources: the indigenous power of symbols on the one hand and the local obsession with names, hierarchy and status on the other. This obsession is reflected in the Asian approach to

Brand Loyalty or Mental Illness?

Brand development at Castrol rests upon the company's perspective on the market for its lubricants as a pyramid structure formed of three levels. The base comprises "price end" and the middle chunk the "mass segment." Castrol then places itself in the small top sector – as a premium-grade master brand. Within this latter segment the company splits itself yet further – with products such as SLX acting as figureheads, the flagship brand of a quality name. The company's corporate heritage rests on images of high technology and performance. It is said that during the 1920s four out of five British car races were won on Castrol oil. Being self-perceived as "best in class," the company balks at pricing competition. The key to Castrol's success is seen in differentiation – engaging price simply to reinforce the brand image, the price sometimes being as much as 80 percent higher than that of the nearest local competitor.

So strong is the brand, especially for its employees, that there have been two cases, both in Australia, where Castrol employees expressed their wish to be associated with their company colors even in death. Specifically, one Castrol sales manager asked to be buried with the red and green Castrol flag draped over his coffin, while another employee – a service engineer – requested that he be buried in his serviceman's uniform. But does this serve to demonstrate an unprecedented attainment of branding strength? When this question was discussed among the company's indigenous management team, such a request was unanimously perceived as expressing more a subtle form of mental disease. Among Westerners in the company, however, it was looked upon as a manifestation of Castrol's corporate team spirit and its policy of caring for its people.

motorcars, in which the local stratification of domestic markets provides an ideal feeding ground for the promotion of Western prestige marques as an external reflection of one's rank within society. In the Southeast Asian environment big cars of quality origin (Mercedes-Benz, BMW, Daimler-Chrysler, and so forth) furnish one with the all-important concept of "face."

Further, and as noted in a recent article by Sreshthaputra (2001), Asian consumers tend to be highly appearance-conscious as a result. It is therefore somehow logical that even as the region recovers from the recent crisis, brands or models attached to a level of prestige are still doing well and recovering slightly faster than the "average" makes (despite crushing import duties of up to 200 percent). Hence, whereas most manufacturers in the West are striving to offer cheap vehicles at an increasingly cheaper price, the ASEAN bloc seems to be witnessing a steady price escalation. Cars in the region are first and foremost status symbols, the ultimate expression of one's terrestrial rank. But in a sense they are also quasi-homes within the gridlocked city thoroughfares of

Manila, Bangkok, Jakarta, and so on, with local managers spending far greater chunks of time within their personal cars than their counterparts in the West – or anywhere else. This is why it is almost natural that their cars feel so important, with comfort, noise and climate being deciding factors to be added to brand strength.

However, many local managers have disputed this increasing attachment to brands, deriding it as a "passing phase" in the long-term development of the region's economies. Perhaps surprisingly, the view from these regionally based strategists was that once consumers reach a certain level of sophistication they become *more* cynical about foreign brands and *less* likely to remain loyal. But what does this suggest about the future of the global brand in ASEAN? The consensus among our informants is that consumer–brand relationships within the region would indeed prove enduring in the long term – yet many opined that they would gain importance only when these developing economies "settled down." The current near-obsession with being seen in quality labels, the kind of mentality to have spawned a myriad of brand-counterfeits, is perceived as merely that – as a "fad," a teenage-like flirtation.

This view has been compounded by the crash of 1997. Years of growth have made nonprice factors more and more important. MNCs were shifting stress toward their global branding objectives when, unforeseen, the downturn struck their predictions for the region's performance. But over time, and in an increasingly uncertain world, the brand as key nonprice factor *will* reassert itself, if only as a reassurance, a reducer of decision-risk. More practically, the long-term strength of the global brand within the region will be achieved only with the rise and sustenance of a big enough, stable middle class for whom the marginal extra cost is a small price to pay for these benefits.

Traditional practice

In terms of their approach to marketing strategy, Asian companies have traditionally tended not to invest in the packaging and promotion necessary to build a strong brand image. To start with, brand development is considered to be a risky and intangible process. As one local manager expressed it, "We need to focus on reality – you cannot eat a brand name here, you cannot eat an *image*. Branding is important, yes, but we need to stay with what our customers want . . . sales pay our salaries."

Traditionally ASEAN firms have focused on short- to medium-returns, tending to push any notions of brand building way down their list of priorities. Top Asian executives will be preoccupied in other areas, largely dismissive of a "soft," "fuzzy" concept perceived as an excessive drain on limited resources. Further, during the boom years of the 1980s and early 90s it had seemed that this local resistance to global branding methods was entirely justified – with the local units of some of the world's foremost multinationals expressing record sales and profitability growth levels on the back of traditional, relations-based working practices.

Against the backdrop of economic success, incumbent MNCs of this period were largely content with this "polycentric" approach to organizing operations on a country-by-country basis within the region. The approach allowed individual country managers to tailor marketing strategies to local peculiarities. Product adaptations and modifications were obviously a part of this, again as a tool catering to the specialist needs and wants of local customers. To this end, the global brand values of any corporation could – within reason – be kept on a back burner, along with notions of regional coordination, even economies of scale, on the strength of rocketing domestic sales. Products were then targeted primarily at secure market niches, relying on deft sales-led strategies for increasing market share. Piecemeal, "gut instinct" marketing tactics enacted as and when environmental factors shifted pricing were defended as incorporating the speed, efficiency and flexibility deemed to hold the key to years of competitive success.

Traditional pricing methods

In many ways the Southeast Asian manager's "take" on the issue of pricing ties back to dated Western marketing theory textbooks. Price positioning stems from a company's perception of itself within its target market, for example as the market leader, challenger, follower, nicher, and so forth. In the classic oligopolistic environment – in which multinationals typically compete – one member of the industry usually emerges as leader and its pricing moves are duly acknowledged by its competitors. The tendency to play cat and mouse with competitors on the issue of pricing, founded on quick, instinctive shifts, neatly fits in with this analysis. Price, as local managers stress, is after all the sole element of the marketing "mix" to produce revenue for the company – the others merely add cost. To this end the price element is usually taken as being the core of any marketing strategy and therefore set independently, the others being viewed as there merely for support.

In the wake of the regional economic collapse this tendency has been reinforced – at least in the eyes of the indigenous marketing teams. Cutthroat price competition reigned at this juncture, particularly among the locally based companies, serving to reduce the marketing margins of all major players across the respective industrial board. Price competition was reinforced as the optimal means of dealing with stagnant, even contracting market demand, raising itself as an effective strategy for holding up market share among increasingly cost-conscious consumers.

In terms of structure, prices have traditionally been formulated from the top down. The respective local marketing chief would decide what was required in terms of either sales or net profit – whether or not this was in theory the province of corporate head office. A series of "margins" would then be added to the base cost of the product, accounting for cost of sales, transport, tax, and so forth in order to arrive at a final "price-to-market" figure which would satisfy consumers on the one hand and then – at this time – indulgent Western parents on the other. With the leeway granted to them in the precrisis boom period, local managers tended to stress flexibility and market share over brand strength and positioning. Hence, pricing was prone to change along a wide bandwidth, with a line-by-line approach incorporated into each product range for maximum flexibility – habitually kept on a "word-of-mouth" basis among trusted sales and marketing aides.

Executive Insights: Battling Price Control

"Sometimes, when managing companies in Southeast Asia, you need to stick your neck out but you also need a bit of luck. I remember June 1981 very well. The then Thai Prime Minister – His Excellency Premsakdi Tinsulanonda – had agreed to address a joint foreign chambers of commerce meeting at the Oriental Hotel. A day or so before the event it was announced that he would be bringing the key members of his ministerial cabinet. I called the then chairman of the British Chamber of Commerce, David Welham (also chairman of the Shell Group in Thailand), and told him that I'd like to ask a question about price control on lubricants, which had been in effect since the OPEC oil crisis of 1979. David said, 'OK, I'll put you down for one of the British Chamber questions.'

"Naturally, when the day came, the ballroom of the Oriental Hotel was full. After Prime Minister Prem's speech the time came for questions, and with some trepidation I said, 'Your excellency, during the past eighteen months the cost of lubricating oil has increased by six and a half baht per liter, but the price control mechanism has only allowed us to increase prices by two and a half baht. Does the government have any plans to abolish price control on lubricants?'

"The applause was deafening and I was shaking all over when I got back to my seat. General Prem said, 'I would like my deputy, Khun Boonchoo [Rojanastien], to answer this question.' Boonchoo took the microphone and said, 'No, I think the Commerce Minister, Khun Tamchai [Kamtabo], is the correct person to reply.' The microphone then went along to Tamchai, who said that he would like his deputy, Khun Visit, to respond. Khun Visit, who had previously worked for Esso, had to get up from a table in front of the audience, and he insisted that the question be answered by the Commerce Minister himself. So the microphone went back again to Khun Tamchai, who gave a wooly answer which failed to address the question. The meeting moved on, but afterwards many of my Rotary friends suggested that I was unlikely to be in Thailand for Friday's meeting, and then a number of our competitors in the oil industry came up and thanked me for asking the question. One guy who'd been in Thailand a long time said, 'That was the gutsiest thing in years, your chairman must be in town!'

"In my budget and marketing plan for 1982, which had already been sent to the shareholders, I'd made the assumption that price controls would be abolished on the first of October 1981, the start of the new Thai fiscal year. Not only did I make Friday's meeting of the Rotary Club Bangkok South, but price control on lubricants was lifted on the sixth of October 1981. So I was lucky.

"Incidentally, following the meeting at the Oriental, it was reported that the Prime Minister had ordered that the question and responses be expunged from the official tape recording. The Commerce Minister, Tamchai, was also asked the same question in a television interview later that evening and had given a similarly nonconsequential answer. I suppose that the lesson from this episode is that if you need to ask an important and difficult question, then you have to choose a public and proper forum, ask it in a noncontroversial way and, above all, be polite. In a democratic country like Thailand you don't have to be frightened to speak the truth."

Multinational brand repositioning strategies

The underlying marketing philosophies of the global MNC were effectively reincorporated and imposed upon the crisis-era ASEAN bloc – no longer the jewel in the corporate fold. The perceived erosion of loyalty toward major foreign trade names – Shell, McDonald's, Coca-Cola, Procter & Gamble *ad infinitum* all taking hits – was inevitably the result of the local, newly cash-strapped consumer seeking the "best deal."

Within this context many corporate respondents stressed the need for taking – then imposing – clear in-house decisions on where their respective companies wished to position themselves in the new environment. Substantial numbers of expatriate marketers sought a restatement of their "differentiation focus" to avoid the risk of being "stuck in the middle" or – worse – resigned to cost and pricing competition.

This revision of overall positioning commitments was founded on reemphasizing underlying corporate tenets. The majority of MNCs we spoke to restated their belief that the (Southeast) Asian consumer essentially mirrors his developed Western counterpart in all but the most superficial of desires. This was held to be especially the case with the younger generation looking for "new" experiences, innovation, quality and, above all else, value for money. Future, long-term brand development in the region should thus be focused upon this burgeoning sector of the local populace – with over half the indigenous population being under 30 years of age – as a major global marketing target (particularly as education levels have continued to rise).

Once the dust had begun to settle, the economic downturn was perceived by nearly all global corporations as representing an opportunity for them to consolidate their respective market positions and emerge from the crisis stronger than they went into it. Computer chip-makers such as Intel and Cisco have utilized the recession to both gauge and then build upon the extent to which their brand names were "engraved" upon the minds of local consumers, even those only semiliterate in IT knowledge (McKinsey, 2001). More generally, comprehensive programs of brand repositioning were launched in order to "upgrade" the relatively "low-margin" image of local business units, aiming to ensure that positioning within the varied domestic markets of the region remained consistent with corporate objectives. In the wake of this transformed trading environment, prominent MNCs across the board have sought to clarify their master brand positioning, deemed their "most important asset" in building extra value among local consumers.

The practical measures imposed in order to enact these tenets varied from organization to organization, although there were a number of key focal points raised across the regional corporate landscape. To begin with, the dissemination and proposed (re)adoption of corporate branding guidelines was a consistent and widely pushed factor. Within these documents, global indices were often restated for added clarity, relating the corporate brands both to the competition and to their respective units across the world.

Such guidelines were brought to life via relevant training programs. A major aim was to reinforce respective corporate "core values" and to ensure they were being both understood and acted upon in an appropriate manner. Most Western MNCs used the occasion to remind both their expatriate staff and senior local marketing managers that ASEAN customers expect Western products to have a stylish image, be well designed, be periodically improved and be more reliable than their local counterparts. It was also widely posited that strengthening product brand control *now* would have important beneficial knock-on effects for the long-term future of respective master brands within the region. To this end the rise of e-commerce was also mooted across a broad range of organizations; the feeling being that with the rise of the Internet, branding would become even more essential than in traditional retailing practice.

At the lubricants company Castrol, it was decided to initiate a "master-brand protection" program for the region. The aim was to converge perceived disparate brand imaging and standardize corporate market communication practice. Included in the program was the "brand portfolio analysis" framework used in the West to divide competitor positioning policy into "top-end," "premium" and "best value." Castrol units across the region were instructed to avoid the latter "economy/ volume" category in future – corporate strategy being to specialize only in small-volume, high-margin trade.

In rolling out its own brand reinforcement/duplication policy, another oil firm, Caltex, drew upon stated support from a number of key operational units. To begin with, a new "Retail Operations" support unit was given the task of selecting the right representatives, ensuring that their roles were clearly defined, and of training them in a redefined, corporate-guided manner. Brand segmentation itself was also addressed in a formulated fashion that involved analyzing and segmenting customers, developing differentiated brand positionings for each market, and keeping tabs upon international brand positioning convergence. To reinforce these measures, communication and promotional tactics manuals were also distributed across the region, including integrated action plans for each of their respective subsidiaries.

Brand harmonization

In the postcrisis ASEAN marketplace, increased competition and overcapacity pressures have reinforced the trend toward regional standardization in line with global norms. Hence, rather than produce all products for each domestic market, corporations have instead opted to harness their regional resources to gain scale economies. This has in turn reinforced the harmonization of brand positioning. As global MNCs seek to further consolidate their operations there is effectively less and less room for local blends, packaging, and so forth.

This is aptly illustrated by the Anglo-Dutch consumer goods manufacturer Unilever. With its portfolio of household brands – including Lipton tea, Sunsilk shampoo and Pond's cosmetics – Unilever has traditionally prided itself on developing new brands for consumers in specific countries. With claims to be "international by design" and a multilocal multinational, Unilever uses its deep roots in many countries to tailor its products on the basis of this acquired cultural understanding. Aiming to be an integral part of the societies in which Unilever operates, the company's local business units are predominantly run by local people, who are felt to be in tune with the values of their communities. In the ASEAN region the company has been an especially prominent player. At one time the company boasted a headcount of some 12,000 people in its local operations and expanded rapidly – indeed, aggressively – across the Mekong Delta with locally adapted variants of Lipton tea, Jinghua tea and Lao Cai culinary products.

Yet in the wake of market downturn and collapsing demand, this situation has dramatically changed. As the largest consumer-goods company in the region, Unilever found its margins shrinking dramatically by the late 1990s as it juggled hundreds of loss-making brands (indeed, at one point it was calculated that over 1,000 of its disparate product brands – many of them small and locally adapted – accounted for only 8 percent of sales, while 90 percent of revenue came from the top 400 best-sellers). At the end of 1999, after announcing that profits had shrunk by almost 15 percent in one quarter, Unilever set about a massive restructuring program founded on the opposing – and almost unheard of – precepts of standardization and portfolio shrinkage. The company has seemingly now ditched the idea of wringing minimal profits from tiny local brands. Instead, it has decided to foster global brands like Dove soap, which has effectively doubled its sales in the past decade and is now marketed in over seventy-five countries across the world.

An added impetus to this stress on harmonization has stemmed from the well-documented advances in electronic technology – and especially regarding multinational product testing and the standardization of global product portfolios. With regard to the former, the World Wide Web has enabled global marketers to test multiple new product variations simultaneously as a result of the enhanced control of information flows between test markets. Furthermore, the task of formulating regional – even global – brand positioning policies has been aided by the transparencies engendered by the Internet, which effectively supports the standardization of price positioning across borders. At the broader level, brand harmonization has been facilitated by the way in which computer-based technology has overcome traditional boundaries of space and time. Consumers worldwide now have increasing access to the products and services of providers from around the globe. E-commerce provides consumers with timely and pertinent information regarding product and price comparisons, enhancing the need for brand image coordination at the cross-national level.

Brand "strength"

"Brand strength" in the Western sense of the word arises from what the majority of global MNCs term a *dominant state of mind* among consumers, in terms of both product quality and product benefits. The key to successful branding traditionally has been to give people what they want. But whereas perhaps a decade or so ago almost anything from the "developed" world would sell, the situation has changed drastically in the wake of the economic downturn, and the Southeast Asian markets have become more competitive and demanding. In marketing terms the region's economies have become progressively more segmented in tandem with the long-term trading up of ASEAN consumers in line with Western standards.

In the immediate postcrisis period MNCs such as Caltex, Mobil, Unilever, Colgate-Palmolive and Castrol were becoming concerned that their regional positioning was increasingly disparate as local business units struggled to cope with deteriorating demand via the use of unheralded price and promotion discounts. The debasement of the brand has always been a prime concern of multinationals in the region, which have traditionally sought to dissuade their local teams from simply lowering prices when the going gets tough. The incorporation of sales discounts in, say, Thailand, would always involve the danger of placing a corporation's master brand at a perceptibly lower level than in Malaysia, the Philippines or Singapore, or even Vietnam. The fear was that this disparate positioning would result in the erosion of brand premiums gained elsewhere as the entire region gravitated toward the lowest common denominator.

Several cases of multinational intervention in the region serve to illustrate these points. Our chief reference corporation, Castrol, sought to ensure that its local units were not "lowering" the global brand name by competing in domestic "economy/volume" market categories. As per global corporate guidelines, Castrol's ASEAN units were to focus exclusively on small-volume, high-margin trade. Differentiation, not cost, was repromoted as the only method via which long-term competitive advantage was to be attained (whatever the circumstances – a view held across the MNC landscape by brands as disparate as Coca-Cola, Renault, Heinz food products and the Procter & Gamble range of household goods). In the attainment of such objectives, "brand strength" was held to be the key priority. Accordingly, senior local sales and marketing executives were advised to rebuild the company's brand strength in the region. A stated future objective was to concentrate on making local consumers *aspire* to buying Castrol lubricants rather than persuading them to switch or maintain their brand of choice on the basis of cost and value. Largely against the wishes of the local management teams, the Castrol name within the region was to be retargeted toward *quality* consumers. To achieve this, a higher proportion of domestic resources was to be set aside for the strategic acquisition of prestige, globally based luxury franchised dealerships, like Porsche and Jaguar.

Within the regional cosmetics industry, one of the fastest-growing companies to emerge from the crash of 1997 has been the Estée Lauder conglomerate. With its product brands run and managed as independent profit centers, Estée Lauder is a prime example of how a company can raise its revenues by more than 50 percent almost exclusively on the strength of its developing brand names. Seeking to coordinate its overall brand fold while at the same time tailoring its local products to each market, the group has expanded its operations to the extent of commanding almost 50 percent of the Thai domestic market alone (see Srinivasan, 2001). Rather than retreat in the face of regional recession, the company has rolled out a score of new brands – e.g. "Bobbi Brown" and "Mac" products – while remaining firmly ensconced within the "prestige" sector. Focusing on product quality and technical advances,

Estée Lauder has sought to personalize its product brands in a way that renders them "unique" to each individual customer. By avoiding the "pricing" trap and by investing heavily in marketing and brand development skills, the company has aptly demonstrated the possibilities for future MNC expansion in the region.

Price revision: positions and formulas

At the overarching level the global MNC seeks to underpin any local pricing policy with a regional foundation of brand/product positioning guidelines. To bolster and support the brand strategy, multinationals were anxious that their extant market share in the ASEAN bloc not be devalued by any hasty discount pricing by the local teams. Guideline pricing strategies imposed at this juncture sought to ensure that price competition not be elevated to a "core" status among local marketing mix tactics. As a general concern, traditional ASEAN-based pricing methods were being roundly criticized during this revision period for their ad hoc, "gut feel" emphasis. Once lauded by Western headquarters for its intrinsic flexibility, Asian pricing was now being dismissed as inappropriate and unprofessional on the strength of its apparent lack of clear formulas to underpin individual unit prices.

Further, such unsystematic methods were held as detrimental to the longer-term future of respective MNC development policies. A number of MNCs therefore drafted in special "audit teams" from among the new marketing executives to try to determine the underlying threads to extant price portfolios. Their findings were of considerable concern. Across a number of key multinational "core" industries – including telecommunications, automobiles and chemical manufacturers – it was discovered that local "price to consumer" figures were often reached by a (deliberately) opaque mix of cost and "markup" calculations. Evidently such unwritten, "instinctive" methods ran contrary to the intricate systematic and statistically founded calculations operated by the typical global conglomerate. Visiting expatriates viewed these antecedent methods as being at best "piecemeal" and at worst "confused" – running contrary to the often intricate and systematic calculations operated by group headquarters.

Criticisms aside, the local methods of pricing were themselves often very complex, tending to be worked on a "line-by-line" basis to allow for maximum strategic maneuver. With each product pack priced independently, and with no scant written record of methodology, corporate attempts to systematize these old practices were fraught with difficulties – so much so that in a number of cases group headquarters were effectively bound to surrender control back to the indigenous methods, at least for a period.

Many MNCs were also confounded in their efforts by the severity of the economic crisis, a force that also compelled them to make further pricing concessions. Within the oil, petrochemical and automotive industries – traditional weathervanes of broader economic health – immediate postcrisis contingency plans witnessed key players being forced to review their product positioning.

A number of oil-based corporations decided to institute a regionally agreed "cost cushion" – of a temporary nature – of perhaps 5 to 10 percent on their current base oil expenditure. These "cost cushions" were introduced by companies independently, so this was not "price fixing" as such. Termed "standard (adjustable) cost" – as opposed to "actual cost" – the cost cushion was designed to provide them with added flexibility to cope with continuing currency exchange rate difficulties. Certain other measures were also introduced by MNCs using prime regional bases to export product to neighboring countries. Unilever, Bridgestone Tyres, Volvo and Castrol are cases in point, all involved in supplying product to Laos from Thailand at a time when the Lao authorities stipulated that all official price lists were in future to be drawn exclusively in US dollars. In order to cope with these changes, the companies involved chose to implement some form of exchange rate "range" for sales to their respective sole distributors. Given at, say, 2.5 percent either side of 40 Thai baht to 1 US dollar, this "range" was set up in order to better cushion themselves against future movements. The typical agreement involved an allowance for the range to either fall short of or exceed the set point for thirty consecutive days, following which a newly revised band would be established.

The underflow: forces for adaptation

In spite of all the MNCs' measures outlined above, there has remained a trickling – though ever-present – stream of indigenous dissent. Much of this has turned on the simple premise that not all global brands can be transferred to the region or be positioned in the same way in ASEAN countries as they are in the West. It was posited to us early on in our research that the so-called "Westernization" of Asian consumer tastes and behavior may in actuality be a myth. Young, affluent Asians, so it is held, are if anything becoming more "modernized" – and for the Asian populace there is a world of difference between the two depictions.

Further, the comparatively huge proportion of funds Western multinationals spend upon the development of their brands is not without its critics. Particular concern was expressed with regard to the perceived Western attitude toward brand and supporting price positioning whereby the corporate group favors the major shareholder at the expense of the Thai divisional balance sheet. Almost all interviewees expressed their doubts as to the long-term commitment of a Western multinational in their country, referring to previous experiences where such corporations tended to "cloak" their profits and shift proceeds overseas.

In their pursuit of integrated brands, MNCs were also berated for their attempts to persuade – even push – local consumers into buying more premium brands – that is, "trading up." Unilever – with its strategy of market dominance – came in for particular criticism from its distributors for such a push in Vietnam and Laos. Procter & Gamble was similarly denigrated for its perceived "overconcentration" on upmarket product lines, again in Vietnam. But this is not to say that local teams were unappreciative of the power of targeted branding tactics. Many managers we spoke to stated their belief in the status and achievement conveyed through the brand. In the East Asian marketing environment, the associative aspects of the societal culture make brand possession especially valid, founded on the indigenous importance attached to signaling one's place within a certain social group. But the main point here is the perceived incongruity of MNCs focusing upon the "top-end" segment in exclusivity.

To an extent this runs back to the multinationals' reemphasis upon product brand harmonization – a move that was itself criticized by the vast majority of local sales and marketing officers. Once again, we were regaled upon this topic with tales of Western MNC insensitivity to the needs of the local consumer base. In the light of its changing direction, Unilever – to our surprise – came in for a vast amount of criticism. According to members of the company's sales and distribution teams, the prevailing attitude of the firm was simply that "if a product works in Mongolia, then it'll work in the Lao PDR" – and so forth.

More broadly, the case for adapted product types – and their corollary brands – was reiterated and promoted by the majority of our local marketing informants. Representatives from the prestige cosmetics sector leaned upon the "you can't do the same thing with Chinese eyes and Chinese hair that you can with Caucasians" tack while their counterparts from the consumer goods industry pushed for the restocking of locally favored goods – an example here being that of salty toothpaste, playing on the local custom of using salt to clean teeth. One strong illustration of the apparent strength of the local product brand came in the form of Coca-Cola's energy drink Bolt, marketed through much of the region. Although extremely successful in Vietnam – for which it was originally formulated – Bolt essentially bombed in Thailand, Malaysia and Singapore, exacerbated by both varied domestic tastes and the Vietnamese script on the packaging. Coca-Cola's "Schweppes manao soda," by contrast, has been especially popular in Thailand, but far less so in Vietnam.

A similar domestic exclusivity confounded the consumer goods MNC Unilever, with its regionally developed range of tamarind-based shampoos. Originally conceived and manufactured in Thailand, the "tamarind" range took over two years to perfect and was eventually supplied in the color yellow, green, orange, black, blue and clear. Bizarrely, however, and in spite of an equidistribution of promotional coverage, only the black variant really ever took off in both Vietnam and Laos, leaving Thailand to soak up the majority of the other colors. Because of such domestic – let alone regional – market idiosyncrasies, the vast majority of our local corporate respondents remained in favor of products suited to the "ordinary local consumer."

The MNCs' upmarket emphasis was further criticized on a number of more general grounds. To begin with, the regional collapse in consumer purchasing power seemed to favor the local stress upon price marketing as a means to maintain valuable market share. In this context Castrol's aim of seeking to make its local customers "aspire" to buying its premium-branded products seemed nonsensical. Regional managers were adamant in their belief that mere "aspiration" alone was hardly going to figure in the monthly sales volume – or indeed profitability – figures. As one senior Thai sales manager reiterated,

> "Who from our customers, or from all of the Thai people, is going to be interested about this kind of thing, especially in this present bad [economic] situation? . . . they [corporate HQ] should try to remember that nobody can eat this 'aspiration' story, nobody can eat an 'image'."

Furthermore, and in spite of what was perceived as "headquarters propaganda," it was held that the mass/value end of markets within the region comprised the bread and butter for the vast majority of local MNC units. Hence, while the local teams adhered to the need for developing brand strength, they were also of the opinion that this should be placed on a back burner in the sluggish postcrisis environment. For the likes of Toyota, Honda and even Ford and General Motors, the reality of consumer demand for automobiles in the region was focused primarily on cheap cars and motorcycles with low fuel consumption and strong design.

As the recession wore on into its second year, price effectively surpassed brand as a deciding factor in product choice among hard-hit motorists. As a consequence of this, many ancillary industries such as petrochemicals, automotive parts and oil were also adversely affected. Within the motor lubricants sector the major multinationals, Shell, Esso, Castrol, Mobil and Caltex, felt especially threatened by the changing, price-conscious consumer climate. A flood of cheaper mineral brands progressively muscled in on their ASEAN markets, as low-cost, often illegal local distributors have been the only suppliers to benefit from the ongoing economic downturn. This preference for cheaper, buyer-friendly indigenous goods was also bolstered by the various government-sponsored "Buy Thai/Malay/Filipino/Indo/Vietnamese" campaigns, which have appeared especially persuasive against any further encroachment of the "global brand." Profits in many MNCs were, however, maintained at respectable levels, but only at the expense of some painful retrenchment in staff numbers.

Local methods: the defense

Indigenous counterproposals have tended to focus on revised notions as to what constituted the "right" products at the "right" price – with an undisguised emphasis upon domestic customization. It appeared that the typical MNC preoccupation with a coordinated, efficient overall structure was being pitted once again against the indigenous, traditional emphasis on flexibility, adaptation and intuition. To this end, notions of cross-border product brand differentiation and standardization were largely demoted down the priority list in favor of unadulterated "customer orientation."

Nonetheless, the localized emphasis on tailored goods was not pushed in a vacuum. In order to secure a viable longer-term strategy alternative, several key business mores were promoted in support. Foremost among these was the age-old stress on local company–customer relationships. More precisely, the long-standing, often informal networks that pervaded the corporate environment in Asia between individual managers and clients were held as comprising the traditional *equivalent* to Western notions of "branding." Further, and perhaps more interestingly, such claims were made not solely for the industrial sectors – where business-to-business relations have been universally important – but also, and even especially, for the domestic *consumer* market base. Quite simply, the concept of *reputation* within the relevant local networks effectively acts as the Asian equivalent of the concept of *branding* in the "developed" world.

For the local marketing teams the clearest means by which to "develop" – that is, enhance loyalties toward – the "brand" is to focus in the first instance upon maintaining, reinforcing and then expanding these established company–customer networks. Developing customer communication channels at a time of continued economic instability continues to be pushed as the sole method of ensuring brand strength in the ASEAN marketplace. MNCs would do well to recall that, in any case, the vast majority of regional consumers away from the few big cities remain relatively uneducated as to the notions of "brand positioning," often basing their attitudes on an unquestioning acceptance of product claims. At this stage of market development, the local retailer will, if anything, have far more influence over any purchasing decision than any globally promoted brand name. In this context the local equivalent to a "brand positioning strategy," on the basis of the remarks above, would focus on reining in MNC territorial ambitions in the selection of the most *favorable* ground over which a product can consolidate its sales, then expand. In positioning terms the multinational should therefore pay far less attention to where it perceives that the brand *should* be in the market – and instead divert its resources to identifying where it can *win*. In fact Castrol's market strength in up-country Thailand can be traced to a decision taken thirty years ago to have English on one side of the pack and Thai on the other.

Price competition

Newly imposed moves in favor of regionally decided, globally approved price positioning policies – to "coordinate" and "bolster" brand strength

– were severely criticized by the local marketing teams of incumbent Western MNCs. Depicted as a "straitjacket" in the Southeast Asian trading environment, the perceived rigidity of a regional pricing standard was deemed an unavoidable hindrance to traditional market success. The prevailing view was that any move toward corporate "harmonization" would in practice serve to bind the local sales managers, against their instinctive knowledge of both the market and their customers.

A host of indigenous managers stressed that in Southeast Asia the traditional method of using price backed by the relations-linked "personal touch" was the *only* real way to communicate with the local customer. By virtue of its speed and flexibility, their habitual "gut feel," user-friendly pricing was deemed to have been the major factor in accounting for the tremendous sales growth in the precrisis years. The Western obsession with "structures" was derided as culturally incongruent in an environment where notions of flexible price "haggling" were so deeply ingrained in the minds of the indigenous customer base. Western-style retailing founded on the "fixed" price in the local department stores and supermarkets has largely been an innovation of the past decade and a half (Singapore and parts of Malaysia excepted).

Further critiques centered on the perceived overemphasis of the brand name by foreign MNCs. According to local managers, this was just one more expression of Western naïveté in a culturally distant host market. For one thing, it was put to us that the whole idea of brands in Southeast Asia was to some extent a "fad" linked exclusively to the younger generation. As one executive put it,

> "Like so many other things from the US, the idea will die down and then the young will forget all about it. Especially in the problem situation we have since the economic slowing . . . this thing about the foreign brand name will pass . . . [because] it's not really suitable here on the long term, it doesn't suit how local people really think."

This appeared to be supported by other comments made to us on the subject. Added to the decline of the "novelty" period was the inevitable entry of more and more foreign competitors all bent upon the same "brand-focused" course of action. This, it was held, would expedite the unavoidable lowering of prices to support continued sales growth – again, particularly in the recent unstable market environment.

In this uncertain climate, the MNCs' tendency to hold firm to their global brand positioning has led to a further series of negative side effects. For one thing, the failure to lower prices in an era of lowered consumer confidence has undoubtedly served to exacerbate the local gray trade in imitation Western-branded goods. Sellophane bags of consumer goods manufactured by the likes of Procter & Gamble, Colgate-Palmolive and Unilever have often been subject to emptying, repackaging, stapling and then repricing in the same bags, and to good effect – with customers drawn to a perceived "realistic price."

The gray trade has also been effectively encouraged over time by the unwillingness of certain MNCs to *adapt* their prices within the ASEAN bloc. The classic illustration here concerns the corporate use of Thailand as a base with which to serve the emerging economies of the Mekong Delta, notably the Lao PDR. In contrast to the depth and long-term potential of the Thai economy, Laos was recently ranked the thirteenth poorest country in the world, only barely off the United Nations list of the "least developed" countries. Nonetheless, premium-graded MNCs such as Castrol have been criticized by their Lao agents and retailers as being unrealistic, inflexible and plain unwilling to adjust their prices and halt the swathe of illegal border sales via the more powerful Thai concessionaires on the border. This type of "gray trade" coming across the Mekong River from Thailand into Laos has been a major bone of contention between local agents and their multinational principals. According to a prominent Lao-based agency, in their refusal to lower their prices adequately, foreign MNCs were encouraging the practice of big-volume Thai-based distributors (Makro et al.) shipping their excess consignments illegally across the river at a price below that offered to the agent. The general MNC retort – that they were already offering a "special price" to their Lao agents – was dismissed as of no consequence, as in practice it was still failing to stamp out the illegal shipments. In response to this the multinationals tended to reiterate the fact that – "whatever the case" – the gray trade would always be practically impossible to stop completely.

But this was not always the case. Certain big consumer-goods multinationals – e.g. Kimberley Clark, Unilever and Colgate-Palmolive – have actually *lowered* their Lao prices to make them on a par with or even lower than those of the big Thai concessionaires. This was accomplished via the calculation of a final Lao "price to customer" (i.e. cost and freight plus import duty, added to the agreed CBKP margin plus VAT) so that it equated to the cheapest Thai wholesale price in operation. In practice the Lao distributors for these MNCs were effectively being subsidized in order to dissuade retailers/wholesalers from crossing the river into Thailand to buy product and then channeling it back into the country.

Pricing Strategy in the Lao PDR I: The Case of Castrol

As the self-proclaimed "lubricants specialist" – and in line with the company's premium imaging – Castrol's ASEAN positioning strategy has hinged upon targeting imported, prestige motorcycle consumers. As a long-term concern Castrol aims to "trade up" the region's consumers to using its higher-quality motor oils – mostly via "educating" them in order to lengthen their oil drain intervals, hence saving them money. In the more developed markets such as Singapore – and, to some extent, Thailand and Malaysia – the group has already partly witnessed this trend materialize, as increasingly stringent pollution regulations have gradually shifted buyers toward more expensive, environmentally friendly synthetic oils – for which Castrol is renowned.

Wishing to avoid any "dilution" of the global master brand, as elsewhere in ASEAN, Castrol decided to duplicate this strategy in the Lao PDR, focusing its products away from the mass-market brands in Laos and into a specialist, premium price niche all to itself. Yet this strategy – effectively duplicated from that adopted in the Thai market – was the major stumbling block for its sole distributor in Laos. Although to some extent conscious of these local difficulties, Castrol decided nonetheless to try to "persuade" local dealers – and hence consumers – to accept the long-term benefits of its premium oils.

Although seeking to make initial concessions to the poorer Lao consumer, Castrol still insisted it make a trading profit of at least 10 percent on every pack sold, less than half of what it would normally expect to accrue in Thailand. Beyond this initial adaptation of its prices, Castrol decided that it would not be able to "flex" its regionally set pricing policy any further. Concerned with the positioning and its overall control of the brand in Laos, the company was wary of compromising its premium brand image, regarding its master and product brands as being among its most valuable assets. As one executive stated,

> "They build extra value for our products and help differentiate us from our
> competitors, which has always been our route to competitive advantage . . .
> we are supposed to be the lubricants specialist and that is how we want all
> our consumers anywhere in the world to see us . . . the idea of economy
> simply does not fit in with our image."

Instead of seeking the traditional "maximum profit flow" objective, the "adapted" brand goal in Laos was held to be that of making the local consumer aspire to buying Castrol products. This was implemented via the initial training of the designated Lao team at Castrol (Thailand)'s head office in Bangkok. Castrol Thai executives sought to warn the agent away from being too concerned with simply "shifting units" and stressed that the agent should focus on developing the company's image as an initial target, and be content to sell smaller than anticipated volumes of high-margin product.

However, Castrol's official agent for the country, claiming to speak on behalf of its customers, expressed incredulity at Castrol's attitude as well as its own total lack of interest in stocking any "top-drawer" product range. The agent's desire was to concentrate on the company's "lower-end" products such as those used in the poorer, fragmented agricultural regions of Thailand. The view was quite simply that the Castrol strategy, whereas quite possibly suited to the richer cities of the region, was patently incongruent for the world's thirteenth poorest country. To begin with, the transport infrastructure in Laos is notoriously underdeveloped, an environment which renders the notion of vehicle "performance" pale in comparison to the twin factors of "robust design" and "large ground clearance" (see also Jurado, 1998). Added to this is the bottom-end per capita income of consumers, reinforcing the local desire for low fuel consumption and sturdy build quality as the norm. In a similar vein the regulatory preoccupation of the Lao authorities is in marked contrast to the "environmentally friendly" trends gaining ground across the rest of the region. Certainly there has been a marked lack of governmental interest in implementing exhaust emission standards – leading to a continued demand for only the cheapest mineral lubricants.

Taking these above factors into consideration, even Castrol was forced to accept a partial dilution of its original "brand establishment" objectives for Laos. Although Castrol managed to persuade the agent to at least *stock* its "flagship" product brands in the agent's office premises, there was an overwhelmingly dismissive disinclination on the part of the Lao agent to "take these products any further"; the agent stated that for the local customer such premium goods were simply a "fantasy." Many of the indigenous Lao retailers responded to Castrol's market approach with almost contemptuous dismissals. As one representative expressed it to us,

> "We have to be clear about this. Laos is not your average industrializing ASEAN market, it's one of the poorest undeveloped countries in the world. If your product is simply not affordable to the Lao consumer then you're in dreamland here; whatever your so-called brand development objectives are, whatever your product benefits, your strategy just will not work. People in Laos have problems even in paying for imitation oil, you'll see them leave their bikes in these oil shops for three days, maybe a week at a time as the only money in their pockets must be spent on food for the family. As a middle class in Laos are virtually nonexistent, then 99.999 percent of the population will think only as far as tomorrow, and get a cheap repair when their engine beaks down."

Trade and corporate research documentation seems to support the agent's comments concerning income structure differentials. To place Laos's very limited vehicle parc (meaning the total number of vehicles in the country) in perspective, whereas in Thailand the ratio of motorcycles to people was something like 1:6 in 1999, the corresponding figures for Laos were barely 1:40. This gives a practical idea of the widely differing levels of purchasing power. Although this differential was slightly reduced with the onset of economic crisis, the resulting drop in the Thai baht's value, the increase in VAT, and the sharp rise in oil and electricity charges boosted the already elevated transport and production costs involved in exporting lubricants to the Lao PDR. This then tended to exacerbate the contention surrounding Castrol's stated pricing policy.

Perhaps more intriguing here is the apparent contradiction in the detailed price formulation adopted by Castrol for the Lao domestic territory – "contradictory" in the sense that it appears to run counter to the group corporate literature. Castrol from the outset has based its price to the Lao distributor on a cost-plus-plus basis in the attainment of its minimum 10 percent trading margin. The calculated agent price CIF (cost, insurance and freight) was scaled upward by Castrol to include tax and the various retailer/wholesaler "cuts" in arriving at a final pricing bandwidth it wished to see presented to the local customers. But whereas the final consumer prices were around 10 to 15 percent lower than the equivalent price in Thailand, they were still as much as 35 percent higher than those of the rest of the competition in Laos.

Castrol's stated *corporate* pricing strategy runs against this, however, advocating "market pricing," which is almost diametrically opposed to the type of structure built for Laos. Corporate literature emphasizes the avoidance of "cost-plus" pricing strategy as "creating an easy opportunity for competitors." Cost pricing – it is held – will only embody "what a market will bear" as opposed to the favored "market pricing" which, by contrast, embodies what a market is *willing to pay*. Market pricing in Laos would seem to indicate a need to encompass the low levels of purchasing power based on equally low income levels, a point accepted by the majority of Castrol sources questioned on the point. Respondents from group headquarters were also prepared to accept the fact that despite the corporate "blurb," the Thai unit was utilizing uncharacteristically simplistic pricing methods for the Lao market, a fact they were uneasy with. It was further suggested that this idiosyncratic structure expressed a deeper division and lack of clarity concerning the group's overall intentions for both its product and its sole distributor in Laos.

Further disagreements arose concerning Castrol's regional strategic focus, which was tightly concentrated upon consumer lubricants and away from any diversification into areas perceived as unrelated to or "diluted" from the perceived corporate core strengths. The Lao agent's wish to target the supply of industrial lubricants into the Lao beer factory on an "exclusive" package with the plant was rejected on these grounds. Agency requests for certain greases and in particular a specialist lubricant for sewing machine oils – for the local Singer plant – were also dismissed. The agent's retort that this was unfair to Laos – in that such Castrol oils were readily marketed in Singapore – was countered with the statement that in Castrol's view Laos should follow the same market curve as that pursued by Thailand, on the basis of the cultural and historic similarities between the two nations.

Pricing Strategy in the Lao PDR II: The Case of Unilever

Unilever takes no prisoners in the furtherance of its "full-spectrum dominance" policy. To this end the company's long-term goal in the Lao domestic market is simple: "market supremacy." In this respect the company – and its patient shareholders – are not seeking to make money from the outset, but are prepared to wait ten – even fifteen – years to secure a satisfactory return on assets. Unilever's strategic thrust rests in part upon the importance group executives attach to "first mover" status within any given territory. The advantage of effectively being a pioneer in far-flung emerging economies is that it has allowed Unilever to tailor a strategy designed to "sew up" a market before the likes of Procter & Gamble and Colgate-Palmolive can follow suit.

Once within the market, the company's traditional route to capturing 95 to 100 percent market share stems from its policy of domestic product adaptation. In practical terms Unilever's soap powder, detergent and toothpaste are the company's top sellers in Laos, effectively funding the more rural, up-country marketing of its other household items. Rather than seeking to overcome the essential economic variations between its Thai and Lao consumers, Unilever has sought to tailor its product range on the basis of usage requirements and package size. For instance, unlike in Thailand, soap powders in Laos are used not merely for washing clothes but also for washing hands, hair and cutlery – being considerably cheaper than soap or shampoo. Unilever also developed a local product development program for its shampoo range, which finally found expression in a black-and-yellow-packaged shampoo variant tailored specifically for the Vientiane customer base. Furthermore, in terms of package size differences, although Unilever's range of shampoos come in size of 500, 200 and 100 ml and sachets, it was only the sachets that ever really sold, accounting for over 90 percent of total shampoo sales. Because of the very low income levels, buying patterns among the Lao are dominated by the "enough for today, the devil take tomorrow" attitude.

This final point accentuated the overall success of the company's domestic pricing policy in Laos. Unilever's first move was to effectively subsidize its agent – via reduced cross-border price sets – in order that they both avoid hefty excise and customs duties. By pricing its products at among the cheapest in Asia, Unilever has sought to acquire and then maintain a wide and loyal domestic customer base. Having secured the requisite "brand loyalty," the company could then begin to edge prices upward in order to reap the rewards of long-term investment. In contrast to the Castrol stress upon profitability flows, Unilever's initial working objective of market share expansion essentially kept its agent, dealers and customers satisfied – at least until now. This was reflected in the annual doubling of the company's sales volumes during its first three years of operations. Through the adept exploitation of its first-mover advantages both Unilever and its agent have largely attained their joint objectives of Lao market domination.

"Cross-verging" brand perspectives

Over the course of the postcrisis period, the diverging brand priorities outlined in the above sections have to an extent been enmeshed and compromised in the emergence of a set of "cross-vergent" positioning practices. These have been depicted to us in a number of varied – though converging – definitions and suppositions. As a senior marketing executive with the US oil giant Caltex expressed it,

"Essentially, your strategy in the Southeast Asian market has to be built on twin pillars, pillars of priority . . . that must always be referred to, no matter what you do. The first of these is your brand, the international brand equity of your company. The second is a positioning strategy in line with local realities. It's about balancing the two forces in the best way you can."

To summarize the sentiments of a host of both local and expatriate marketing managers, the branding strategy of the foreign MNC must "fit" the level of development of the domestic market. This "fit" has been described in varying terms, one of them being the catch-all claim to target the "right" products to the "right" people. The more specific issue of "sensitivity" to local cultural mores was also expressed on numerous occasions as an underlying balance to the push for regional standardization. Within the varied domestic markets of the region, obviously the basic needs and underlying motivations of consumers change only very slowly – reinforcing the need for adapted marketing strategies. At the same time, fashion and more superficial needs tend to change much more quickly – hence the opportunity for globalized strategies linked to localized behavior adaptation. A cross section of Japanese and Western MNCs are progressively seeking to identify and explore a potential blend of the necessarily local and the ideally global in order to manage their respective brands across the region.

In practical terms the typical contemporary MNC must plan and announce its long-term market and financial objectives from a central – increasingly global – source. This is partly in order to set challenging and measurable goals to work toward; partly to impress the shareholders and financial analysts. Downstream at the business unit/host-market subsidiary level, however, the organization must also ensure that its own goals are based to an extent upon local customers and their buying behavior, and also on the local competition (as well as the unit's own skill and resources levels). In accounting for these local market variations the foreign MNC may well engender a "relative" – as opposed to "absolute" – positioning strategy in acknowledgment of domestic realities. To use a previous example, although the troubled UK retail group Marks & Spencer serves the mass-market segment in its home base, across much of Southeast Asia it is positioned in an altogether different bracket: that of "high" or "top end." But in this context the brand image was "raised" only to the extent that it was held unchanged across markets with contrasting levels of purchasing power. A more "active" example of relative brand positioning concerns the Danish beer manufacturer

Carlsberg, whose beer is brewed in ASEAN under license. Positioned in Thailand to compete in the mass-market segment alongside the likes of the local brand Singha, Carlsberg decided to change the color of its bottle from green to brown to reflect this shift. With the progressive rise in income levels, however, for the long term the company has radically changed its direction in order to better "balance" its brand positioning along the global–local continuum. Hence the return to the green bottle alongside both its MNC competitors, such as Heineken and Becks, and the premium local brand Kloster. We should also note here that interestingly, despite the changes in packaging, Carlsberg never once lowered the actual quality of the bottle contents – regardless of consumer perceptions.

The progressive emergence of hybrid brand positioning strategies in recent years has to a degree been the tale of global corporate concessions to the Southeast Asian marketplace. These have been facilitated by the explosion of Internet-based global pricing capability among the larger MNCs. Improved computer-based technologies have permitted them to improve their information bases with regard to currency changes, international tax adjustments, and transparent cross-cultural differences in price elasticity, crucially increasing the ease with which regional markets can be segmented (see also Lazer and Shaw, 2000).

At the broader level, Western MNCs have reconsidered their corporate "top-end" positioning emphasis, diluting certain such policies in deference to the continuing uncertainties of local consumers. This is clearly illustrated by a number of MNCs within the domestic oil-related industries – the likes of Castrol, Mobil, Ford and Shell. Castrol corporate guidelines for Thailand were effectively repositioned in order to amalgamate the differing global–local areas of emphases, in practice devoting more resources to the "mass-market," bread-and-butter segments traditionally served by the "lower-end" standard products such as Super 2T for motorcycles and LT40 for automobiles. Although the change was only of a few percentage points, this expenditure switch agreed between the newly separated sales and marketing departments and the regional head office was welcomed by senior local executives as a sign of a mutually beneficial postcrisis rebuilding strategy (acknowledging – "at last" – the *traditional Thai* policy of targeting contextual consumer preferences).

Similarly, in Vietnam the Shell group has sought to compete in and capture part of the lower-margin "cheap lube" segment – again without compromising its premium brand image. In attaining this objective Shell has adopted a radically different tack, however, shifting further toward the "local" end of the positioning spectrum. In practice a strategy was put in place whereby Shell could maintain – even raise – the positioning of its corporate/premium brand imaging on the one hand while undercutting the prices of its local competitors on the other. Simply and cleverly, the latter part of this strategy was implemented via the formulating and adoption of the Molla product for the mass motorcycle segment. Blended from the cheapest base oils, the Molla range targeted the lower end of the domestic market, the local "man in the street" for whom the Shell-branded equivalent remained a distant fantasy. But on the Molla range itself there was no mention of the Shell master-brand connection – either in the advertising and promotion or on the product packaging. In this way the Shell corporate fold of brands remained uncompromised.

The local Lao retailers' reaction to the development of Molla – perceived as an apparent corporate "ploy" – was at best lukewarm. Cautiously welcoming of the realistic opportunity Shell was providing for them to compete in the domestic mass market, these customers remained partially resentful of not being able to do so using the weight of the global Shell master-brand symbol in support. The feeling was that Shell would have done better to have competed "up front" at the "bread-and-butter" end of the market, as a mark – among other things – of "respect" for the Vientiane populace. However, it should also be noted that the majority of retailer comments were expressed less as an indication of what they themselves thought and were more about how they perceived their *own* customers/end users would react.

In one respect, and perhaps surprisingly, the premium-brand "lubricants specialist" Castrol actually moved closer to a genuine local product variant using its own master brand on the packaging. This came in the form of a low-end mineral oil tailored specifically for the Mekong Delta – the kind of motor lubricant common in the UK as far back as the 1950s! The Shell company equivalent was, if anything, stocked well away from the road engine range and apparent in the fishing boat oil FB40 – again for Vietnam exclusively. But in terms of longer-term corporate concessions to local realities, a more fitting example stems from another US oil major, Conoco. In a distribution agreement with the local supermarket chain Tops, Conoco has sought to gain considerable leverage in the longer-term growth of the "supermarket" supply chain. According to Conoco, this strategic tie-in with such a local partner would enable it to build indigenous brand loyalties via cooperative positioning strategies.

Further down the supply stream, concessions and compromises have also been witnessed in the practical field of product pricing. Taking stock of initial postcrisis resistance on the part of the local sales teams, a number of Western MNCs, including Castrol, have decided to rebuild their *own* price formulas "from the inside" – on the basis of an eighteen-month record of individual pack pricing movements. This strategy has been operationalized via negotiations held between local managers and corporate marketing envoys and representatives. Still with nominal responsibility for the final "price-to-consumer" tag, the local sales and marketing team were eventually given an ongoing "free hand" with individual pack prices via the use of monthly set promotions and discounts. Yet the broader price positioning has still in practice been set by regional marketing representatives through the utilization of a pricing "bandwidth" for each segment, in line with the corporate brand portfolio framework. Subsidiary consensus would then be sought and secured on a theoretical basis, so long as the market price remained anywhere within this predetermined range. In practice this might involve a reclarification of market objectives, typically followed by a joint price positioning survey of the territory by both corporate and subsidiary representatives. Realistic sales targets with corresponding volumes could then be drawn, again on a mutually agreed basis.

Essentially, local managers were being reinvested with the power to fine-tune individual pack pricing in line with their short-term customer priorities. Furthermore, this "bilateral" agreement as to priority and strategy signaled in part the return to consensus decision making in line with ASEAN business norms. But in retaining corporate control of regional positioning bandwidths it was also an illustration of the strategic blends of priorities increasingly prevalent in the postcrisis period.

In the gradual convergence of accepted branding and product-range practice, concessions were also sought – and even proffered – on the part of the local subsidiary unit. Take the aforementioned "about-turn" of the consumer goods MNC Unilever, which retrenched perhaps 50 percent of its locally formulated product range. Quite simply, as time has worn on, even Unilever's skeptical local representatives across the Mekong have had to accept that in many of these cases the move was a justifiable one. Unilever was simply supplying far too many different product sizes, many of which sold only in token volumes. Previous examples of shampoo packs in Laos provide a classic illustration. A similar fate has accompanied the sales of the company's toothpaste across the Mekong Delta, where only the smallest two sizes ever sold.

Similar cases have emerged from the field of product price-positioning strategy, where time has often served to prove that the MNC premium stance has been the correct route to follow in the sustenance of long-term competitive advantage. Certainly, local concerns have needed more attention than has typically been afforded them. For one thing, the notion of premium pricing by *local* – as opposed to global – brackets remains a valid avenue of compromise. Positioning should always, inevitably, be determined by *both* strategic brand positioning *and* consumer empathy. Hence, if sales fail to show up in the short term, then local sales teams, as well as their corporate marketing counterparts, should hold firm – "elevated" pricing may not always be to blame.

Fortunately for the global MNC, there are discernible trends within the region toward a more internationally oriented business environment. An increasing number of local companies have been voicing their unease with what they perceive to be their relatively "blurred" positioning policies within the domestic territories – at least when compared to their Western counterparts. We also note with interest the frequency with which the indigenous marketing managers of global MNCs have themselves begun to stress the need for "differentiating products" and "adding power" to the brand name, encouraging the input of resources into developing brand awareness and product imaging, innovation and design as being tangible long-term assets for their organizations. This is well illustrated by the recent tie-in of the Malaysian national automaker Proton with the prestige Lotus group. In financial terms the acquisition of its stake in the British supercar has been a substantial burden, especially in an already depressed economic context (the Lotus Group has, after all, been losing money for years, even in its home market). The move itself is hence indicative of the wider shifts in Asian attitudes toward the importance of product design, technology and, of course, branding. The current Proton Satria GTI now sports a small silver badge on its boot upon which the phrase "Engineered by Lotus" is suitably inscribed – lending the Malaysian brand what has been described as "real performance car credibility" (Bickers, 2001).

Branding in Thailand: The Case of Blacktec

In aiming to strengthen its top-end postcrisis brand positioning in Thailand, Castrol decided to develop a new, regionally marketed premium automotive lubricant. In its quest to accomplish this shift in emphasis, the plan was to effectively scrap the locally conceived flagship product brand Blacktec. The latter product had been developed and sold exclusively in Thailand since its launch in 1995, yet had been increasing cause for concern for the parent group. Corporate doubts centered in particular on the overall positioning "fit" of the product in the regional hierarchy of products. This in turn stemmed from the racy, arguably sexist promotion and packaging of the product – flames, black leathers and a scantily clad model being among the composite ingredients. Concern was also expressed with the marginal sales figures engendered by the product.

Toward the end of 1997 the local Thai management were briefed on the corporate plan to replace the product altogether with a higher-positioned international alternative already in use through much of the region (including Malaysia and Singapore). Local reaction to these home office efforts was predominantly emotional, based on the attachment held to a product brand that had been developed and packaged internally, and free from UK "interference." Blacktec was depicted as a "premium Thai product for the premium Thai people" and jealously guarded by the senior marketing team. The corporate plan to replace the product with a higher-positioned regional alternative was also criticized for its insensitivity in the depressed economic environment.

Resentment to the idea of giving up their "baby" (as it was described) prompted Castrol headquarters to strike a compromise deal with the local marketing team. In simple terms a decision was made to effectively transfer the resources earmarked for the originally proposed new product launch toward a heavily promoted *re*launch of Blacktec. Minor repositioning facets were incorporated, along with a higher-quality blend, although the local name was kept. Although slightly higher-positioned than its predecessor – and subject to a corporate-directed reblending – New Blacktec was largely acceptable to the local management team in that it retained the former name, image and basic packaging and would thus be perceived by the local consumer more as an "update" than a replacement.

10 Advertising and promotion

- The traditional dilemma
- Corporate advertising and promotion retrenchment
- Indigenous resistance
- Intra-ASEAN promotion strategy
- Advertising and promotion strategy "cross-vergence"

Taken as an integrated whole, the variety of activities that comprise corporate advertising and promotions strategy is often deemed to be the most important of cross-national marketing tools. Certainly the host of MNCs we spoke to considered advertising and promotions strategy to be the principal means through which the corporation communicates its core "differentiation" message to the regional/domestic market base. Due prominence will be given to advertising in this chapter as the most visible promotional activity. But localized sales promotion activities – such as trade fairs, adapted billboards, public relations and publicity, and the usual corporate paraphernalia – will also be discussed at length. A major concern for global MNCs is that these component tools together project and deliver a consistent message and image, particularly in the emerging markets of ASEAN, where certain elements of the promotional armory may not yet be available.

The MNC promotional "mix" – whether developed on a global basis or for a specific region – is traditionally implemented by local employees. As Johansson (2000) notes, local salespeople are necessary for running promotional schemes such as in-store displays, free samples and contests. Because of the added complications of widely differing local trading regulations and cultural mores, promotional activities have always presented especially valid objections to being "standardized" – whatever the superficial financial incentives involved. However, with the recent growth of computer-generated technology, the global reach of Western media has become a technological reality and the incentives for seeking to coordinate advertising and promotions strategy have never been stronger. Those incentives have been compounded by the concurrent growth of the "global brand" and catalyzed by the economic crash of the late 1990s.

Against this backdrop the following discussion focuses upon the postcrisis attempts by – predominantly – Western multinationals to retrench and harmonize their ASEAN promotions mix strategies. We retrace the traditional dilemmas involved, corporate procedures for restandardization plus the indigenous reactions to these proposals, concluding once again with some of the longer-term "hybrid" practices that have emerged.

The traditional dilemma

Because of both technological and cultural constraints, of the promotional activities utilized in Southeast Asia, personal selling and outdoor emplacements have traditionally been the most important. The heavy traffic and bustling crowds typical of most ASEAN cities ensure large audiences for outdoor messages such as billboard advertising. Indeed, their affordability, exposure and long life (typically six months or longer) make billboards a most popular form of outdoor advertising. Bus shelters, telephone cabins and panels on the bodies of buses and trolleys are also used extensively for advertisements throughout these cities.

However, in line with global technological advances the possibilities for the dissemination of information in ASEAN have multiplied. Concurrent with these advances have been the overall increases in consumer spending up to the present day (crisis notwithstanding). Greater per capita incomes, particularly within the urban centers, have expanded television set ownership levels. As the affluence of countries grows, new products and services have appeared, and customers feel they need more information. Advertising becomes more important, and advertising expenditures as a percentage of GDP typically increases markedly.

Further, the structure of the typical ASEAN-market advertising "spend" has altered considerably in the past decade, with consumer goods having replaced industrial products as the major object of advertising focus. A similar fate has affected advertising message *content*, instanced by the cases of both the cosmetics and the food industries. Heavily pushed in urban areas over the past few years, the message accompanying these products has one of modernity and technology association, indicating a fascination with cultural values considered "Western." Added to this has been the progressive introduction of new types of advertising vehicles within these host markets. Traditionally they have been a billboard stronghold, but locally based advertisers looking for "flashier" displays have turned *en masse* to the idea of neon signage, particularly in the larger cities. As the number of skyscrapers continues to increase, this desire for neons is exacerbated by the potential for roof signs visible for miles around.

More generally, as the host economies of Southeast Asia continue to integrate, the opportunity for pan-regional communication strategies continues to gnaw at incumbent MNCs anxious for further scale efficiencies. But the practical realizations of such corporate priorities are rooted deeply within the multidomestic fabric of the region. This is well illustrated by the varied perceptions of the importance of the advertising function itself across the East–West divide. A large cultural gap exists between Western corporate clients and their global advertising agencies on the one hand and their ethnic Chinese counterparts on the other. This is partly a result of differing business traditions. The predominant view of the indigenous ASEAN managers is that their own advertising agents, with little expertise beyond that of media procurement, simply do not merit much remuneration. Traditionally utilizing their resources in other ways, these local teams are now understandably reluctant to start spending relatively vast sums of money on multinational agency houses such as Saatchi & Saatchi. Conversely, Western MNCs demand advertising expertise according to their own standards and are loath to "cut corners" in host markets, no matter what the prevailing attitude may be.

To take an example, as the world's largest advertising spender, the US consumer-goods giant Procter & Gamble has always hinged its global strategy upon the optimal promotion "mix" for its fold of products. Yet this strategy has come up against some stiff local resistance in – among other places – Vietnam. More precisely, its local JV partner, the Phuong Dong company, had always relied on its state distribution ties to get its products to consumers in what it termed a concrete, practical way. The incoming corporate stress upon advertising spend as a core concern was largely dismissed as impractical and incongruent – as a inefficient use of their joint resources (see also Quang, 1998).

Beyond this, however, much of what Western MNCs have implemented in the way of campaign advertising has been accepted in local markets.

This is not to say that pitfalls do not exist – they do, and many of them concern culture. These are often compounded in the ASEAN bloc by its cultural diversity, especially in those countries with indigenous as well as Chinese and/or Indian immigrant communities. Nonetheless, precrisis period MNC advertising in the region effectively complied with standard international marketing theory in that domestic campaigns were thoroughly researched in order to conform to local sensibilities and avoid potential conflicts with indigenous societal values. Expatriate managers spoke to us of the need for close monitoring of evolving cultural and social values; essentially, of the need to develop an advertising strategy that is *responsive* to the needs of the target population.

As one incumbent expatriate CEO expressed it,

> "In my experience, if your advertising strategy is really going to touch the people you want it to . . . [then] it has to come from the heart, based on not just your knowledge and experience but also of your *feelings* for the indigenous people. This goes for PR events as well; relying on engineered campaigns from head office which are just shaped at the edges is just asking for trouble or, even worse, indifference. One way of making sure your campaigns stand a better chance of local success is through using local staff – both your own and those from the agencies."

Many of the MNC branch units we talked to boasted a local as head of PR for just this reason. Similarly, a goodly host of global advertising agencies present in the region – typified by Ogilvy & Mather – tend to employ local staff, perceived as understanding their own culture more deeply than the average expatriate ever could.

Corporate illustrations: advertising

Among the many examples of MNCs' adaptation of advertising, the consumer goods manufacturer Unilever's attempt to woo the rural populations of its target markets stands out – not least for the lengths the company has gone to to empathize with its consumers. To begin with, Unilever has often decided to shun traditional media – press, television, etc. – in its emerging markets on the grounds of their being in themselves culturally incongruent. The developing markets of the Mekong Delta house very high rates of illiteracy and very low per capita income figures. Quite simply, the rural majority cannot afford television sets and do not read billboards or T-shirts. To deal with these factors Unilever utilizes "unconventional" media to contact its customers. For one thing, it typically seeks to establish a *physical* presence wherever people frequently gather in numbers. This means that hoardings advertising color photographs of its brands are seen at markets and along riverbanks where, in the very poorest areas, people still wash their clothes. A supporting strategy is to provide free samples of company product, for example via regular distribution among the visiting crowds on market days.

The flooding of local markets with corporate imagery has also been the mainstay of Castrol's marketing strategy within the region – notably in emerging markets such as Vietnam (as well as in Thailand years ago). Positioning the Castrol "red and green" at frequent intervals – say 50 metres – around the cities and larger towns, the group sought to establish brand awareness in the visual memories of domestic citizens as part of its stated ten- to fifteen-year developmental perspective.

At a more general level, in terms of advertising program design Western MNCs have traditionally had to be very wary in their portrayal of the female form. Region-wide advertisements have been especially difficult to disseminate for this reason. The traditional dress for Vietnam, for instance, is the *ao-dai*, a tight body-dress split at the thigh but with trousers worn underneath. In terms of generalized acceptance, whereas this may be acceptable for use in Cambodia (where the design is similar), it most certainly is not in the neighboring Lao PDR, where the Lao *sinh* is quite distinct. Further afield, the markets of Indonesia and parts of Malaysia are territories subject to the constraints of the Muslim religion, and due care must therefore be taken with the covering of women's heads as a matter of some urgency. Bedroom shots for shampoo and health-care products must also be thoroughly checked in order not to cause offense across the region.

Corporate illustrations: promotions

Unilever has always been noteworthy for its innovative promotional activities in the region. In Thailand, for example, the company staged the world's biggest catwalk, sporting a thousand models to promote its wares. In neighboring Cambodia the world's longest washing line was created in Phnom Penh for VISO detergent. Both these events were subsequently recognized by the *Guinness Book of Records*. In Myanmar the company has typically utilized the local penchant for video halls – a peculiarity to the country – where films are shown in a shop-house type of environment, instead of the more usual cinema houses. Unilever will then insert product-brand video clips during the main film and on-hand sales staff will promote and hand out giveaways. During program intervals an MC will typically enhance the spiel given to advertise the company's products.

Across the border in Thailand the annual motor show provides another stark illustration of the continuing importance of locally driven promotions events, often of a kind that would be inconceivable at the home bases of the sponsoring corporations. Reporting on the Twenty-Second Bangkok Motor Show – in an article entitled "Heels on Wheels" – Sreshthaputra (2001) depicts the "lovely lady presenters," along with the professional dancers hired for short performances, as being "just as much a draw as [the] cars themselves." Female presenters are further portrayed as an apparent "must" at every corporate stand, adding their "beauty, charm and communications skills" to the total "bodywork" of the vehicle on offer.

But such tactics are not the exclusive terrain of local companies (such as Proton from Malaysia). On the contrary, among the global auto manufacturers, present were the likes of Toyota, Peugeot, GM, Ford, BMW, Volkswagen and Mercedes-Benz – apparently with the blessing of their headquarters operations. In the words of the local Peugeot-Citroën director, as a marketing concept the feminine presentation of a car makes sense: "the . . . concept of a car is as a she . . . [and] so it's like presenting two beauties side by side." Cars are deemed to be the "fruit of technology" and synonymous with masculine qualities such as strength, performance and robustness. Women counterbalance this with the addition of the "elegance" and "refinement" characteristic of the premium-brand images – the term "softness" itself being used by one of the Toyota "Pretty-5" dancing girls (ibid.).

Promotion campaigns as a whole within the region have traditionally been utilized as a vehicle with which to boost certain products in certain areas, usually those deemed to be underperforming. As a case in point, within the motor oils industry Castrol has taken advantage of such promotions to target the supply of – for example – "gold coins" in special packs to such "problem" areas. Other methods employed by oil companies in Southeast Asia have involved, typically, the use of giveaway coupons, gifts and lucky draws at their respective gas station outlets. The general feeling among the local marketing managers is that customers were happier with what they could get "on the spot." Hence the penchant for gizmos for car interiors, tissue boxes, even drinks such as Coca-Cola and beer (!).

Corporate advertising and promotion retrenchment

Although they are domestically customized to reflect local cultural mores, the very endurance of internationally recognized "motor shows" in the region illustrates the potential for future convergence in advertising and promotion – at least to the multinationals. One of the major markets to have seemingly "opened itself up" to international promotions practice during this period is Vietnam – and in part via the progressive softening in its attitude to the portrayal of its women. The beauty contests and calendars sanctioned by the state in recent years have been interpreted by the international business community as meaning that Vietnam is "open for business." The progressive habit of displaying feminine smiles and female bodies serves as an attractive advertisement for the new Vietnam (as Pelzer noted way back in 1993, the "foreign investment law" is simply not photogenic!). True to prediction, Vietnam has been home to some of the most favorable regulations in Asia for foreign capital investment. In order for its authorities to disseminate this fact in a more visual manner, beauty queens with a typically "come hither" look portrayed in local company and state calendars help to project the image of promise and availability (ibid.).

In a similar vein, once established in the local market, incumbent MNCs have progressively been able to utilize the urban Vietnamese woman both in advertisements and – increasingly – as consumers of their products. Western MNCs have spearheaded the large-scale promotion of techniques developed elsewhere to harness women's sexual allure in order to advertise their products – examples being the "Marlboro girls" utilized by the Philip Morris group (Fahey, 1998). More generally, the burgeoning urban centers of Vietnam – Hanoi and Ho Chi Minh City – are demonstrating their commercial role in the opening up of Vietnam by the increasing use of billboards along the main thoroughfares, advertising Western consumer goods.

This is a trend claimed by MNC expatriates to be of increasing prominence throughout the ASEAN trading bloc. As a general response to these developments, and in line with regional demographic trends, foreign corporations have increasingly refocused their marketing in Southeast Asia toward a generally younger audience than they would at home. Multinationals across the industrial spectrum have traditionally sought to play to this audience by – for example – setting up a user-friendly Web site. Local companies have until now been relatively slow to pick up on the Internet as an effective tool for advertising. Against this backdrop, the likes of Coca-Cola, Pepsi, Procter & Gamble and Unilever have appeared especially responsive to Internet advertising. Hence, of the total Internet advertising spend in Thailand in the past few years, over four-fifths has gone toward brand awareness, increasing traffic and positioning in line with MNC priorities – with only a small amount going directly toward sales or encouraging purchases. Multinationals have also sought to employ television campaigns replete with local soap opera stars.

Taken as a whole, however, the wholesale use of "modernist," arguably "Western," promotional techniques has remained a source of contention in host markets. We begin analyzing this debate in practice with the overall shift toward the standardization of advertising and promotion attempted by MNCs in response to the Asian economic crisis.

Crisis response measures

In general terms, the immediate postcrisis environment in ASEAN appears to be littered with corporations looking to centralize their corporate functions in the region: purchasing, supply chain, research and development and, of course, advertising and promotion. Much of this reflects the core values of the "typical" Western MNC. For example, the two Anglo-Dutch giants Shell and Unilever both expressed to us their underlying belief that there are – or should be – "no boundaries" between nations. In this sense the corollary assumption is that societal cultures are in any case converging, and that we shall all be eventually embodied in the generic, catch-all term "the consumer." Appealing to the global consumer tends to suit the multinational, which can then play down national divisions in the promotion of one single global brand name, brand image and brand heritage.

The trend toward globalization has been further facilitated by the climate of "corporate integration" in recent years, of mergers, takeovers and strategic alliances. Within the Castrol fold, for example, it was assumed by all concerned that BP's acquisition of the group would further propel BP toward the global standardization of its advertising and promotion. True to form, BP rolled out its stated strategy of "internationalizing" its own domestic units in the wake of the regional economic crisis. A host of MNCs across the industrial landscape have also progressed a number of recommendations to their various divisions – claiming, for instance, to want to simplify their advertising as a means to global integration.

In organizational terms, the oft-witnessed separation of local subsidiary sales and marketing functions in the postcrisis era has engendered its own, more detailed impact upon domestic advertising strategy. With corporate-sponsored control of the advertising budget, many units at this stage have sought to transfer their accounts away from locally founded agencies and toward the likes of Saatchi & Saatchi in adherence with global guidelines. Future plans for television and radio campaigns have tended to be kept away from the traditional sales in a number of organizations – right up until the stage of implementation.

The renewed push toward more standardized regional – even global – campaigns at this juncture was also very marked. In their reemphasis upon formulating standardized advertisements, many MNCs have leaned toward the blander type of innocuous advertising that can be shown anywhere. As a result, a substantial number of purely local campaigns were jettisoned. In the precrisis years Shell had developed localized advertisements at its Vietnamese subsidiary, including one for a popular national radio station. But even in the context of one of the cheapest coverage costs in the region, the company decided in 1998 to simply dub its Thai-based advertisements for the surrounding Mekong Delta – including Vietnam – and then rely on localized promotions for domestic markets. Within the richer Thai market itself, many companies were still looking to press for greater standardization in advertising and promotion.

In the implementation of such corporate guidelines, many MNCs utilized their central advertising "forms" at their local branch units, allowing an arm's-length control of local practice. Local subsidiaries were often pushed to return back to core corporate concerns, for example being centered on the English-language daily newspapers for advertising coverage, rather than their local counterparts. Such moves were to come under fire from local staff, who felt that any remaining budgets following the corporate restrictions should be split equally between local and foreign media vehicles. But there was another, far more serious, divergence of priority to come.

As a result of their collective experience of economic downturns in their home environments, the majority of MNCs took the decision to maintain – even increase – their advertising spend in the immediate postcrisis period. Even some corporations that initially cut their advertising and promotion budgets then reinstated them to their full levels in the months that followed (McKinsey, 2001). But to local managers this was not merely shocking, but disrespectful – bearing in mind that these same corporations were simultaneously ridding themselves of whole swathes of personnel as a means to "cut costs."

MNCs' rationale for such "irregularities in priority" was simply that they were taking the necessary steps to build their brands via "share of voice" initiatives within the beleaguered market environment – so that when the upturn came, they would be in a much stronger position to grab further market share. Much of the former advertising spending was nonetheless being transferred to new methods during this period, and in particular to the cheap advertising rates on the Internet. Adopting the longer-term strategic perspective, MNCs held to the belief that, crisis notwithstanding, the Internet would emerge from the arcane specialty it was perceived as being during the precrisis years and blossom into an integral part of regional consumers' everyday lives. This was held to be especially the case with special Web sites for the young, professional Asian customer.

In terms of promotions strategy, the major change demanded by MNCs of this period was of an altogether more practical nature, although again it was disliked and resented by interviewed respondents. Initial corporate dissatisfaction stemmed from what was perceived as the time and resources "wasted" by local staff on the adaptation and customization of corporate promotional literature for each domestic market – instanced by leaflets, billboarding, stickers, caps and T-shirts. For this reason a host of redundancies occurred within the sector – instanced by local "publicity managers" and the like, who had effectively created work by seeking to adapt centrally distributed promotion material unnecessarily. The general corporate directive here was to scrap all local practice in favor of regional/global duplication – again a part of a broader aim to standardize resources on the back of a globally coherent brand.

More specifically, many foreign MNCs sought the stricter on-the-ground integration of their brand signalization and merchandising material. This was viewed as an essential corollary to the long-term "trading up" of local customers. The uniform appearance of corporate promotions material was to include the use of Western Pantone specifications for all ink coloring, following a number of concerns raised with regard to local signage and billboarding – especially across the more rural regions. Measures were also implemented to try to standardize domestic unit "giveaways." Concern was expressed at a number of MNCs as to the practice of intraregional swapping of items such as diaries, calendars, pens, calculators and watches between senior sales and marketing managers, again seen as a waste of resources.

Additional corporate critiques revolved around the issue of local promotional methods traditionally employed for their respective products. The multinational oil corporations form a case in point, all of which – Shell, Mobil, Caltex, Esso, and so forth – were critical of the local penchant for handing out gifts at their respective service outlets. Utilized as part of an "on-the-ground" means of nurturing and maintaining local custom, such gifts ranged from soft drinks, tissues and toy models – even to premium beer. Yet although on the face of it this was a sensible adaptation ploy, corporate headquarters were concerned that such methods imbued them with a "tacky" image, one that they would be better off without in the new "globalizing economy." Again, it was felt that only via the development of a viable international master brand could a company enjoy long-term success – ahead of any "quick-fix" measures for survival.

Further measures enforced during this period addressed the issue of perceived "corruption." More precisely, MNC headquarters across the industrial spectrum were concerned with the "corrupt" methods by which domestic ASEAN promotion campaigns were traditionally administered. At the general level, sales promotions were habitually utilized not only as a price discount strategy but also as a means to jump-start product figures in areas viewed as underperforming. Such objectives were often accomplished via – to cite one example – the strategic targeting of "gold coins" in special packs for cargo bound for the territory in question. Claiming to have long been "suspicious" of such local practices, the MNC in question took advantage of the crisis as a catalyst with which to "audit" these promotion procedures.

Finally, corporate home office dissatisfaction also lay with the broader issue of the ad hoc monitoring of campaign objectives. Quite simply, they were deemed to be severely lacking in postcampaign evaluation, hence results and market trends were being obscured. Future local promotions were therefore placed under international campaign guidelines with the stress upon detailed, objective postcampaign reports. The digested view of Western MNCs was that the traditional Asian failure to adhere to global "regulations" had effectively negated the promotion method as a valid device for sampling the market. In this it was effectively condemned as serving only to divert resources away from the more "essential" regional activities, namely brand development and long-term segmentation analysis.

Indigenous resistance

In organizational terms, MNCs' practice of shifting responsibility for advertising toward newly appointed "experts" was initially – and expectedly – resented by local employees. Implemented as a means of dealing with the crisis-engendered regional environmental instability, the effective bypassing of local sales-driven mores came as a shock to teams of managers habituated to decades of success. However, as a whole the foreign MNC cohort tended to refrain from simply "bulldozing" their newly standardized advertising campaigns into place. Most companies sought to soft-sell the concept in terms of its alignment with the traditional sales emphasis. Looking for a consumer-friendly approach, a number of MNCs – Shell included – created local Web sites in order to provide end users with a means of two-way communication. Again, one of the major sticking points was the refusal of Western multinationals to cut their expenditure on advertising and promotion – a refusal regarded as both insensitive and unethical. The corporate response to these critiques – that this was the norm for downturns in the West – was itself criticized as being "arrogant" and "imperialistic," as well as dangerously presumptuous.

Concurrent local defenses were made of traditional promotions methodologies. The so-called rigging of promotional competitions in favor of "targeted" areas was deemed wholly acceptable and even welcomed in the indigenous cultural environment. The lack of a standard word for the Western concept of "corruption" in several of the region's languages was pointed to as offering practical evidence. When probed further on this matter, local managers tended to shrug on the issue, claiming simply to not understand why MNC headquarters were being "so serious" about this topic. Throughout indigenous Southeast Asian society much of the way communal affairs – including public administration and regional business – are conducted has always been labeled "corrupt" in the West, whereas to the local customer such methods are entirely acceptable, and even commendable.

The Western notion of monitoring or "tracking" each promotion campaign was also greeted with an overwhelming feeling of incomprehension among the local Asian sales and marketing management. Although we have gauged no specific, detailed objections to the proposals, the overall impression given was that in Southeast Asia there was simply "little point" in seeking to comb over or evaluate an event that had been "dealt with and gone" – it was simply not "the done thing." Again, the feelings expressed were of a culturally embedded nature, it being suggested to us that owing to the Buddhist-type nature of much of Southeast Asian society, the tendency was for people to seek to live in the present, with the idea of "looking back to the past" as at best a mistake, at worst a "cultural sin."

MNCs were especially criticized for their decisions to ditch domestically adapted promotions material. Local objections to this perceived change in head office priorities turned upon the cultural "insensitivity" of which it was held to be indicative. Proposals to duplicate future material were further derided as being an essentially short-termist, blinkered approach to solving a long-term issue. The local perspective on this matter was that the immediate advantages in terms of saved cost to corporate figures would be more than lost by the longer-term refusal to make the necessary modifications to an Asian market wholly different to that of – for example – the USA. It was also deemed to be liable to cause deeper and more dangerous rifts with the local dealers and end users accustomed to sporting a brand name seen as "friendly" to the local-market way of life.

Indigenous marketing managers reemphasized the need to have their own materials tailored by the *domestic* subsidiary for the *domestic* consumer. They were encouraged by the partial retreat into nationalism following the regional crisis of 1997, which in many cases found expression in anti-Western sentiment via a whole host of local actions. We may note here the push to repaint English-language billboards with only locally scripted messages in the various regional domestic markets. At the same juncture, Thailand's Boonrawd brewery developed the slogan "My country, my beer" to advertise its locally produced number one seller, Singha.

Local fears concerning the "creeping cultural pollution" afforded by the West and promoted by the crisis found particular resonance among the Islamic populations of Malaysia and Indonesia. As a reaction against the perceived threat of "Westoxification" of their traditional cultures, a strong section of the growing middle class deliberately focused on the dangers for family life produced by modernity and, specifically, "modern" sexualities (see also Forbes and Cutler, 2000). The critique of the potential compromise such "Westoxification" may hold for the

Indo/Malay woman has become crucially centered on the issues of modesty, chastity and sexuality. As Stivens (1998) notes, in practice the meanings deployed around the figure of the traditional Islamic woman have become inseparable from a critique of the ills of Western modernity. Hence the creeping push toward reworked, "modern" versions of traditional Indo-Malay women's dress in glitzy shopping centers has been kept closely held in check. Unlike their male business counterparts, women are constructed as bearers of a recreated nationality/nationalism and/or Islamic piety in their everyday dress.

Similarly, where MNCs have sought to produce standardized advertising campaigns for the entire region, they are having to tread extremely carefully as regards their portrayal of the female form. Hence, although in the postcrisis period the vast majority first sought to "regionalize" their campaigns, in practice most are forced to go market by market depending on culture and the state of each country's development. In some cases this has made it necessary to keep using advertising agencies, particularly where the host government stipulates local content requirements. Whatever the case, and as admitted by expatriate managers, the global agency itself can only ever be as effective as its local people on the ground.

Intra-ASEAN promotion strategy

Increasing global competitive pressures coupled with the continuing fallout from the recent economic recession have acted as the triggers for a major realignment of Western corporate strategies. In contrast to the "adaptation" mindsets of the past, contemporary MNCs are focusing more upon the perceived inevitability of ASEAN market integration. Yet this creeping assumption of regional homogeneity is one that should be treated with caution. Consider the coupling of Thailand with Laos. On the surface the countries should be the closest of brothers and a ripe source of cross-border marketing duplication. The countries share a heritage, close economic ties, linguistic and religious ties, and numerous cultural similarities. Yet beneath the surface the two nations are separated by generations of ideological conflict. Whereas Laos served as a colonial territory for both the French and – latterly – the Soviet governments, Thailand has remained a US-friendly, pro-business powerhouse for incoming MNCs entering the ASEAN bloc. Because too of the huge differences in wealth and power between the countries, the Lao authorities have remained highly suspicious of the "cultural pollution" creeping in from Laos's Thai neighbor. Seeking to protect their national heritage from Thailand's perceived "rampant consumerist culture," the Lao continue to struggle to retain their own identity. In general marketing terms the Lao government continues to regard any advertisement commissioned from Thailand as being culturally unacceptable – as "decadent" and "offensive," and a threat to the indigenous Lao culture.

Nonetheless, given that the Lao are faced with the inviting prospect of watching Thai television, which is beamed across two-thirds of the Lao indigenous territory, many Western MNCs have been reluctant to adapt their material for such a small, undeveloped economy. According to the Lao authorities, such television spillovers simply represent the sole remaining illegal means by which Thai-based companies can disseminate their names in Laos. But in view of the huge popularity of Thai programs – especially soap operas – among the Lao populace, such "piggyback" promotion remains a special bonus to companies such as Unilever and Castrol, which traditionally advertise heavily via this particular media channel.

Indeed, the contrasting approaches of Castrol and Unilever form an illustrative case as to the pros and cons of domestic adaptation of advertising and promotion. Unlike Castrol, the regional Unilever representatives gradually came to heed the vociferous view of the Lao authorities, particularly as they witnessed the achievement of their initial annual sales targets in Vientiane. Adopting a far longer-term perspective, Unilever began to realize that it would not be politically astute to allow the "spillover" situation to persist if it were to garner long-term cooperation from the Vientiane municipal authorities. Hence, as a corollary to the "free" advertisements from across the border, Unilever decided to progress with the development of material deemed culturally congruent by the Lao domestic authorities. To begin with, material was adapted from that used in countries such as Indonesia or Malaysia, and then overdubbed. This was acceptable to the Lao authorities in that it featured material that concurred with the local regulations concerning the depiction of women; that is, that only "proper," traditional apparel be allowed, with figure shots being only of the head.

However, as the company rapidly expanded its presence in the market, a further agreement was sealed for Unilever to make wholly Lao-commissioned television adverts in future, carefully ensuring that all local cultural and linguistic traditions were respected in the process. Similar arrangements were then progressed with regard to all other forms of promotional material, such as billboards, stickers, newspaper ads, T-shirts and posters. Much of the billboard advertising was subject to painstaking negotiation, apparently stemming from the Lao authorities' unwillingness to see their capital become a "glorified Christmas tree" – a thinly veiled reference to how the Thai authorities had dealt with Bangkok. But in keeping with the company's policy of market development subsidization, Unilever nonetheless went ahead with their reputed Lao advertising budget of between 2 and 3 million dollars for their first three years of operations. Along with its pricing policy, it was prepared for a five-year trough in returns as a means toward its long-term goal of domestic market dominance and expansion of its geostrategic strength into southern China.

In practical terms the unprecedented "localization" policy of Unilever in Laos was met with a myriad of bureaucratic regulations. Owing to the complexity and ad hoc nature of the municipal system, Unilever, along with its sole distributor during this era, had drafted an unprecedented and exclusive five-year billboard advertising contract. This agreement was drafted in conjunction with the Ministry of Information and Culture in 1996. In essence, the agreement spanned regulations governing all stages in the billboarding process, from planning through design and then production. Even the formats and fonts used in the execution of the posters had to be approved by the requisite ministry. More specifically, the agreement authorized CBKP (on Unilever's behalf) to employ billboard advertisements for the designated fifteen types of imported branded consumer goods as per a detailed product breakdown summary in the preliminary article. A separate article then denoted the types, dimensions and quantity of billboards, as well as the specific installation sites authorized by the ministry. Subsequent articles and clauses often go into incredible detail as to the particulars of the above arrangements, exemplified by their allowance of a maximum of five billboards of 2×4 metre dimensions to be used for each main province, and two per smaller province (to a maximum of 15). This particular size of billboard was then to be installed only in the vicinity of trading markets. Similar details were also expressed with regard to smaller billboards, which were to be used only on the outside of designated distributor-owned offices and trading outlets. Detailed regulations were then delineated for the design and usage of stickers, shelfboards, T-shirts, hats and bags. A further article consisted solely of official restrictions on the use of language, centered on the stipulation of the Lao language for all types of billboards and posters listed above. Regulations stated that if a product name in English were required on the same board, then it "shall be of equal or smaller size to the Lao language" and must be positioned either "after or under" it.

Hearing of the complexities of this agreement via its distributor, which it shared with Unilever, Castrol's Thai representatives balked at the idea of pursuing a similar "exclusive" arrangement. Scanning Unilever's arrangement – and its list of fifteen included product brands – Castrol's local marketing manager inquired as to whether a sixteenth item couldn't be scribbled underneath (i.e. "Castrol"!). In practice, however, Castrol was unwilling to progress such an agreement and was faced with a myriad of restrictions once "in the field." To begin with, Castrol's exportation of sundry promotional items – e.g. stickers, fly-posters, T-shirts and umbrellas – was deemed unacceptable owing to these items' neglect of the Lao script in favor of either English or – worse – Thai. The agent – in conjunction with the local authorities – reiterated to Castrol the importance of ensuring that all promotional script was first translated into Lao. To this end the recovered items were quickly taken to local printing shops to have the Thai input adapted into Lao and the billboards partially repainted. However, Castrol was dissatisfied with the results of the latter – the classic Castrol red and green being "off-color" owing to the unavailability of the correct Pantone dyes in Vientiane. Principal corporate representatives emphasized that the correct red and green Castrol logo acted as a signature for the company and a perceived guarantee of value for the company's products. A further deterioration in Castrol's relationship with both agent and government came with the former's flat refusal to invest in domestic television advertisements, either wholly composed in Vientiane or else dubbed into the Lao language.

The Vientiane boat races: contrasting methodologies

As one of the world's foremost specialists in developing markets, Unilever supports a variety of standard promotional events across the region, and Laos is no exception. Like the majority of incoming MNCs to have entered the country since the opening of the Thailand–Laos road bridge in 1994, Unilever agreed to provide promotional support for the dissemination of the company's products and advertisements at the traditional Vientiane boat races. Boat racing is a very popular national pastime in Laos, the regatta in Vientiane having been held since "time immemorial" and being well attended by people from across the region. The stated aim of the festival is to strengthen unity among the Lao ethnic groups as well as helping to promote a closer relationship with the Thai people living on the banks of the Mekong River (Vientiane Times, 1996). As a forerunner to the increasingly lavish opening campaigns of – for example – Coca-Cola and Colgate-Palmolive, Unilever had put a lot of thought into its initial campaign coverage.

Adopting a varied portfolio of ideas and methods, Unilever successfully demonstrated an effort to make its presence appear congruent with the cultural traditions of the festival. This was typified by the company's provision of branded T-shirt sponsorship for several favored teams of rowers, notably in Lux soap or Sunsilk shampoo color – usually reserved for women's teams – and Viso detergent shirts for the men. Perhaps more memorable – at least in terms of direct observation – was the company's novel sponsorship of one of the traveling *mor lam* troupes. In basic terms these are traditional Lao singing and dancing groups, always extremely popular with the masses, who arrive for the races from the rural towns and villages. As well as simply sponsoring their brightly colored attire for the duration of the events, Unilever instructed its Lao representatives to become even more involved, interspersing the various acts with product advertising jingles, even including branded lyrics in the songs themselves. Lauded in local business and governmental circles as representing a "positive cultural gesture," the practice of novelty sponsoring was imitated by numerous other MNCs, notably by US representatives Colgate-Palmolive and Coca-Cola, in the late 1990s.

By way of contrast, the premium-branded lubricants specialist Castrol carved a domestic approach very much grounded on its own *modus operandi*. Following the company's initial dabbling in Laos at the beginning of the 1990s, Castrol Thailand decided to sponsor the annual Vientiane boat races at the end of 1996 as part of an unspoken "relaunch" of the brand in Laos. Yet unlike the majority of its Western counterparts, Castrol – again as a "top-end" marketer – decided against the targeted variety approach to sponsorship, opting for a more "hands-off" approach via the blanket financing of prizes.

Castrol was also unwilling to diffuse its marketing efforts beyond the capital city of Vientiane. By contrast, the "mass-market" approaches of both Unilever and Coca-Cola led them far into the up-country provinces. Back inside the capital, Unilever in particular was also very supportive of the *That Luang* festival – basically a trade fair but with a strong religious overlay. The country's second largest cultural event, the festival was a further opportunity for Unilever to demonstrate its cultural interest in the market. Supporting the event via a notably generous raffle – the prizes were motorcycles, televisions, rice cookers, fans and Unilever branded products – the company also became involved in organizing locally inspired games and entertainment. Its stand is held to have been the biggest crowd-puller over a number of years. Unilever's approach was eventually – and unsurprisingly – imitated by the likes of Colgate-Palmolive, the latter scoring particular success with its promotional giveaway of gold chains.

Environmental congruency

As depicted in the Introduction, there is a marked need for caution regarding the oft-espoused intraregional standardization of the strategic marketing mix (*à la* Powpaka, 1998). Our own findings support this. Taking Thailand and Laos as an illustrative case, we find that even these two apparently closely related cultures need to be treated independently. Notwithstanding the more obvious economic differentials and fundamental political idiosyncrasies, there is a more subtle, partially hidden and perhaps surprising variation in sociocultural mores between the two nations, particularly with regard to social attitudes and values. These latter discrepancies are especially relevant within the realms of advertising and promotion methodology, where differing aesthetic perspectives are illustrated by the need for adapted language and font-size packaging.

At the more general level of analysis, our Laos-based respondents' critiques of both case-study corporations (Castrol and Unilever) centered on their underlying assumptions, which they regarded as inherently ethnocentric and presumptuous. As one executive expressed it,

> "The main problem for us with these big corporations is that they view the Mekong area as being one single entity in terms of customer base. . . . They believe that we're all really just the same under the outside and so the borders between countries do not matter, either now or more strongly in the future. So they look at all populations here as being the same, as the Mekong Customer or the Asian Customer – and this is not reflected in reality. They're always going to have big problems if they view the region here in these terms, if they're not looking at – and so underestimating – the cultural

differences. Remember that what you have as success in one country
doesn't always fit in another, especially like Laos and Thailand,
which have many problems with each other."

Even Unilever – traditionally a staunch advocate of the multidomestic
approach – was apt to make the odd culturally incongruent blunder.
According to its Lao representative, the company was – at least for a
while – determined to pursue the same promotions strategy in Laos as the
one successfully used in Myanmar. However, the strategy of targeting
the video halls, used in Myanmar, was simply not capable of being
applied in Laos; the conditions for replication were simply not there.
Unilever's reported response – "well, then we'll create those conditions"
– was then much criticized as both impractical and presumptious.

A similar fate awaited the company's decision to launch a new shampoo
variant in Laos. As the shampoo was to be colored black, the original
idea was to use the color of black and yellow as the theme of a parade
down the main avenue, ending at the local stadium, where an
entertainment event was to be held. Unfortunately, the day chosen also
commemorated the death of a former president, a fact Unilever's Thai
reps had overlooked in their prior research. The Vientiane authorities
were concerned about the color Unilever was proposing to use, and duly
ordered the removal of all adverts and so forth, and halted the event
completely. The idea of using a black and yellow-painted helicopter
overflying the city and dropping leaflets was also forbidden for reasons of
security – interpreted by Unilever reps as meaning "originality,"
something of which the local government was deemed "afraid."
Curiously, a number of the local *samlor* motorcycles painted especially
for the occasion are still to be seen running the streets of the capital.

Castrol's auspicious decision to sponsor the Vientiane boat races for the
very first time in 1996 was also soon marred by a major cultural blunder
in its own exported promotional material. To begin with, Castrol shipped
a dozen or so life-sized cutouts of its local beauty queen, "Miss Castrol
Thailand." Held by the municipal authorities to be salacious and sleazy,
these cutouts were seized by Lao customs officers at the border, attendant
CBKP representatives being cautioned and threatened with arrest as the
official importer of "inappropriate material." Further, a promotions team
sent up for the occasion, as well as including the incumbent CEO and
Lao market development managers also included Miss Castrol herself,
who was to appear in the flesh – again to the obvious dismay of the local
authorities (although her forthcoming appearance was warmly welcomed

Kiss of Death? Miss Castrol Thailand

Castrol's corporate decision to impose a series of postcrisis changes upon its subsidiaries was focused in Thailand upon the continuing usage by the unit of an annually selected "Miss Castrol" beauty queen for its advertising and promotion campaigns – not only on company billboards and brochures but also "in the flesh" at product launches and motorsport events. The original "Miss Castrol" concept was developed during the 1980s via a competition advertised through the local Thai newspapers. Castrol's Thai local advertising agency drew up an initial shortlist of candidates, who were to be screened by a panel consisting of half a dozen representatives – one male and one female from the advertising agency, three males and one female from Castrol Thailand's executive committee. The stated criteria for ultimate selection were "personality," "confidence," "attractiveness," "a pleasing voice" and some ability in English (although the latter requirement was "sometimes dropped if the winner was outstanding in other respects"). Further, in her role as a – at times *the* – perceived Castrol representative in Thailand, the young woman in question was bound to be effectively "beyond reproach." Ensuring that this was the case was not always as straightforward as it might appear. In one year a prospective candidate turned up at the advertising agency in a brand new BMW. Yet when the agency executive made the usual visit to acquaint her parents with what she would be doing in the company, he found that it was an extremely poor household – and, crucially, that there was no clear reason why the daughter should be driving such an expensive vehicle. In such circumstances the candidate was eliminated from the contest.

By Castrol's own standards the criteria fixed were strict. As a former company executive notes, "Many of them were extremely nice people and went on to progress to worthwhile careers in PR, modeling, TV commercials. Many formed very successful and happy marriages and have remained in contact with the company until this day."

Utilizing the economic crisis as the stated trigger for change, however, Castrol home office issued a directive to Thailand expressing concern at the damage being done by Miss Castrol to the global image of the corporation. Deemed to be "dated" and "inappropriate" to consumer perception objectives, Miss Castrol Thailand would lay the corporation open to charges of sexism, as well as associating the Thai unit with the country's seedier image, of which the company had always sought to steer clear in its maintenance of favorable governmental relations.

Not surprisingly, these statements were hotly disputed by the sales managers for several key reasons. To begin with, it was claimed that among local customers – and especially the franchised motorcycle and automotive dealers – Miss Castrol's presence at launch parties, soirées and motorsport events gave Castrol an edge over its rivals in an environment where face-to-face contacts and informal events tended to be exclusively male and (arguably) chauvinistic. There were also tie-ins with the larger wholesalers, who were encouraged to assist in the Miss Castrol selection process. Finally, the local Thai media – among which there were long-standing contacts built up over time – were held by respondents to be very much in favor of such beauty contests, and had continued to give Castrol excellent media coverage on the back of Miss Castrol Thailand's ongoing presence.

The home office and the Thai unit remained at loggerheads over much of the immediate postcrisis period, but an emergent compromise was eventually laid out. Essentially, the working policy was to discard the "Miss Castrol" image for calendars, billboards and packaging – thus, essentially, in any *written* form. However, corporate representatives heeded the points made concerning "in person" appearances at company launches and dinners, and Miss Castrol was kept in attendance as per tradition. This newly merged programme of revision has over time been almost unanimously approved across the corporate–societal divide.

by the local populace). Ironically, within the years to come it was not so much the Lao authorities questioning the concept of a Miss Castrol as the Castrol group itself.

Advertising and promotion strategy "cross-vergence"

The year-long standoff in the case of Miss Castrol was essentially mirrored across the spectrum of MNCs' advertising and promotion strategies in postcrisis ASEAN. As a generalization, we found that the corporate "standardization/harmonization" push in the immediate postcrisis period was progressively relaxed over time – reconceding some level of control back to the local sales/marketing managers. Broader moves were also noted with regard to an increasing (re)turn toward local advertising agencies – held as being cheaper and domestically driven. As recounted to us by a former Shell Vietnam executive, the general feeling has been that head office can be "overly worried" as to the regulation of strict corporate branding guidelines.

Further concessions were made as regards the local setting of the advertising and promotion budget. Basically, so long as the local managers were demonstrably operating within a home office-imposed "bandwidth," then home office would leave them to "fine-tune" their own advertising budgets. As the dawn of this new millennium has witnessed a steady – albeit fragile – economic recovery in the region, controversial moves by MNCs to maintain advertising spend have become less of an issue.

A progressive "cross-vergence" of MNC headquarters–subsidiary priorities has also redefined the practical application of corporate promotional guidelines in the region. Often under the auspices of a visiting Western- or Japanese-based marketing team, corporate recommendations have effectively been incorporated with regard to regional promotional campaign tracking and analysis. However, concessions have been made to "Asian-style" business practices of, for example, "regulated" prize targeting, judged a worthy gift to the host economy's cultural norms.

More generally, a number of "Western" methods and practices have been accepted by the local sales and marketing team. This is partly a reflection of the "Westernization" of many MNC marketing departments by US- or British-educated external recruits more attuned to occidental marketing methods. Further, over time, many of the once resentful sales executives forced to relinquish responsibility came to "appreciate" the added time and resources with which this new state of affairs was to provide them; they became better able to concentrate on their monthly sales targets and commission-based rewards.

Much of this new-found acceptance of Western methods among local marketing teams concerned the avoidance of advertising adaptation and modification in favor of cheaper, straightforward "duplication." Again, this was partially a result of the concessions that emerged from MNC headquarters and their corollary local counterparts. For example, in Castrol's case many of its ASEAN units have been allowed to maintain their signalization in domestic country script/design. But this concession has come only on the back of each unit's subjugation to strict global Pantone color coding. Designs for T-shirts and caps and the like are similarly regulated by this new and mutually agreed code of practice; that is, *standard* color but with *customized* script.

This "cross-vergence" of regional promotions methods was especially evident within the oil industry regarding the progressive distribution of free gifts for service-station customers. In the wake of a worsening economic environment, many local service stations had begun to offer free soft drinks, candies and tissues in a ploy to maintain or boost customer expenditure at respective company sites. At first – and not surprisingly – these measures were roundly criticized – and effectively forbidden – by brand-oriented Western MNCs for being "tacky" and inappropriate to their corporate images. But the local management teams vociferously defended these crisis measures, emphasizing the practical benefits of handouts to the average Southeast Asian consumer. Part of their argument was that giveaways actually served to enhance the provision of better services. As one Vietnamese executive pointed out,

"Our local customers now used to this, to receiving this extra service in this bad situation – even if just some water to drink or something to eat. Now they used to it and we are the leader . . . we should develop this, not try to stop it . . . in this business situation we all must listen to the most important person here . . . the customer, the Thai customer."

On the strength of such arguments, many regional units simply refused in practice to desist from the "giveaway program." Fortunately, however – and increasingly aware that local motorists had by now become habituated to receiving gifts at gas stations – the majority of MNC representatives tacitly agreed to its continuance, albeit with certain well-defined restrictions. To begin with, only corporate-branded merchandise was ever really encouraged, as opposed to the handing out of Coca-Colas or, worse, bottles of the local beer. The crux of this policy revision was that branded merchandise – including caps, umbrellas and T-shirts – based on a "coupon literage" system were in future to be substituted for the miscellaneous drinks and candies held as being "unsuitable" and "unprofessional" by regional corporate headquarters. Pledged to "consistent modernization" of their operations, Western MNCs became increasingly happy with this trend – "novelty" giveaways being seen as an effective long-term marketing tool with which to attract the region's all-important young consumer market.

In an increasingly unstable, changing marketing context no single medium, no single promotional method regardless of merit, is likely to satisfy all the complex demands of the ASEAN regional marketplace. Rather than trying for complete uniformity, MNC promotions strategy should therefore seek to identify the optimal compromise between cost-efficient global/regional standardization on the one hand and locally adapted customization on the other. The "cross-vergent" examples delineated in this chapter perhaps hold the key – juxtaposing unified slogans and visualization with local execution (i.e. as regards language, spokespersons and copy).

11 Distribution

- Traditional ASEAN distribution
- Distribution chain subversion: global corporate fightbacks
- "Cross-verging" distribution practice

Of all the "marketing section" categories discussed in this book, the function of local distribution has proven to be the most complex and controversial. The following analysis of postcrisis MNC local strategy in Southeast Asia brings to a head some of the clearest remaining divides between business culture thinking in the East and that in the West. Global corporations face a plethora of challenges when designing globally coordinated channels through which to market their products – and especially, so it would seem, within the ASEAN bloc. Even greater problems are encountered when seeking to implement such designs in practice.

As noted by Johansson (2000), at the general level, channel strategies successful at home may be neither effective nor feasible when implemented in foreign markets. The functions and availability of alternative market intermediaries may also be at odds with home office experience. Distribution channel management is a mixed reflection both of societal culture and of industrial development – and hence a very local concern. In practice, establishing your distribution network is a costly and time-consuming process – it takes so long, in fact, that during its construction, foreign companies may find themselves unable to seize otherwise viable market opportunities. Local subsidiary managers play extremely important roles in implementing regional distribution strategy – particularly in gaining viable access to suppliers, middlemen and retail outlets.

In Southeast Asia the prohibitive lack of foreign access to supply chains has been a traditional concern to incoming multinationals. Partly this comes down to geography, with mountain ranges, webs of rivers and dense terrain in evidence. MNCs have typically had to rely upon the cooperation of local distributors; that is, wholesalers, large retailers and (non)exclusive agents. Dependency on such partners is of particular import in some of the region's developing markets, where it is estimated that over one-third of all consumer purchases are based on a retailer's recommendation. Rural ASEAN consumers tend to be relatively ignorant of brands and will therefore ask for products by type. This then makes them dependent on their choice of retailer, and so retailers emerge in such a context as powerful intermediaries. The relative access to and support from indigenous distributors impacts directly upon an MNC's long-term success levels within any given domestic territory.

This is illustrated by several brief examples from the field, beginning with that of Estée Lauder in Thailand. For years the indigenous Princess cosmetics company was the runaway market leader in Thailand, with a proven history of successful client rapport. The surprise success of a foreign entrant – Estée Lauder – in the market has been dubbed a trademark example of just how vital local ties can be. Established initially in 1991, the marque was helped enormously in developing its brand presence through its links with the Central retail chain, which in the crucial early days ensured its distribution by persuading stores to stock the products (Srinivasan, 2001).

Elsewhere across the region, US software giant Microsoft was so determined to establish viable channels within the region that in markets such as Malaysia the company significantly reduced its wholesale prices in order to attract respondents. As stated by the company, this short-term reduction in margins was a small price to pay for the foundation of long-term distribution aides. In a similar vein Coca-Cola has placed a premium on developing decent channel standards within the Mekong Delta, in order to help build "sustainable traffic," incidence and transaction size across the region. Companies such as Unilever have also sought first-mover advantage as a means to secure channel networks. These firms tend to enter with a high-powered team and a minimal number of expats in order to develop JV partners for reasons of distribution access.

The importance of securing good distribution access has tended to enhance the selection of a *good* local partner – for example as part of a JV agreement. The ability to select appropriate distributors from the outset will form a key plank of any successful marketing strategy, as exemplified by Unilever's rapid domination of Vietnam, Laos and Cambodia. The flip side of the coin can be a formidable local competitor, emergent on the back of an agreement going wrong. Take Procter &

Gamble in Vietnam – reliant on a local firm which for a time was found to be still peddling a direct competitor's products (Quang, 1998).

Traditional ASEAN distribution

One of the determining characteristics of the ASEAN region has been its skewed distribution facilities, which are hampered both by a lack of infrastructure and by the marked difference in infrastructure grading between the urban centers and the up-country provinces. Southeast Asia houses a host of nations with extreme "primacy indexes" where the single largest city dominates the country. Metro Manila, Phnom Penh, Bangkok, Vientiane and Rangoon are all preeminent examples of the primacy phenomenon. Bangkok, as the most extreme example, is widely thought to be over thirty times the size of second city, Nakhon Ratchasima, and fifty-one times the size of Chiang Mai. It accounts for 95 percent of Thai foreign commodity trade and nearly half of GDP (Goss, 2000).

Aside from the figures, primacy is argued to cause inefficient and inequitable distortions of the national political economy in question, as well as diseconomies of scale within the primate city itself. In Thailand, Malaysia, Indonesia, the Philippines and Vietnam, state policies are being developed to facilitate a more balanced economic structure. In the meantime, local MNC units formulate unusual, often ingenious methods to deal with the lack of rural infrastructure. The Pepsi company, for one, has come up with the novel idea of developing portable "backpack dispensers" to distribute its beverage across the up-country regions – also now utilized in both Singapore and the Philippines for sporting events.

Ethno-domination

A major characteristic of ASEAN corporate distribution is what has been termed the "ethno-domination" of regional marketing channels. By this is meant the control of export/import, wholesale and retail channels by people who belong to a different ethnic group than the majority of people in a society. Specifically, we refer to the role of the ethnic Chinese in the domination of Southeast Asian trade channels. The Chinese have traditionally acted as intermediaries between Western trading houses and – latterly – corporate bodies and indigenous consumers. Indeed, ethnic Chinese migrants are common across the region, even down to the level

Executive Insights: Pizza Wars

"Tricon International – the food marketing arm of the PepsiCo Corporation – made an expensive mistake in challenging William E. Heinecke's hold on the Thai market for pizzas. Heinecke's Minor Food Group bought the Pizza Hut franchise many years ago, utilized motorcycle deliveries to beat the notorious Bangkok traffic, and guaranteed delivery within thirty minutes (or the pizza was free). But when he tried to renew the Pizza Hut franchise recently, he was obliged not to operate any chicken or burger outlets in Thailand (or anywhere else for that matter), and the draft contract further stated that he could not go into any other food business without Tricon's approval. Being a public company with 6,000 employees, Heinecke's Minor Group prides itself on being multibrand and therefore could not accept a restriction imposed by Tricon that was tantamount to restrictive practice.

"The court case itself cost Heinecke's company millions of dollars. Yet instead of simply giving in – and at considerable additional cost – Heinecke rebranded his 116 restaurants as The Pizza Company. Redesigned uniforms for staff and motorcycle delivery boys, new recipes, a new telephone order number and a hefty advertising campaign have all contributed to The Pizza Company achieving 70 percent of a growing market in the year 2001.

"Heinecke – who has been living in Thailand for thirty-eight years – has had to work harder to achieve 70 percent market share from scratch, yet he gives most of the credit to his people. After all, he says, they built the brand in the first place and have now done so again. Tricon, although possessing the original brand, simply don't have the people to compete. Knowing the Thai market so well is not the only advantage Heinecke has over his US corporate rivals. Minor Foods also has its own cheese-making factory in Thailand, which eliminates high import duties on dairy products.

"But the real winners are justice and the consumer. Heinecke has fought against what amounts to restrictive practice on the part of PepsiCo, and is winning. He is now free to go into any food enterprise, so don't be surprised if he expands The Pizza Company into other parts of Southeast Asia."

of the local village shop (Speece and Igel, 2000). Through their hugely disproportionate ownership of regional business outlets, Chinese traders supply and trade in products from across the consumer spectrum.

Generations of distribution experience and control have enabled these sizeable – and often very powerful – Chinese-led conglomerates to develop. Moving upward through the supply chain via accumulated capital assets, these ethnic Chinese have progressed into broader business activities such as manufacturing and finance. The Thai-Chinese group Charoen Pokphand – to take one example – has in this way shifted its focus from trade *per se* and expanded into commercial operations as diverse as the automotive sector, telecommunications, banking and petrochemicals (Speece and Igel, 2000). Perhaps more importantly, such conglomerates often hold many of the contacts and much of the market weight with which foreign multinationals are so keen to become associated. The vast majority of indigenous ASEAN joint venture partners are Chinese owned or controlled, able to flex the strength of their local "ground-floor" influence upon the all-important domestic supply chain.

Thailand is traditionally very tolerant of outside people and values, and its relatively small cultural distance from the Chinese has resulted in their strong and widespread assimilation into domestic Thai societal culture. But elsewhere within the region the indigenous populace has been less welcoming – even hostile – to this Chinese "hijacking" of domestic supply chains, instanced by cases of cultural segmentation in Indonesia and Malaysia. In Vietnam, corporate representatives from the Shell company noted tension between Chinese *guanxi* networks on the one hand and the ethnic Vietnamese on the other – often coming to a head within the retail channel milieu. Part of this hostility stems from the Chinese themselves. Even in Thailand they are perceived as favoring business relationships with similar Chinese groups rather than, say, non-Chinese Asians or Westerners. Quite simply, the Chinese view themselves as handling money much more carefully than their local/indigenous counterparts within the Southeast Asian region.

An example in practice is the Castrol (Thailand) business unit's foray into Laos. Seeking to "relaunch" the branch, the group decided to try to mimic the success of the Castrol Pitstop program as successfully pursued in Thailand. Essentially the Pitstop was a selected auto workshop then supported by Castrol in terms of both material and equipment in return for exclusive supply and commitment to the brand – essentially Pitstops were the company's visible "flagshop" outlets. Yet when it came to selecting a Lao representative, the Chinese-dominated Castrol marketing team were loath to relinquish any control to any outlet owned by an indigenous Lao. Hence the selection made was – by default – the only Chinese-owned motorcycle workshop on the shortlist. The existence of such an ethnic compatriot also briefly served to temper the Thai-Chinese marketing management's skepticism toward the entire "Lao project."

Supply chain characteristics

The ethnic Chinese distribution channels so dominant within the region are founded primarily upon flexible, informal but highly resilient networks (often referred to as "bamboo" or *guanxi* networks). Whereas Western business contacts are based upon professional referrals and legal contracts, these are far less of an issue to the indigenous supply chain conglomerates. Within Southeast Asia, friendships, mutual trust and familial contacts are the essential pillars upon which business relationships are based. Such informal but morally binding "agreements" come with an unwritten obligation to maintain them throughout the bad times as well as through the good. Further, and unlike in the West, these relations tend to be personal between *individuals* rather than between *organizations*. Hence, so long as the individuals remain within their respective functional roles, the agreement is expected to continue. Even nonfamilial customer links are usually bound at a level beyond what was considered the "norm" at Western head office. Not surprisingly, the great majority of expatriate managers working in the region have serious difficulty in understanding the deceptively complex forms of social etiquette and are therefore almost entirely precluded from building any kind of local patronage network.

Within this context local sales managers have thus been particularly incensed by their corporate parents' proposals to effectively tear up these nurtured ties. Their anger is exacerbated by the fact that many of them had personal equity interests in their clients' business establishments. In some cases even the profound nepotism that appeared to regulate certain sales rep–dealer links was admitted to as another block in the push for continued local flexibility. Indeed, many of the region's supply chain dealerships right across the industrial spectrum were found to be mere offshoots of some extended family conglomerate.

Further – and in contrast to the perceived "short-termism" of the Western business approach – Chinese managers simply do not value the Western corporate propensity for job rotation, preferring instead to cement relations that cut across the cycles of business. *Guanxi* takes its time to work, and once established is hard to break. Oftentimes the expatriate envoy tends to suspect such "loose" and "old boy" ties of being inherently corrupt and unprofessional, yet is bound to work within their confines should the company seek to establish a viable foothold.

Wholesale power: the gray trade factor

Held to be the direct result of local distribution mores – and in particular the huge power of domestic/regional wholesale groups – the proliferation of gray trade activity continues to be a major problem for extant MNCs in Southeast Asia. During the research for this book we have noted many instances of angry multinationals discovering the existence of products produced in one country being illegally available in another. For example, the Unilever Vietnam management team become incensed with their Lao distributor on finding Lao tax stamps upon locally sold shampoos and detergent. Within the realm of theory such gray trading is prohibited in MNC agency agreements across national borders, with sole distributors being forbidden to "knowingly sell or dispose of their product to any person or persons residing or carrying on business in the territory with a view to the same being sent or exported to any place, country or state outside [the named country]" – and so forth.

In practice, however, such transit trade is often nigh on impossible to control. Indeed, local agents tend to resent being lumbered with the responsibility of controlling it. As the agent in question phrased it, "How can we be expected to take the blame for something which, when it leaves our warehouse, is then out of our control?" There have also been accusations from agents that their respective MNC principals are guilty of both inflexibility and double standards on the issue. These stem in particular from their perceived unwillingness to stop their own wholesalers from "palming" excess stocks across borders – for instance across the Mekong into either Laos or Vietnam from Thailand.

The increasing power of the larger ASEAN wholesalers has become a major worry in itself for the incumbent foreign corporations. It is coupled with the overall nature of the traditional local supply chains themselves. Serious concerns have focused on the presence of rent-seeking middlemen, who clog the networks and siphon profit. Their power within the systems permits them deliberately to embed extra costs into the final price of goods, saddling both consumers and producers with a distorted pricing structure. Western MNCs have therefore sought to circumvent these distribution networks, building ways to work around or even reduce the influence of the local Chinese trade chains.

Unilever's Rural Networks

Almost 80 percent of the ASEAN populace live in small, often tiny, villages and hamlets. Colonizing this "nest" of evolving consumerism is pivotal in acquiring dominant market share. Yet the dire lack of infrastructure has traditionally rendered such strategies nigh on impossible – and in particular to the foreign MNC. The vast majority of local consumers are simply very hard to reach – in every sense. Across the Mekong Delta, more than half do not have access to road transport, so product is shifted instead via bicycle, cart or even bullock. Modern media – and in particular television – also reach barely 50 percent of these people.

Within lower social brackets almost two-thirds of household income gets spent on bare necessities. Many houses also lack direct access to water – which on the surface is one important factor keeping companies like Unilever and Colgate-Palmolive, with their array of household products, far away. Not surprisingly, the latter firm has largely shunned the rural sector, focusing its strategy upon the region's urban centers (see also Cohen, 2000a). In direct contrast, Unilever sees long-term potential in these poorer village roots. To capture market share the firm has set about developing some idiosyncratic distribution tactics, as we shall see. Moreover, it has become commonplace to witness Unilever trade stands set with satellite dishes in village squares, alongside company "jingles" slotted in among local songs and music.

Broadly speaking, Unilever has developed an extensive and effective rural distribution network, playing to the domestic appreciation of its strategic adaptation. Within the emerging markets of the Mekong river basin much of this was achieved by using squads of so-called motorcycle cowboys. These riders typically earn commission rates of 2 percent on safe delivery of Unilever branded product – often boxed in jumbles piled high on their backs and under their arms (Cohen, 2000a).

Yet the replication of such distribution methods is not without its problems. Although tried and tested through much of India and Thailand, the use of motorcycle squads through much of the region met with several key barriers. To begin, the infrastructure challenges across the Mekong subregion effectively rendered impractical the widespread use of motorized transport, particularly as regards the overall state of the roads. The subsequent switch to tricycles, boats and even rickshaws to reach far-flung, often mountainous villages met with notable success across Cambodia and Vietnam.

Yet problems remain, for instance with the hiring of indigenous staff to man the various transport modes. One is the presence of local banditry, which is spread through much of the Mekong countryside. But other concerns stemmed from an unexpected source of cultural hindrance – namely, the refusal of the indigenous Lao to peddle produce from one village to another (as indigenous Thais, Indians and Vietnamese do in their respective countries).

Because of this curious difference, although it has become normal to see Vietnamese immigrants peddling the length and breadth of Laos selling a variety of produce, there is a notable dearth of indigenous Lao doing the same thing. As one expatriate remarked, "Only a couple among Laotians have ever been seen doing it. And yet the Vietnamese are everywhere – we've seen them everywhere, on roads, along fields, even halfway up a mountain on the track up north to Luang Prabang."

Even with a network of traveling vendors in place, there has still not been the same rush to buy these products in the Lao countryside. Indeed, the average Lao consumer appears actually to *prefer* making the trip to the social milieu of the marketplace, despite the five- to six-hour round trip this can often involve. Quite simply, the idea of buying product from a traveling salesman has never taken off in Laos.

Distribution chain subversion: global corporate fightbacks

In the immediate postcrisis environment all major distribution channels were subject to a marked downturn in business. Within the pivotal automotive industry the wholesale and retail outlets that survived the downturn were still cutting their monthly orders to the tune of 50 percent and more through the regional trough of 1998. Though still replenishing their stocks, many such outlets were notoriously plagued by bounced stocks and overdue payments, and saturated with bad financial accounts. More generally, the ASEAN distribution setup was depicted as a huge house of cards just waiting to collapse. In this sense the economic crisis was viewed less as a nightmare and more as a timely catalyst for change. Many foreign corporations had for some years deliberated how best to reform their own incumbent supply chain inefficiencies, seeking ways around the locally embedded inefficiencies.

One way to gain a tighter grip upon local operations is to buy up local assets, an avenue to which MNCs were increasingly to turn. Prompted by fallout from the economic crisis, domestic governments across the region relaxed their foreign ownership laws. In view of the devaluation of local currencies, this became an attractive option – and not just for the manufacturing multinationals. Ironically, many Western retail chains were themselves anxious to break into and/or develop their presence in the region – instanced by the case of Tesco, Marks & Spencer and Boots from the UK and C. R. C. Ahold from the Netherlands. Since the late 1990s these ambitious foreign chains have become some of the heftiest investors in the regional economy. With their better management, advanced technology and effective customer-orientation strategies, companies such as Tesco have been quickly able to gobble market share. Purchasing in bulk and dealing directly with their suppliers, these firms effectively eliminate layers of rent-seeking middlemen from the equation.

In doing so they alter the entire power relationship of the supply chain, making distribution cheaper for supplier and retailer alike.

In almost complete contrast to these retailers are the number of firms that have adopted a policy of partial withdrawal in order to "get around" the local distribution networks. Pharmaceutical MNCs such as Bristol Myers Squibb are following one method and outsourcing their logistics operations, transferring them to Diethelm and in the process trimming excess staff. Elsewhere, firms are choosing to subcontract production, especially within the footwear and garments industries. In this situation, instead of building their own branch plants like most electronic firms, these companies get local producers to manufacture for them. In this way the MNC producer minimizes its own local commitment, obviating the need to invest in constructing its own factory. Hence, although providing less security for local employees, this type of arrangement is ultimately much more flexible for the MNC. The major drawback with the approach is that it also gives the multinational much less control over its "coalface" operations.

At the more detailed level we turn to the working practices employed by MNCs within their existing subsidiary units "on the ground." Within the ASEAN corporate subsidiary the market commitment of the parent multinational has, to a large extent, already been established. Any revision of existing distribution arrangements is thereby – almost by default – of a much more practical nature in terms of both channel design and execution – and always tailored within the confines of existing business culture mores.

One common change promoted by anxious MNCs in the light of the 1997 downturn has been to try to render systematic the existing channel support mechanisms practiced by their local corporate subsidiaries. One major criticism of endemic precrisis methods was the perceived ad hoc, haphazard method by which promotional support was given to individual wholesale/retail outlets – with resource expenditure rarely proportionate to relative generated revenue. The Thai lubricants industry provides a good illustration of this issue. Premium Western suppliers such as Shell, Castrol, Dupont and Esso have traditionally channeled their product through a half-dozen or so major outlets, typically via spare-parts shops, independent gas stations, exclusive company outlets, automotive dealerships (franchised and nonfranchised), department stores and wholesalers. Yet in practical terms, aside from company-owned outlets a handful of key wholesale accounts have tended to swallow a huge 60 to

Executive Insights: The Conoco–Castrol Thailand Tie-in

"Conoco's entry strategy into the Thai petroleum market was well thought through and hence very successful. They already had their parent – Dupont Chemical – well established but decided to opt for a strategic alliance with Castrol, a rapport between the two companies which had been in existence in other markets for some two decades already. Quite simply, they recognized that the oil market was quite different to the ones which Dupont were in. Conoco wanted to open service stations in Thailand using the Jet brand, which had already gained respectable market shares in the UK and continental Europe. In particular, they had enjoyed a successful relationship with Deutsche Castrol for many years, with Castrol being sold on all their sites in what was then West Germany. A long-lasting relationship existed between Klaus Koslowski, Deutsche Castrol's Automotive Sales Director, and Franz Erhardt of Conoco. Franz was a very unusual executive who acted best alone. He was not the type to fit comfortably into the normal corporate structure, and was given a pioneering job developing possible new markets. I was asked to meet him in Bangkok and spent some time briefing him on the Thai business environment in what was then the late eighties.

"Jet wanted to build a chain of service stations with Jiffy convenience stores, and wanted Castrol as their premium brand to help them with quick customer recognition, and to have Jet lubricants as the lower-priced brand. Music to the ears of any Castrol man! The major oil companies such as Shell, Esso and Mobil would never normally allow a competitive brand to be sold on their service station forecourts.

"Michael Loew – a tall, fair-haired, blue-eyed Swede – came to Thailand in 1990 and we spent many hours together talking about Thailand and the local trading environment. Conoco recognized that their expertise was in refining and had an investment in Malaysia with Petronas, plus their existing supply deals in Thailand. Their aim was to run low-cost, low-price gas stations and to make money from volume throughput and what they saw as a growing potential for their Jiffy convenience stores. A selected range of Castrol lubricants would be sold on the forecourts and in the Jiffy stores. The stations would each have a Castrol sign at the drive-in and exit, and the product range would also be available at Castrol Pitstops established on sites in high-traffic residential areas as a kind of quick-lube operation.

"A big opening celebration was planned for September 1991, with a large number of the Conoco board members plus wives traveling to Thailand in the corporate jet. Tragically, the plane crashed in a mountainous area of east Malaysia in a severe storm, with the loss of all passengers and crew. The loss of so many senior people not only put additional pressure on Michael Loew but probably delayed Conoco's plans by up to a year.

"In any event their entry strategy was very successful. Mike Blackburn took over as their Thai unit CEO when Loew was transferred to London but the momentum continued. Since the 1997 crash the number of service stations has shrunk, but Conoco, who boast the biggest sales per station of all operators in Thailand, continue to grow their network. However, they now no longer sell Jet lubricants as they make more money selling Castrol which, when I last checked, outnumbered sales of their own brand by a factor of five to one."

70 percent of total volume sales – something that was being seemingly overlooked by local managers armed with their own culturally bound agendas. Indeed, it was often the case that the support for the key accounts barely rose above a quarter of total budget – with disproportionate amounts of funding being handed to the smaller-type outlets characterized by workshops and spare-parts dealerships.

But why this huge variation? By (almost) all accounts, the differential appears to be rooted in culturally founded priority variations. The vast majority of corporate representatives across the board expressed their suspicions of "unprofessional" familial links between clients and Thai sales representatives as having a major bearing on the perceived diversion of distribution budget support. Parent guidelines as to the regional/domestic "realignment" of distribution support mechanisms were thus a prime feature of the immediate postcrisis era. Concerned multinationals were anxious to secure a firmer grip upon their subsidiaries' distribution unit expenditure with policies of methodology convergence aimed at opening up the "volume/resource" account information and thereby making it transparent. In practical terms this tended to involve the redistribution of resources in favor of the larger, more formal wholesale and franchised outlets and away from the small, more traditional family-run shops such as those that supply oil and spare parts, and carry out motor repairs.

More generally, visiting envoys from a host of multinationals – again often in the context of economic collapse – were sent to outline the proposed adoption of new, unequivocally "Westernized" sets of planning tools that were held to improve the efficiency levels of consumer supply chains. Again we can use the examples proffered from the regional motor lubricants industry. Part of this new strategy was to include a number of tie-ins with other Western chains. An example is Castrol's decision to pursue Conoco fuel station outlets for the mass distribution of its specialist product on an exclusive basis, both in Bangkok and up-country. Western MNCs were keen to operationalize the enhanced exercise of head office control over the "riskier" smaller outlets. To this end – and in spite of often tiny volume sales – "corporate priority" was effectively being stamped upon these new agreements, with delivery arrangements to be similarly engineered in favor of the Western purchasers. The corollary to such arrangements also involved organizational changes with the indigenous sales and marketing departments, with resources again being shifted toward these new distribution channel concerns.

At a broader level, many Western suppliers to the ASEAN region have to an extent taken advantage of the recession to rethink some of their longer-term marketing distribution strategies. Many have also benefited from the relaxation of foreign ownership restriction – lifted across the region in the light of business meltdown. Within specific domestic markets, oil majors such as Caltex and Shell have in this way sought to cut the number of their dealer-owned and dealer-operated service stations, looking to maintain a tighter control on the way operators manage their businesses (from marketing strategy right through to station upkeep). The number of dealer-owned and operated stations will continue to decline further over the medium term as contracts begin to expire. Benefiting from the continuing relaxation of foreign ownership laws, companies will operate more of their own, dealer-operated stations, which will facilitate the control-oriented, hands-on type arrangement currently in vogue for multinational suppliers.

A further source of concern to a majority of MNC oil corporations within the region has been the increasing use of supplementary domestic income earners, largely as a response to the heightening competition in the post-economic crisis period. A host of ancillary sales techniques are being brought into play upon the region's gas pump forecourts as a method with which to ensure the very survival of motor oil marketers. Held to be the future of service station operations, the provision of on-site amenities such as convenience stores, ATMs and even coffee shops has begun to take hold in the postcrisis regional environment, as part of longer-term moves to differentiate branded retail outlets from each other. Although aware of the possibilities, MNCs have traditionally been very wary of losing brand control in the wake of these localized tactics to shore up market share. As already noted, the means by which they have come to terms with these developments has been to expand their own exclusively owned retail outlets.

There are several less prominent ways by which MNCs can seek to retilt the traditional supply chain power base in their favor. In the pharmaceutical industry – and specifically vitamin supply – the likes of Hoffmann-La Roche have developed the notion of selling products in package bundles rather than as stand-alone items. In this way the distributor can be given discounts on specific brands in order to stave off the competition successfully, while maintaining the desired price positioning for the other goods. In practical terms this places the distributor in a weaker position than before. Should the retailer opt for a competitor's single product, then a company such as Hoffmann is able to retaliate by raising its prices for all the other products for which it is the sole or prime supplier. In this vein Unilever has also sought to increase its bargaining power with the larger wholesalers via initial contract demands for specified market share targets – typically around 5 percent to be achieved within three months (reportedly initiated at the Makro chain).

Strategic alliances

Unilever adopted a markedly different approach, and one that illustrates the collaborative method taken by some Western MNCs within Southeast Asia, instanced by its symbiotic rapport with Kimberley Clark in terms of regional distribution. Supply chain collaboration is also markedly prevalent across the traditional industrial divides – notably in Vietnam, where multinationals such as Shell and Procter & Gamble have formed distribution arrangements with the likes of Unilever and Coca-Cola, particularly as regards the design template to be adopted through the country.

Further examples of MNC alliances are to be found further down the supply chain, for example at the level of the retail outlet. Specifically, within the Thai domestic market, the Dutch supermarket chain C. R. C. Ahold and the US oil firm Conoco have formed an expansion partnership via the former's grocery retailing outlets. The partnership – reportedly the first of its kind in the region – commenced with the provision of grocery logistics services via C. R. C. Ahold's operations into the Conoco-owned Jiffy convenience stores at its 120-plus Jet service stations. It has been cemented by the companies' joint development of the "Jiffy Kitchen" by Ahold's Tops supermarket chains, a new buffet section within Jiffy stores that offers fresh meals, bakery products, fruit, sandwich items and drinks, along with seating facilities.

In general terms, both C. R. C. Ahold and the US-based Conoco view the alliance as a key component in the facilitation of upward sales concurrent with downward costs. The latter are especially useful as regards the resulting savings, which can then be passed on to consumers, in turn serving to render the company's prices more competitive and more nearly in line with those offered at the emerging discount superstores. Perceived as the key future threat to sustained market share, such discount outlets are increasingly being targeted as the main rivals, against which Ahold is looking to the new Jiffy tie-in to help it fight back successfully. Against this backdrop the partnership should help provide it with the innovative edge it is seeking in what has become a highly competitive domestic retailing business.

Multinational tie-ins are also increasingly – though less visibly – found at the level of the sole agency/distributorship specifically contracted to serve the export market. The case of Unilever and the US trading house Connell Brothers provides a case in point. Beginning its entry into the Lao market with the indigenous KP company, Unilever witnessed a rapid expansion of sales of its Lux soap within the capital, Vientiane – so rapid, in fact, that the company quickly sought to build upon this success by expanding into the domestic up-country provinces. The arrival of Connell Brothers in support of the KP group gave Unilever's development push an added impetus. However, toward the end of its first year of operations Unilever became increasingly concerned with the cashflow difficulties experienced by the renamed CBKP venture – mostly occasioned by the late payments of up-country subdistributors. More important for Unilever was the apparently "passive" nature of these subdistributors' selling activities – exemplified by their flat refusal to take on the company's full product range (they claimed that in Laos it was the norm simply to order what one was convinced one could sell). Anxious to achieve market dominance "before the competition move in," Unilever was keen to promote an expanded product range throughout the country yet was increasingly unhappy with the indigenous side of the CBKP venture. Unilever's envoys – mostly from Thailand – began pushing for the US Connell side to take a more active part in the joint venture, effectively taking over the management of provincial distribution. Not surprisingly, the Lao-based team voiced their deep offense at the nature of some of the comments made by certain corporate representatives of the era. Further, the local Lao managers were also dissatisfied with what they perceived to be the aggressive nature of certain Unilever envoys, and similar allegations of "bullying" were made by the local dealers and subdistributors. Among the specific complaints voiced to us was the insistence by Unilever on its products being displayed either exclusively or prominently in each holding outlet. Many also claimed to feel looked down upon, and in particular by the company's visiting Thai executives.

Rise of the "cyberintermediary"

To return to our analysis of MNC distribution tactics, mention must be made here of the ballooning impact of computer-based technology on the future mechanics of the supply chain. Multinationals headquartered in the West and Japan remain committed to the potential of extranet communication systems, looking to directly link up trading partners through the computer matching of inventory requirements with individual suppliers. It is argued that the Internet, held to provide a more efficient means of contacting consumers, will progressively reduce the importance of traditional intermediaries in international marketing.

The Thai–Lao Supply Chain: Indigenous Critiques

Agent–principal tensions concerning distribution strategy (design and execution) have been rife across the Thai–Lao border in the years following the construction of the Friendship Bridge linking the two countries in 1994. The CBKP joint venture forms a classic case in point. CBKP was formed a year later in 1995 between the Lao KP family and the US trading house Connell Brothers. Among its armory at the time were the likes of Unilever, Castrol, 3M, Volvo Trucks, Bridgestone Tyres, Toyota and Cormix. Yet from this wide variety of interests one can isolate two main critiques from CBKP with regard to its principals' distribution methodology.

The first of these concerns shipments. Specifically, CBKP often bridles at the refusal of its various principals to participate in "mixed" product shipments (i.e. the sourcing of small orders of company product with their other interests in a single truck). Although this would possibly be cheaper for all parties concerned, both Castrol and Unilever were suspicious of CBKP's intentions – perceiving it to be avoiding the maintenance of "adequate" inventory levels. Hence, despite the country's well-documented paucity of purchasing power, the incoming MNCs were insistent on running their own exclusive freight deals – in some cases utilizing the smallest half-truck for a meager consignment. According to CBKP, the end result of these "single brand" shipments was excess stock, constricted cash flow and lost opportunities in developing portfolio sales.

CBKP's second critique was one upon which resolution has now been achieved. We focus here upon delivery lead times, as well as upon the implied expectation of stock level maintenance. Regarding the former, whereas two weeks was the norm for shipments anywhere in Thailand, CBKP representatives bemoaned the "two to three months" it was taking for their orders to arrive at the Lao border. However, over time, all principals agreed to speed up their internal turnaround processes, eventually cutting these lead times back to a maximum of four weeks. In turn this enabled revised stock-level agreements to be incorporated, whereby CBKP was in theory allowed to cut back inventory to 15 percent of the previous levels.

Hence, for traditional distribution channels to be able to compete, they will need to offer a quite different set of services. Western MNCs generally hope that in future such hard-to-penetrate chains of intermediaries will no longer be able to add value via their current distribution activities, but will rather need to focus on the collection, collation, interpretation and dissemination of vast amounts of information. This new breed of so-called "cyberintermediary" will need to house data management as its critical resource, and help dilute the tendency for the ethnic Chinese closeting of supply chain access.

"Cross-verging" distribution practice

Attempts by Western MNCs to seek to standardize the ASEAN supply chain system drew the largest and most sustained response from all respondents concerned. Most critiques were centered upon the perceived need for adapted cultural compliance. Some of these will be explored in detailed case examples. But first let us begin outlining the notable "successes" of foreign corporations in progressing their own distribution agendas.

The trend whereby multinationals seek to progress their own channel methods has been enhanced in the wake of the regional crisis. As an example, Castrol has successfully sought to widen its servicing arrangements with foreign-based franchise dealerships via the internal development of a "premium first-fill" team, targeting the likes of Jaguar, Honda and General Motors. Implemented via regional headquarters, these arrangements have effectively bypassed the grip of the local sales managers and their rapport with domestic outlets.

Even among the local supply chains there appears to have been an increasing propensity to try to "professionalize" their business practices in line with international standards. Several of the larger family-owned networks (often incorporating a diverse set of interests) have been actively seeking ISO 9002 quality certification, for example, in order to boost their export potential. To some extent the "informal contact" power base held by indigenous sales and marketing managers is being compromised from within. Furthermore, this "professionalization" of traditional distribution outlets has rendered them more attractive to the MNC community, anxious to circumvent wholesaler power. Many multinationals have sought to formalize agreements with these rapidly changing retail chains, for example by drawing up a shortlist of interested outlet owners, depending on their resources and attitude. In the case of Castrol these candidates were then invited to pass a set of examinations. Training would then be provided within the relevant Castrol units.

More generally, there is a perceived sense of optimism with regard to the explosion of computer-based technology – and more specifically for its distribution potential. MNCs look to Internet information flows to help engender the rationalized, centralized future supply of regional goods and services. The Internet's impact, they hope, will facilitate the negation of much of what has served to build the traditional inefficient chains of supply in ASEAN. What we now must turn to stems from the powerful and vested set of interests that will seek to stop this happening.

Indigenous resistance

There were several major reasons why the MNC-sponsored changes outlined were rejected by indigenous management teams. Partly their rejection of them was due to dissatisfaction with stated corporate objectives. Much of it involved the methods by which such change was to be implemented. To begin with, MNC home office envoys were castigated for their lack of cultural sensitivity, and in particular for their narrow and deficient understanding of traditional supply chain tenets. Multinational corporate proposals designed to try to circumvent existing distribution networks were held to be unsuitably "rigid" in an environment characterized by being fluid, informal and, above all, flexible. Attempts to try to "systematize" proportionate support to company outlets came in for particular dissension; they were held to be a naive swipe at the some of the long-standing relations developed between reps and dealers that had helped ensure success in the first place – relations they regarded as both nonquantifiable and unique in every case.

As one senior Thai marketing executive expressed it,

> "To my mind you simply cannot function without at least some form of localized distribution strategy. You simply cannot standardize the 'customer-edge,' it's what the local team do best. . . . Each business relationship needs its own special nurturing . . . [it] has its own individual needs, and trying to drive a wedge through these contacts is self-defeating . . . it's as simple as that."

Within each ASEAN domestic market, over 90 percent of local respondents interviewed felt very strongly that only a locally born

Business "Stream" Restructuring: Taking Aim at Thailand's Bamboo Networks

The notion of business "streaming" marks a seismic shift in corporate plans for global organization structures. Moving away from the traditional geographic "matrix" system, companies such as Castrol have sought to reshift their reporting structures toward a more functional, product-oriented focus – partially in order to facilitate global business practice convergence. Moreover, the resulting management structure was designed to further weaken the senior sales hold upon the regional territories and to end some of the perceived politicking among the Asian fiefdoms by a more balanced allocation of global resources.

The Castrol corporation provides a prime illustration of the business streaming phenomenon. It was implemented at its ASEAN divisions through much of 1998, and we focus in particular upon the problems later encountered within the Thai domestic structure. Before the onset of "streaming," the typical Castrol unit consisted of two divisions: the larger Consumer division on the one and the composite CIM (Commercial, Industrial and Marine) division on the other, each with its own director of operations. With the onset of business streaming, however, these two existing divisions were to be split into four corporate "streams" by making the previously integrated CIM side into three separate areas of business. In order to bring about the new structure, domestic reporting lines were essentially scrapped and then redrawn – much to the chagrin of the existing divisional directors. Specifically, the former CIM director's scope of responsibility was narrowed down to one single – usually Industrial – stream of operation, instead of the traditional CIM triumvirate. Furthermore, instead of reporting to the domestic CEO, each deepened stream was now elongated in terms of its chain of command – from domestic manager to regional head and right up as far as the global controller. The idea of an all-powerful CEO was then rendered practically obsolete, with each domestic unit now fronting a renamed "country manager" with diminished levels of responsibility, who again reported directly to the Asia-Pacific area streaming controllers.

On paper the program appeared to be airtight in its design. At the stage of implementation, however, a number of key criticisms were leveled. To begin with, the project was viewed as culturally incongruent with prevailing business practice. In contrast to the practically borderless regions of the European Union – or even North America – the national divisions within the ASEAN bloc were held to be "far more complex." Thailand, for one, was held to be culturally distinct, never having been colonized by a Western power. The process of having to involve a regional chain of ascending managerial levels was seen as particularly inappropriate. Traditionally, the self-contained and highly successful Thai subsidiary was habituated to using its own, informally styled/"off-the-record" means of resolving personal staff–customer crises. The fear was that in future these kinds of decisions would be subject to time-consuming and inflexible consultation with a regional headquarters perceived as both unsympathetic and culturally misinformed. Further, traditional one-to-one communication modes were perceived as being under threat by regional plans to integrate electronic and video modes of respective "stream" meetings. Such means were derided as impractical and inappropriate in a local commercial environment characterized by intense, instinctive and flexible decisions made on the back of face-to-face debate. Thailand, it was held, should remain as one single, integrated concern.

The second major reservation expressed reinforced the country's idiosyncratic commercial structure. In contrast to Western norms – and even to the more developed markets of ASEAN – nearly all the lubricant distribution outlets in Thailand are under the extended grip of one of several Chinese-run family conglomerates. This is where the problems began. Instead of there being the usual separation between a consumer-based motorcycle workshop on the one hand and an industrial-based sugar mill on the other, such theoretical divisions simply do not hold in Thailand. In practice, *both* will generally be under *one* family, and that one family will have built up long-term relations with *one* senior sales manager and/or *one* sales representative.

In this contact-oriented environment the imposition of distinct business streams was held to draw artificial divisions in the extant company–client structure, detrimental both to existing relationships and to long-term business success:

> "Having three salesmen visiting one family is not the good way to develop the business here – or even to hold their business. They will think you are playing the game with them. In Thailand it is necessary to keep the relationship stable – this is the most important thing the Western style never understand."

national sales manager could ever seriously hope to gain the local customer knowledge necessary to operate effectively.

The postcrisis regional business environment witnessed a generalized backlash by traditional, local family retailers against the increased multinational impingement upon their territory – instanced by the likes of Tesco, Makro and C. R. C. Ahold. Within the retail trade itself even resident expatriates were beginning to deride the strategies of these latter Western incumbents – criticized for their prices (over and above the "odd discount"), delivery systems and overall service. The service element was particularly castigated – standardized global methods falling way short of the "smiling, gentle, attentive," Asian approach.

Traditional family distributors were also making headway in the export markets, typified by the less developed markets of the Mekong subregion. Seeking to subvert their perceived grip on the Lao domestic market, Unilever looked for cheaper networks of retailers in order to lessen its dependence on the CBKP agency. Yet Unilever's offer of a 5 to 6 percent trading margin was quickly rejected by the smaller retail outlets, which claimed that they simply could not survive on such a meager cut –

especially from such a wealthy, internationally renowned supergroup. Typically, however, the KP Lao group *was* able to deal with such figures, because it had the requisite distribution network, trucks, equipment and staff already in place. As a result of its undoubted market reach and knowledge, KP could make its money on volume sales to compensate for the diminishing principal margins and thereby retain its status within the Lao domestic market.

Finally, local managers have been inherently dismissive of Western plans for strategic market collaboration – specifically as a means to circumvent existing channel ties. The feeling was that in practice any extant MNC would still have the traditional networks to deal with, no matter how far it pursued any allied distribution agreements between them. This was borne out by the widespread cases of indigenous resistance, turning the resilience of local distribution networks into a self-fulfilling prophecy. Disgruntled sales and marketing executives across the region sought to "work around" corporate postcrisis arrangements, not so much via open

Executive Insights: Tesco Lotus in Thailand

"One of the biggest investors in Thailand in the post-economic crisis period has been the British group Tesco/Lotus, who continue to compete very aggressively with the likes of Makro, Carrefour, Big C and Foodland. Successful marketing is giving the customers what they want, and stores like Tesco/Lotus do this with notable efficiency. Their stores are spacious, well lit, air-conditioned and carry a full range of food and household necessities which are well displayed and clearly priced. Further, the checkout rows are efficient and the car parks adequately sized.

"Make no mistake, their stores are full, and 98 percent of the clientele are indigenous Thais. However, there have been many complaints in the Thai press that the corner 'mom and pop' stores are being put out of business. But this has happened everywhere, for such big stores are great for the weekly shop. However, the local ministores and specialized shops will still flourish if they efficiently satisfy niche markets.

"Perhaps what is most disturbing is the recent spate of attacks on Tesco/Lotus stores in the latter half of 2001 by certain individuals held to have previous connections to the military. Indeed, in late 2001 one activist actually died after firing an antitank rocket at a Tesco store, supposedly in defense of 'Asians exploited by rich Westerners.' The Lotus/Tesco team in Thailand, led by CEO Michael Raycraft, wisely avoid public comment about such attempts at intimidation, seemingly content to let the local authorities deal with the issue. But if they don't deal with it effectively, what effect will such incidents have upon future foreign investors both in Thailand and in the region as a whole?"

conflict as through the covert maintenance of certain long-established contacts. The so-called bamboo-network formed among favored suppliers, clients and departmental employees kept for local management an informal, flexible but highly effective grip on traditional territory "patches." Hence, in the long run – and whatever the merits of these MNC-oriented measures – the sales–client network proved too elusive and resilient for corporate representatives to track their viability on any regular basis. Over time, individual local assistants, coordinators and finally even the Western expatriates had little practical alternative but to heed traditional working practices.

Compromise measures

Within these initial trails of resistance, emerging avenues of compromise between MNC headquarters and their ASEAN subsidiary managers have been progressively developed. One such blend of both priority and method concerned the forecast balance of resources being spent on each distribution channel/outlet. As outlined already, initial MNC plans involved the "ironing out" of the perceived idiosyncrasies of indigenous management practice, whereby support was offered to dealerships on the basis of informal, unsystematic personal contacts and client–sales rep relations. Instead, MNC directives stated that the resources devoted to each outlet/channel should be proportionate to the revenue generated – thus adhering to Western-oriented professional norms. However, in practice this was shown to be exceedingly difficult to implement. A compromise of sorts was often reached whereby in return for more regular and transparent data on distribution support expenditure, the informal networks were left largely as they were, within each domestic territory.

More specific corporate concessions were made within certain key industries – illustrated here within the MNC oligopoly that forms the Southeast Asian motor oils market. It will be remembered that Castrol Thailand had operationalized a tie-in with the US major Conoco for distribution of its premium oils at all Jet station forecourts. Although this deal was soon to be formalized, in order to placate the local management team a number of options with Thai suppliers recommended by local managers were also considered. Further, initial local fears concerning the proposed transfer of unit resources away from the smaller, more traditional family-owned outlets were also largely mollified. Local sales and marketing chiefs, far from being shut out of the new deal, have become active participants – quickly building healthy relations with the Western gasoline chain's locally based management. Home office representatives decided to give back responsibility and control over much of the distribution structure to the Thai executive committee, including the ability to set resource handouts between the traditional outlets and the Jet chain. This perceived reinvestment of confidence in the local employees gave local respondents the boost they claimed to have awaited, especially as they had by now become largely accustomed to the new distribution arrangements.

This willingness for long-term compromise was also evident in some of the changes made to initial MNC "product-territory" reorganization initiatives. Essentially these were designed to express corporate shifts toward a global distribution framework – freed from the constraints of localized customs. Unsurprisingly, they were resented among indigenous teams for taking no account of regional disparities and personal network contacts. They were also demonstrably unworkable in practice – and again for all the reasons that have been discussed in this book. In order for all sides to be pleased, a compromise agreement was progressively developed. Hence, while on the one hand senior management were retained in their newly designated corporate roles, on the other hand the traditional domestic geographic structure was essentially left intact – as were the lower-level managerial teams. This optimal "mixed system" arrangement effectively allowed the Western MNC to emphasize *both* its long-standing commitments to local customer relationships *and* its parent-based global product focus.

At ground level, traditional local ASEAN dealer/retail networks were in practice left largely as per tradition. These perceived concessions by foreign MNCs in the redrawing of their domestic channel strategies were welcomed among the ranks of indigenous managers. Corporate distribution revisions were applauded in that they permitted this essential continuance of traditional long-term relationship strategies between individual managers and their clients. But even within these MNCs themselves, there were growing calls for the overhaul of extant supply chain partnerships – even within their home territories. Typified by the actions of the US oil venture Caltex, the revised goals of global corporations were to encourage a much more open rapport between their sales managers, their dealer and their so-called brand representatives, the all-important retail outlets.

More generally, increasing numbers of MNCs within the region are embracing the Asian-style concept of customer relationship management (CRM). In the context of an increasingly unstable, fragmented world, many corporations are concerned at the way in which their

Executive Insights: Reverse Culture Shock

"One MNC, the well-respected Hong Kong and Shanghai Banking Corporation [HSBC], has a long history founded in East Asia, where it has been successful in understanding both its indigenous customers and its competitors. In the 1990s HSBC acquired the British high street bank Midland – a sort of culture shock in reverse, since Midland had never been an international operation.

"I remember going to settle my daughter into Canterbury University [strictly, the University of Kent at Canterbury] in the UK in 2001, and on a day of dealing with domestic issues paid a visit to the HSBC branch on-campus. I explained that my daughter was starting a four-year law program, showed them my HSBC bank cards and our passports, and gave the lady a cheque for 500 pounds sterling to open the account. She retorted that as my daughter had no proof of either British or German government funding we were being refused an account – despite my having been an HSBC customer for over twenty-two years. I asked if I could speak to the manager and she said that to do this I would need to go "into town," probably wasting two hours of an already very busy day. She could not let me talk to him over the telephone, as she was not allowed to "allow anyone into our booth." Very disappointed, we left. Next door was the campus branch of the Natwest Bank, where I explained what had happened. "No problem," they said, and within thirty minutes had pretty much everything arranged to our satisfaction.

"Back in Bangkok a few weeks later I happened to meet the CEO of HSBC Thailand, Richard McHowatt, in an Irish pub, where he was having lunch with colleagues. I asked him whether the Bank's chairman was still John Lumsden as I wished to write him a (constructive) letter about the obvious missed marketing opportunity of gaining customers at the beginning of their careers. Richard asked me to write him the details of what had happened, which I did. He had previously been seconded from Hong Kong to Aberdeen to help with the integration of Midland Bank, and so had a lot of contacts in the UK. The relevant area manager quickly made amends. They located my daughter, escorted her to their Canterbury branch, opened her account, somehow managed to close the one with Natwest, and – importantly, as she'd never previously lived in the UK – gave her a list of contacts in case she ever had any problems.

"This story shows that expansion from Asia into Europe can likewise have its teething troubles, and that the way in which a corporation deals with customer complaints – quickly, efficiently and courteously – can have a positive and lasting impression. Our experience had identified a gap in corporate training guidelines and operating procedures which should help make the former Midland part of the HSBC group more international in its outlook."

business–customer rapports have effectively broken down over the years. They have therefore begun adopting the sales-oriented nurturing of existing clients, backed by related figures demonstrating that acquiring a new customer is anywhere between five and ten times more costly than retaining an old one (Burns, 2000). CRM is regarded as one of the "buzzwords" of the moment (ibid.), and its bottom-line advantages are helping to turn corporate management thinking toward the "Asian way" – yet enacted using the latest corporate technology. Specifically, many MNCs have begun to install computer software and systems designed to assist all parts of a firm respond coherently and consistently toward its customers.

Adopting a radically new set of initiatives are the Western MNCs actively seeking to merge concrete distribution alliances – not so much with their corporate compatriots, more with their indigenous former competitors. General Motors is a case in point, as the company's Asian divisions seek new networks with Japanese carmakers in the hope of sharing distribution channels (Wilhelm and Dawson, 2000). Intriguingly, the Toyota connection has also proven beneficial to the likes of Castrol inside the Lao PDR, as an offshoot from the KP family ran the official Toyota dealership. Stocking Castrol oils exclusively, the company has for a while now been Castrol's single biggest customer in Laos, keeping alive the Castrol brand within the Vientiane district. Indeed, bolstered by such regional tie-ins, a host of MNCs now hope to find lasting success within the ASEAN market.

Finally, indigenous conglomerates like the Bangkok Bank corporation in Thailand are now stating that in order to maintain their current positions they can no longer rely exclusively back on the "old ways" of getting their products and services to the market. An increasingly competitive global banking market is held to necessitate higher margins, set alongside the age-old customer orientation. According to Bangkok Bank representatives, it is within the former area that foreigners have the edge, based on their technology and products (Keenan et al., 1999). Yet in the latter area the indigenous company – in whatever industry – will tend to hold the long-established customer networks essential to the development of any business enterprise. With the huge advantage encapsulated in informal, relationship-based market knowledge, much of Southeast Asia's corporate landscape is sure to be framed within traditional ethnic networks for many years to come. In the banking industry, as in any other, both indigenous and foreign-based corporate managers are waking up to the need for an optimal compromise of business objectives and methods.

Shell in Vietnam

Through much of the latter half of the 1990s the Shell corporation sought to effectively clip the wings of its unwieldy Vietnamese distribution network. Yet in the attainment of this objective the company, far from cutting distributor numbers, actually *increased* them from just eight in 1995 to thirty-eight by 2001. Why? In order to try to shorten the domestic supply chain as much as possible, thereby facilitating the maintenance of a tighter grip upon each individual distributor. Generally speaking, as for most other Western incumbents, much of the challenge in securing an efficient distribution network lay in circumventing the power held within the habitually large, family-driven ASEAN wholesale/retail conglomerates. Typically such groups would reign supreme over a given territorial area within the country – Vietnam being no exception. Hence, by increasing their number Shell reasoned – correctly as it turned out – that with each holding a smaller territorial patch, their power base could progress only so far, and then no further.

Practically reinforced by sponsored modes of transport, Shell's handpicked distributors traveled almost solely by motorcycle (with a van as rare backup). This effectively reduced the physical scope of each motorcyclist to no more than, say, around 50 to 60 kilometers in one single day (taking account of the local heat and humidity). In temporal terms a maximum of between 1 and 1.5 hours a day was also loosely envisaged – again as a reflection of the difficult climate and topography. Traveling for any longer than this rule-of-thumb time frame could lead to territorial "trespass" and meet with serious reprisals.

At the end of the 1990s Shell began to move to direct distribution in major cities, cutting out the traditional middleman. A Shell-contracted workforce – around twenty strong in Ho Chi Minh City – would leave the central warehouse in the former Saigon with two or three boxes of lubricants. This form of distribution is especially favored by the Vietnamese Shell unit, operating on a purely cash-on-delivery basis and with a total lack of credit facility. The system was locally run by local staff, and it was rumored that head office were for a long time unhappy with it – until they had watched it bring in the forecast sales, without any spiraling of debt.

A number of other MNCs in Vietnam have been pursuing a concurrent policy of distributor restructuring, seeking to render their respective supply chains as short, as simple and as straight as possible. This is well illustrated by Shell's employing one former Coca-Cola employee to operationalize its Ho Chi Minh depot-based network. Beyond the Shell confines, its premium lubricant competitor Castrol was also expanding its distributor network – up to around sixty members at the time of going to print. Elsewhere the consumer giant Unilever was pursuing essentially the same strategy on a grand scale – scaling up its Mekong Delta operation to an astonishing forty-six exclusive distributors, 2,000 wholesalers and 20,000 retailers – from only 7,000 wholesaler-retailers in 1995 (Cohen, 2000a).

Castrol in Laos

As of late 2001 the capital of the Lao PDR, Vientiane, still accounts for over 60 percent of domestic motor lubricant sales, with the southern trading centers of Savannakhet and Pakse, plus Luang Phabang in the north, accounting for a further 30 percent between them. Choosing to mirror these statistics, the Castrol Thailand company has until now refused all agency requests to develop an up-country presence – preferring to remain focused exclusively upon the capital.

Within Vientiane itself, much of Castrol's extant business stems from an informal agreement to supply Lao Toyota at its local headquarters – as well as a stable, though meager, trade that continues with a handful of dealer clients. However, one other mode of distribution progressed by the company in Laos, at least for a time, was its exclusive Pitstop programme (successfully developed in neighboring Thailand). But seeking to duplicate the same rules and conditions, the company quickly ran into difficulties. Respondents claimed that owing to the economic situation in Laos, the condition of material and equipment support from Castrol in return for its supplying premium-end Castrol lubricants in exclusivity was unrealistic. Owing to the low purchasing power of Vientiane consumers, even potential Pitstop vendors claimed that they would be compelled to stock other, low-end brands for their "bread-and-butter" sales. Individual vendors were effectively bound to stock other brands to ensure their own survival – even if this was increasing their sales by an additional 1 to 5 percent. Concerned for its regional brand positioning, Castrol was in theory unwilling to budge on this issue, and over the course of several months a number of faxes were sent and telephone calls made in order to convey this point. However – and as with so much of business strategy enacted in the ASEAN bloc – in practical terms such directives were essentially impossible to monitor.

Conclusions

- The dialectic of "cross-vergence": closing summary
- Globalization: toward an integrated redefinition
- Facing the future

This book has sought to examine how and why the strategy, structure and culture of multinational corporations in the ASEAN trading sector have changed and continue to change. The past decade – spanning the dawn of this new millennium – has witnessed a confluence of forces leading to the fundamental reappraisal of corporate operations in this emerging and strategically critical region. Among these are the economic meltdown of 1997, the growth in electronic technology, regional market integration, changing levels of education, business process standardization and transparency measures, the rise in "corporate governance," and targeted political developments.

We began this text with an overview of these and other macro marketing trends, followed by a detailed analysis of the changing structure of business operations and the emergence of foreign MNCs with their various modes of entry into the region. We then shifted to the core thrust of the book in subsequent chapters devoted to analyzing the postcrisis programs of organizational restructuring widely attempted by Western MNCs of the era. Specifically, we focused on the downsizing and consolidation of subsidiary operations in Southeast Asia before examining the corollary human resource, electronic and quality issues being reassessed at the same juncture.

In line with the objectives of the Working in Asia series, our research has been founded on real-life case study histories recounted by insider executives, often with unprecedented access to in-depth data drawn directly "from the trenches." In this respect the core of the material presented here has been derived primarily from the testimony of practitioners working in the relevant sectors. Adopting this insider perspective, we have sought to elucidate both how and why the relevant organizational changes alluded to above have taken place. In the depiction of such changes we quickly came to recognize the essential dialectic that has lain at the heart of these and all subsequent chapters in the book. Specifically, we have outlined the initial corporate programs of change (the "thesis"), followed them with an examination of the local resistance to such programs (the "antithesis"), and ended with the essential – and continuing – set of "compromise" or cross-vergent business measures and managerial practices that have emerged (hence, the "synthesis" or resolution). At each stage of this process we sought to explore the critical cultural determinants that have influenced the various courses of action – founded at the societal, national and organizational levels.

With the organizational aspects covered, we shifted our attention toward the MNC and its host environment, specifically its relations with its indigenous customer base, recounted through our chapters on the marketing function and ensuing "mix." Again, essentially the same dialectic was seen to emerge through the recounted experiences of our respondents, this time founded on the marketing "convergence" or "standardization" policies pursued by MNCs in the postcrisis period, the resistance generated in the host nations and the blended compromise to have emerged over time.

In all cases our exploration of the determining causes has been founded upon qualitative respondent case study reports, and our results must be viewed accordingly. Nevertheless, it is hoped that our in-depth empirical observations may shed new light upon the strategic "standardization/adaptation" practice of multinational corporate strategy in Southeast Asia, and upon the culturally bound perception of a corporation's international business values and practice. Also, it is hoped that where appropriate, future courses of action may suggest themselves in light of the case studies presented here. In practical terms they might also serve as a source of valuable practical data for practicing and potential international business executives seeking to build or maintain culturally distant markets overseas.

Again in line with the objectives of the series, we have composed this book with a view to providing management students with a fresh dimension to their reading of the standard academic texts in the field. Our hope is that this has been largely achieved through the real-life experiences of working managers on the ground, demonstrating how and why they perceive the ongoing tactics of foreign multinationals to be changing. In this concluding chapter we seek to make general predictions on how working in and with corporations in the region will change in the near future.

The dialectic of "cross-vergence": closing summary

Status quo ante

Through the precrisis growth years of the 1980s and early 1990s the vast majority of foreign multinationals in Southeast Asia adhered to all the implicit guidelines of business process adaptation. In the context of unparalleled market growth and prosperity, locally based subsidiaries and joint ventures were left pretty much to their own devices and were therefore free to run their day-to-day operations using their own indigenous business methods. Multinational corporations of the era tended to pride themselves on their "multidomestic approach" toward the region, underpinned by the oft-stated need to "live, breathe and feel" these markets on a daily basis. A major plank of this "locally inspired" business philosophy was that each domestic unit responsible for a given domestic territory should be run in the "domestic" (i.e. Thai, Filippino, Malaysian, etc.) style. In this manner many of the region's subsidiary corporations became textbook baronies with unprecedented levels of independence, and – often – unprecedented levels of profit. Conversely, over the years corporate headquarters' knowledge and control of its local operations became progressively weak and opaque.

Crisis control

In the wake of the shattering economic meltdown of the late 1990s a sea change in MNC attitudes was to occur. Triggered into often frantic activity by the sudden reversal of high East Asian exposure levels, many multinationals felt compelled to radically streamline and reevaluate their local ASEAN operations. With the local middle classes reeling from sudden asset deflation and entrepreneurs "groaning under the weight of spiraling debt" (Godement, 1999), older and rising young managers alike within these markets were suddenly being torn between conflicting perceptions and emotions (ibid.). External bodies and local analysts together were quick to emphasize the fact that in light of the economic crisis, increasing competition, global trading pressure and computerization, the region's domestic private sectors and governments were now being effectively compelled to reprioritize their attitudes to business – finally coming to grips with the importance of product quality, innovation, worker productivity and internal cost structures (ibid.; see also Toews and McGregor, 1998; Yuthamanop, 1999).

Foreign multinationals were also quick to realign their ASEAN units, reorganizing their *modi operandi* in order to provide quicker, globally calibrated products and services. In the attainment of these objectives, multinationals such as Bristol Myers Squibb, Microsoft, Castrol, General Motors and Unilever have sought to "converge" or standardize their regional offerings in line with worldwide corporate norms. Once renowned for its locally focused advertising and promotions campaigns, Unilever, the maker of Bird's Eye foods and Dove beauty products, announced to a shocked marketplace the progressive retrenchment of over 75 percent of its existing product portfolio in order to better concentrate on its global "top earners." To many an observer such practices suggest that global competition has at last emerged, to put paid to the traditional "Asian way" of working. Furthermore, such changes are also depicted as a justification for the usage of Western-oriented so-called "best practice."

But does this signify that this rise of global business norms – along with its corollary value system – has actually "won over" the region and buried the former working methods? Much of our rationale for composing this book has been to demonstrate that this is most certainly *not* the case. Indeed, taking into account the fact that for most individuals one's value system is acquired by adolescence, then the so-called "evolution of values" that a global business system would require would take ten or even twenty years – perhaps even generations. The local business culture could certainly not be transformed overnight. It will be remembered that cultural conditioning in Southeast Asia is still very deep and difficult to overcome, something that in turn helps to shape local consumers' perceptions and approaches to purchasing decisions. In this respect the "maturity" of the indigenous customer in, for example, his or her perception of brands, status symbols and added value is founded in the domestic education system and the ensuing changes in mentality it may one day engender.

However, this is not to deny that there can be a sharing and borrowing of ideas and practices. But there are also very real constraints on the kind of "convergence" programs being implemented by foreign MNCs of the era, founded in themselves upon the questionable assumption that all managers are driven by the same desire for efficiency, regardless of societal context (Lubatkin et al., 1997). On this basis alone, the very notions of "convergence" or "universalism" need to be questioned as to their relevance in the transitional and less developed nations of the ASEAN bloc. As Orru et al. note with some clarity, the business economies found in each of the Southeast Asian economies should therefore not be judged mere "corruptions" of technically ideal organizational forms, but represent "qualitatively distinct conceptualizations" of what constitutes appropriate economic activity (Orru et al., 1991). Within this context, socially constructed, accepted models of "correct" market thinking and behavior shape interfirm relations, prompting firms to interact both with their environments and with each other in characteristically homogeneous ways. In simple terms, in order to be "technically efficient," incumbent MNCs *must* consider and comply with the institutional setting in which they find themselves embedded.

Forces for adaptation

In practical terms the vast majority of Western- and Japanese-headquartered MNCs chose to ignore these tacit warnings and instead sought to bulldoze through their centrally formulated agendas. On the ground, such programs of change were met with an often silent but extremely resilient backlash from the region's indigenous management teams. Taken aback by the strength and depth of local leverage these teams held with key domestic clients, corporate head and regional offices were progressively forced across the board to "soften," "dilute" and otherwise compromise their original methods and objectives.

More generally, multinationals in the region have been confronted with the blunt realization that seeking to implement new technology and working methods on a global, organization-wide basis works far less effectively in culturally distant markets. In order to justify the higher customization expenses required, MNCs would do well to apply the old adage of formulating business lessons *globally* but then applying them *locally*. At the critical stage of implementation, foreign corporations in ASEAN need to learn to impose their designated policies, procedures and rules in a flexible, adaptive manner rather than with the usual iron rod. Bearing in mind the general point of how indigenous managers tend to work for a person – as opposed to a company – the overall style of management employed by incoming MNCs should be conciliatory; they should tailor their local units to indigenous working mores and conditions.

During the course of researching this book we have found overall that corporations that remain rigidly held to uniform management policies and practice tend, in the longer term, to be the least successful. Any continuing assumptions of market homogeneity in Southeast Asia should therefore be treated with caution and subject to detailed on-the-ground evaluation – witness the problems we have outlined through this text concerning MNCs seeking to transpose their marketing plans from Thailand to neighboring Laos. Although the two countries are supposedly geographic and cultural brothers, the example of Thailand and Laos provides the clue to how varied markets can be across this diverse and changing subcontinent.

The key is to listen to the voice depicted time and time again by indigenous managers as the most important influence on business strategy, namely the "man on the street," the local consumer. So although the foreign MNC needs to explore regionally based synergies wherever possible, each market should be addressed individually to ensure that local opportunities are being maximized. Executives must guard against the simplistic assumption that marketing strategy across the ASEAN trading bloc equates to marketing one strategic "mix" to many similar countries bounded into an integral unit. The role of the nation-state – and in particular its shared cultural norms and practices – will continue to be highly significant even as new technology progressively homogenizes working practices. The right blend of business strategy components should therefore be used in the right markets where they are shown to be most relevant.

At a deeper level, such realities attest to the impossibility of choosing between globalization and universal values as a tool for renewed modernization and growth on the one hand, and the preservation of Asian cultural relativism on the other. Indeed, for the past century, East and West have tended to converge, yet have never actually coincided. The economic crash of 1997 has thrown many of these tensions into relief, specifically calling into question the suitability of Western managerial values in the context of the domestic ASEAN market environments. The generation gap among the extant managers in the region has been particularly exacerbated. Typified in the ethnic Chinese-dominated subsidiary partners in Thailand and the Philippines, the older generation of top managers have remained true to traditional notions of "trust" and "loyalty" within their indigenous business cultures. In contrast, however, the newer generation of managers tend to stress acquired ideas concerning management "professionalism," ability and performance, while also maintaining the basic values stressed by their elders. A fair proportion of up-and-coming executives in Southeast Asia have been educated abroad, typically in US schools of management. Not surprisingly, in the wake of unprecedented local economic meltdown, many of these youngsters remain torn between traditional Confucian-oriented customs and the demands of a competitive and ever-changing technology.

And the indigenous norms remain strong. As Godement observes, any "changeover" rendering Southeast Asia into "the rest of the West" flies in the face of every anthropological, cultural and political reality (Godement, 1999). The key to "modernizing" ASEAN consumer markets is on the contrary to be found in the local susceptibility to adapting incoming influences – the way in which external norms are successfully blended into the fabric of local business conduct – as opposed to any wholesale "adoption" of foreign influence.

Resolution: business practice "cross-vergence"

The aim of any foreign MNC in the region must be to understand its consumers, customers, partners, governments, and other players in the market. The more an incoming corporation can identify with the thought patterns of its host-market partners, the more deeply it can benefit over time. This accounts in part for the continuing importance of the international joint venture as a vehicle for two-way understanding and communication, as a concrete means for the integration of local cultural idiosyncrasies with Western management techniques.

In this context, managers who can instill the requisite blended managerial values within entrenched local work practices are at a premium. Such individuals are able to work within the given organizational and cultural constraints, finding ways similarly to motivate the local workforce. The value now being placed upon such "cross-cultural" executives is evidenced by the case of Texaco Asia's substituting local managers at the helm of its Thai operations in place of the extant team of Western expatriates. While not being explicit on the subject of cultural "cross-vergence," an increasing number of Western MNCs incumbent in the region have begun to explore the potential synergies to be garnered from seeking to blend "best" practices from both East and West. Across the spectrum of Western industrial interests, corporate managers are now mooting the need to understand the domestic trading culture as being of the same practical import as possessing the requisite professional skills and knowledge of the industry.

Called the *halo-halo* or *mestizo* (mixed) approach in the Philippines, corporate practices to accommodate local cultural values and sensitivities as part of a two-way assimilation of values could have positive, far-reaching implications for global corporate culture design (Amante, 1997). Similarly, many local analysts have – using a host of synonymous terms – come to advocate this cross-vergent "balance" of Eastern and Western business strengths as being the key to optimal and sustainable competitive advantage in the ASEAN bloc (Ashayagachat, 1998).

Globalization: toward an integrated redefinition

The very existence of cross-vergent managerial practices has concurrent implications for the future of globalization theories. At the general level, the prevailing connotations ascribed to the term should be adhered to with some caution – particularly as regards the seemingly inexorable spread of Western- and Japanese-headquartered multinational corporate influence. The lack of any "standard," universally accepted definition of globalization – or even of how "globalization" works – is widely acknowledged (e.g. Held et al., 1999; Hirst and Thompson, 1999). Broadly speaking, the term is used to delineate the increasing global integration of consumer markets, production, labor, technology, investment and – critically – management culture and practices (Lall, 1999; O'Neill, 1991). Such a phenomenon has its adherents and detractors, but on all sides there is always the acknowledgment – however tacit – of the concurrent increase in the size and scope of multinational corporations and their entrenched methods of business practice (ibid.; see also Levitt, 1983; Ohmae, 1990).

Of course, to an extent, this contemporaneous force is making for gradual business practice and regulatory convergence – notably via the opening up of previously closed markets and the rise of economic deregulation. Furthermore, competitive pressure from the G7 industrialized economies is forcing a real change in Southeast Asian business cultures due to the real increase in foreign investment in the light of the Asian economic crisis. Indigenous business managers have themselves been claiming that they need to compete more aggressively in a "Western style" in order to maintain both their domestic and their overseas market shares – especially in the wake of the progressive computerization (or "technical globalization").

However, in the light of our findings, we maintain that this shift can never represent a total negation of local values in favor of those emanating from the West (or anywhere else). In this respect, whereas the regulatory and attitudinal changes behind the Asian shift toward newer, cross-vergent management processes marks an important compromise with the Western way of doing business, they should not be assumed to comprise just another step on the road to "globalization" (as conventionally perceived). Certain key cultural determinants – climate, geography, natural resource types and levels, and so forth – simply do not evolve, over a time span of hundreds or even thousands of years, and thus remain entrenched as continuing barriers to organizational change.

The analysis of the emergence and development of cross-vergent managerial practices outlined in this book demonstrates that distinctive knowledge and understanding of culture-specific business practices and values is a continuing key success factor for sustained competitive advantage in the ASEAN bloc. In accounting for the existence of cross-vergence, the developmental process needs to be reconsidered. As companies move away from the culturally embedded difficulties of seeking to impose a global set of seamless, Western/Japanese miniature replicas, we can begin to question the very association of "globalization" with increasing multinational corporate power, and the attendant implications of ethnocentrically imposed managerial practices and values.

In its place we wish to substitute a more integrated concept of the term, one that is characterized by polycentric managerial behavior based on the working collaboration of differing cross-border perspectives. Expressed throughout this study as a process of change negotiation, cross-vergence in this wider context comprises simply a practical, "ground-floor" means by which this continuing synthesis in worldwide management styles – "globalization" in its purest form – is taking place. In this sense, global business success will rest on the ability to listen, understand and thereby profit from the very best of host-market business culture norms. The long-term multilateral assimilation of globally synthesized best practice will then progressively find expression in the increasing usage of hybrid managerial practices and values such as those explored within this book.

In organizational terms this will inevitably negate the use of the single structural principle, of seeking to impose the "one size fits all" mentality across an entire global corporate network. Interestingly, business culture theorists – including Hofstede – actually began developing "compromise" corporate structures as far back as the early 1980s, promulgating a "patchwork" layout: certain markets would be self-tailored whereas others would go along with the need for regional – even global – coordination of business functions (Hofstede, 1980). Against this backdrop, instead of merely seeking to iron out the host market's cultural idiosyncrasies, the corporation could work with and alongside them, establishing a balanced two-way communication process at the corporate–subsidiary interface. Bridging inherent societal divides, this patchwork structure would also provide a flexible base on which to conduct organic organizational modification in order to suit the changing needs of increasingly destabilized markets.

Facing the future

Macro-level forces

At the macro level the less developed economies of Southeast Asia are finding themselves progressively competing with the People's Republic of China (PRC) to attract continuing inward investment. Rising production costs – and in particular labor costs – are forcing some of ASEAN's multinationals to switch their low-margin manufacturing operations and resources to the cheaper regions of the PRC. Indeed, it is predicted that in future the whole light industrial sector currently based in Southeast Asia will be taken over by new sites being constructed in ASEAN's larger neighbor (see also Goad, 2000b). However, despite its predicted reduction in importance, the ASEAN bloc will continue to be the strategic crossroads between Europe, India and the Pacific Rim, leading the way in a whole host of industries, notably the automotive, electronic and chemical/pharmaceutical sectors (Bangkok Post, 2002).

At the global level the terrorist attacks of 11 September 2001 have accentuated the global turmoil and uncertainty confronting the world's foremost multinationals at the dawn of the new millennium. Faced with a host of unprecedented external forces, managers are having to navigate essentially uncharted global waters characterized by instantaneity, risk and uncertainty (see also Lazer and Shaw, 2000). More worrying still is the apparent failure of traditional corporate methods to deal effectively with this new environment. Traditional Western-oriented tools to deal with change are characterized by notions of scenario and impact analyses, statistics to predict future trends and cross-impact graphing. Yet the underlying premise on which such measures are founded – that planning ensures change *instigation* rather than change *subjection* – may now be increasingly untenable.

Toward a new global management mindset

In order to deal effectively with an increasingly destabilized global economy, a new corporate mindset is patently needed – and nowhere more so than in the culturally distant markets of Southeast Asia. In line with our cross-vergent framework garnered from the region, we advocate a similar blend drawn from the best of both Eastern and Western business cultures. Traditionally, Western corporate strategists have been characterized by a measured approach founded on market analysis, prediction and control. Relatively mechanistic in operation, such techniques can be justified in the context of stable and largely predictable business environments. Their main focus, after all, is on regulating inputs to achieve clearly defined outputs. But against a backdrop of increasingly unstable, disorderly, even chaotic global market conditions, such approaches may be of dwindling relevance.

In dealing effectively with future global marketing conditions, a mindset attuned to dealing with unexpected, unstructured, less predictable marketing situations is required. Developing the new mindset necessitates a break from the past, and so global corporate managers must seek to go beyond the limits of their traditional strategy formulas. Grounded in market intelligence garnered from volumes of knowledge, traditional strategy plans, although suited to the mind of a computer, can only ever be tethered to the past, and so are inherently limited. Only by attuning themselves to the ever-changing movement of markets will corporate managers ever be freed from the pattern of thought and memory, and permitted the ingress of an intelligence that stems from constant renewal.

In practical terms the cross-vergent managerial mindset advocated in this book provides one tentative pointer to a radically new approach to global corporate strategy. In the midst of global turmoil and uncertainty this "third way" for corporate managers seeks to mold the best of Western and Eastern management strategy, effectively pursuing the optimal point along the standardization–customization continuum in order to navigate the strategic constraints of the twenty-first century effectively. Its strength lies in its globally tailored orientation, drawn from the blending of theoretical constructs with empirical experience across the East–West business strategy divide. Taking the "best" from both cultures, multinationals can realistically hope to gain a sustainable presence in the tempestuous markets of Southeast Asia. To take a couple of illustrative examples, from the *Western* value-set we would regard the emphasis on brand development as essential. Brands are an essential tool for responding to uncertainty and rapid change in that they nourish the increasing "appetite for trust" among a worried consumer cohort – trust being the precondition of loyalty.

From the *Eastern* side – and far more controversially – comes the approach toward "strategic planning." In total contrast to the Western emphasis upon linear trend prediction and planning, we would advocate an Asian-embedded "rapid response" approach, grounded in the designated "bamboo networks" outlined in this book. The agility and flexibility afforded by such a mindset stems from a perception of the environment as "unknowable" and time as a cyclic process. Given the confluence of destabilizing global forces, a nimble mindset attuned to dealing with chaotic, unpredictable and fast-moving changes will be a key weapon in any future corporation's strategic arsenal.

Coda

The "cross-vergence" framework developed through this book has been garnered from the integrated practice of corporate management in Southeast Asia – from the overarching internal corporate structure right through to the business-level strategies enacted on the ground. The kernel of an agenda-setting approach to future business practice in the region, cross-vergence is characterized by the synergistic inclusion of both corporate home office and societal culture influences to form a unique value-set, one that is different from those supported by either corporate or national ideology.

The means for teasing out these two value-sets has its roots in the unique sequence of events that occurred in Southeast Asia toward the end of the 1990s. As we have demonstrated, a multinational such as Unilever (Thailand) Ltd represents a melting pot of the Western-oriented values of the Unilever corporation on the one hand and those of the Thai populace on the other. But inextricably bound in everyday practice, such managerial values have traditionally formed an uneasy couplet based on the underlying failure of the twin poles to successfully "cross-verge." Enter the resounding collapse of the ASEAN economic bloc, which forced the multinationals to drastically reimpose their own "international" priorities and methods – often in the teeth of cohesive indigenous resistance. We have acquired access to the dividing lines of these twin organizational culture elements. Not only can we now visualize the methods and forms by which Eastern and Western business cultures conflict and divide, we now *also* have the potential to see how they may successfully "cross-verge" into a defining set of best corporate practices. We envisage that this "merging" of business cultures across the multinational corporate spectrum, steeped in the progressive global uncertainties of this new millennium, will effectively set the agenda for the years to come, not least within those most diverse and intriguing of nations that comprise the ASEAN bloc.

References

Agence France-Presse (1999) "E-commerce: Potential for Growth in Asia Remains High," *Bangkok Post*, July 21.

Amante, M. S. V. (1997) "Converging and Diverging Trends in HRM: The Philippine 'Halo-Halo' Approach," *Asia Pacific Business Review*, Vol. 3, No. 4: 111–132.

Andrews, T. and Chompusri, N. (2001) "Lessons in Cross-vergence: Restructuring the Thai Subsidiary Corporation," *Journal of International Business Studies*, Vol. 32, No. 1: 77–93.

Ashayagachat, A. (1998) "Anand Sees Merit in Shared Values," *Bangkok Post*, February.

Backman, M. (1999) *Asian Eclipse: Exposing the Dark Side of Business in Asia*, Singapore: John Wiley.

Bangkok Post (2001) "PERC's Survey: Expats Prefer Cold Northeast Asia to South," *Bangkok Post*, April 12.

Bangkok Post (2002) "Auto Production: Revamp of Operations in ASEAN," *Bangkok Post*, January 4.

Bartels, F. L. and Freeman, N. J. (2000) "Multinational Firms and FDI in Southeast Asia," *ASEAN Economic Bulletin*, Vol. 17, No. 3: 324–342.

Bartlett, C. A. and Ghoshal, S. (1989) *Managing across Borders: The Transnational Solution*, Boston, Mass.: Harvard Business School Press.

Bickers, C. (2001) "Lotus Starts to Blossom for Proton," *Far Eastern Economic Review*, July 26.

Bigoness, W. J. and Blakely, G. L. (1996) "A Cross-national Study of Managerial Values," *Journal of International Business Studies*, Vol. 27, No. 4: 739–753.

Borton, L. (2000) "Working in a Vietnamese Voice," *Academy of Management Executive*, Vol. 14, No. 4: 20–29.

Bunyamanee, S. and Yuthamanop, P. (1998) "Thai Approach to Debt Urged," *Bangkok Post*, June 30.

Buranakanonda, A. (1998) "Business Leaders Must Give Staff a Vision of the Future: Consultant," *Bangkok Post*, May 26.

Burns, S. (2000) "The Name Game," *Far Eastern Economic Review*, September 7.

Chandranoi, K. (1998) "Housecleaning in the Academia," *Bangkok Post*, September 20.

Charoenwongsak, K. (1998) "Thai Culture: Strengthening the Community," *Bangkok Post*, August 9.

Cohen, M. (2000a) "Village Leverage," *Far Eastern Economic Review*, August 24.

—— (2000b) "Foreign Cover," *Far Eastern Economic Review*, August 3.

—— (2000c) "Anyone for Coffee?" *Far Eastern Economic Review*, November 2.

Corona, S. (2001) "ISO 9000," www.agcohio.com

Crispin, S.W. (2000a) "Out of the Driver's Seat," *Far Eastern Economic Review*, August 17.

—— (2000b) "More Secure, Less Free," *Far Eastern Economic Review*, May 11.

Erramilli, M. K. (1996) "Nationality and Subsidiary Ownership Patterns in Multinational Corporations," *Journal of International Business Studies*, Vol. 27, No. 2: 225–249.

Fahey, S. (1998) "Vietnam's Women in the Renovation Era," in K. Sen and M. Stivens (eds.) *Gender and Power in Affluent Asia*, London: Routledge.

Far Eastern Economic Review (2000) "Interview with Doug Daft: Coke's New Formula," *Far Eastern Economic Review*, April 20.

Forbes, D. and Cutler, C. (2000) "Vietnam, Cambodia and Laos," in T. Leinbach and R. Ulack (eds) *Southeast Asia: Diversity and Development*, Englewood Cliffs, N.J.: Prentice-Hall.

Gilley, B. (2000) "Pulling Away," *Far Eastern Economic Review*, February 10.

Goad, G. P. (2000a) "What the Future Holds," *Far Eastern Economic Review*, June 15.

—— (2000b) "Anaemic ASEAN," *Far Eastern Economic Review*, September 7.

Godement, F. (1999) *The Downsizing of Asia*, London: Routledge.

Goss, J. (2000) "Urbanization," in T. Leinbach and R. Ulack (eds) *Southeast Asia: Diversity and Development*, Englewood Cliffs, N.J.: Prentice-Hall.

Granitsas, A. and Bickers, C. (1999) "Telecommunications: Opportunity Calls," *Far Eastern Economic Review*, February 11.

Hafner, J. A. (2000) "Thailand," in T. Leinbach and R. Ulack (eds) *Southeast Asia: Diversity and Development*, Englewood Cliffs, N.J.: Prentice-Hall.

Headlam, B. (2001) "How to Email Like a CEO," *New York Times*, April 8.

Held, D., McGrew, A., Goldblatt, D. and Perraton, J. (1999) *Global Transformations: Politics, Economics and Culture*, Cambridge: Polity Press.

Hirst, P. and Thompson, G. (1999) *Globalization in Question*, Cambridge: Polity Press.

Hofstede, G. (1980) *Culture's Consequences: International Differences in Work-Related Values*, Beverly Hills, Calif.: Sage.

Holland, T. (2000) "Moment of Truth," *Far Eastern Economic Review*, November 23.

Holmes, H. and Tangtongtavy, S. (1995) *Working with the Thais*, Bangkok: White Lotus.

Hugo, G. (2000) "Demographic and Social Patterns," in T. Leinbach and R. Ulack (eds) *Southeast Asia: Diversity and Development*, Englewood Cliffs, N.J.: Prentice-Hall.

Johansson, J. K. (2000) *Global Marketing: Foreign Entry, Local Marketing and Global Management*, Boston, Mass.: McGraw-Hill.

Jurado, T. (1998) "New Markets: The Mekong Region," *Asian Automotive Industry: Strategies beyond 2000*, Bangkok: EIU Publications.

Keenan, F. (1999) "Companies: Join the Club," *Far Eastern Economic Review*, June 3.

Keenan, F., Daoreung, P. and Tasker, R. (1999) "To the Ramparts," *Far Eastern Economic Review*, July 22.

Keeratipipatpong, W. (1998) "Financially Shot at Dawn," in *Bangkok Post 1998 Mid-Year Economic Review*, June 30, Bangkok: Post Publishing Co.

Kittikanya, C. (2000) "Internet Slow to Make Inroads into Business," *Bangkok Post*, http://www.bangkokpost.com/MidYear2000

Kositchotethana, B. (1998a) "Shell Plans to Shed 150 Local Jobs," *Bangkok Post*, August 7.

—— (1998b) "More Thais Are Rising to the Top," *Bangkok Post*, September 18.

Lall, R. (1999) "Rethinking Asia: Time to Get Wired," *Far Eastern Economic Review*, August 19.

Lawler, J. L. (1996) "Diversity Issues in South-East Asia: The Case of Thailand," *International Journal of Manpower*, Vol. 17: 152–168.

Lawler, J. L., Siengthai, S. and Atmiyanandana, V. (1997) "HRM in Thailand: Eroding Traditions," *Asia Pacific Business Review*, Vol. 3, No. 4: 170–196.

Lazer, W. and Shaw, E. (2000) "Global Marketing Management: At the Dawn of the New Millennium," *Journal of International Marketing*, Vol. 8, No. 1: 65–77.

Legewie, J. (2000) "Cars Get No Vroomm from AFTA," *Far Eastern Economic Review*, May 4.

Leinbach, T. R. and Bowen, J. T. (2000) "Industrialization and Trade," in T. Leinbach and R. Ulack (eds) *Southeast Asia: Diversity and Development*, Englewood Cliffs, N.J.: Prentice-Hall.

Levitt, T. (1983) "The Globalization of Markets," *Harvard Business Review*, May–June.

Lewin, K. (1951) *Field Theory in Social Science*, New York: Harper.

Lim, L. Y. C. (2000) "Southeast Asian Chinese Business: Past Success, Recent Crisis and Future Evolution," *Journal of Asian Business*, Vol. 16, No. 1: 1–15.

Long, G. (1999) "Y2K a Pest for Local E-commerce Projects," *Bangkok Post*, August 7.

Lubatkin, M. H., Ndiaye, M. and Vengroff, R. (1997) "The Nature of Managerial Work in Developing Countries: A Limited Test of the Universalist Hypothesis," *Journal of International Business Studies*, Vol. 28, No. 4: 711–735.

Luo, Y. (1999) "Dimensions of Knowledge: Comparing Asian and Western MNEs in China," *Asia Pacific Journal of Management*, Vol. 16, No. 1: 75–93.

—— (2000) *Multinational Corporations in China*, Copenhagen: Copenhagen Business School Press.

McKinsey, K. (2001) "Advertise Now, Gain Later," *Far Eastern Economic Review*, August 2.

Marukatat, S. (1999) "Moving Forward Blindfolded," *Bangkok Post*, August 18.

Muralidharan, R. and Hamilton, R. D. (1999) "Aligning Multinational Control Systems," *Long Range Planning*, Vol. 32, No. 3: 352–361.

Neal, M. (1998) *The Culture Factor: Cross-national Management and the Foreign Venture*, London: Macmillan.

Niratpattanasai, K. (1997) "Sequencing of Business: East and West," *Thailand Tales*, March.

Nivatpumin, C. (1998) "Thailand Has Six Months to Exploit Advantages," *Bangkok Post*, July 1.

Nivatpumin, C., Sivasomboon, B. and Chaimusik, J. (1997) "Reengineering: It Pays to Put People First," *Bangkok Post*, July 6.

Ohmae, K. (1990) *The Borderless World*, London: Collins.

O'Neill, O. (1991) "Transnational Justice," in D. Held (ed.) *Political Theory Today*, Cambridge: Polity Press.

Orru, M. M., Biggart, N. W. and Hamilton, G. G. (1991) "Organizational Isomorphism in East Asia," in W. W. Powell and P. J. DiMaggio (eds) *The New Institutionalism in Organizational Analysis*, Chicago: University of Chicago Press.

Pelzer, C. (1993) "Socio-cultural Dimensions of Renovation in Vietnam: *Doi Moi* as Dialogue and Transformation in Gender Relations," in W. S. Turley and M. Seldon (eds) *Reinventing Vietnamese Socialism: Doi Moi in Comparative Perspective*, Boulder, Colo.: Westview Press.

Peters, T. J. and Waterman, H. (1982) *In Search of Excellence: Lessons from America's Best-Run Companies*, New York: Harper & Row.

Phongpaichit, P. and Baker, C. (1998) *Thailand's Boom and Bust*, Chiang Mai: Silkworm Books.

Powpaka, S. (1998) "Factors Affecting the Adoption of Market Orientation: The Case of Thailand," *Journal of International Marketing*, Vol. 6, No. 1.

Quang, T. (1998) "A Case of JV Failure: Procter and Gamble vs. Phuong Dong in Vietnam," *Journal of Euro-Asian Management*, Vol. 4, No. 2.

Quelch, J. A. (1992) "The New Country Managers," *McKinsey Quarterly*, Vol. 4: 155–167.

Ralston, D. A., Holt, D. H., Terpstra, R. H. and Kai-cheng Yu (1997) "The Impact of National Culture and Economic Ideology on Managerial Work Values: A Study of the United States, Russia, Japan and China," *Journal of International Business Studies*, Vol. 28, No. 1: 177–207.

Index